Critical Essays on
KAY BOYLE

CRITICAL ESSAYS
ON
AMERICAN LITERATURE

James Nagel, General Editor
University of Georgia, Athens

Critical Essays on
KAY BOYLE

edited by

MARILYN ELKINS

G. K. Hall & Co.
An Imprint of Simon & Schuster Macmillan
New York

Prentice Hall International
London   Mexico City   New Delhi   Singapore   Sydney   Toronto

G. K. Hall & Co.
An Imprint of Simon & Schuster Macmillan
1633 Broadway
New York, NY 10019

Library of Congress Cataloging-in-Publication Data

Critical essays on Kay Boyle / edited by Marilyn Elkins.
       p.   cm.—(Critical essays on American literature)
    Includes bibliographical references and index.
    ISBN 0-7838-0012-6 (alk. paper)
    1. Boyle, Kay, 1902–   —Criticism and interpretation.   2. Women
and literature—United States—History—20th century.   I. Elkins,
Marilyn Roberson.   II. Series.
PS3503.09357Z58   1997
813'.52—dc21   97-8361
                                                               CIP

The paper used in this publication meets the minimum requirements of
American National Standard for Information Sciences—Permanence of Paper
for Printed Library Materials. ANSI Z39.48-1984. ∞™

10 9 8 7 6 5 4 3 2

Printed in the United States of America

for my parents, Blake and Mary Gene Roberson

Contents

◆

General Editor's Note

♦

This series seeks to anthologize the most important criticism on a wide variety of topics and writers in American literature. Our readers will find in various volumes not only a generous selection of reprinted articles and reviews but original essays, bibliographies, manuscript selections, and other materials brought to public attention for the first time. This volume, *Critical Essays on Kay Boyle,* is the most comprehensive collection of essays ever published on one of the most important modern writers in the United States. It contains both a sizable gathering of early reviews and a broad selection of more modern scholarship. Among the authors of reprinted articles and reviews are William Carlos Williams, Katherine Anne Porter, Malcolm Cowley, Sandra Whipple Spanier, and Vance Bourjaily. In addition to a substantial introduction by Marilyn Elkins, which reviews Boyle's career and the history of criticism of her work, there are also five original essays commissioned specifically for publication in this volume: new studies by Linda Wagner-Martin on Boyle as a poet, Dianne Chambers on female roles and national identity in the fiction of Edith Wharton and Boyle, Abby H. P. Werlock on Wharton's influence on Boyle's *My Next Bride,* Burton Hatlen on the gender politics of literary form in *Monday Night,* and Christine H. Hait on Boyle's innovations in the autobiographical tradition in *Being Geniuses Together.* We are confident that this book will make a permanent and significant contribution to the study of American literature.

JAMES NAGEL
University of Georgia, Athens

Publisher's Note

♦

Producing a volume that contains both newly commissioned and reprinted material present the publisher with the challenge of balancing the desire to achieve stylistic consistency with the need to preserve the integrity of works first published elsewhere. In the Critical Essays series, essays commissioned especially for a particular volume are edited to be consistent with G. K. Hall's house style; reprinted essays appear in the style in which they were first published, with only typographical errors corrected. Consequently, shifts in style from one essay to another are the result of our efforts to be faithful to each text as it was originally published.

Acknowledgment

◆

I want to thank Maureen Boyd for her invaluable assistance in preparing this volume for publication.

Introduction

◆

MARILYN ELKINS

When Kay Boyle was asked to create a self-portrait for the *San Francisco Chronicle* in 1978, she sketched a winged angel who supported both a halo and an aristocratic nose reminiscent of Boyle's. The whimsical, soaring figure also transported two live hand grenades. Beneath her drawing, Boyle placed the following caption:

> Since receiving several volumes of censored data through the Freedom of Information Act, I see myself as a dangerous "radical" (they themselves put it in quotes) cleverly disguised as a perfect lady. So I herewith blow my cover.[1]

Somewhat belatedly, literary critics have begun to lift another of Boyle's disguises, for beneath her refined language lies explosive subject matter. Sometimes overlooked because of its elegant surface, Boyle's writing is as loaded as the hands she drew in her self-portrait. She consistently used her art as a political weapon in an attempt to change the world around her.

Following her death on 27 December 1992, the *New York Times* referred to her as "a short-story writer and novelist renowned for her deft and powerful style and her keen insights into human nature," adding that her work had "commanded admiration from critics for more than half a century."[2] As the last surviving member of the "lost generation," Boyle had certainly lived to see a revival of interest in her writing, but this attention had eluded her during long periods of her 70-year career. Indeed, her literary reputation fluctuated greatly throughout her lifetime, perhaps as a result of the great variety of strategies, techniques, and genres that she used to reach an unusually wide range of audiences. Ironically, even her stylistic artistry made her seem suspect to some critics. A prolific novelist, short-story writer, poet, and essayist, Boyle also wrote memoirs, translations, and children's stories. She published almost 50 volumes, including the books for which she was the ghostwriter,

1

Relations and Complications, Being the Recollections of H. H. The Dayang Muda of Sarawak (by Gladys Palmer Brooke) and *Yellow Dusk* (by Bettina Bedwell). Her short stories and poems appeared in such diverse publications as *transition,* the *Nation,* the *New Yorker, McCall's,* and the *Saturday Evening Post.*

Boyle's writing certainly brought her recognition and honors: two O. Henry Awards (1935 and 1941), two Guggenheim Fellowships (1934 and 1961), a San Francisco Arts Commission Award (1978), a Senior Fellowship for Literature from the National Endowment for the Arts (1980), the Before Columbus Foundation Award (1983), the Celtic Foundation Award (1984), the *Los Angeles Times* Kirsch Award (1986), an endowment from the Fund for Poetry (1987), the Lannan Foundation Award (1989), and honorary doctorates from Columbia College (Chicago), Southern Illinois University, Skidmore College, Bowling Green State University, and Ohio State University. She was elected to the Henry James chair of the American Academy of Arts and Letters in 1979.

Despite this public recognition of her talent, Boyle's place in twentieth-century American literature remains somewhat uncertain. When literary historians describe the expatriate movement of the '20s, they invariably mention Boyle's name, but they rarely discuss her writing as though it merits attention equal to that of many of her contemporaries. Instead, scholars frequently focus on Boyle's friendships and political activities rather than on her literary achievement. When they do examine Boyle's literary significance, they usually classify her as among the best American short-story writers of the twentieth century, although she worked in various genres. In his introduction to her collected short stories, David Daiches accurately describes her work in that genre:

> [T]hese stories show one of the finest short-story writers of our time counterpointing imagination and experience in different ways as experience took on new forms and imagination shifted its role and scope to meet it.[3]

Expertise as a writer of short fiction does not, however, guarantee a writer's place among those of the highest standing, for the short story remains somewhat suspect as a form able to establish a writer's place among the literary giants. Unless its practitioners have gained recognition for their work in other genres, they are less likely to be ranked among the first tier of American writers, regardless of their skill with short fiction. Because Boyle's novels have just entered a phase of reconsideration, assessing their success and, by implication, Boyle's overall literary significance remains somewhat premature.

When Boyle began writing in the '20s, her fiction was frequently praised by other writers, and she was considered a significant modernist.[4] Her early poetry and fiction fit both the content and stylistic expectations of modernism and afforded her early publication in the avant-garde literary magazines of the '20s.

Her career and eventful life offer an imposing, if somewhat unsettling, profile of the twentieth-century American woman as writer: three times married, mother of six and step-mother of two, and an unrelenting political activist who was jailed for her opposition to the Vietnam War when she was in her 60s. Born on 19 February 1902, in St. Paul, Minnesota, and reared in a number of locales before finances forced the family to settle in Cincinnati, Ohio, Boyle attributed her artistic and political ambitions to her mother's tutelage. An active leader in the Farmer-Labor party, Katherine Evans Boyle instilled Kay with a respect for human rights and a high regard for her own artistic endeavors. Mrs. Boyle read the youthful Kay's writing aloud to dinner guests, along with works by Gertrude Stein, treating the writings as though they were of equal worth.[5] Boyle maintained that she could become a writer "because my mother brought me up in that quite simple feeling."[6]

Although Boyle studied briefly at the Cincinnati Conservatory of Music, the Ohio Mechanics Institute, and Parsons School of Design, her only formal training as a writer was a short course in fiction writing that she took at Columbia University when she was serving as Lola Ridge's editorial assistant at *Broom* after moving to New York in 1922. During this eventful year, she became friendly with Marianne Moore and William Carlos Williams; had her first poem, "Monody to the Sound of Zithers," published in *Poetry;* and married Richard Brault, a French engineer. When they sailed for France in 1923 and settled in Le Havre, after spending a harrowing summer with Brault's bourgeois family, Boyle continued to write and paint.

During the period of Boyle's apprenticeship, her poetry and short fiction began appearing in *This Quarter, transition, Broom, Poetry,* and *Contact,* alongside the work of William Carlos Williams, Ezra Pound, James Joyce, Stein, Djuna Barnes, and Ernest Hemingway. Because she had been mistakenly diagnosed with tuberculosis, Boyle went to Grasse in the south of France in 1926 as the guest of Ernest Walsh, editor of *This Quarter,* with whom she had been corresponding about writing. While their mutual interest in literature initiated their friendship, the two soon fell in love, and when Walsh died from tuberculosis within the year, Boyle was pregnant with their daughter, Sharon.

She continued her apprenticeship, writing poetry, short stories, working on a novel, and ghostwriting to survive financially while she lived in England and Paris. While in Paris, she briefly joined Raymond Duncan's artist colony, made friends with Nancy Cunard, Harry and Caresse Crosby, Robert McAlmon, Archibald MacLeish, Joyce, and Samuel Beckett, and signed the "Revolution of the Word" issue of *transition* that proclaimed "the plain reader be damned" (1929). By the end of the '20s, she had begun her relationship with Laurence Vail, whom she would eventually marry in 1932 and with whom she would have three children. Black Sun Press published much of her fiction of this period—some of which had already appeared in *transition* and *This Quarter*—in her first volume, *Short Stories,* in a limited edition of 165 copies (1929).[7]

No first book by a relatively unknown writer could have received a more positive reception than the criticism of this volume that William Carlos Williams wrote for *transition*. He linked Boyle's writing to that of Emily Dickinson and pronounced Boyle's work of a "high degree of excellence," predicting that the very quality of her stories, their assault on the sleeping consciousness of Americans, would ensure their failure to find an audience. Williams described Boyle as a writer who "has a comprehensive, if perhaps disturbing view of what takes place in the human understanding at moments of intense living, and puts it down in its proper shapes and color," and evaluated her work as "equal in vigor to anything done by a man but with a twist that . . . carries the mind completely over until the male is not the seeing agent but the focus of the eye."[8] Williams's observations that Boyle's work was too advanced for an American audience seem prescient, just as his recognition of the importance of Boyle's "female gaze" seems contemporary in its feminist consciousness. While the sexuality of her women characters may have been initially disconcerting for her American audiences, it is a quality that many critics have found engaging.[9]

The decade of the '30s was Boyle's most prolific and most artistically successful period. She began this period by adding six stories to the seven included in *Short Stories* to form the manuscript for *Wedding Day and Other Stories* (1930). In this collection, Boyle begins exploring one of the themes that would continue to dominate her work throughout her career: the pain of unfulfilled communication and love when people meet with insurmountable psychological, physical, or societal barriers. Expressionistic in nature, her physical settings are often used to reflect the characters' troubled internal states, and the stories frequently employ experimental language to further the presentation of intense inner turmoil.[10]

The volume met with qualified success. In his review for the *Nation,* Gerald Sykes proclaimed Boyle's writing as "potentially valuable because it is possible—as it is so rarely possible—that she may write something that has not been written before." He commented on Boyle's ability to "put nearly every other emancipated woman writer who has attempted to deal with this subject" [presumably sexuality] to shame; yet he called her work derivative and, therefore, nourished by the "repetition of a repetition."[11] An anonymous reviewer for the *New York Times* declared that "the best of Kay Boyle is quite good," but complained that some of the writing is "queer jumbles, calling for such an alertness at untangling them that it is not quite worth the effort." However, the reviewer praised "Miss Boyle's effort in such jumbles to catch all the fleeting impressions of a moment of living."[12]

Boyle followed this publication with her first novel, which fictionalized her early married life with Brault, *Plagued by the Nightingale* (1931).[13] In her treatment of a young American wife's search for a way to retain her sense of self and to form a sense of relatedness to her new French husband and his bourgeois family, Boyle handles the novel's resolution in a somewhat ambiguous manner. But clearly her heroine still envisions a married life in which she will be a contributing partner and an active artist—an uncommon resolution for a novel of this time. Because of Boyle's style, the novel often operates more like poetry than fiction, uniting compression, lyricism, and ellipsis. In both its style and content, the book is a significant precursor to Boyle's later works, which frequently focus on the important question of how an artist who is also a woman can express her artistic individuality within a heterosexual relationship. Boyle also seems to be wrestling with her own aesthetic question: how to wed her experimental style with themes that are central to women's domestic and artistic lives.

For many reviewers, such questions were seen as slight or trivial, and the novel's reviews were quite mixed. A complaint that would haunt Boyle's reviews throughout her career began to surface in objections to the refinement of her language, often followed by an insistence that the effect of her style was mannered or overwrought.[14] Unlike many of these early reviews, Katherine Anne Porter's criticism of Boyle's first two volumes, which appeared in the *New Republic,* seemed to understand and appreciate Boyle's experimentation. Porter praised Boyle's superb manner of telling, stating that "there are long passages of prose which crackle and snap with electric energy, episodes in which inner drama and outward events occur against scenes bright with the vividness of things seen by the immediate eye." She also commended Boyle's "masterful use of symbol and allegory," before concluding that Boyle's writing was "a magnificent performance" and suggesting that its content had much to offer as well.[15]

With the publication of her second novel, *Year before Last* (1932), Boyle began to receive accolades from reviewers who were not her writing peers.[16] This novel—which recasts Boyle's relationship with Ernest Walsh, their difficulty finding housing because of his tuberculosis, and his eventual death— seems to have found an audience among both the literary and the general reading public in part because it treats a small, manageable private tragedy in language that is by turns lyrical and stark. Boyle adapts the fallen-woman script but assigns death to her male partner. The narrative argues that a woman has the right to choose a sexual partner outside the bounds of a stultifying marriage without suffering death or exile because of her actions.

Writing for the *Nation,* Robert Cantwell concluded that the novel "states its case as few contemporary novels do" and called the book a distinct advance over her earlier volumes.[17] Myra Marini, in a review for the *New Republic,* commended the novel's power and emotional sincerity, finding Boyle's prose "as highly charged as poetry" and suggesting that such intensity is praiseworthy.[18] And in the *Saturday Review of Literature,* Gladys Graham argued that Boyle "shows conclusively that both her style and her analysis are completely under her control," stating that the "disquieting, poetic beauty" of Boyle's style works in conjunction with the novel's "emotional and psychological vortex."[19]

In 1933 Boyle published two volumes: *The First Lover, and Other Stories* and *Gentlemen, I Address You Privately*.[20] Dedicated to Eugene Jolas, the first was a collection of 14 short stories that continued Boyle's "revolution of the word" through her experimentation with language and subject matter, while much of her focus continued to be on the theme of individuality versus love. Writing for the *Boston Transcript*, Karl Schriftglesser concluded that the stories are "the matured work of an avowed experimentalist who has standards and subjects that are worth experimenting with,"[21] while other reviewers continued to complain that her work was too "precious" or "pastel."[22]

The reviews for *Gentlemen, I Address You Privately* were not uneven; they were uniformly bad. One of the earliest novels about homosexuality, the work rejects common assumptions about gender roles within same sex relationships as well as about gender-defined characteristics. The novel has two love triangles: a married woman and a former priest competing for the love of a vagabond sailor, and the daughter of a Madame and a prostitute who vie for the love of a cross-dressing lesbian. Both triangles make a wry comment on this standard plot device as it appears in romantic literature, but the subject matter only appeared shocking and confusing to Boyle's readers and reviewers. A review in the *Nation* suggested that perhaps Boyle was suffering from "metaphorical spots on the eye which consistently get in the way of the object and her proper perceptions of the object," and others found the novel equally distasteful in its subject matter.[23]

The reception of her next novel, *My Next Bride* (1934), was only slightly more positive.[24] Set in Paris and based loosely on Boyle's time in Raymond Duncan's artist colony, the novel's heroine is a young American idealist who believes that she can help change society's antiquated, inhibiting structures through friendship and art. The novel reflects the importance of women's friendships as a means for survival and contains a realistic handling of the difficulty in attaining safe abortions. This subject matter, which also includes an unsentimental look at the difficulty of the female American artist's economic and physical survival in the Paris of the '20s—while it may interest today's readers—appeared shallow to the proletariat readers of the '30s, who were uninterested in stories about decadence in the Paris of the previous decade. The young Mary McCarthy wrote that Boyle's prose could not save "her anachronistic novel from the category of peep-hole, wish-fulfillment literature into which it inevitably falls" and recommended the book to "adolescents and spinsters," who, she suggested, were the only audience who could agree with the novel's point of view.[25] Another reviewer, while admitting that Boyle's craftsmanship is exquisite, stated that she makes one "wonder what use she is going to make" of it and that Boyle's use of such trivial material was upsetting for those who had been quick to recognize her as "one of the most gifted and interesting" of the younger writers.[26]

The subject matter of Boyle's writing during this phase, with the exception of *Gentlemen I Address You Privately*, was highly autobiographical, yet critics seemed to feel that a young woman's quest for selfhood, artistic freedom, and sexual involvement was not weighty enough to serve as appropriate content for a novel. To see one's innermost concerns dismissed as superficial must have been painful, and perhaps Boyle internalized her reviewers' assumptions; after the rather poor reception of *My Next Bride,* she rarely treated her own experience and feminine concerns—or those of her female characters—with the same level of respect for their significance. Regardless of her motivation for the shift, she began to write about issues that were more public in their focus.

Her movement into a period that centered more on political concerns began with *Death of a Man* (1936), one of the earliest fictional treatments of the growth of Nazism.[27] The novel indicts such movements in a non-doctrinaire way, subtly delineating their insidious nature by showing how they attract young idealists like the novel's Dr. Prochaska, who works in a children's hospital for infectious disease; it also explores the "sexual politics of Nazism," Burton Hatlen's term for the parallels that Boyle draws between the patriarchal structure and Nazism.[28]

With the exception of Geoffrey Parsons's response, reviewers were generally still displeased with Boyle's subject matter and suspicious of her delicate style, disagreeing with Parsons's assessment that "surely a talent so great is entitled to choose its own path" and his pronouncement that the book's flaws are "negligible by comparison with the central achievement."[29] Alfred Kazin's review was much more typical, decrying Boyle's lack of "significant material." Although Boyle's novel concludes with the assassination of Dollfuss, Kazin complained that her style is so overbearing that we remember her subtlety rather than her subject matter. He concluded that the book "decomposes into trivial effects and still-life pictures."[30]

Although the title story of *The White Horses of Vienna, and Other Stories* (1936) won the O. Henry Short Story award for 1935, the collection's reviews also seem to reflect many of the same sentiments about the insignificance of Boyle's subject matter—even though these stories clearly show Boyle's movement toward including more overtly political and public worlds in her writing.[31] Despite the complaints about Boyle's exquisite style, however, some reviewers seemed pleased with the volume. In a mostly positive review, Elizabeth Hart declared that the stories displayed Boyle's artistry to its best advantage, and R. W. Seaver commented on the power of the writing, declaring the volume "a writer's book" that would be "thoroughly appreciated for its craftsmanship by a very exclusive audience."[32]

The critics were not much kinder to *Monday Night* (1938), Boyle's admitted favorite among her novels.[33] Boyle adopts a male protagonist, and the novel follows the aesthetic dictates of modernism closely; the novel is essentially a male bildungsroman that underscores the universality of this male experience with mythical and literary allusions. It also uses experimental form and structure, and the plot line, while reminiscent of detective novels as well, revolves around a male writer's search for subject matter and self. The writer's aspirations and the frequent allusions to mythology are balanced against the seediness of contemporary Europe, and the hero is alienated from both his native land and his adopted country.[34] Like that of Joyce's *Ulysses,* the novel's action takes place in a 24-hour period, suggesting that it is also a modern epic.

Most of these aspects of the novel eluded the contemporary critics, who concentrated their remarks on the novel's ending. They felt it failed to deliver a satisfying climax to the story's chaotic and terrifying actions. From the general condemnation, Louis Kronenberger, Phillip Hartung, and the anonymous reviewer for the *London Times Literary Supplement* dissented to some degree, with Kronenberger saying the book is "full of astute touches and sly descriptions" and finding it to be "a step forward from the often too delicate and attenuated studies in sensibility which Miss Boyle has written in the past."[35] Hartung, writing for *Commonweal,* called Boyle "a stylist of first rank and an artist in American prose," and the *London Times Literary Supplement* commented on the "*tour de force's*" "strange visual beauty" and "subtle perception."[36]

Boyle's book of poetry, *A Glad Day* (1938), met with greater critical success—perhaps because most of its reviews were written by practicing poets.[37] Babette Deutsch, writing in the *Nation,* remarks on Boyle's "surprising, vivifying perceptiveness, her capacity for seeing things in new relations, for combining them and making them act upon each other in new ways."[38] Louise Bogan was equally laudatory, commenting upon Boyle's "great talent for language, sharp senses, and . . . rich subconscious. . . . The love poems are intensely moving and the general fantasy frequently superb."[39] Boyle continued to please the serious practitioners of her craft, even though critics were less generous.

The critics and writers joined ranks, however, when they reviewed Boyle's volume *The Crazy Hunter: Three Short Novels* (1940).[40] A collection of three novellas, the volume is often considered to be Boyle's finest work in fiction. For once, Boyle combined style with content in a way that other writers, critics, and readers could all approve. Set in England, the first novella, "The Crazy Hunter," tells the story of a young girl who fights to save the life of her blind horse. Boyle's symbolism allows the novella to speak of the plight of the individual who comes up against unalterable circumstances but refuses to forsake worthy ideals simply because they are not practical or economical. The second story, "The Bridegroom's Body," reiterates Boyle's theme about the necessity of women's bonding against harsh circumstances as a means of survival and the difficulty of communication between two people—even when both are female. The third story, "Big Fiddle," focuses on a young American boy who is equally lost in Devon and Capri.

Reviewing the collection for *Books,* William Soskin called the title story "one of the finest modern novelettes to be found anywhere"; Olga Owens said the story "shakes the heart," suggesting that it can be taken as a fable "of the tenderness and human understanding in a menacing world"; and Otis Ferguson called the work "simply fine writing in both senses of the word, controlled to the point of elegance but still running as free as you please. . . . [I]t is at its best in 'The Crazy Hunter.' "[41] Peter Monro Jack, writing for the *New York Times,* summed up the praise succinctly when he wrote that Boyle "demonstrates that she is one of the best short-story writers in America, and probably the most careful, percipient and unusual."[42] Only Clifton Fadiman, writing for the *New Yorker,* seemed qualified in his approval; after he praised Boyle for her "rarefied art," one of his primary complaints was the "veterinary atmosphere" of the title story, which he felt was wasted because he knew nothing of horses. But he conceded that the title story was "original" and "moving" and called "The Bridegroom's Body" "as original a tale as I have read in years, somber, completely removed from conventional life, existing in a world of its own."[43] Besides signaling a high point in Kay Boyle's critical acceptance, the book of novellas served as another marker as well. It was the last time that Kay Boyle would write a longer piece of fiction that was not connected in an immediately apparent way with the political realm of the public world.

During the '30s, Boyle and Laurence Vail had lived in Austria and briefly in England before they settled in the French Alps in Megeve. These homes provided Kay Boyle with firsthand information about the political scene in Europe, and with the onslaught of World War II, she began to incorporate the European political situation into most of her fiction. Boyle's change to a more overt politicization is evident in her writing of the '40s and in the years to follow. While some of her works written after 1940 would feature women, her heroines would now be involved in social and political issues that went beyond the realm of the sexual and artistic. As a resident of Europe, being, as Glenway Wescott states, always "more completely abroad than the rest of us [American expatriates],"[44] Boyle understood the political implications of events in that sphere with greater clarity than did her American contemporaries. She had witnessed the more subtle ways in which Europeans' daily personal lives were being transformed. This knowledge gives her writing about the European conflict an immediacy of detail that often escapes other American writers' presentations of the subject matter.

Primer for Combat (1942) evidences this perspective fully in its treatment of the theme of coexisting with the enemy, looking at the psychological and practical effects of both collaboration and resistance and at the ways in which outside forces can engulf and destroy personal relationships.[45] Written as a diary, the novel describes the life of an American woman in a French village during the summer of 1940, when the French were beginning to realize that they would be defeated by the Germans. Again, the critics were generally receptive to Boyle's work. The review in the *Atlantic* declared that "nothing better has been written on France since the Germans got there"; in a mixed review, Malcolm Cowley pronounced the book "accurate, honest and much better informed than most of its predecessors"; Robert Littell said that "the piling up of little incidents, the words and faces of the people numbed by despair, but each one behaving in his characteristic way, are skillfully and movingly done."[46]

Boyle's contemporary reviewers would never again be this accepting of one of her novels. Part of the shift in critical reception can be attributed to Boyle's deliberate change of approaches for her next work of fiction. Eager to reach a broader American reading public and to explain the French reaction to the German invasion to Americans, who seemed to feel that the French had simply given up, Boyle agreed to serialize her next book for the *Saturday Evening Post;* she also desperately needed the money. Always aware of her intended audience and her goal, Boyle adapted her style and story line accordingly. This change did not sit well with her usual audience, who felt betrayed by what they considered to be her commercialism. A page-turning account of a young woman, half French and half American, who returns to France and becomes involved in the French Resistance, *Avalanche* (1944) spelled almost unanimous critical rejection for Boyle—a rejection that would haunt her literary reputation for years.[47]

Struthers Burt accurately predicted in his review for the *Saturday Review of Literature* that "a number of Miss Boyle's admirers . . . are going to rebuke her for this story, and although they are going to be right technically, they are going to be enormously wrong theoretically and practically."[48] Writing his first column as Clifton Fadiman's replacement at the *New Yorker,* Edmund Wilson was at his most caustic, dismissing the book as "nothing but a piece of pure rubbish," calling it "the usual kind of thing that is turned out by women writers for the popular magazines."[49] Diana Trilling was no kinder, terming the book "offensive in the extreme against the serious truth because . . . [Boyle] pretends to more and better than pot-boiling."[50] Boyle maintained that she wanted "to reach as great a number of Americans as possible," knew that she was not writing literature, and did not need a critic to point this out to her.[51] Elizabeth Bullock was quick to side with Boyle, castigating Wilson for missing "the frankly stated intention of author and publisher." Comparing Boyle's novel to works by Graham Greene and labeling it as "literary adventure," Bullock argued that as such the novel succeeds. She suggested that reviewers were responding more to their prescription that Boyle must "write for Art, for the chosen few" and were upset because Boyle had stepped out of character and could no longer be easily pigeonholed.[52] Ironically, although the novel's critical reception damaged Boyle's career as a serious writer, *Avalanche* brought Boyle her first large reading audience.

A Frenchman Must Die (1946) shared much of its construction and style with *Avalanche* and received reviews that were similar.[53] Even more daring than Boyle's first action heroine, the French double agent Danielle continually bests the novel's half-American Resistance fighter. Such unquestioning bravery usually is typical of the action novel, but Boyle certainly risked her literary reputation by giving this attribute to a woman and by placing her so firmly at the center of this standard male script. When she returned to this mystery-adventure genre much later in her career, with the publication of *The Seagull on the Step* (1955), the critics were again upset, complaining that they expected more from Kay Boyle.[54] One reviewer charged that Boyle's "once hard and original prose style, with no fresh ideas to support it, has softened into dullness."[55]

Published in 1946, *Thirty Stories* seemed to be a corrective to the period's general evaluation of Boyle's worth as a writer.[56] Many of these stories were accounts of the effect of the war on the individual. Most had already been published in magazines before they were collected for the volume, and "Defeat" had won the 1941 O. Henry Award for its perceptive treatment of the French survivors and their mood after the armistice had been signed between the Germans and the French. Struthers Burt proclaimed that the volume showed Boyle to be one of the best short story writers alive, and suggested that her expertise is similar to that of Henry James, complimenting her "eerie gift of bringing completely to life the European background."[57]

Boyle's earlier attempt to treat the problems of confused national identity created by the war was eventually published in 1948; *1939* was actually written prior to her work on *Avalanche* and *A Frenchman Must Die,* but Boyle had difficulty finding a publisher willing to take on such a short, uncommercial novel.[58] Divided into two sections that present an American woman's and an Austrian man's response to war and its impact upon their relationship, the story covers the 24-hour period just following the man's military induction into an French interment camp for foreign nationals. Boyle juxtaposes the immediate action with the couple's ruminations about their relationship. Offering an unusual perspective on the European situation in 1939, the book emphasizes the special difficulties involved when wars are fought by people whose geographical borders make them neighbors. Writing for the *Atlantic,* Edward Weeks called Boyle one of the finest stylists of the day, but complained that she had chosen characters who were undeserving of the reader's attention, as did Nona Balakian in her review for the *New York Times* and the anonymous reviewer for the *New Yorker.*[59] Only Walter Havighurst and Florence Haxton Bullock seemed to dissent. Havighurst found the book to be worthwhile, commenting upon Boyle's "miraculous freshness" and "austere understanding," and Bullock declared Boyle "a master hand at giving full value not only to the explicit words spoken and the scene described, but to the delicate overtones that hover around and above her so-innocent seeming statements."[60]

The xenophobia displayed by the French in *1939* becomes an American characteristic in Boyle's final World War II novel, *His Human Majesty* (1949), in which Americans appear no more trusting and accepting of other nationalities than the French.[61] The novel focuses on European émigrés in a Colorado training camp, who are awaiting their chance to participate in the eventual assault upon the Nazis who were responsible for their emigration. While critics did not question the value of the novel's subject matter, Boyle is taken to task for her inability to write about men in a realistic way, with the only compliments going to her superb ability to capture the cold, barren setting.[62]

Boyle's responses to the war's aftermath were considered to be much more worthwhile. Her volume of short stories that focus on the aftereffect of the war, particularly the American occupation of Germany, *The Smoking Mountain: Stories of Postwar Germany* (1951), met with greater critical success, as did her novel that treats the same subject material, *Generation without Farewell* (1960).[63] The short-story volume was uniformly praised for its penetrating historical analysis and style, and it elicited a laudatory review from Harry T. Moore in the *New York Times*. Moore praised Boyle's skillful observation and careful prose, concluding that the stories have "the added virtues of dramatic presentation and that fusion of theme, symbol and character which enables fiction to be a powerful agent for revealing truths."[64]

Although *Generation without Farewell* received praise for its reflective exploration of the relationship between the occupied and the occupiers, it also received its share of criticism for Boyle's lyricism, which some reviewers continued to describe as overwriting.[65] Set in the American Occupied Zone of Germany in 1948, the novel argues against the use of national characteristics as a way of defining individuals. In the *New York Times Book Review*, Virgilia Peterson declared that Boyle had "never written more poignantly, never come closer to absolute pitch than in this new novel . . . and has surpassed herself." William Stuckey found the characters unconvincing but felt that Boyle rendered the novel's scenes in a believable manner. The reviewer for *Time* praised Boyle's "cameralike shots of war's destruction."[66]

While Boyle was composing her chronicles of war and its aftereffects, she lived in a variety of locales. In 1941, she had returned to the United States, already romantically involved with the Baron Joseph von Franckenstein, an Austrian baron who had participated in anti-Nazi activities in the Haut Savoie. When she divorced Laurence Vail in 1943 in Reno, Nevada, she immediately married Franckenstein; she had already borne one child by him and was pregnant with their second. In 1947, she joined Franckenstein, who was by then a U.S. Foreign Service officer, in Germany, where she worked as a correspondent for the *New Yorker*. Because of McCarthyite loyalty charges, Franckenstein was dismissed from the Foreign Service in 1952, and the couple moved to Connecticut, where they taught school and fought his dismissal. Reinstated in 1962, Franckenstein died a year later, and Boyle moved to San Francisco to join the faculty of San Francisco State University, where she basically remained until her retirement in 1980.

During the '50s and '60s, Boyle continued to write, but as Elizabeth Bell points out, Boyle began to focus more on nonfiction, although she continued to write in other genres.[67] She was also forced to seek new publishing venues as a result of McCarthyism; even the once-faithful *New Yorker* refused to publish her work. Only the *Nation* continued to print her writing. She would eventually collect much of her nonfiction into two volumes of essays: *The Long Walk at San Francisco State and Other Essays* (1970) and *Words That Must Somehow Be Said* (1985).[68]

These collections treated such topics as the arms race, the teaching of writing, and student unrest, along with Boyle's personal musings about writing and writers. Reviewers were receptive, particularly for what the essays revealed about Boyle's own personal commitment to both her politics and her craft. Anne Chisholm's response to *Words That Must Somehow Be Said* in the *London Times Literary Supplement* reflects the general tenor of critical response to these volumes. She stated that Boyle deserves celebration "for her indomitable spirit and for the tradition she upholds: the radical intellectual streak in American culture, now unfashionable, which holds that dissent on grounds of conscience is not anti-American but essentially American."[69]

Boyle's continued political involvement during her final years is reflected in her last novel, *The Underground Woman* (1975).[70] A fictional rendering of internment of Boyle, together with singer Joan Baez and her mother, for blocking the entrance to the Oakland draft board, and of Boyle's daughter's frightening involvement with a Manson-like cult that took over Boyle's home, the novel combines these subjects with frequent allusions to Greek mythology. It received diverse reviews; the *New Yorker* called it "a reflective, well-written novel" whose heroine is "an intelligent, affecting, and memorable creation," while other reviewers found the novel fundamentally unconvincing. The reviewer for *Newsweek* insisted that the volume "shouldn't have been a novel at all."[71]

Still the innovator, Boyle created a new form of nonfiction with her 1968 publication of a dual autobiography: a reissue of Robert McAlmon's reminiscences of Paris in the '20s interspersed with newly written chapters of her recollections of the period. The volume of joint memoirs, *Being Geniuses Together 1920–1930* (1968) was praised for the duality of its perspective by most reviewers. Malcolm Cowley wrote a laudatory response for the *New York Times Book Review*. Commending Boyle's writing, Cowley stated that she seems "bound to the craft like a medieval apprentice," and considered the collaboration "amazingly successful" because of its "impression of depth and substantiality that have been lacking in other memoirs," including McAlmon's original version.[72]

During the last twenty years of her life, Boyle slowly gained a new generation of followers though the publication of collections of her short fiction and poetry and through reissues of earlier novels, such as the Virago Press Series' publication of *Plagued by the Nightingale*, *Year Before Last*, and *My Next Bride*.[73] Boyle wrote the introduction for *Plagued by the Nightingale*, and Doris Grumbach wrote afterwords for the other two volumes of Boyle's trilogy of the young American female abroad. In 1989, New Directions reissued *Death of a Man,* with an important introduction by Burton Hatlen,[74] which received generally positive responses.[75] Throughout Boyle's lifetime, *Three Short Novels* went through various editions, and Boyle edited the 1991 reissue of *Gentlemen, I Address You Privately.*[76]

The collection *Fifty Stories,* which appeared in 1980, drew upon Boyle's work in short fiction from 1927 through 1966.[77] The locales were as varied as Boyle's had been: the Midwest, Atlantic City, France, England, Austria, occupied Germany, New York, and San Francisco. Writing for the *New York Times Book Review,* Vance Bourjaily called the collection a "wonderful exhibit of techniques and themes in evolution." He also stated that no assessment of Boyle's career would be complete without looking at her poetry and novels and he declared that this collected volume "should serve to get that assessment off to a strong start."[78] Carole Cook called the book Boyle's "best," stating that Boyle forces the reader to "suspend our grudging disbelief in man's honor and to share in her passionate idealism."[79]

Copper Canyon Press published the *Collected Poems of Kay Boyle* in 1991.[80] While the reviewers were short on analyzing Boyle's poetic technique, they appreciated the underlying spirit of her work. Writing for the *Antioch Review,* Molly Bendall called the volume "an important document, not only of a public and private writer, but of our 20th century."[81] Ellen Kaufman characterized the poems as "uninhibited and passionate" astounding in their forthright treatment of political issues. Kaufman found Boyle's "eroticism . . . most compelling" but complained that the poems are uneven and can lapse into pretension and appear derivative.[82]

While the reviews of her work constitute a somewhat problematic barometer of Boyle's estimation during her lifetime, they certainly reflect the inconstancy of that valuation. After the initial positive criticism from William Carlos Williams and Katherine Anne Porter, literary scholars have been slow to recognize Boyle as important, and she has only recently begun to gain the recognition that many other writers have long maintained is her due. That movement seems to be growing, and Boyle's literary reputation again appears to be ascending.

Boyle received brief, but complimentary, critical attention in Harlan Hatcher's 1935 assessment of the creation of the modern novel; he described her work as uneven, but complimented Boyle's brilliant facility and "vivid prose that stings and delights the mind with its sharp clarity and its cadenced vehemence."[83] He placed Boyle in the school of poetic realism and cautioned that "her fine craftsmanship, expended upon too specialized and unimportant materials, protrudes as craftsmanship."[84]

This claim is certainly one that appears in the reviews of Boyle's work as well, and the criticism written in the '50s and '60s attempted to answer this charge. Richard C. Carpenter's article, "Kay Boyle," published in 1953, is the first serious critical assessment of Boyle's proper literary place, using an approach that Carpenter continued in his "Kay Boyle: The Figure in the Carpet," published in 1965. In the former, Carpenter writes a convincing assessment of Boyle's literary career through the publication of *The Smoking Mountain,* concluding that more readers would benefit from seeing that "Miss Boyle not only can dazzle us with style but also can move us to a deeper understanding."[85] The latter offers a compelling analysis of both "The Crazy Hunter" and "The Bridegroom's Body" and suggests that Boyle's greatest accomplishment as a writer is her acknowledgment of "the paramount value of love for fallible and limited human beings, for whom nothing else is a proper substitute." Carpenter argues that Kay Boyle demonstrates in these stories that "she is an artist deeply involved with one of literature's most enduring and significant concerns."[86]

Harry T. Moore's insightful introductory essay to the 1966 reissue of *Plagued by the Nightingale* gave Boyle's work serious consideration,[87] as did his essay on Boyle's fiction in his volume *Age of the Modern and Other Essays,* which appeared in 1971.[88] Moore sees Boyle's value primarily as an American writer of the international theme and argues that "[s]ince James, no American except Kay Boyle has concentrated so thoroughly upon that theme."[89] He interprets Boyle's mixed critical reception to be the result of her writing about subjects that were unfashionable for the times, arguing that Boyle's proper place is "among the fine women authors of our time who do not write like men (as, say, Willa Cather does), but operate through a distinctly feminine vision (as Dorothy Richardson does), to capture and project experience in a unique and important way."[90]

Sandra Spanier's groundbreaking, book-length study of Boyle, *Kay Boyle: Artist and Activist,* which was originally published in 1986, provided the first in-depth assessment of Boyle's entire writing career. A comprehensive critical biography that includes perceptive analyses of most of Boyle's work, the study is invaluable for its insights into Boyle's writing and for its carefully argued connections about the relationship between the work and both the period in which it was written and Boyle's life. Spanier's book reasons persuasively that "[d]espite the surface diversity of her works . . . hers is a unified vision . . . motivated by what she calls 'the crusading spirit.' "[91] Spanier concludes that "in her strong stands against war and any brand of personal or social oppression, she continues to express her belief in the absolute necessity for human beings to connect with one another."[92] Spanier's introduction to Boyle's volume of previously uncollected stories, *Life Being the Best and Other Stories* (1988), also helped to awaken new interest in Boyle's work, as did the "Kay Boyle Issue," which Spanier edited for *Twentieth Century Literature* (fall 1988).[93]

In addition to personal portraits of Boyle written by her friends, this special issue contained a number of important critical articles: Deborah Denenholz Morse's "*My Next Bride:* Kay Boyle's Text of the Female Artist," Edward

M. Uehling's "Tails You Lose: Kay Boyle's War Fiction," and Elizabeth S. Bell's "Call Forth a Good Day: The Nonfiction of Kay Boyle." Morse's essay makes a strong statement for reading *My Next Bride* as a female *Kunstlerroman,* connecting her novel to that developing genre in 1930s England. Morse concluded that Boyle's text shapes a new version of this form, one that requires the artist to incorporate into her artistic vision compassion for a world in pain. In his analysis of Boyle's short fiction about war, Uehling elucidates the way in which Boyle portrays the full cost of war through her disquieting portrait of survivors. He argues that Boyle's presentation of the gap between public utterance and private thought suggests ways in which both language and moral courage fail in the spiritual aftermath of combat. Bell suggests that the essays of Boyle's later years serve as the completion of the circle that Boyle began in the '20s; Boyle continued to speak for those who are unempowered, using whatever form is necessary to reach new audiences.[94]

Two authors of other excellent essays from the 1988 volume further developed their essays for other forums, allowing them to reach an even broader audience with their call to reevaluate Boyle's literary career. In her thought-provoking analysis of women's role in the experimental writing of modernism, Suzanne Clark's *Sentimental Modernism: Women Writers and the Revolution of the Word* (1991) devoted an important section to Kay Boyle's rewriting of the new word and the ways in which her newness differed from that of her male contemporaries. The chapter, "Revolution, the Woman, and the Word: Kay Boyle," contends that Boyle's "innovations qualify her as a revolutionary of lyric language" and submits that Boyle opens up language to the "pressure of emotion" in ways that are simultaneously "modernist and womanly."[95]

Burton Hatlen converted his essay into an introduction to the reissue of *Death of a Man.*[96] In his important, feminist reading of the novel, it becomes "an integrated work of art, in which every detail works toward a subtle, complex effect" which "deserves a new generation of readers, both for the delicacy of its arts and the power of its political and psychological insights."[97]

Martin Meyer's 1990 essay "Kay Boyle's Postwar Germany" affords a more international perspective on Boyle's success in depicting post-1945 Germany. He argues that Boyle's belief that Germany had been spiritually exhausted by the war made her seem wary of Germany's recovery, but that it also allowed her to portray Germans as creative enough to build a better society. He praises Boyle for her ability to see opportunities for change when most Americans still envisioned Germans as evil incarnate, and he suggests that Boyle shows her readers that what happened in Germany was not impossible elsewhere.[98]

Elizabeth Bell's *Kay Boyle: A Study of the Short Fiction,* published in 1992, analyzes Boyle's contribution to this genre and suggests that she is among the best writers of short fiction of the twentieth century. The volume offers sensitive interpretations of most of Boyle's major stories and presents a lucid survey of Boyle's career in this genre. In addition, it includes reviews of the fiction collections, articulate recollections of Boyle composed by her writer friends, and an interesting group of Boyle interviews.[99]

The present editor's *Metamorphosizing the Novel: Kay Boyle's Narrative Innovations* (1993) provides analyses of all of Boyle's novels, proffering readings of books that had previously received only cursory examination. The study indicates that Boyle's longer fiction is revolutionary not only with its experimental language but also in its presentation of alternative scripts for female characters. It maintains that while Boyle was certainly not an avowed feminist, she created feminist characters, placing them in transformative plots, and, therefore, scripted new possibilities for both the women writers who followed her and their readers.

In addition to these recent book-length examinations, contemporary critics are beginning to write essays that connect Boyle with other female writers of the period. Donna Hollenberg's 1994 essay, "Abortion, Identity Formation, and the Expatriate Woman Writer: H.D. and Kay Boyle in the Twenties," posits that Boyle was revolutionary in her treatment of the subject matter of women's abortions and that both Boyle and H.D. used expatriation as an opportunity to explore "the impingement of gender roles upon their lives and aspirations."[100]

Boyle's life as a writer has recently received new consideration as well. Joan Mellen's biography provides a wealth of new information about the details of Boyle's life. While much of it was gleaned from interviews and from the Kay Boyle collections at the University of Delaware and Southern Illinois University libraries, far too much of it is inferred from Boyle's fiction and poetry. Mellen often reads the fiction as though it is strictly autobiographical, leading to interpretations of this material that are disconcerting. Both Alice Hall Petry and Bettina Berch have commented on the unreliability of Mellen's analyses and have voiced concerns about the intent of the volume, with Petry concluding that "anyone with a particular interest in Boyle's writing would be better served by Sandra Whipple Spanier's *Kay Boyle: Artist and Activist*, a thoughtful critical biography."[101] Mellen seems to suffer from a recent phenomenon regarding biography: a penchant for presenting writers in an unfavorable light whenever possible.

Interest in Boyle has taken other scholarly forms as well. Boyle has been the subject of three special Modern Language Association sessions (1979, 1987, and 1991), and with the help of a National Endowment for the Humanities Grant, Sandra Spanier is currently preparing Boyle's letters for publication. The availability of this correspondence will further our understanding of the seriousness of Boyle's intent—both as a writer and as an activist who hoped to use the power of words to improve the general conditions under which people lived. The letters should also illuminate the ways in which Boyle connected the private with the public in her life and work. Because Boyle was so involved with the political and literary issues of her time, the letters will afford an opportunity to look at the century through her perceptive and observant eyes. Spanier's edition of Boyle's letters should also do much to correct some of the misrepresentation of Mellen's biography. Perhaps the letters and other previously unpublished materials—some of which have been unavailable until now because of Boyle's own stipulations—will fuel other biographies that present us with an even richer, more comprehensive picture both of Boyle and of her literary output.

Certainly, Boyle's writing offers a myriad of possibilities for further investigation. The concluding essays in this volume are only a first step in that direction. Because so little has been written about Boyle's poetry, Linda Wagner-Martin's essay on Boyle's poetic vision offers an important beginning to our reassessment of Boyle's work in this genre. The essay also helps us understand the importance of poetry in the formation of Boyle's fiction style.

Within the tradition of the American woman writer who moves abroad to live and write, Dianne Chambers connects Boyle's work to that of Edith Wharton, Boyle's literary foremother, whose work she claimed to dislike, and illuminates both writers' treatment of the resulting cultural clashes in terms of motherhood, family values, and women's roles. Her essay, "Female Roles and National Identity in Kay Boyle's *Plagued by the Nightingale* and Edith Wharton's *Madame de Treymes*," compares the writers' treatment of expatriation and cultural identity and argues that Boyle's and Wharton's willingness to explore cultural and gender differences in both fiction and memoir provides contemporary readers with a more complete version of the expatriate experience. Abby H. P. Werlock explores Boyle-Wharton connections as well, but she focuses on the ways in which Boyle continues the work begun by Wharton: the provision of powerful and empowering legacies for women. She postulates that within the confines of a single work, Boyle's *My Next Bride* incorporates most of the gender-based dilemmas that Wharton treated in a number of novels. For Werlock, Boyle's novel expands the horizon of possibilities for women.

In his analysis of Boyle's admitted favorite among her novels, Burton Hatlen repositions *Monday Night* in "an intertextual space" between the two broad literary currents of the period: French surrealism and American novels of the "tough guy" and "innocents abroad" school. He suggests that Boyle successfully combines these schools and interprets the novel as an exploration of the ways in which the cultural circumstances of America and France structure the modes of male desire. He proposes that Boyle is unique among her female contemporaries in her literary mix of feminism and sexual warmth toward men.

Christine H. Hait's essay "Life-Giving: Kay Boyle's Innovations in Autobiography in *Being Geniuses Together* analyzes how Boyle's additions to *Being Geniuses Together* work to "redeem and recollect another." Hait submits that Boyle's approach is itself self-consciously modern by problematizing the actions of memory and recollection through her open recognition of their pit-falls. Boyle's work, then, becomes a kind of meta-autobiography, honest and direct as it calls attention to its inability to be so.

These new essays, prepared especially for this volume, join the others in this book in an attempt to correct the continued underestimation of Boyle's contribution to American literature and culture. It is to be hoped that this book will aid in the growing interest in her work and in our need to reclaim her as an important writer of the twentieth century, who wrote longer, more prolifically, and more politically than her peers, managing to outlive most of them as well.

Before the revisioning of American literature that began with the femi-nist and civil rights movements of the '70s, Boyle's reputation suffered from many of the same problems confronting the literary standing of other women writers. Her reclamation has not been as extensive as that of many of these authors, however, and Boyle continues to be a worthy candidate for further reevaluation—for a return to the literary stature that she once enjoyed among, and along with, her now more famous peers.

As Sandra Spanier has pointed out, Boyle "had little patience for the high art of alienation and despair. She believe[d] that there are still responsi-bilities to be taken and choices to be made."[102] Willing to take literary and personal risks for her beliefs, Boyle was dedicated both to her art and to her liberal political principles. Her political insights and motivation in her writ-ing were carefully matched by her innovative use of language and form, reflecting her ability to take such issues into the realm of art. Consequently, Boyle never took the safe and easy route, but always ventured into the high ground, taking her political beliefs into artistic arenas that other writers often deemed too dangerous or too unseemly. This blending of what more tradi-tional critics regard as disparate realms may be partly responsible for her con-tinued undervaluation. Surely, this aspect of Boyle's work merits additional research.

Perhaps Boyle's iconoclastic approach to the roles of woman and writer—her insistence that a woman can be a feminist, an active heterosex-ual, and an artist—has also helped to keep her hovering at the margins of the modernist canon. Using the established experimental style of modernism, she challenged ideas about gender roles, often employing themes that centered on women's experience. As many of the more recent essays in this volume attest, this combination of woman-centered text and modernist style makes Boyle an important literary foremother. While this unusual blending may complicate the easy categorization, assessment, and placement of her achieve-ment, it provides a worthwhile challenge for literary scholars, especially femi-nists.

Kay Boyle's revolutionary words offer a unique chronicle of the major public and private concerns of twentieth-century life. The typewriters that she transported throughout Europe and the United States could prove to be as powerful as the imaginary weapons Boyle placed in her hands in her 1978 self-portrait. It is time for scholars to treat her as the "dangerous" literary "radical" she has always been. Her innovations offer us the opportunity to do groundbreaking work of our own.

Notes

1. Merla Zellerbach, "When Writers Give Themselves Away," *San Francisco Chronicle,* 15 March 1978.

2. Eric Pace, "Kay Boyle, 90, Writer of Novels and Stories, Dies," *New York Times,* 29 December 1992.

3. David Daiches, introduction to *Fifty Stories,* by Kay Boyle (New York: Doubleday, 1980), 9–14.

4. See, for example, William Carlos Williams, "The Somnambulists," *transition* 18 (November 1929): 145–46; Katherine Anne Porter, "Kay Boyle: Example to the Young," *New Republic,* 22 April 1931, 278–79.

5. For Boyle's recollections of her mother's role in her formation as an artist, see Robert McAlmon, *Being Geniuses Together 1920–1930,* revised with supplementary chapters and an afterword by Kay Boyle (San Francisco: North Point, 1984), especially 18–23. Joan Mellen's recent biography criticizes Mrs. Boyle for pushing her daughters to become successful artists, describing the mother-daughter relationship as psychologically harmful to Kay Boyle. See Joan Mellen, *Kay Boyle: Author of Herself* (New York: Farrar, Straus and Giroux, 1994), especially 26–46. Mellen treats Mrs. Boyle as a kind of stage mother who is "disappointed in [her] husband" and, therefore, revolves her life around her daughters, training Kay to be shallow and selfish. Yet Mellen also states that the young Kay, as a result of her mother's political and artistic activism, thought that "the poet's role was to expose and reform an unjust world where the innocent suffer, a view she was to hold all her life. The artist searches out the pain of those who cannot speak for themselves" (p. 35). This belief hardly seems selfish and narcissistic. Replete with such inconsistencies, the biography presents Kay Boyle as self-seeking and a bad mother, personal characteristics that other accounts of Boyle's life never mention. In her review of Mellen's book, Bettina Berch states that Mellen's "mean-spiritedness masquerades as well-intentioned truth-seeking" (review of *Kay Boyle: Author of Herself,* by Joan Mellen, *Belles Lettres* 24 [fall 1994]: 64–65).

6. Quoted in Sandra Whipple Spanier, *Kay Boyle: Artist and Activist* (Carbondale: Southern Illinois University Press, 1986), 8.

7. Kay Boyle, *Short Stories* (Paris: Black Sun Press, 1929).

8. Williams, 145–46.

9. For example, see Spanier, *Kay Boyle;* Elizabeth S. Bell, *Kay Boyle: A Study of the Short Fiction* (New York: Twayne, 1992); and Marilyn Elkins, *Metamorphosizing the Novel: Kay Boyle's Narrative Innovations* (New York: Peter Lang, 1993).

10. Spanier describes this early collection as a "sampler of Kay Boyle at her best," commenting on Boyle's "finely wrought style" and "skill in manipulating" (*Kay Boyle,* 56).

11. Gerald Sykes, "Too Good to Be Smart," *Nation,* (24 December 1930), 711.

12. "Kay Boyle's Experiments," *New York Times,* 16 November 1930.

13. Kay Boyle, *Plagued by the Nightingale* (New York: Jonathan Cape and Harrison Smith, 1931).

14. See, for example, reviews of *Plagued by the Nightingale*, in the *Nation*, 6 May 1931, 509; Viola Meynell, *The New Statesman and Nation*, 1 August 1931, 144; L. A. G. Strong, *Spectator*, 18 July 1931, 93.

15. Porter, "Kay Boyle," 278–79.

16. Kay Boyle, *Year before Last* (New York: Jonathan Cape and Harrison Smith, 1932).

17. Robert Cantwell, "American Exile," *Nation*, 20 July 1932, 60.

18. Myra Marini, review of *Year before Last*, by Kay Boyle, *The New Republic*, 13 July 1932, 242.

19. Gladys Graham, "Inescapable End," *Saturday Review of Literature*, 9 July 1932, 827.

20. Kay Boyle, *The First Lover, and Other Stories* (New York: Harrison Smith and Robert Haas, 1933); Kay Boyle, *Gentlemen, I Address You Privately* (New York: Harrison Smith and Robert Haas, 1933).

21. Karl Schriftglesser, review of *The First Lover, and Other Stories*, by Kay Boyle, *Boston Transcript*, 25 March 1933.

22. See, for example, review of *The First Lover, and Other Stories*, by Kay Boyle, *Forum* 89 (May 1933): vi; Louis Kronenberger, review of *First Lover, and Other Stories*, by Kay Boyle *New York Times*, 25 March 1933.

23. Review of *Gentlemen, I Address You Privately*, by Kay Boyle, *Nation*, 29 November 1933, 630. See also Louis Kronenberger, "Kay Boyle's Story of a Moral Crisis," *New York Times*, 12 November 1933. When Boyle revised the book for its 1991 reissue, she removed most of the novel's overabundant modifiers; she seemed to have agreed with the comments of many of these critics and often referred to the book as overwritten (quoted in Spanier, *Kay Boyle*, 72; see also Elkins, 65).

24. Kay Boyle, *My Next Bride* (New York: Harcourt, 1934).

25. Mary McCarthy, "Romance of Paris," *Nation*, 26 December 1934, 746.

26. Edith H. Walton, "Miss Boyle's Irony," *New York Times Book Review*, 11 November 1934, 6.

27. Kay Boyle, *Death of a Man* (New York: Harcourt, 1936).

28. Burton Hatlen, "Sexual Politics in Kay Boyle's *Death of a Man*," *Twentieth Century Literature*, 34 (1988): 347–61.

29. Geoffrey Parsons, "Kay Boyle's Profound and Poetic Style," *Books*, 11 October 1936, 3.

30. Alfred Kazin, "Kay Boyle's New Novel," *New York Times*, 11 October 1936.

31. Kay Boyle, *The White Horses of Vienna, and Other Stories* (New York: Harcourt, 1936).

32. Elizabeth Hart, "The Style of Miss Kay Boyle," *New York Herald Tribune Books*, 9 February 1936, 5; R. W. Seaver, review of *White Horses of Vienna, and Other Stories*, by Kay Boyle, *Boston Transcript*, 13 February 1936.

33. Kay Boyle, *Monday Night* (New York: Harcourt, 1938). Boyle frequently stated that this novel was her most satisfying (see McAlmon, *Being Geniuses Together*, 291; Dan Tooker and Roger Hofheins, "Kay Boyle," in *Fiction! Interviews with Northern California Novelists* [New York: Harcourt Brace, 1976], 15–35; and Bell, *Kay Boyle*, 93).

34. The character, Wilt Tobin, is apparently based on Harold Stearns. For a thorough discussion of this connection, see Spanier, *Kay Boyle*, 126–27.

35. Louis Kronenberger, review of *Monday Night*, by Kay Boyle, *Nation*, 30 July 1938, 111.

36. Phillip Hartung, review of *Monday Night*, by Kay Boyle, *Commonweal* 28 (19 August 1938): 432; review of *Monday Night*, by Kay Boyle, *London Times Literary Supplement*, 15 October 1938, 665.

37. Kay Boyle, *A Glad Day* (Norfolk, Conn.: New Directions, 1938).

38. Babette Deutsch, "An Unhabitual Way," *Nation,* 12 November 1938, 514.

39. Louise Bogan, review of *A Glad Day,* by Kay Boyle, *New Yorker,* 22 October 1938, 95.

40. Kay Boyle, *The Crazy Hunter: Three Short Novels* (New York: Harcourt, 1940).

41. William Soskin, review of *The Crazy Hunter: Three Short Novels,* by Kay Boyle, *Books,* 10 March 1940, 2; Olga Owens, review of *The Crazy Hunter: Three Short Novels,* by Kay Boyle, *Boston Transcript,* 9 March 1940, 1; Otis Ferguson, review of *The Crazy Hunter: Three Short Novels,* by Kay Boyle *New Republic,* 8 April 1940, 480.

42. Peter Monro Jack, "Three Unusual Stories by Kay Boyle," *New York Times,* 17 March 1940.

43. Clifton Fadiman, review of *The Crazy Hunter: Three Short Novels,* by Kay Boyle, *New Yorker* 16 (9 March 1940): 88–89.

44. Quoted in Hugh Ford, *Four Lives in Paris* (San Francisco: North Point Press, 1987), 224.

45. Kay Boyle, *Primer for Combat* (New York: Simon and Schuster, 1942).

46. Raoul De Roussy De Sales, review of *Primer for Combat,* by Kay Boyle, *Atlantic Monthly,* December 1942, 152; Malcolm Cowley, "Lost Worlds," *New Republic,* 9 November 1942, 614; Robert Littell, review of *Primer for Combat,* by Kay Boyle, *Yale Review* 32 (winter 1943): viii.

47. Kay Boyle, *Avalanche* (New York: Simon and Schuster, 1944).

48. Struthers Burt, "Kay Boyle's Conscience and Melodrama," *Saturday Review of Literature,* 15 January 1944, 6.

49. Edmund Wilson, "Kay Boyle and *The Saturday Evening Post,*" *New Yorker,* 15 January 1944, 66–69.

50. Diana Trilling, review of *Avalanche,* by Kay Boyle *Nation,* 22 January 1944, 105.

51. Quoted in Spanier, *Kay Boyle,* 163.

52. Elizabeth Bullock, "*Avalanche:* The Book Versus the Critics," *Chicago Sun Book Week,* 23 January 1944, 2.

53. Kay Boyle, *A Frenchman Must Die* (New York: Simon and Schuster, 1946).

54. Kay Boyle, *The Seagull on the Step* (New York: Knopf, 1955). See, for example, Sidney Alexander, review of *Seagull on the Step,* by Kay Boyle, *New York Times,* 8 May 1955.

55. Review of *Seagull on the Steps,* by Kay Boyle, *London Times Literary Supplement,* 9 December 1955, 737.

56. Kay Boyle, *Thirty Stories* (New York: Simon and Schuster, 1946).

57. Struthers Burt, "The Mature Craft of Kay Boyle," *Saturday Review of Literature,* 30 November 1946, 11.

58. Kay Boyle, *1939* (New York: Simon and Schuster, 1948).

59. Edward Weeks, "The Sitzmark," *Atlantic* 181 (April 1948): 108; Nona Balakian, "Two Cards at a Time," *New York Times,* 15 February 1948; review of *1939,* by Kay Boyle, *New Yorker,* 13 March 1948, 123.

60. Walter Havighurst, "Avalanche in the Haute-Savoie," *Saturday Review of Literature,* 28 February 1948, 12; Florence Haxton Bullock, "The Man Without a Country," *New York Herald Tribune Weekly Book Review,* 15 February 1948, 4.

61. Kay Boyle, *His Human Majesty* (New York: McGraw-Hill, Whittlesey House, 1949).

62. See, for example, Peter White, review of *His Human Majesty,* by Kay Boyle, *Commonweal* 50 (20 May 1949): 155; Nona Balakian, review of *His Human Majesty,* by Kay Boyle, *New York Times,* 10 April 1949.

63. Kay Boyle, *The Smoking Mountain: Stories of Postwar Germany* (New York: McGraw-Hill, 1951); *Generation without Farewell* (New York: Knopf, 1960).

64. Harry T. Moore, "In Germany the Ruins Still Smolder," *New York Times,* 22 April 1951.

65. See, for example, Belle Pomer, review of *Generation without Farewell,* by Kay Boyle, *Canadian Forum* 40 (June 1960): 66; Melvin Maddocks, review of *Generation without Farewell,* by Kay Boyle, *Christian Science Monitor,* 21 January 1960, 5; Max Cosman, review of *Generation without Farewell,* by Kay Boyle, *Commonweal* 71 (8 January 1960): 425; William Hogan, review of *Generation without Farewell,* by Kay Boyle, *San Francisco Chronicle,* 22 January 1960.

66. Virgilia Peterson, review of *Generation without Farewell,* by Kay Boyle, *New York Times Book Review,* 17 January 1960, 4; William Stuckey, "Some Recent Fiction," *Minnesota Review* 1 (1960): 119; review of *Generation without Farewell,* by Kay Boyle, *Time,* 25 January 1960, 94.

67. Elizabeth S. Bell, introduction to *Words That Must Somehow Be Said: Selected Essays of Kay Boyle,* 1927–1984, by Kay Boyle (San Francisco: North Point, 1985), ix–xiv.

68. Kay Boyle, *The Long Walk at San Francisco State and Other Essays* (New York: Grove, 1972).

69. Anne Chisholm, review of *Words That Must Somehow Be Said,* by Kay Boyle, *London Times Literary Supplement,* 27 September 1985, 1076.

70. Kay Boyle, *The Underground Woman* (Garden City, N.Y.: Doubleday, 1975).

71. Review of *The Underground Woman,* by Kay Boyle, *New Yorker,* 20 January 1975, 97. For less favorable responses, see Gail Harlow, review of *The Underground Woman,* by Kay Boyle, *Library Journal* 100 (1 February 1975): 309; review of *Underground Woman,* by Kay Boyle, *Newsweek,* 13 January 1975, 67A.

72. Malcolm Cowley, "Those Paris Years," *New York Times Book Review,* 9 June 1968, 1.

73. Kay Boyle, *Plagued by the Nightingale,* (1931; reprint, London: Virago Press, 1981); *Year Before Last* (1932; reprint, with an afterword by Doris Grumbach, London: Virago Press, 1986); *My Next Bride* (1934, reprint, with an afterword by Doris Grumbach, London: Virago Press, 1986).

74. Kay Boyle, *Death of a Man* (1936; reprint, with an introduction by Burton Hatlen, New York: New Directions, 1989).

75. See, for example, Steve Kettmann, "Old Novel Offers Insights into Nazism," *San Francisco Chronicle,* 14 September 1989.

76. Kay Boyle, *Three Short Novels* (Boston: Beacon Press, 1958; reprint, with an introduction by Margaret Atwood, New York: Penguin Books, 1982; reprint, with an introduction by Doris Grumbach, New York: New Directions, 1991; *Gentlemen, I Address You Privately* (1933; reprint, Santa Barbara, Calif.: Capra Press, 1991).

77. Kayle Boyle, *Fifty Stories* (Garden City, N.Y.: Doubleday, 1980).

78. Vance Bourjaily, "Moving and Maturing," *New York Times Book Review,* 28 September 1980, 9, 32.

79. Carole Cook, review of *Fifty Stories,* by Kay Boyle, *Saturday Review* 7 (September 1980): 70.

80. Kay Boyle, *The Collected Poems of Kay Boyle* (Port Townsend, Wash.: Copper Canyon Press, 1991).

81. Molly Bendall, review of *The Collected Poems of Kay Boyle,* by Kay Boyle, *Antioch Review* 50 (fall 1992): 780.

82. Ellen Kaufman, review of *The Collected Poems of Kay Boyle,* by Kay Boyle, *Library Journal* 116 (August 1991): 105.

83. Harlan Hatcher, *Creating the Modern American Novel* (New York: Russell and Russell, 1935), 258–61.

84. Hatcher, *Modern American Novel,* 260.

85. Richard C. Carpenter, "Kay Boyle," *College English* 15 (November 1953): 81–87.

86. Richard C. Carpenter, "Kay Boyle: The Figure in the Carpet," *Critique* 7 (winter 1964–65): 65–78.

87. Harry T. Moore, introduction to *Plagued by the Nightingale,* by Kay Boyle (1931; reprint, Carbondale: Southern Illinois Press, 1966).

88. Harry T. Moore, "Kay Boyle's Fiction," in *Age of the Modern and Other Essays* (Carbondale: Southern Illinois University Press, 1971), 32–36.

89. Moore, "Kay Boyle's Fiction," 32.

90. Moore, "Kay Boyle's Fiction," 36.

91. Spanier, *Kay Boyle,* 219–20.

92. Spanier, *Kay Boyle,* 220.

93. Kay Boyle, *Life Being the Best and Other Stories* (New York: New Directions, 1988); "*Kay Boyle Issue,*" *Twentieth Century Literature,* 34, no. 3 (fall 1988).

94. Deborah Denenholz Morse, "*My Next Bride:* Kay Boyle's Text of the Female Artist," *Twentieth Century Literature* 34 (1988), 334–46; Edward M. Uehling, "Tails You Lose: Kay Boyle's War Fiction," *Twentieth Century Literature* 34 (1988), 375–83; Elizabeth S. Bell, "Call Forth a Good Day: The Nonfiction of Kay Boyle," *Twentieth Century Literature* 34 (1988), 384–91. All are reprinted in the present volume.

95. Suzanne Clark, *Sentimental Modernism: Women Writers and the Revolution of the Word* (Bloomington: Indiana University Press, 1991), 127–54.

96. Burton Hatlen, introduction to *Death of a Man* (reprint, 1989), v–xii.

97. Hatlen, introduction to *Death of a Man* (reprint, 1989), xii.

98. Martin Meyer, "Kay Boyle's Postwar Germany," in *Germany and German Thought in American Literature and Cultural Criticism,* ed. Peter Freese (Essen: Verlag Die Blaue Eule, 1990), 205–29.

99. Bell, *Kay Boyle.*

100. Donna Hollenberg, "Abortion, Identity Formation, and the Expatriate Woman Writer: H.D. and Kay Boyle in the Twenties," *Twentieth Century Literature* 40 (1994): 499–517.

101. See Berch, review; Alice Hall Petry, review of *Kay Boyle: Author of Herself,* by Joan Mellen, *American Literature* 67 (1995): 164–65.

102. Spanier, introduction to *Life Being the Best and Other Stories,* xvii.

REVIEWS
◆

The Somnambulists

WILLIAM CARLOS WILLIAMS

There is, in a democracy, a limit beyond which thought is not expected to leap. All men being presumed equal, it becomes an offense if this dead limit be exceeded. But within the opacity which encloses them the American people are bright, active and efficient. They believe in science and philosophy and work hard to control disease, to master the crime in their cities and to prevent the excessive drinking of alcohol. Alcohol is the specific for their condition, thus they fear it; to drink to excess breaks the shell of their lives so that momentarily, when they drink, they waken. Or they drink, under subterfuge, as much as they may desire, but it is a public offense, for all that, which the very drinkers themselves acknowledge.

When one wakes from that sleep, literature is among the things which confront him, old literature to begin with and finally the new. In the United States let us say first Emily Dickinson and then Kay Boyle. To waken is terrifying. Asleep, freedom lives. Awake, Emily Dickinson was torn apart by her passion; driven back to cover she imprisoned herself in her father's garden, the mark of injury she deplored, an opacity beyond which she could not penetrate. And in literature, since it is of literature that I am writing, it is the mark of our imprisonment by sleep, the continuous mark, that in estimating the work of E. D., still our writers praise her rigidity of the sleep walker—the rapt gaze, the thought of Heaven—and the structural warping of her lines, the rhymelessness, the distress marking the place at which she turned back. She was a beginning, a trembling at the edge of waking—and the terror it imposes. But she could not, and so it remains.

It remains with us the wilderness, the Indians, the forest, the night, the New World—as already pointed out. Kay Boyle was quick to take up this realization. A woman, as fully impassioned as was her famous compatriot, but trembling today on the other side of waking, her short stories assault our sleep. They are of high degree of excellence; for that reason they will not succeed in America, they are lost, damned. Simply, the person who has a comprehensive, if perhaps disturbing view of what takes place in the human understanding at moments of intense living, and puts it down in its proper shapes and color, is anathema to United Statesers and can have no standing with them. We are asleep.

In some moods it may be charming, a breaking and holding that reminds one of surf on rocks. But good God, it is the breaking of the barriers to our lives that is human, not the dashing of ourselves to pieces on granite that we should praise. We try and yet we do not lift a finger. In what country will such freedom of intercourse exist among school children? And in what country, on the other hand, is the fear of genius so pronounced in the midst of such over-powering wealth? In what other country, its potential home, could a jazz opera by a German composer be received and paid for while not the faintest flick of support and encouragement is accorded to a man like George Antheil, an out-standing genius among us, whose works Germany and France both have hon-ored? The German work which we have accepted is pale, abstract, removed from direct contact with our lives, an opera in a foolish dream. Antheil's work hits home. It is one of our characteristics that we distrust each other and are rivals to show how appreciative we are of foreign distinction. Antheil is antipa-thetic to us. It is that we fear to awaken and in sleep all are equal.

The phenomenon of our attitude toward the work of George Antheil and what must be Kay Boyle's reception; the brilliant newspapers actively trem-bling under a veil; the work of the poet H. D.; the young wife that walked six blocks asleep in her husband's pajamas one winter's night, the pants' bottoms trailing in the mud; the boy that, thinking himself in an airplane, dived from a window in a dream head down upon the gravel path—this is America accu-rately delineated. It is the School Board which, to make a rule, made a rule that forbids themselves from smoking at their evening meetings in the school building in order that they might prevent the janitors from smoking in the building while cleaning up the dirt after school. Fear to vary from the average, fear to feel, to see, to know, to experience—save under the opacity of a mist of equality, a mist of common mediocrity is our character.

The quality of Kay Boyle's stories has in it all of this strain. They are simple, quite simple, but an aberrant American effect is there in the style. There is something to say and one says it. That's writing. But to say it one must have it alive with the overtones which give not a type of statement but an actual statement that is alive, marked with a gait and appearance which show it to be the motion of an individual who has suffered it and brought it into fact. This is style. Excellence comes from overcoming difficulties. Kay Boyle has the difficulty of expression by Americans firmly in her mind and at the same time the female difficulties to make them more difficult. And yet, showing all this, the work may be done simply and directly; not with the hor-rible contortions, the agony of emission, the twisting and groaning and deforming effort of statement, seeking to disclose what it dare not acknowl-edge, the style of the repugnant Jurgen, tortured without relief in his quiet

Richmond library—free from interruption. Kay Boyle has succeeded in writing of difficult matters clearly and well and with a distinction that is outspoken and feminine—not resorting to that indirection and tortured deformity of thought and language, that involved imagery which allows us to lie and hide while we enjoy, the peep style of a coward.

Why do American artists go to France and continue to do so and when there to drink, if they are wise, heavily? It is not postwar hysteria as the newspapers and monthly reviews would make us believe—for it has always been the same. It is not, to repeat, postwar hysteria. We do not go there out of courtesy to the French. We go out of our direct need. Paris is the one place in the world that offers the West its compensation, and opportunity, in all its deformity of spirit to awaken. Drink breaks the savage spell of nonentity, or equality as they call it, which chokes them in the great western republic. In France, they find themselves, they drink and they are awakened, shocked to realize what they are, amazed loosed—as, in fact, they on their part shock and arouse the tenderest sentiments of astonishment and tolerance among the French. They are, in fact, for the first time in their lives—and it is curious—with the sound frequently of slops emptied from a bucket. Not always; however. Possibly, it will be enlightening, if something of spiritual worth is uncovered. But most that appears is stale, mediocre, not equal to the continental. The women, Americans, get to show their bodies—I don't mean the contours only—and American women in Paris have been anonymously very successful in latter years. At their best they are perhaps always anonymous. They seem delightfully exotic with their natural faces, pretty legs and feet and shoes.

Kay Boyle, in her stories, reveals herself, her body, as women must in any art and almost never do in writing, save when they are exceptionally distinguished. It is France again and she, partly from her own tragic history, more by France and alcohol, is awake. She has shown more than the exterior of her purely American female body. I don't know any other place where this has occurred. I speak of a work of art as a place where action has occurred as it occurs nowhere else. Kay Boyle has profited by her release to do a stroke of excellence which her country should honor her for. It never will.

It is a false hope, pathetic and amusing at the same time—like an old woman dying of a worn-out heart, broken over the loss of a pet dog, who refuses treatment but keeps a chicken wish-bone between her swollen feet under the bedclothes—that a man should think he can solve the everlasting and everpresent problem of making of literary excellence in a quiet, sane and orderly manner, using the same old wordbound ideas that have been successful with writers in the past, by the virtuous exercise of reason alone. The new is disorderly and lacks, it may be, all correlation with a ready body of listeners—who must be sacrificed—but it does not at least pretend to believe that out of old wrecks of thought, once successful, it can constitute by substitution and rearrangement alone that which is living, young and able.

Surely excellence kills sales. Why is an outspoken statement of this plain fact, known the world over to publishers and writers, always so carefully avoided? I know it is a cover in which writers hide their pique and, naturally, just because a work does not sell does not prove it good. But it certainly is known that even when excellence has a market, such a success is rarely its own but must be suspect, from the artist's viewpoint. Nearly always some quite accidental and therefore unimportant genre which such a work shows will be found to be the cause of its popularity. It is worthwhile in considering the extraordinary modeling and sure technique of Kay Boyle's work, what she has avoided and what included, to know that she has also written two novels (being hard pressed for cash) which two prominent New York publishers (one of them had given her his word that he would print her first novel) with typical cupidity have turned down.

This is the sum and sum again of the publishing situation in America. Plain it is and has always been and must be to anyone that the best is untimely as well as rare, new and therefore difficult of recognition, without immediate general interest (any more than a tomato was until prejudice had been knocked down) therefore, dependent on discerning support (without expectation of money benefit) from the able; scantily salable—and without attraction for the book trade. While wonders are advertised. And it is at the same time true that the only thing of worth in writing is this difficult, priceless thing that refreshes the whole field which it enters, perennially, when it will, the new.

The great and blackguardly American publishers, catering to the somnolence, think always and only of cash and, bat-blind, seeking to seem to favor the new out of fear lest they must toot for new that which is first salable, new in appearance only, but mediocre and trite in fact. There is nothing to be done about it, nothing except to continue to envision the fact and to continue, difficult as it may be, to build a new means of access to new work separate from the agents in control and their fashionable pimps.

Few women have written like this before, work equal in vigor to anything done by a man but with a twist that brings a new light into the whole Sahara of romanticism, a twist that carries the mind completely over until the male is not the seeing agent but the focus of the eye. The dirty tradition of women's modesty and the cringing of women behind law and tradition gets an airing that certainly calls for a protest from the corrupt puritans. The usual reader will not be used to fairness from a woman, this straightforward respect for the writer's trade. Nearly all the noteworthy women writers of the past that I can think of, or nearly all, have been men, essentially. Perhaps I should have said, all the women writers acceptable to the public.

Too Good to Be Smart

GERALD SYKES

Kay Boyle is the outstanding young woman member of that group of American writers who make their headquarters in Paris and whose work until recently has appeared for the most part in the pages of *transition*. This volume of short stories [*Wedding Day and Other Stories*], her first, was originally published in a special edition at Paris. Anyone who reads it and whose standards of the short story are not the standards of the correspondence school will appreciate that the work of Miss Boyle, for simple craftsmanship, is superior to most of that which is crowned annually by our anthologies. Anyone with an ear for new verbal harmonies will appreciate that Miss Boyle is a stylist of unusual taste and sensibility. It is time, therefore, to cease to regard her as a mere lower-case *révoltée* and to begin to accept her for what she is: more enterprising, more scrupulous, potentially more valuable than nine-tenths of our best-known women authors.

She is potentially valuable because it is possible—as it is so rarely possible—that she may write something that has not been written before. When we have read these few brief stories we realize that they sprang from a genuine inner necessity, that the author was helplessly obliged to communicate them with that blind honesty which is the best augury for the future. We also realize that she has an original gift. This gift is a sexual one. With the first sentence of the first story—"the horses . . . stamping and lashing themselves with fury because she passed by them"—we are thrust into the presence of feelings which could have been generated in no other place than a woman's body. And those pages which come to life prove almost invariably to have been written either by or about desire. This is a difficult subject to handle. Miss Boyle's solution, which for the most part is mischievous, not only stakes out a new field for herself but gives the clearest evidence of her integrity. For although she has allowed herself absolute freedom on one of the most delicate of all subjects she has not written an offensive line. In fact, she has put to shame nearly every other emancipated woman writer who has attempted to deal with this subject: she is by comparison so simple, so honest, so pure. It is

Reprinted with permission from *The Nation* magazine (December 24, 1930): 711–12. © The Nation Company, L.P.

probable that the two stories in which she has given comic treatment to sexual themes, Episode in the Life of an Ancestor and Summer, mark the highest stage of her development.

In view of her virtues it is all the more unfortunate that her work abounds in mannerisms, that it lacks a face of its own, that it bears so continually the stamp of fashionable influences. It is unfortunate that she has expended so much of her freedom in exile toward the development of an impeccability of style which is after all but the testimony of her admiration for Hemingway, Cocteau, and others. The result of her smartness is that even her best work has its roots in nothing, being nourished by the repetition of a repetition. Surely we must all be aware by this time that we cannot hope to grow orchids in America until we have had our hardy perennials. One wonders if Miss Boyle is aware that she has only to look within herself to find strong and deep roots for her art. Does she know that she is much better when she describes a lover's kiss—"his mustache tasting of snow"—than when she repeats the jumbled password of the advance guard?

Kay Boyle: Example to the Young

KATHERINE ANNE PORTER

Miss Kay Boyle's way of thinking and writing stems from sources still new in the sense that they have not been supplanted. She is young enough to regard them as in the category of things past, a sign I suppose, that she is working in a tradition and not in a school. Gertrude Stein and James Joyce were and are the glories of their time and some very portentous talents have emerged from their shadows. Miss Boyle, one of the newest, I believe to be among the strongest. At present she is identified as one of the *transition* group, but these two books just published should put an end to that. What is a group, anyhow? In this one were included—as associate editors and contributors to *transition*—many Americans: Harry Crosby, William Carlos Williams, Hart Crane, Matthew Josephson, Isidor Schneider, Josephine Herbst, Murray Godwin, Malcolm Cowley, John Herrman, Laura Riding—how many others?—and Miss Boyle herself. They write in every style under heaven and they spent quite a lot of time fighting with each other. Not one but would have resented, and rightly, the notion of discipleship or of interdependence. They were all vigorous not so much in revolt as in assertion, and most of them had admirably subversive ideas. Three magazines sustained them and were sustained by them: *transition,* Ernest Walsh's *This Quarter* and *Broom.* The tremendous presences of Gertrude Stein and James Joyce were everywhere about them, and so far as Miss Boyle is concerned, it comes to this: that she is a part of the most important literary movement of her time.

She sums up the salient qualities of that movement: a fighting spirit, freshness of feeling, curiosity, the courage of her own attitude and idiom, a violently dedicated search for the meanings and methods of art. In these short stories and this novel there are further positive virtues of the individual temperament: health of mind, wit and the sense of glory. All these are qualities in which the novel marks an advance over the stories, as it does, too, in command of method.

The stories have a range of motive and feeling as wide as the technical virtuosity employed to carry it. Not all of them are successful. In some of the

Reprinted from *New Republic* (April 22, 1931): 279–80.

shorter ones, a straining of the emotional situation leads to stridency and incoherence. In others, where this strain is employed as a deliberate device, it is sometimes very successful—as notably in "Vacation Time," an episode in which an obsessional grief distorts and makes tragic a present situation not tragic of itself; the reality is masked by drunkenness, evaded by hysteria, and it is all most beautifully done. "On the Run" is a bitter story of youth in literal flight from death, which gains on it steadily; but the theme deserved better treatment.

In such stories as "Episode in the Life of an Ancestor" and "Uncle Anne," there are the beginnings of objectiveness, a soberer, richer style; and the sense of comedy, which is like acid sometimes, is here gayer and more direct. In "Portrait" and "Polar Bears and Others," Miss Boyle writes of love not as if it were a disease, or a menace, or a soothing syrup to vanity, or something to be peered at through a microscope, or the fruit of original sin, or a battle between the sexes, or a bawdy pastime. She writes as one who believes in love and romance—not the "faded flower in a buttonhole," but love so fresh and clear it comes to the reader almost as a rediscovery in literature. It was high time someone rediscovered it. There are other stories, however—"Spring Morning," "Letters of a Lady," "Episode in the Life of an Ancestor"—in which an adult intelligence plays with destructive humor on the themes of sexual superstition and pretenses between men and women. "Madame Tout Petit," "Summer," "Theme" and "Bitte Nehmen Sie die Blumen" are entirely admirable, each one a subtle feat in unraveling a complicated predicament of the human heart. "Wedding Day," the title story, is the least satisfactory, displaying the weakness of Miss Boyle's strength in a lyricism that is not quite poetry.

The novel, *Plagued by the Nightingale*, has the same germinal intensity as the shorter works, but it is sustained from the first word to last by a sure purpose and a steadier command of resources. The form, structure and theme are comfortably familiar. The freshness and brilliancy lie in the use of the words and the point of view.

It is the history of an American girl married to a young Frenchman, and living for a short period in the provinces with his wealthy bourgeois family. There is Papa, a blustering old fool, though Bridget never says it quite so plainly; Maman, a woman of energy, good will and appalling force of character; three unmarried sisters, Annick, Julie and Marthe; Charlotte the eldest sister, married to her cousin; Pierre the elder brother, a young doctor; and Nicholas, Bridget's husband. A taint in the blood causes eccentrics and paralytics to blossom like funeral wreaths in every generation. Nicholas is warned by his weakened legs that the family disease is likely to be the main portion of his inheritance. He is dependent on his people, his wife is dowerless. Charlotte's husband is little better than an imbecile, but he is wealthy. Uncle Robert, a perverse old maid of a man, is also wealthy, and he amuses himself by tampering with family affairs; the victims endure him in the hope that he may give someone money sometime. First and last it is the question of money that agitates the family bosom.

The three younger daughters are waiting, each in her own way, for a proposal of marriage from Luc, an idolized young doctor, who nonchalantly enjoys the privilege of the devoted family without asking to become a member. Bridget is a vigorous personality, with powerful hates and loves, a merciless eye, and a range of prejudices which permits no offense against her secret faiths to be trivial. She has gayety and charm, and at first she is ingenuously fond of this household of persons so closely and tenderly bound, so united in their aims. Nicholas feels quite otherwise. He hates his dear good sweet people who are so warmly kind in small things, so hideously complacent and negligent in the larger essentials. He needs help, restitution really, from this family that has brought him disabled into the world. His father brutally— that is to say, with the utmost fatherly kindness—tells Nicholas that he will give him fifty thousand francs when Bridget has a child. Charlotte's five beautiful children are weak in the legs, but they are "the joy of existence" nonetheless. One's duty is to procreate for the family, however maimed the lives may be.

Bridget, caught in a whirling undercurrent of love and hatred and family intrigue, begins first to fear and then to despise these strangers as she realizes the ignoble motives back of all the family devotion. She sees her husband gradually growing hostile to her as he identifies her with his family, no longer with himself. She is confirmed in her instinctive distrust of situations and feelings sanctified by the rubber stamps of time and custom; she defends herself by mockery and the mental reservation against the blind cruelties and wrongs which are done under cover of love. Luc complicates matters by falling in love with her instead of asking for one of the sisters, but even so he does not speak until it is too late—until it is safe for him to speak, when marriage to one of the sisters is no longer the best investment he can make. And Bridget, who has wavered, been pulled almost to pieces by the tearing, gnawing, secretive antagonisms and separate aims of the family, comes to her conclusion—a rather bitter one, which in the end will solve very badly the problem. Of her own will she takes to herself the seed of decay.

This is no more than a bare and disfiguring outline of the plan of the novel. The whole manner of the telling is superb: there are long passages of prose which crackle and snap with electric energy, episodes in which inner drama and outward events occur against scenes bright with the vividness of things seen by the immediate eye: the bathing party on the beach, the fire in the village, the delicious all-day excursion to Castle Island, the scene in the market when Bridget and Nicholas quarrel, the death of Charlotte, the funeral. Nothing is misplaced or exaggerated, and the masterful use of symbol and allegory clarify and motivate the main great theme beneath the apparent one: the losing battle of youth and strength against the resistless army of age and death. This concept is implicit in the story itself, and it runs like music between the lines. The book is a magnificent performance; and as the short stories left the impression of reservoirs of power hardly tapped, so this novel, complete as it is, seems only a beginning.

Inescapable End

Gladys Graham

The short story has seemed the perfect medium for the microscopically detailed analysis of emotion with which Kaye [sic] Boyle's work has been concerned since the very beginning. Her style, too, seeking always the last refinement of phrase and rhythm, suggested shorter forms than the novel. But in "Year before Last," a full-length novel, Miss Boyle shows conclusively that both her style and her analysis are completely under her control; she can bend them to whatever task she chooses. There are no uncertainties in the book, no experimentations, from the first page to the last the story moves along as relentlessly as time itself on some tragic mission bent. And the style, despite its disquieting, poetic beauty, remains purely the medium for communication of the emotional and psychological vortex from which the book is builded.

The story is told from the point of view of Hannah, but the character most vividly given is that of Martin. It opens abruptly on the day that Hannah joins him at the château on the French Riviera. From Hannah's thought, from scraps of their conversation, the past very slowly takes form for the reader. There is a husband in England whom Hannah has left to be with Martin. There is a wealthy aunt whom Martin has had to give up to be with Hannah. Each knows almost nothing about the other, except the strange necessity that has drawn them together. In the brilliant sunlight with their bright new love Martin's cough seems to mean very little, and they scarcely notice their complete lack of funds. With the old car, the three dogs, and Martin's brave chamois cape they seem almost safe against the world.

The most important thing in the world to Martin—and both accept this fundamental fact—is his magazine. That must go on—a refuge for the beauty and truth that more commercial journals will have none of. For Martin his publication is both a mission and a symbol. And the money for its being is dependent upon his aunt, the aunt who offers him his choice, either Hannah or the magazine, not both. There is no money even for living ex-

Reprinted by permission of *The Saturday Review* 9 (July 9, 1932): 827. © 1932, S.R. Publications, Ltd.

penses, they are put out of the château. They compromise, they sacrifice each other, but circumstance will have none of it and throws them back upon one another, still without money and now with very little hope. They begin the long, agonizing trip along the bright Riviera towns where Martin's hemorrhages force them from one sorry hotel to another, on and on to that inevitable end that neither Martin's will nor his gay chamois cape can hold at bay.

Every day, almost every hour, of the time covered by the story is suggested if not described with an intensity usually reserved for only the dramatic moments. All events stand out clear and hard in a brilliance of illumination that leaves their shadows deep and black beside them. A sound, a gesture shows in sharp significance against the tenseness of the situations growing out of three personalities in contest. Yet nowhere is there any sense of strain in the writing, no feeling of overdoing or exaggeration; the strain, the almost unbearable intensity lies within the situation itself, inescapable.

With this book it may be hoped that Kaye [sic] Boyle will reach the larger public she deserves. Here, while she loses nothing of her own peculiar and personal distinction, she does achieve a fuller-bodied work that will have a wider appeal than any of her work that has appeared before.

Kay Boyle's Story of a Moral Crisis

Louis Kronenberger

It is only recently that we have had much fiction in English whose predominating note is that of sensibility. Our older novelists flirted with the same note; but Meredith, Jane Austen, Henry James impress us, in the long run, as really psychologists or novelists of manners. It is among certain recent women writers—Katherine Mansfield, Elizabeth Bowen, Virginia Woolf and latterly Kay Boyle—that sensibility seems to dwarf all other characteristics. The world they present to us has been refined and smoothed down; it is a world under glass, so to speak. They convey to us a special and overexquisite feeling for life; and it is not life itself we are most keenly aware of in their work, but this special and delicate approach to it. Perhaps even "approach" is an inaccurate description; there is often a kind of withdrawal in their attitude.

Among these writers it is Kay Boyle who cultivates the purest order of sensibility. Unlike Bowen and Woolf, she is not, for example, a wit. She throws her whole weight in one direction: toward turning up, with infinite precision, the delicate roots of temperament and interaction. She is a kind of surgeon, though her surgery is always performed with one tool: a scalpel. Her work accordingly has a great deal of inadequacy.

In a book like the present one [*Gentlemen, I Address You Privately*] the finesse displayed only brings out the inadequacy the more sharply. For Miss Boyle has invaded the harsh, dark, tangled precincts of the moral world where whole and merciless vision is demanded, where the attributes of culture can only play a minor part. She has seized one man at a crisis in his development and, pinning him fast, hurled another man into contact with him. Munday, bred in the ascetic ways of the church, has broken with the church when the story opens, and turned to his music for compensation. At that moment (with undue theatrically) the sly, magnetic, effeminate Ayton bursts into Munday's life and insists upon joining it to his own. Munday, his starved body answering before his mind is able, consents; and at once he is drawn into a homosexual relationship with Ayton. Soon he finds himself much more deeply drawn than he could possibly have foreseen: for Ayton has deserted his

Reprinted with permission of *The New York Times Book Review* (November 12, 1933): 9.

ship and committed thefts, and Munday is forced into hiding with him. Up to this point, in spite of being overlaid with verbal décor, Miss Boyle's pattern is almost mathematically clear; beyond this point the tracings grow more and more blurred. A number of other characters move into the narrative, and it loses sight of its major objective. For Leonie's love for Ayton, her getting with child by him, Ayton's final diving back into the dark waters of adventure from which he at first emerged, all seem strung out as linked-up incidents; they do not give the book any real plot, any real centre; and they do not constitute a working out of its theme.

For Ayton is the spectacular figure of this novel, certainly Munday is the important one. Ayton's character, subtle and complicated as it is in the nervous sense, is nevertheless a fairly clear and simple one: he is an inveterate experimenter with life, a man who lives dangerously, wanting all sensations and all experiences. In naïve hands he would doubtless symbolize some spirit of evil, but realistically (and Miss Boyle is a realist in her intentions if not always in practice) he is simply unmoral, unprincipled and mischievous. He is merely the reef against which Munday founders; the moral issues of the book are centred in Munday. But once posed, they are never solved. For one thing, Miss Boyle never carries the book toward its indicated destination. For another, Munday is hopelessly unreal. He is a collection of fragments that are never integrated. The real people in the book are two secondary characters: Quespelle and Leonie.

Because its theme never flowers, because its hero never breathes, this book for all its minor excellences fails to be important. And the fault lies, not in a lack of talent, but in a lack of coordination. Ornament is substituted for architecture. Miss Boyle's writing lives for the moment; each separate burrowing is more an end in itself than part of something larger and continuous. The result is a lack of fiber, of weight, which in a book like this one is fatal. Life cannot be properly revealed through sniffing and snipping; one must drink and smell.

Yet it would be wholly unjust not to commend Miss Boyle for what she does give to us. It amounts, at moments, to revelation: her subtleties of insight are such as no other writer of our time, in English at least, can match. Her style, when she has it in control, is enchantingly fluid and lovely; in some of these pages Brittany comes alive as in a sensitive poem. But the mature novelist gives us something beyond subtleties, beyond style; he makes us see life through the magnifying lens of the glass, not—as Miss Boyle has done— through the lens that contracts.

Miss Boyle's Irony

Edith H. Walton

Several years ago Kay Boyle published a short story, "Art Colony," which contained the kernel of this ruefully ironic novel [My Next Bride]. Outlines which she sketched briefly then have been filled in, and Sorrel, the leader of the colony, has moved from the shadowy wings to the centre of the stage. Miss Boyle, incidentally, makes the conventional statement that all her characters are imaginary, but Sorrel, with his tunics and sandals, his craftwork, his dead wife—in the short story she was his sister—who wanted to teach the whole world to dance, so inevitably suggested Raymond Duncan that one may be pardoned a polite skepticism.

The seamier side of idealism receives scant shrift from Miss Boyle, though her wickedest digs are tempered by a lurking sympathy. Sorrel's colony in Paris, sheltered in a dingy and slackly kept house, has disintegrated sadly since the days of his wife, the dancer. The remaining members are a wrangling, ill-fed, second-rate lot; fewer disciples visit him on Sundays to prance rhythmically in Grecian tunics; the sale of hand-made scarfs and vestments and rugs has fallen off in his shop. Sorrel himself, his shining, filleted hair snow-white, is an aging and a rather weary man.

The scheme of Miss Boyle's novel demands that this pseudo-Utopia be viewed freshly from the outside, and the spectator she has chosen is a young American girl who drifts accidentally into Sorrel's orbit. Victoria arrives penniless in Paris and is unable to find a job. She is rescued by two Russian ladies, half-starved, half-crazy remnants of the old aristocracy, who board in the same gloomy house as herself and who know that Sorrel will offer shelter to strays. They introduce Victoria to him, and she is attracted at once by his lean, benignant Middle-Western face. It is agreed that she shall work for a tiny salary in the shop and share the sternly vegetarian meals of the colony.

Victoria is something of an idealist herself and at first she is mesmerized by Sorrel's gentleness and dignity, his air of sweet saintliness. She refuses indignantly to believe that he has been, and still is, a lustful man, and she consoles herself for the disorder of the colony by blaming—quite justly—his unworthy followers. She defends Sorrel, protects him, steals off with him in

Reprinted by permission of *The New York Times Book Review* (November 11, 1934): 6.

quest of the ice-cream sodas which he so childishly and pathetically covets. She shuts her eyes to the charge that he has a snobbish, mercenary streak, and only admits it when, instead of relieving the poverty of his colony, he lavishes a sudden windfall of money on a fine new automobile. Even then she but half condemns him. For all his flaws, he has a quality of nobility which cannot quite be denied.

It is a grave defect of "My Next Bride" that Victoria is allowed to steal a story which does not rightfully belong to her. Parallel with her adventures in the colony runs the tale of her love affairs—and it is not a very significant or credible tale. She falls in with a wealthy young man, Anthony, who is really desperately in love with his glamourous wife, Fontana, but who permits himself platonic nocturnal excursions with Victoria and talks a lot of involved poppycock. Knowing he is not for her, Victoria turns in desperation to promiscuity, becomes pregnant, and is rescued, in Anthony's absence, by the understanding, all-wise Fontana. There is something suspiciously Michael Arlen about this pair, and all the episodes in which they are involved are so hollow, false and tinselly that one blushes for Miss Boyle.

Fortunately, what one will remember in the book is the picture of the colony—Sorrel the contradictory; the ribald music hall dancers who live in the same house but who are not among the members, the grave, thin children who bear the astonishing names of Hippolytus, Prosperine, Athenia and Bishinka, the silly American women who flutter round the shop. One will remember also the two starving Russian ladies, with their prim black muffs and fur-pieces, their piteous greediness for food, their fierce pride. Muted humor, tinged with pathos, is the keynote of Miss Boyle's book, and she has contributed some matchless sketches of fantastic waifs and strays.

Even when one grants her all this, however, "My Next Bride" raises some sober questions as to the future of Kay Boyle. Her last novel, "Gentlemen, I Address You Privately," was distinctly a disappointment to most of her admirers. So, presumably, will this one be. That Miss Boyle is an exquisite craftsman few are blind enough to doubt, but one begins to wonder what use she is going to make of her craft. If she continues to spend herself on trivial material, to foster her tendency toward precociousness, to move further and further away from ordinary life, it will be a sad blow to those who have been quick to recognize her as one of the most gifted and interesting of the younger writers.

The International vs. the Local Outlook

A type of novel that is in complete contrast with *Crippled Splendour* and the other romantic and objective novels is Kay Boyle's *Monday Night*. And, on another side, in complete contrast with *Monday Night* is Stephen Vincent Benét's booklet, *Johnny Pye and the Fool Killer*. But these two last could only have been written by Americans. Readers who are always on the lookout for the great American novel, for the especially American novel, might ask themselves if the distinctive American fiction is not, on the one side, the international novel and, on the other, stories like Mark Twain's *Huckleberry Finn* and this recent booklet by Stephen Vincent Benét—books that come out of a local, out of a folk, life.

In their very different ways the stories by Kay Boyle and Stephen Benét are, technically, highly accomplished.

What might be termed the action in *Monday Night* consists merely of telephone calls, taxi drives, and drinking in bars. Its wrapper describes it as the sort of tale Edgar Allan Poe would write if he were to come back to the world today. But, while the comparison is not impertinent, one might with equal appropriateness have imagined it as coming out of the mind of Henry James. The story deals with Americans in Europe, Americans thrown into contact with an old, complex civilization, as were Henry James's. But James's Americans were cultivated people of leisure, with a sophistication different from that of Europeans; they were, in fact, uncommon people. Kay Boyle's have a superb ordinariness; they are men with agile wits and uncultivated minds—or even uncultivated minds without the wits. The world she reveals in this story is a patternless one, where the disconnected and the inconsequential reigns, where action and thought have only a passing significance.

Monday Night belongs to a new genre of fiction and is essentially different from the classic European novel, such as that of Thackeray or Dickens, Balzac or Flaubert, Turgenev or Tolstoy, where the characters have a definite locality and a definite national life for their backgrounds. The master of this

Reprinted from *Forum* 100 (October 1938): 165–66, with permission from *Current History* magazine.

special kind of American novel is Ernest Hemingway, and *The Sun Also Rises* may be regarded, so far, as its classic. Kay Boyle is Hemingway's successor, though she has not that piercing if patternless emotion which is what we remember of Hemingway at his best. It is significant that both writers received their literary training in Paris, as did Henry James, that they are familiar with deracinates and those casual sojourners in Paris whose search is for the exciting and the momentary. Each has the observational facility of the newspaperman, with the poet's power of meditating on life; their work stands out from any other type of fiction written in any other country, in both content and technique.

Monday Night leads off with a casual encounter of two Americans in Paris—one a down-at-heel newspaperman, Wiltshire Tobin, who describes himself as a writer but who has never achieved a book; the other a Midwestern hobbledehoy, St. Bernard Lord, otherwise Birnie, who has just graduated as a doctor and who has come to Paris on a pilgrimage of his own. Wilt takes Lord in hand because the newspaperman in him somehow senses a story behind Birnie's pilgrimage to see the great toxicologist, Dr. Sylvestre; also, it happens that Wilt had had the same sort of mystic desire to meet famous writers, Anatole France and George Moore.

The story is concerned with the search for Sylvestre, and from it results a series of adventures that really do recall a Poe tale, with its strangeness and terror. But the manner of presentation is widely different. The traditional narrative manner has no place in a book like this; it does not start with a story, like the modern best sellers, or with an emotion, as does Homer; every incident comes out of some psychological complex that inheres in the characters; all that is disclosed comes out of their conversation and their actions. From the babbling of the Doctor's butler, Wilt is able to build up the toxicologist's career, though he never once comes face to face with him; from the details that the butler gives, he is able to sense the fact that Dr. Sylvestre is a frustrated man capable of avenging, in strange and even in insane ways, his own frustrations.

The art of this story recalls a superb invention in another medium, that extraordinary film that was given no successors, *The Cabinet of Doctor Caligari*. Like the film, it has an eye of extraordinary range and detachment, an eye that can give a drugstore or a railway station, by its fixity, the aspect of a nightmare scene; and it has further affinity to a film in that it is really made up of a series of speech records combined into a continuity.

In the continuity that is the story, there are subsidiary stories which are a sort of symbolic comment on the main story. As Birnie is being taken to the train for Lyons, Wilt tells him an inconsequent and fantastic tale. It is about a ship's cook who is employed in Africa by butterfly hunters whose boat is drifting down a river. The cook remembers that a chief somewhere in these parts was given an American horse. He tries to land from the boat, but is repelled by a beast that starts up from beside the river. The creature has teeth like tombstones, ears like an ass, eyes like a dog and is of an immense size. To make a long story short, this is the American horse that was given the chief some years back, but the horse's lower lip has been bitten off by an alligator, thus giving to the animal a fantastically terrifying appearance.

All around us, Kay Boyle seems to imply, there are torpid alligators; they wake up from time to time and take a bite out of us, and ever after we are unrecognizable beasts. Everybody in the book, symbolically, has been bitten—except, perhaps, Birnie, who has not enough in him to get near the alligators' lairs. The power in this novel of Kay Boyle's, *Monday Night,* is such that for a while after reading it we see men and women as an unrecognizable kind of creatures.

An Unhabitual Way

Babette Deutsch

It was Aristotle who said that for the poet "the greatest thing by far is to have a command of metaphor." William James defined genius as "little more than perceiving in an unhabitual way." Whatever else is wanting in Kay Boyle's poetry, it shows her to possess that "greatest thing." It is touched with genius.

Most of these poems [in *A Glad Day*] are about ten years old. One remembers having read them in the expatriate magazines of the post-war period. Removed from that setting, and assembled in one slight volume (there are only twenty-four pieces here), they tend to date. The drunken fluency of some, while delighting by its impetuousness, annoys by its incoherence. But if their faults become more apparent, so do their beauties. They shock ear and eye with a more splendid vigor. They pierce below surfaces with a more penetrating intensity.

Half the time it is impossible to say what these poems are "about." Some exceptions are the brief image Hunt, the objective and slightly sentimental Funeral in Hungary, the elaborate Statement for El Greco and William Carlos Williams, and the Communication to Nancy Cunard, which might better have borne its original title, Scottsboro. This untranslatableness, itself a mark of good work, applies to one of the most memorable pieces in the book: A Complaint for Mary and Marcel.

The substance of these poems is the response of a sensitive, cultivated woman to the excitements of this cockeyed world, and, more often, to the tragedies of expatriate artists (and amateurs) caught in the toils of contemporary living. The unique character of Miss Boyle's work lies in the way she has handled this refractory material. She has been called an imagist, and though she avoids the hard clarity of pure imagism she does have a flair for conveying sensation, for producing atmosphere, for making the moment real in a physical way, that is a hallmark of the school. More often she employs or approximates surrealism, organizing objects, about an emotion, and telescoping her figures, dream-fashion. Sometimes she combines passages of surrealist prose

Reprinted with permission from *The Nation* magazine (November 12, 1938): 514. © The Nation Company, L.P.

with snatches of simple balladry and ill-concealed iambic pentameter in a curious and arresting manner. But what chiefly distinguishes her work and makes it valuable is her surprising, vivifying perceptiveness, her capacity for seeing things in new relations, for combining them and making them act upon each other in new ways. Her metaphors explode brilliantly, dissolving before they are fully formed and arising anew in unexpected shapes. Illusion becomes as present as reality; reality takes on the magnified character of illusion. Here, if anywhere, we have "imaginary gardens with real toads in them." The fewest of her images may be isolated, and those do not give the peculiar quality of her writing but are worth noting, as this, of a love-song:

> It may be sung without rehearsal any night
> At bars or cafe tables; it may suddenly rise
> The way a statue in the falling dark
> Discards its marble and its classic eyes.

Or this passage from the opening poem:

> There is another season after spring when lights as
> white as fountains spray the north, and leaves like tar
> drip thickly from the bough and cast a cloak of elegance
> around. When odor leaps full-blown upon the stalk and
> music runs in hard steep flights of sound, when taste lies
> slow as honey in the mouth and drifts of snow lie change-
> less at the pass.

Experience is so thick with disorder that it is not surprising if the artist, seeking to communicate it, should occasionally babble. Miss Boyle has not imitated those Gothic tribes who were said to have debated matters of state once drunk and once sober, drunk that they might not lack vigor, sober that they might not want discretion. One would not wish her to be more discreet, but the strength of her writing would be greater if it were not sometimes so loose. These poems remain vital because Kay Boyle has perceived certain events in an unhabitual way and, to however limited a circle, communicated her unique perception.

Three Unusual Stories by Kay Boyle

PETER MONRO JACK

Miss Boyle is an expert in the psychiatry of fiction and there is no story of hers that does not send a delicate thrill of apprehension and recognition of the neurotic even in the most normal reader. The lines from Mr. Eliot's tortured Love Song of J. Alfred Prufrock should accompany her stories:

> It is impossible to say just what
> I mean!
> But as if a magic lantern threw
> the nerves in, patterns on a
> screen:

That is what Miss Boyle does, to throw the jangled nerves in delicate patterns on a screen that is only indirectly and often obscurely reflective. It is a technique developed (in the short story) through Chekhov and Katherine Mansfield and it is evident in the work of Katherine Anne Porter (to whom this book [*The Crazy Hunter: Three Short Novels*] is dedicated) and Djuna Barnes, whose early story, "A Night Among the Horses," has perhaps some relation to Miss Boyle's extended story of the crazy hunter. Possibly it is a peculiarly feminine art, a nervous exacerbation combined with a small but most acute perception of character and style.

"The Crazy Hunter" takes the space of half the book, a long short story stopping short of the development of a novel. It is followed by "The Bridegroom's Body," a story of average length—not, as the publishers say, a short novel—and one of Miss Boyle's best; and by an unsuccessful hugger-mugger called "The Big Fiddle." The first two are of English county life, as distinguished from her earlier French or Austrian sophistication; but of English county life as only a visitor would see it in all of its clarity and ambiguity, as Henry James saw it, for instance, in "The Turn of the Screw." Miss Boyle's excellence is her extraordinary and unfailing knowledge. If it is horses that turn the story, then Miss Boyle knows all about horses; if it should be swans, then Miss Boyle knows them from cob to pen, better than their owners.

Reprinted by permission of *The New York Times Book Review* (March 17, 1940): 5.

The first long story is about a horse, an unhappy marriage, and a young sensitive girl, almost a compendium of Miss Boyle's work. The husband is a pleasant impecunious Canadian painter who has married a moneyed English-woman and fallen under her domination. Her hobby is pedigreed horses, about which he knows nothing; but in an effort to assert himself he buys with her money, and he gives to their daughter a stag-faced hunter that turns out to be stone-blind. His wife insists that it should be "put down," killed, imme-diately. The daughter, who has fallen in love with her blind horse, wins a delay while she hopes to prove that he can still be a useful animal.

But while the daughter has gone down to London (and here is the begin-ning of the love story that Miss Boyle has not developed into a novel) her mother determines to kill the horse, and her father, fortified with whisky and an unusual sense of responsibility, overcomes his fear and keeps vigil over the horse for his daughter. Miss Boyle's men get drunk too easily and rather implausibly and there is a general sense of unreality in the last scene. What remains in the memory is Miss Boyle's uncanny feeling for the animal life of a horse and the tender and disciplined, though overstrained, solicitude of the girl. The strain lies in Miss Boyle's writing, with its burden of emotional words and its Irish rhythms that have a sort of intellectual blarney to them.

But for the second story, "The Bridegroom's Body," there can be nothing but praise. All of Miss Boyle's undeniable artistry in the short story, all of her intuitions into the curious motives of human behavior and her startling and peculiar guesses at animal behavior, even her studied mannerisms and tricks of style seem to come to the proper terms of her narrative. With the savage sexual life of the swans as a counterpoint, Miss Boyle delicately, meticulously and admirably suggests the impotent desire of the owner of the swannery, Lord Glourie; the restless, unsatisfied energy of his wife; the tenacious habits of the old swanherd; the new blood of the young farmer; and, to focus all this, the clear and honest innocence of a young Irish nurse who comes up from a London agency. Of course there is a certain ambiguity and symbolism, with-out which Miss Boyle would not be herself, but here it seems natural and as if it wrote, so to speak, its own ticket.

The last story is a made-up story and reminds us too violently of Miss Boyle's worst fault of artificiality, and her habit of making a neurotic excitation take the place of a sober and more difficult realism. Sentences like "the fragile, the peaked, the almost-ailing, almost-tainted quality of her flesh lured him speechlessly and terribly toward love" and "the childish neck turned, the small breakable white jawbone visible, beneath the skin" are made up for the psy-chology of a crime story; they never ring true, the intention is too obvious, and Miss Boyle is caught in her own network of alarming words.

But at her best in this book Miss Boyle demonstrates that she is one of the best short-story writers in America, and probably the most careful, per-cipient and unusual.

Review of *Primer for Combat*

RAOUL DE ROUSSY DE SALES

Primer for Combat is the first book written about the fall of France which conveys a sense of reality to those who were not caught in that disaster.

Kay Boyle is neither a journalist nor a political polemist. She does not think that the ability to use a typewriter and to record what she sees can be called writing. She believes that even the cataclysmic dislocation of a great orderly nation in the space of a few weeks should be described with care. In other words, Kay Boyle remains as much of an artist in this book as in those she wrote in more tranquil times about less dramatic subjects.

And through all her experience, Kay Boyle remains what Rebecca West would call an "idiot, from the Greek root meaning a private person," while men are afflicted with "lunacy," which makes them so "obsessed by public affairs that they see the world as by moonlight." They see the "outline of every object but not the details indicative of their nature."

Primer for Combat is a novel in the form of a diary. It covers about one hundred days, from the twentieth of June to the second of October in 1940. These hundred days are probably the most horrible that the French have ever lived through, both as "private persons" and as a nation, if it can be said that the French did live at all during that period. Most of the story takes place in a small village called Pontcharra in Haute-Savoie. It describes what happened to the people there, what they said, what they thought, and how they tried to adapt themselves or to resist.

A love story runs through the book. An Austrian ski-instructor, whose outstanding feature seems to be his remarkable golden hair, is in love with Phil, the American woman who writes the diary. She wants to get him out of the Foreign Legion to America to escape the Nazis, but he has a French wife, who is a niece of Pétain, and his wife thinks he might as well use this protection and stay in France. In spite of the appeals of Phil and freedom, the ski-instructor apparently decides that it will be less trouble to follow his wife's advice. The whole affair is lamentable, and one wonders why both these exceptional women waste so much love over this ineffectual hero.

Originally published in *The Atlantic Monthly* 170 (December, 1942): 152.

But this love story is not important. The value of *Primer for Combat* is in the numerous unforgettable scenes and characters it describes, and in its authenticity. It will not satisfy those whose maudlin nostalgia for France makes them revel in a kind of falsified picturesqueness. They are in no danger of having seen that for the last time: it can always be reconstructed for them with Hollywood technique. Kay Boyle speaks only of a small corner of France, and of a few people of France, and her book is short. But nothing better has been written on France since the Germans got there.

Kay Boyle's Coincidence and Melodrama

STRUTHERS BURT

This book [*Avalanche*] disarms criticism because of its setting and its theme and because toward the end there is something in it that must bring every American up full-standing, his heart in his throat. But then that is a stupid phrase, "disarms criticism," because it implies abeyance of objective standards, and that isn't what I mean at all. Not in this case. Indeed, I will state at once, that taken at its simplest valuation, this is one of the most exciting stories I have read in a long while, ranking, so far as I am concerned, along with "Rebecca" and "Escape." If it hasn't the careful and interwoven texture of both of these, the convincing psychological undercurrents, and, especially, as with the latter, the extraordinary analysis and convincingness of plot, it has on the other hand, well as those two books were written, Miss Boyle's beautiful and eerie command of language and sensitiveness toward scene and scenery, toward atmosphere of place and person, as if the finger-tips of her mind and spirit had been filed to an almost agonizing thinness. And so nothing that she writes can be taken at its "simplest valuation"; it is too important, actually and potentially.

Nor can it be dismissed easily or briefly for the same reason. Certain writers—a very few—are always "on trust." And I think the trouble with "Avalanche" is that Miss Boyle, breaking abruptly with her past, was too determined to accomplish a tour de force and as a result, misprizing her material, seized too readily upon shopworn ingredients and coincidences too perfectly synchronized, including a hero whose sense of timing is to say the least uncanny. And a person like Miss Boyle hasn't a right to do this.

Not that life isn't filled with coincidences. And the older you grow, the more you know it, perhaps because your own circle for possible coincidences widens. And God knows there are plenty of coincidences at present, incredible ones. But they don't seem to happen so invariably on the side of good. I wish they did. For the most part their arrangement is neither logical nor necessarily well-intended, and that's where the motion-pictures go wrong, and

Reprinted by permission of *The Saturday Review* 27 (January 15, 1944): 6. © 1944, S.R. Publications, Ltd.

that's what makes the use of the word melodrama in a derogative sense legitimate.

Life, properly viewed, is just as melodramatic as it possibly can be, always subjectively, sometimes out in the open and on the surface, and at times like the present it is unashamedly and nakedly melodramatic, but the difference between melodrama, twisted to an author's ends, and life, is that indigenous melodrama does not, any more than coincidence, which is largely the stuff of which melodrama is made, work consciously to the advantage of better people. To the contrary, both it and coincidence seem to have an entirely cold and aloof attitude toward the morals of the case, and like rain, to fall equally upon the just and the unjust. Too often the heroine, tied in the grove of a buzzsaw, is cut in half.

In only one plane of human conduct, so far as I can make out, do coincidence and melodrama, like some sleepy and indifferent gods, suddenly roused to indignation and closeness, take a culminating and determining course as if directed by an observing intelligence, and that is when the weak, the wicked, or the desperate behave in such a notorious fashion that neither life nor their fellow-men can stand them any longer. The Greeks knew about this, and they called the form of it tragedy, and the conclusion, nemesis.

I would like to continue the discussion of nemesis, but it would not be fair to Miss Boyle's story, satisfactory as the end of her well-concealed villain is. However, I wonder if even a Gestapo agent walks so obstinately and with such wide-eyed innocence toward what anyone could tell him is sure death. I know they are violently and cosmically stupid, Gestapo agents and the nation from which they come, for all their initial detailed shrewdness. That has been proven, and never in history has there been a clearer case of nemesis than the vast and bloody downfall now happening, too much mixed up with pretensions and thick skulls even to be a dignified Götterdämmerung. And their's is an inherent stupidity, too, so colossal that it causes men to try to walk across volcanoes because they think they are superior to fire, or across water because they think they are superior to water. And so death, horrible and contemptuous, overtakes them, and you laugh even as you retch. But I wonder if individually, for all their inhuman vanity, they haven't more simple self-protectiveness.

All of this, however, is really not so important, for the real importance is that a number of Miss Boyle's admirers, unless I am mistaken, are going to rebuke her for this story, and although they are going to be right technically, they are going to be enormously wrong theoretically and practically. I hope Miss Boyle is engaged in a serious pursuit. She might even start a much needed revolution. Nobody could do it with more authority than she. But first of all she will have to reconsider the worthiness and dignity of plot.

The view from a single window is of great import and interest, depending of course upon the import and interest of the person looking out. But, anyway, the sum total of the views from single windows adds up to something worthwhile. However, eventually even the most searching gazer should go down in the street and look up, not down, and along, not across. For a number of years American writing has suffered from magnificent emotion and a sort of demonaic, centripetal concentration upon self, a sort of national narcissism, just as formerly American writing suffered from all plot and no emotion. But the point is that great novels have always had a plot; and many of them most exciting plots. So now maybe it might be a good idea for first-class American writers to try to combine the two.

But once more, Miss Boyle disarms criticism, at least where I am concerned, for never in my life have I come across such descriptions of mountains. Never. Not even in that totally different book, "Primer for Combat." And I say this as a mountain-man. Her sentences about mountains go up and up to snow-peaked beauty almost unbearable, just as great mountains do, or swoop down like glaciers and snowfields, or are close and warming and exciting like snow in a village. Never have there been such descriptions of mountains.

The Mature Craft of Kay Boyle

STRUTHERS BURT

M iss Boyle is a storyteller, a superb one: by and large, the best in this country, and one of the best now living. This somewhat belated point of view concerning her work emerges clearly, it seems to me, in this present volume of her collected tales [*Thirty Stories*], especially as they have been arranged chronologically and according to background; according, that is, to the country in which they are laid. Here is the grouping.

Early Group: 1927–1934. Austrian Group: 1933–1938. English Group: 1935–1936. French Group: 1939–1942. And then finally, three stories, all recent and well known, "The Canals of Mars," "The Loneliest Man in the U. S. Army," "Winter Night," American Group: 1942–1946. These last were written after Miss Boyle's return to this country in 1941 from nineteen years of residence in Europe, principally in the three countries which engage her attention: France, England, and Austria. The background of the Early Group is mostly American, too, but that of an America not yet at war. Of the nine stories in this group, all but three, "Wedding Day," "Rest Cure," and "Keep Your Pity," have an American background. One, "Kroy Wen," which happens to be "New York" spelled backwards, as you often see names on a life-preserver, looked at from certain angles, takes place on a ship, to be sure, but it is an American ship bound for Italy, and the leading character is an American motion-picture director, with all the, by now, well-established rules as to what those abused characters must be. (Motion-picture directors as a whole are extremely sensitive, intelligent men, a beneficent leaven in Hollywood. It is not from them that the fantastic place derives its fantastic traditions.)

These early stories are mostly interesting as a study in the emergence of an artist; an artist with a beautiful command of language, a unique gift for striking metaphor, granted as a rule only to poets, and a passionate, impelling drive. An artist, original, rebellious, and bitterly observant. No wonder Miss Boyle was a sensation: at first, acclaimed only by the cognoscenti, later on

Reprinted by permission of *The Saturday Review* (November 30, 1946): 11. © 1946, S.R. Publications, Ltd.

received, but with reservations, by the general reading public. On the whole, these stories are not completely successful. That was the way they struck me when I first read them many years ago; and that is the way all but one, "Friend of the Family," strikes me now. "Friend of the Family" is a beautiful story, delicate, straight-moving, and filled with implications, and is Miss Boyle at her best and in full control of her equipment. But the remainder of this group seem to me all implication, vague and confused, and not at all clear in the mind of the author.

There is no going deep down below the multitudinous impressions: swift, following upon each other, tumultuous like winds in a storm. But below any winds is the earth and people walking about on it. "Keep Your Pity," for instance, is a splendidly told story, as are all Miss Boyle's stories, early or late, and the characters, on the surface, are as sharp as etchings, but they haven't the distance or depth that etchings should have. It seems to me that Miss Boyle has misplaced both her philosophy and psychology, and has substituted contempt and loathing for the pity the title implies.

It is when she goes to Europe, or, rather, when she begins to write with a European background, that she comes into her own. Like Henry James, like many American writers, something seems to have been released by the European scene, and European character, and the contrast between the latter and the American in Europe. These stories have a sure touch: the touch of a master craftsman. A sure direction. They go places, whether you do or do not always agree with them: whether or not you find, at times, the faults, the reverse side, of Miss Boyle's virtues, too much metaphor; at moments, too much calorescence, too much heat. She has an eerie gift of bringing completely to life the European background: Austrian, English, French, and of bringing to life the people who live there. When she ascends mountains, she is superb. She has an affinity for snow, storm, glaciers, and high places, very moving to those who feel as she does. But once again, the more of a story she has to tell, the better she is, so much so that one of the best stories in the book is "Let There Be Honor," which appeared in that painstakingly non-esoteric magazine *The Saturday Evening Post.*

There has been a lot of nonsense talked about this, of course, ever since writers, to their loss in some ways, ceased having patrons and were cast upon the world to fend for themselves. All great writers have written to be published, to be read, and to make as much money by so doing as compatible with honesty and integrity. What I have said will no doubt offend some of Miss Boyle's numerous admirers, especially the early ones. I trust Miss Boyle will understand the compliment intended. It was George Moore, wasn't it, who said that storytelling was "the pure gold of literature"? Surely it is rare gold, like the gold of melody in music or poetry, and certainly it is historic, stemming down from the Sagas and from Homer: the oldest gold there is. I imagine Miss Boyle will agree. In a foreword she has written:

In the past twenty years I have written a number of short stories—at least three times as many as are included in this book. Some were written for love, and some for money; some out of anger, out of compassion and grief, some out of despair. But whatever the impulse behind the writing of them, one factor remained constant: I wanted to write these stories. Some of them have appealed to a small public, some to a wider public, but this was not the standard of judgment brought to them for this present volume. I chose these thirty stories not because they speak out for any particular people, or any particular thesis, but because, on rereading, they held my interest—and I believe this to be one of the primary obligations of a short story. An equally important responsibility of the short story is that it attempt to speak with honesty of the conditions and conflicts of its time; that it attempt to reflect with honesty the state of the author's mind and his emotions at that time. . . .

This is good criticism: lucid, intelligent, mature.

Avalanche in the Haute-Savoie

WALTER HAVIGHURST

On a sunny September afternoon in 1939 Madame Corinne Audal filled her rucksack in the village and climbed alone to the chalet under the snowfields. Just the day before, in a neighboring town, Ferdl Eder stood in the prefecture of the Haute-Savoie and then was led to the train that would take him away from the mountains. This is the immediate compass of Kay Boyle's flashing and relentless story of how the world's violence came to two persons on an end-of-summer day in 1939. It left Corinne alone in the high bright Alpine silence, still fighting in her mind for her lover's chance at dignity and freedom. It took Ferdl from the mountain snows, the space and solitude, and sent him, without status or identity, to a concentration camp.

In this beautifully wrought novelette [1939] Miss Boyle has dealt with the problem of a man's responsibility to his time and the choices he must make. The simplicity of the story is a simplicity of art rather than of substance. There are many complexities in the character of the French woman who left her army-officer husband for an Austrian ski teacher, and of the athlete whose championships could not serve him on that September day. There are many ironies in their story, all encompassed in the larger irony of the high mountain silence through which beats upon these people the unheard, growing din of Europe's downfall.

The story mounts in meaning as steadily as the old zigzag lumber road that climbs to the chalet. It reaches its final, ineluctable statement in the wonderful metaphor of Tarboux's card game—the game about the herbs he gathered on the slopes and mixed in the back room of his chemist's shop. "You have to know which card you want, and then you call for it by name. But only for one. You can't ask for two cards at the same time." That is the rule which Ferdl, champion skier, chess-player, and swimmer, had refused to learn. He had chosen to be both an Austrian and a Frenchman; he wanted both freedom and a woman's love. He had tried to live uncommitted, and he had failed.

Reprinted by permission of *The Saturday Review* 31 (February 28, 1948): 12. © 1948, S.R. Publications, Ltd.

It was just ten minutes that Ferdl stood in the prefecture, but it was long enough for his life to overtake him. He began with what he had to reassure himself with: "I make use of what ways and means there are for what I want." But that wasn't enough now. For him the main issue had been not to go too far in one direction or another. The time was past for that calculation. He had been a champion at the things men do individually. He had not learned, for all his mountain climbing, that men are relentlessly roped together.

The story is told with a sustained inner tension, and Miss Boyle's style is fully equal to that demand. She observes, selects, and phrases with a miraculous freshness, as though she brought to the task of writing a new equipment. The high, dry mountain atmosphere permeates this little book, filling it with silence and a searching light, and there is an austere understanding that finds the fatal weakness lurking in Ferdl Eder's strength.

In Germany the Ruins Still Smolder

HARRY T. MOORE

The volcano suggested by the title of Kay Boyle's new volume [*The Smoking Mountain: Stories of Post-war Germany*] is the Germany of today which, as the wife of an occupation official, the author knows at first hand. The book, while it does nothing to decrease Miss Boyle's reputation as a writer of excellent short stories, is an unusual blending of fiction and fact. Several of the stories are merely reports or anecdotal sketches, and the longest piece in the book is a penetrating factual history of the trial of Heinrich Baab, a Gestapo sadist. The six or seven genuine short stories, like the documentary items, reveal skillful observation and an expert's careful prose; they have the added virtues of dramatic presentation and that fusion of theme, symbol and character which enables fiction to be a powerful agent for revealing truths.

The truths about today's Germany—use of the plural here is deliberate—are important to every American. In probing the complex tissues of these truths, Miss Boyle shows that she has no patience with Nazis, or with those who helped them by acquiescence, or with those who now call the Belsen pictures propaganda and ask, "What's wrong with saying someone's nice, though a Jew." Sometimes Miss Boyle's Americans are compassionate toward broken human beings, however guilty.

Not all the conquerors in these stories, however, are so humane. In "Summer Evening" a group of military and civilian executives torment an old servant by pretending they can help him go to America. And in "The Lost," one of the wandering boys who chirp G. I. slang learns that he cannot join his soldier friend in America because that friend is a Negro in Tennessee.

The Polish boy, James, like other little Poles and Czechs and Italians who have been absorbing democracy at bivouac level, is a war orphan who stoically accepts misfortunes beyond his control. He sends his dark friend a white lie, a letter in a kind of hillbilly Brooklynese to the effect that he has rediscovered his parents and is returning to them.

The friendliness of another Negro toward children has ironic consequences of another sort in "Home," when this soldier learns that he is being

Reprinted by permission of *The New York Times Book Review*, (April 22, 1951): 5.

victimized by a German child. Yet the man says he does not mind, for he has had little chance to help people at home. This is one of the sketches where the bones of contrivance stick through the flesh of the story. Usually, however, Miss Boyle makes her point more forcibly by subtle deployment of ironies and parallels, as in "Adam's Death," a grim picture of lingering German anti-Semitism. In such stories Miss Boyle usually handles themes of prejudice so adroitly and so understandingly that it is surprising to find her, elsewhere in the book, falling into one of the Nazi ideological traps by speaking of "Jewish blood."

Two of the most effective stories dramatize the author's ideas through descriptions of entertainments. "Cabaret" presents some of the principal themes of the book in terms of a satirical review amid the ruins of a German city. Throughout "The Smoking Mountain," Miss Boyle skillfully uses for her own purposes the particular kind of grimness and horror that have been constants in German art from the Middle Ages to the time of Georg Grosz. The party in the final story, "Aufwiedersehen Abend," is staged by a young American ex-pilot on the evening of a day on which he has heard a courtroom crowd jeer at the denazification proceedings against an obviously guilty Nazi editor. At the party the airman is shocked to learn that one of the musicians is from a town he had bombed: the musician has a shattered face. The danse macabre of two skeleton-thin "entertainers" at the party closes this provocative book with an appropriately disturbing symbol.

Hope out of France

PAUL ENGLE

A young Frenchman is talking to an American girl he has met in his native village:

> "I want to be mayor of Abelin," he said, as if he were saying *I'd like to take the sun down and try another way of lighting for a while.*

This novel [*The Seagull on the Step*] differs from all others about contemporary France in that it offers a new way of lighting the bitter problem of French-American relations. For Michel Vaillant, schoolteacher of Abelin, has learned a great affection for Americans through helping American flyers to escape during the war, and has dedicated his life to diminishing the loathing so many of his countrymen feel toward the USA, and the ignorance so many of us have for France.

Everything Kay Boyle writes has fluency of prose and imaginativeness of conception. This has more of both those qualities than some others of her books. It is as if she had fired the story with all of her unique insight and devotion toward the country where she lived so long. The taste and smell and intonation of France are here, and along with them, a troubled concern for her own country. When Kay Boyle describes a harbor with the fishing boats going out, or a conversation on a bus along the Mediterranean, the cast of the net and the cast of the voice are French.

It's a wonderful story Kay Boyle tells. An American girl, studying art in Paris while keeping an eye on her boy friend in the diplomatic service, reads a letter in a newspaper. It is from a Frenchman on the south coast asking for the American flyer, with whom he walked the dangerous roads at night, to come to his village and see what he is trying to do. She cannot persuade her official friend to go, so she travels herself. The book opens with the bus taking her to the village. The driver is furiously anti-American and his steady attacks on the USA are warmly received by most of the passengers. Going down a steep hill the brakes will not work and the bus plunges over the edge.

Reprinted by permission of *New Republic* 132 (May 16, 1955): 38–39.

The girl regains consciousness in a strange house with a woman who had also been on the bus. The balance of the book is the narrative of the girl's discovery of the village: of Vaillant, who had written the letter; of the cripple Marrakech; of the doctor who treats her and turns out to be a poisoner; of the whole confusion and conflict between propertied and professional villagers on the one hand and fishing people on the other. Through her presence, all of the forces are activated and brought to crisis.

It would be hard to think of a novel which gives a shrewder insight into the dilemma of "ordinary" Frenchmen today, or of a certain sort of official American mind. Vaillant says to Peter Cornish, when he has come down from Paris to find his girl:

> "By profession, we're doomed to function among the intellectuals, but perhaps we haven't the right any more . . . to let it end there. With one quarter of my country voting Communist and the other three quarters split in a dozen ways, I have to speak, I have to act. I have to believe that it's me—the good European—and you—the good American—who together will find the energy and honesty to build our own defense."
>
> "Our own?" repeated Cornish, his eyes baffled and humorless. "I'm afraid that isn't the role an American over here—at least, not an American at my level—is authorized to take."

Admitting that Vaillant's position is unique in its friendliness, the state of mind in Cornish's reply is appalling.

Because she was on the bus at the time of its accident, the girl is blamed for it, on the ground of distracting the driver. The ultimate story of who actually did cut the brake tubes, and of the whole murderous life of the small community, is integrated with the revelation of the still powerful impacts of the war on the villagers and of the struggle for how to use American funds to aid the village. Through it, there is the gradual affection of Vaillant and the girl for each other, and the final scene in which Vaillant and Cornish act out the ancient ritual of the joust from boats, striving to knock each other into the water, in a struggle for the girl. Watching the game, a Frenchman comments:

> "That's what the game was for once, not done for money, or for the tourist trade, but done for a woman. Maybe that gives it a kind of honor again. . . . Perhaps that's what the lot of us are looking for."

There are two flaws. The girl is generalized "girl," a point of view toward action and others, and not an individual. And there is too much deliberate stating of abstractions, as when the girl says to Vaillant, when they meet on a cliff at night as she is escaping from the doctor, who has just shoved Marrakech over, to his death:

"This year, this moment, as you hold my shoulders, Vaillant, I believe that France is just beginning, that this is the new frontier, and everything to be won yet, to be discovered."

The author has put her own conviction too abruptly into the mouths of her characters.

But these are small concerns in a romantic, moving and yet immediate novel. Reading it, this reviewer wishes that the State Department, or the Fulbright authority, would send fewer respectable, uncreative, cautious professors to France, to reach a handful of academic people, and send more Kay Boyles. But that is absurd. There is only one Kay Boyle, whose elegant English, idiomatic French, imaginative energy and personal creativeness are a common glory shared by France and America.

The Light and the Dark

GRANVILLE HICKS

Kay Boyle's "Generation without Farewell" (Knopf, $3.95) also seeks to recreate the atmosphere of a particular place at a particular time. The place is a German town in the American zone of occupation, and the time is the summer of 1948. Most of the characters are Americans: the commander of the post, Colonel Roberts, and his wife and daughter; a lieutenant named Stephany, who falls in love with Millicent Roberts, the colonel's daughter; an idealistic civilian named Honerkamp, director of America House, also in love with Millicent; Mike Dardenella, manager of the post exchange, who has a passion for Lipizzaner horses.

All these characters are seen through the eyes of a young German, Jaeger, who has spent two years in the United States as a prisoner of war. Jaeger has no illusions about the Nazi regime, and he has a warm admiration for America. He would seem to be ideally suited to mediate between the Americans and the Germans, but in fact he is not quite at ease with either. He is a good man, thoughtful, honorable, gentle, but he feels himself to be an ineffectual one.

There is no great novelty in Miss Boyle's account of conquerors and conquered. The colonel, for instance, is like many professional soldiers we have read about—domineering, dogmatic, aggressively masculine. At the opposite extreme is Honerkamp, who is full of guilt because of his part in the destruction of Germany (he was a bomber pilot during the war) and full of good will towards the German people. Then there is Jaeger, in whom we recognize that familiar figure of modern literature, the alienated man.

The love stories, too, follow paths that have been trodden before. One wonders how so delicate and intelligent a woman as Catherine Roberts ever married the colonel, and certainly one is not surprised when she is attracted to Jaeger. Nor is one surprised that their love comes to nothing. Millicent's affair with Christoph Horn, the young groom of the Lipizzaner horses, is a different matter, but this also is in a recognizable tradition.

Reprinted by permission of *The Saturday Review* 43 (January 16, 1960): 59. © 1960, S.R. Publications, Ltd.

If, however, the material seems a little conventional, the manner of telling does not. Miss Boyle has built the novel out of a series of scenes, each lovingly created with the full resources of her style. If the writing sometimes seems too self-consciously artful, it is almost always effective. Scene after scene makes its mark: Millicent and Christoph and the horses, Jaeger and the man resurrected from the ruins, the four crippled veterans, Jaeger and the colonel on the hunting expedition. It is as if Miss Boyle were creating an elaborate tapestry.

The mood is somber, almost murky, and the reader is prepared for the triumph of evil. In spite of Jaeger's effort to secure an iron lung, Christoph Horn dies of poliomyelitis. The colonel lays his tyrannical hand on both wife and daughter. Honerkamp is driven from his post by a heresy-hunting intelligence officer. There may be, as Honerkamp tries to tell Jaeger, some ground for hope, but it seems insubstantial.

To make a distinction of which Hawthorne was fond, "Generation without Farewell" is a romance, whereas "The House in Vienna" is a novel. If Miss de Born relies on precision and clarity, Miss Boyle works with dark powers of suggestion. In "The House in Vienna" no one is wholly good and no one wholly bad, and misfortunes are not irremediable; in "Generation Without Farewell" disaster is absolute, for Miss Boyle is concerned with symbolic rather than literal truth. Her book does not seem to me so brilliant an example of its genre as Miss de Born's is of its; the prose is too mannered and the symbolism too dense; but it is an interesting specimen just the same.

Aristocrat of the Short Story

Maxwell Geismar

Kay Boyle has been one of the most elusive characters in contemporary American fiction. I say this with some feeling, because I have tried to categorize her work in every decade since the early 1930's, and each decade, it seems, I have been wrong.

She is the author of 13 novels, some of them very good, but she is not quite a major novelist. Her major medium has always been the short story and the novelette. (And it is typical of this aristocrat, whose earlier work lay in the tradition of Edith Wharton and Henry James, not to use the fashionable word, novella.) But even here, she was in the early thirties, a writer of superior sensibility—or so I thought—using a foreign scene more successfully than her native one, and belonging, in essence, both to the expatriate line of James and Wharton and to that later "lost generation" of the 1920's.

What this new collection of Miss Boyle's short stories and novelettes [*Nothing Ever Breaks Except the Heart*] does prove is that while all of the speculation above is somewhat true, none of it is really true, or profoundly true. She has all these elements in this new collection of her mature work. But, as in the case of every first-rank writer, she rises above the disparate elements in her work or in her temperament, to become something else. What "Nothing Ever Breaks Except the Heart" proves, in short, is that Kay Boyle has at last become a major short-story writer, or a major writer in contemporary American fiction, after three decades of elusiveness, sometimes of anonymity, almost of literary "classlessness," while she has pursued and has finally discovered her true metier. It is a joy to discover such an event: not a new talent, which is rare enough, but an established and mature talent which has developed and perfected itself—and particularly in an epoch when so many false talents are proclaimed every year.

Unlike her earlier collection of "Thirty Stories," which was arranged chronologically—and that earlier volume is fascinating now to read over and to compare with the present one—"Nothing Ever Breaks Except the Heart" is arranged topically: "Peace," "War Years" and "Military Occupation." And

Reprinted by permission of *The New York Times Book Review* (July 10, 1966): 4, 16.

perhaps one should add, in the selfish concern of pure art, that nothing better could have happened for Kay Boyle than World War II and the periods of military occupation, by the German and then the Allied forces. For even in the present volume, the first section, "Peace," is less effective than the remainder of the book—and still Kay Boyle is less effective about the American than she is about the European scene. When it comes to a story like "Anschluss," dealing with a world-weary Parisian fashion-writer and a marvelously gay brother and sister in a dying Austria, she is superb.

Here, as in so many of her earlier stories and novels, her satiric strain works unrelentingly upon the German character and physique. Here, more convincingly than in earlier books, her romantic lovers are destroyed by the dissolution of a society; and here, just as in her work of the early forties, she dramatizes the pageantry of a dissolute and amoral social scene over and above the sensibilities of her characters.

In Miss Boyle's writing, there has always been a traditional sense of character—romantic, pagan at heart and best exemplified in her heroines rather than her heroes—but the European *Walpurgisnacht* of the late thirties gave her a dramatic social background that she could hardly afford to ignore. Thus, too, in her first novel, "Plagued by the Nightingale," first published in 1931 and just recently reissued, the central theme was of an ingrown and diseased French bourgeois family, of an American heroine's struggle against this family. (Miss Boyle herself was born in St. Paul in 1903, married a Frenchman, and went to live in France in the early twenties; but her "expatriatism," as she recently wrote to me, was enforced by circumstances rather than by choice.)

The style, too, of her first novel is more precious, studied and "literary" than her present, apparently more prosaic, and truly more beautiful style. As late as 1938, she could still turn out such a mediocre novel as "Monday Night," a picaresque mystery, still about that "family romance" which any true novelist must have in his bones, but which, in itself, is never enough. Perhaps it was only with "Primer for Combat," in 1942—which is curiously close to the place and theme of the "Anschluss" story—that the *larger* European scene of social and moral disintegration and corruption appeared so firmly and so incisively and so brilliantly. And it was in "Generation without Farewell" (1960) that she added the American Occupation Forces to her Nazi conquerors, in order to prove that human debasement—the evil soul, the vicious soul, the lost soul—can be a matter of social circumstance rather than of national origins.

Indeed, in "Nothing Ever Breaks Except the Heart," it is a toss-up as to who the true villains are, Germans or Americans or just plain Occupiers— while the heroes, to Miss Boyle, are those who have been conquered and occupied, those who have resisted, those who have put to the acid test their property, their career and their lives. To her earlier vision of sensibility, she has added what every first-rate writer must have, a standard of human moral-ity—and the fact that human morality is usually, if not always, related to a specific social or historical context.

It is this familiar concept, missing in so much current and "new" Ameri-can fiction, that is embodied in the magnificent stories of her maturity. (For conversely, it is of no use to an artist to have a perfect sense of morality with-out an adequate art form to project it.) The title story of the present collec-tion is another beauty: a Hemingway tale, so to speak (about a pilot who is finished), but produced by an intensely feminine talent, and with an anti-Hemingway moral. (By this I mean anti-late-Hemingway, when all that remained in him was the killer pitted against a hostile, menacing universe.) What is so remarkable in these late tales of Kay Boyle, by contrast, is the increased sense of sympathy in them for all the losers, all the defeated persons and peoples of contemporary history.

Here again, an earlier sense of nostalgia in her work has become an intense sense of compassion. I don't pretend to know the secrets of this fine craftsman, but I do realize how many of these stories leave you on the brink of tears. And a world in tears; since Kay Boyle has become the American writer to express the texture of European life after Chamberlain and Daladier and Munich.

There is still a final phase of writing in "Nothing Ever Breaks Except the Heart," still another epoch of our modern history: the period of the Occupa-tion, the black market and the reappearance of the same old people, asking for privilege and power and "deals" all over again, after the heroism, the gal-lantry, the selflessness of the liberation battle. No wonder that the last one of these stories describes an American State Department official returning to a McCarthyite America—ironic sequel to the war for European freedom. And no wonder that the last of these beautiful tales describes an American mother, who agrees with "a terrified race"—the French peasants of the atomic age. " 'I am American,' she said to that unseen presence of people in the silent room, 'and the wrong voices have spoken out for me, and spoken loudly, and I too, I too, am terribly afraid.' "

Those Paris Years

MALCOLM COWLEY

"This memoir," Kay Boyle says in presenting the chapters about her own life that she has included in this new edition of "Being Geniuses Together," "is part of a dialogue that I have never ceased having with Robert McAlmon." But what was McAlmon's part in this dialogue that started 45 years ago and did not cease with his lonely death in 1956? And who in the world, younger readers will ask—in fact have already asked me when I told them about the book—was Robert McAlmon?

Scottish by descent, born in Kansas and raised in South Dakota, McAlmon blew into Paris like a wind from the prairies. That was in 1921, the year when scores of young Americans came storming into the Montparnasse cafes, all bent on having a hell of a good time before they utterly transformed, or so they hoped, the world of art and letters. Ford Madox Ford, who enjoyed their company—so long as they pretended to believe his stories—compared them to a herd of stampeding Herefords.

McAlmon was more like a wild cayuse or its rider. He wore a broad-brimmed hat that wasn't like a cowboy's, but that still made him look as if he had galloped into town on a Saturday afternoon to spend what he had earned in a month by riding the range. He sang Western songs and had enough of a cowboy's energy to carry him through nights of drinking and dancing. He also had self-confidence, a winning smile, and what seemed to the rest of us a generous supply of money, derived from his incredible marriage to the poet Bryher, only daughter of Sir John Ellerman, the shipping magnate.

In 1921 many people thought that McAlmon was destined to have a more brilliant career than any of the other young expatriates. He wrote more and faster than the others, from what seemed to be a richer store of early experiences. He quickly met everyone who counted in the literary world, beginning with Eliot, Pound and Joyce (who was his favorite drinking companion); and he met each of them as an equal—or secretly more than an equal, since he measured them all against an ideal picture of his own talent, and found most of them wanting.

Reprinted by permission of *The New York Times Book Review* (June 9, 1968): 1, 34.

His intimacy with men of genius did not keep him from being generous to younger and needier writers, and it was partly to help them gain recognition that he founded Contact Editions. Though a very small house, with two partners and no employees, by 1929 it had published the work of several famous or soon-to-be-famous authors—Hemingway (his first two booklets), Pound, W. C. Williams, Mary Butts, H. D., Robert M. Coates and Gertrude Stein—as well as seven books of poetry and fiction by Robert McAlmon.

When did everything start to go sour? By 1929 some of the young writers he encouraged—and chiefly Hemingway, whom he regarded as a rival—were leaving him far behind. His marriage had ended; his money was running out; he had given up his publishing house; and, though he was working fast on several books, they seemed likely to remain in manuscript. There were friends of his who insisted—so Kay Boyle reports—"that McAlmon had been exploited, neglected, deceived, and imitated beyond recognition, but anyway preyed on by the vultures of the writing world."

McAlmon seemed to share that opinion, and he did not bear his sorrows like a Christian. When he came to write his memoirs of the 1920's—that is, the original text of "Being Geniuses Together"—he passed so many harsh judgments on famous men, and offered so many reports of their disgraceful behavior, that one is tempted to regard the book as McAlmon's revenge on almost all the writers he had known.

"Being Geniuses Together" was written in Paris in 1934 and was published four years later in London. There was no American edition at the time, partly because the 1920's were then out of fashion, but chiefly because the text fell short of the brilliant title. For all its faults, however, the book was rich in anecdotes and scathing judgments, it was soon to be rifled by others who wrote about those Paris years as they came back into vogue, and after McAlmon's death the copies that appeared on the rare-book market brought a higher price from sale to sale.

It was the last of his manuscripts to be published during his lifetime, and McAlmon was to spend the next 20 years as a solitary and embittered man. But what was the reason for the spectacular neglect from which he suffered? One cannot explain it by talking about "vultures," of which the writing world contains no larger share than the business world, in spite of its being even more bitterly competitive. From what I have read of McAlmon's work, I should hazard what might be the true cause of his failure: that he never in his life wrote so much as a memorable sentence. Phrases, yes, like "being geniuses together," but there were not many of these, and they marked the limit of his skill with words.

Though he lived in a society composed of geniuses and would-be geniuses, he refused to accept instruction. Ezra Pound once offered indirectly to criticize his poems, a service that Pound had already performed for Yeats and Eliot (not to mention Hemingway, who learned from him what to omit).

McAlmon's comment is that Ezra "will be the pedagogue, yearning for pupils to instruct, and I, whether I write well or badly, have my idea of how I want to do it." He was radically unteachable. He could not even learn from his own mistakes, since he seldom bothered to correct them.

Always he wrote at top speed in the effort to set down "what happened"; always he used the first and easiest words that occurred to him, and the result is that his writing never improved; over the years it slowly lost its original freshness. In 1928 Slater Brown, a man who has always loved good prose, summed up what most of the expatriates felt about McAlmon's work:

> *I would rather live in Oregon*
> *and pack salmon*
> *Than live in Nice and write*
> *like Robert McAlmon.*

The couplet was printed in the magazine Transition and was often spoken aloud in Montparnasse cafes. After 40 years Miss Boyle is still indignant about it. She was one of the desperately poor young writers helped by McAlmon, and she has remained one of his defenders, in a select company that also includes Katherine Anne Porter and Ezra Pound. Partly as a gesture of loyalty, she decided some years ago to prepare a new edition of his book. She revised and shortened the text (McAlmon's work always cries for emendation); she consulted the original typescript and restored some passages deleted by the English publisher; then she nearly doubled the length of the book by recounting her own adventures in chapters that are printed alternately with his. By her choice of emphasis, however, McAlmon remains the central figure, and he even acquires a dignity of failure that had been lacking in the story as told solely by himself.

At the same time Miss Boyle's chapters reveal by contrast, and without her intending them to do so, the fact that McAlmon never mastered the craft of writing. Miss Boyle, on the other hand, was bound to the craft like a medieval apprentice. Burdened or blessed as she was by the lack of a college education, she was determined to learn from any book that would teach her. One grim winter in Le Havre, when she was trying to write in a kitchen festooned with wet laundry (of her own laundering), the book was Rebecca West's "The Judge," which she had saved pennies to buy at a secondhand bookstall.

"I read it as a textbook," she says, "studying the shape of the sentences, looking up in the ragged dictionary the words I was not sure of. . . . All that mattered to me was that she was a woman, and that she had written a novel, a very long novel, which is what I was seeking to do." McAlmon, even as a very young man, would have been ashamed to study anyone or anything as a model; he read books to judge them, most often with a hostile and contemptuous eye. His story when set beside Kay Boyle's reminds one of Hogarth's twin fables of the idle and the industrious apprentice.

But a deeper contrast between the two authors is also revealed in this new edition of "Being Geniuses Together." It arises from the different answers they have found to an old question: whether a writer, in Conrad Aiken's phrase, should "give himself away." McAlmon's answer is negative. He is candid about other people, sometimes to the point of being spiteful, but he tells us little about his feelings and almost nothing about his intimate life. Miss Boyle is sometimes less than candid about others, since she wants to protect them, but she "gives herself away" by speaking frankly of her worst follies.

Thus she tells us how she left her first husband to live with Ernest Walsh, the editor of This Quarter, when Walsh was dying of consumption, how she bore him a posthumous child, and how Walsh's former mistress paid for her confinement. She tells how she yielded to self-pity during one summer in Paris and took more lovers than she can now remember, while hating them all and trying to punish herself. By placing the facts on record, without boasting or sniveling, she achieves a sort of selflessness. Apparently she agrees with Conrad Aiken's feeling "that this was one of the responsibilities of a writer— that he should take off the mask."

McAlmon leaves his mask in place, and it is only in Miss Boyle's chapters that we catch a glimpse of the despairing face behind it. Once he burst out to her, after a crazy, boring party at Harry Crosby's summer place: "I'm fed up with whatever it is I'm carrying around inside this skin, rattling around inside these bones!" He struck his chest violently with his fist—so she reports—and his face was hard as stone. "Don't care about me!" he shouted. "Stop it, will you? Let the God-damned pieces fall apart!" There is nothing in his own chapters like that moment of self-revelation.

Yet his memoir is full of entertaining stories about the misdeeds of the great, and I have to report that this collaboration—posthumous in McAlmon's case—has proved amazingly successful. It gives us pictures of two lives—and many surrounding lives—from different angles, as if they had been taken with a stereoscopic camera. Thereby it gives us an impression of depth and substantiality that have been lacking in other memoirs of Paris in the 1920's, and notably in McAlmon's original story.

The Telling of the Story

PHILLIP CORWIN

There is a kind of telescopic intimacy to Kay Boyle's work that manages to relate the grand concerns of the world to the personal lives of individual people in a way that is both touching and magnanimous. That has always been Boyle's strength, and it shines through again in her latest novel, *The Underground Woman*.

For about five decades now, Kay Boyle has demonstrated her literary abilities in a variety of forms: novels, poems, essays, children's books, and memoirs. Throughout that period she has consistently been able to be topical without being superficial, to be radical without being irrational and to be humane without being hypocritical. Perhaps that is because to her generation—she was a member of that distinguished literary set in Europe in the 1920s and 1930s that included Hemingway, Fitzgerald, Stein, Joyce and Pound—there was no contradiction between social conscience and artistic expression. In any case, *The Underground Woman* is a further extension of her lover's quarrel with the world. As such, it is a plea for the exercise of political conscience on the part of the middle class.

The protagonist of the novel is Athena Gregory, a widowed, 42-year-old mother of three daughters (Melanie, Sybil and Paula), who teaches a course in Greek mythology at a college in the San Francisco area and participates in peaceful protests against the war in Vietnam. The novel opens with Athena in a paddy wagon, among a group of demonstrators, all of whom have just been arrested for blocking the entrance to a military induction center. A few pages later Athena and the others are sentenced to ten days in the county's Rehabilitation Center, and it is at the women's compound in that center that most of the novel takes place. A brief period following Athena's release from the center, during which her home is invaded by a group of misfits from her daughter Melanie's commune, closes the book.

This is a novel about women and about femininity as much as it is about politics; but it is not a feminist novel, in the tendentious sense, any more than

Reprinted with permission from *The Nation* 220 (March 22, 1975): 347. © The Nation Company, L.P.

any honest novel could be a propaganda tract. Boyle is too good an artist for that. Indeed, the only avowed feminist among Athena's cell mates is Lou, a harbor pilot's daughter, who is clearly intended to be obnoxious and psychologically disturbed.

This is also, in another way, a novel about a group of freaks walking in the shadows of the epic Greeks, a novel about people freaked out of a society that seems unfit for them; about people who, despite their apparent ineffectuality, try nobly to obey the gods of their consciences, their underground men and women, in order to make their lives more meaningful.

The most consistent set of allusions in the book are to Greek mythology, and actually, they form the framework for the novel. To begin with, there is the matter of names. In addition to Athena, there is a famous folk singer named Callisto and a young woman named Calliope. Callisto emerges as Athena's most trusted friend, and Calliope as an admired companion. There are also repeated references to the Greek myths in Athena's thought and speech. And finally, there is the ever-present specter of intrafamilial strife, the central subject of Greek tragedy.

At a crucial point toward the end of the book Athena tries to tell a friend what significance the Greek myths have for her. She is, at the time, gasping and tearful.

> Mythology transcends the individual. . . . The Greek word, *mythologia*, means more than a simple collection of stories. It also means the . . . the telling of the story. . . . So the narrator . . . and the audience . . . and the whole of humanity . . . they come together as part . . .
> . . . as a part of the echo-awakening process which . . . which is the echoing of history.

In other words, the characters, the struggles, and the issues in this novel are intended to have a transcendency, to be an "echoing of history." And although the characters are undeniably pedestrian, they are meant to be invested with a certain nobility, a stature grander than their conventional lives suggest. Moreover, the person who tells their story, as Athena says in her monologue, is also part of the mythology.

The tension and the movement in this novel derive from various sets of contradictions, both within and outside of the characters. Athena Gregory is a case in point. Named for the goddess of war, she is a fighter for peace. As a woman who once rebelled against her father, she finds herself now the object of a rebellion by her daughter Melanie, who has fled to a commune that is run by a vile fraud named Pete the Redeemer, a kind of Charles Manson. Meanwhile, as a respectable middle-class woman, Athena is constantly hearing the voice of the Underground Woman, who urges her to throw off her restraints, her proprieties, her tendency to remain uninvolved, and to become the opposite of what she is. The Underground Woman is Athena's alter ego, her stifled self.

Once, while lecturing to her students about the myth of Demeter, Athena considers how futile the entire educational system is, how little it has to do with the great problems of the world, and how much she would like to tell her students exactly how she feels. She muses:

> And what if the underground woman at this instant flung aside her disguise? What if she should take my place at this table and say without any show of emotion: "There's really no use in any of us staying here." The underground woman would be the only one with the courage to say this. . . . The underground woman would say: "We have to find some other way." But instead Athena said: "Demeter and her daughter are perhaps closer to our own experience than are the lives of the other goddesses. This is because their grief sets them apart from the immortals." . . .

In *The Underground Woman,* Kay Boyle would have us believe that the grief of the people in her novel sets them apart from those immortal robots who are beyond grief. At times she succeeds and at times she does not. But whatever the final result her effort is a worthy one, and one thoroughly consistent with those of a writer whose energies have always been expended imaginatively and unselfishly in a constant attempt to enlighten her fellow citizens.

Moving and Maturing

Vance Bourjaily

"Fifty stories" is a Kay Boyle retrospective, presenting, pretty much in the order of composition, the writer's choices from 39 years—1927 through 1966—of devotion to the art of writing short fiction.

It is a long, rich progression of work. Even so, it is only a small part of the author's contribution to the literature of her times. Kay Boyle has produced, in what is altogether 50 years of publication, 29 books: 14 novels, eight collections of stories, four books of poetry, three books for children, the compilation of another writer's autobiography, and collaboration in an odd, engaging memoir, "Being Geniuses Together."

This last-named appeared in 1938 as the work of the expatriate writer and critic Robert McAlmon, a rival of Hemingway, companion of Joyce and friend of Kay Boyle. In 1968, she revived his book, adding alternate chapters of her own recollections. In it, we find her discussing McAlmon's conjecture that "both Katherine Anne Porter and Kay Boyle were better writers than Katherine Mansfield, but because no legend had been manufactured for them, their reputations would remain scandalously small. Katherine Anne, Bob said, was in his judgment the sounder writer, for she wrote with greater authenticity, while Kay, come hell or high water, had to romanticize every situation." This conjecture, Kay Boyle adds, "may very well be true."

No. It simply doesn't seem true at all by now. Half a century later, comparing the three is merely capricious; each has been a significant writer in her own very different way. As to the manufacture of legends, Katherine Mansfield's has pretty well faded from consciousness, at least in America (though several recent biographies of her indicate a modest revival). Katherine Anne Porter's reputation is in perfectly good shape, and Kay Boyle remains a central character in that group legend that nourished us all, the literary Paris of the 20's. And of course there is more to their accomplishment than legend; they invented techniques we still practice, and introduced themes that still concern us.

Reprinted by permission of *The New York Times Book Review* (September 28, 1980): 9, 32.

Kay Boyle's "Fifty Stories" is a wonderful exhibit of these techniques and themes in evolution. Among the techniques we have grammatical simplification, rhythmic repetition, the mixing in of vernacular, stream of consciousness, density of impressions, radical imagery and experiments with surrealism that may have originated with Gertrude Stein and James Joyce but became community property of the group.

These 50 stories are set as the author's life was set, and their themes and concerns follow her moving and maturing: There is the Midwest, Atlantic City, France, Austria, England, France again, occupied Germany and postwar New York. Changing as current history changed, the stories deal with childhood and parentage, sexuality, crass exploitation, prejudice, Fascism, war, American values and the disorientation of individuals. Looked at as a whole, they are notably free of a compulsion to romanticize.

Let us agree, if we can, that authentic fiction means fiction in which we hear consistently a particular author's voice that is unaffectedly true to the author's time, place and situation, and tells stories derived from the author's own observation and understanding—stories, that is, firmly rooted in public events and personal experience. Opposed to this mode would be fiction that is contrived or imitated or fabricated or made sentimental—or, at best, purely imagined (what McAlmon meant by a tendency to romanticize; Kay Boyle, he complained, was too easily tempted to "go Irish, twilightly"—the same phrase he used to describe Joyce's poetry and parts of "Portrait of the Artist as a Young Man").

David Daiches, who contributes a thoughtful introduction to "Fifty Stories," holds a different view of Kay Boyle: "The most remarkable thing about the best of these stories," he argues, "is that they combine accurate reporting of the 'feel' of an historical situation with all those overtones of meaning, those probings into the center of man's moral and emotional experience, which we demand of the true literary artist. . . . [They are] compassionate without being sentimental, moral without being didactic, contemporary without being ephemeral. . . ."

Let's look at four of the stories, each from a different decade. In the passages quoted there may be some evidence of the evolution of her style, from high-spirited language-play to a dark, straightforward sobriety as the European situation grew ominous, then to the bitterness felt by so many political activists of the 30's, and finally a return to the spirit of play in art—a play that reflects mature control and creative purpose. There is a particular literary technique that recurs so often in "Fifty Stories" as to be a kind of Kay Boyle hallmark: the technique of surrealism. None of the stories collected here is avowedly surrealistic, but there are controlled and often magical flights of surrealism in most of them.

The story from the 20's is "Wedding Day." Sexuality declares itself in the chief characters, a brother and sister whose relationship is on the threshold of incest. It is the sister's wedding day. Their mother fears things will go terribly wrong. Things don't; so much for romanticization. Before the wedding, however, the siblings go for a walk in Paris, and for several paragraphs it is like a surrealist film: "Here then was April holding them up, stabbing their hearts with hawthorne, scalping them with a flexible blade of wind. Here went their yellow manes up in the air, turning them shaggy as lions." Inexplicably, they are in a little train together. "Here were their teeth alike in size as well as the arrogance that had put the proud arch in their noses. Wallop and wallop went the little train through the woods, cracking like castanets the knuckles of their behinds." Then they are in a little boat, and swans come to stare at them. And then they're back at the wedding with guests arriving peacefully, and the old mother dancing.

"Maiden, Maiden," from the 30's, is admittedly more romantic. It involves a triangle: a couple, illicit lovers, mountain-climbing with a dark, appealing guide. The guide and the young woman have declared their mutual attraction; the guide is killed before it can develop. The surrealist personification of a flock of sheep mirrors what is being said perhaps of the mixture of persons: "There was a scattered flock making their way upward: strong mountain sheep as big as calves, their smooth ebony faces turned to the sight of the people. . . . A few whitish ones walked among the others, and under their eyes were shadows of disillusionment and the long potted cheeks of the old and evil and dissipated."

It's hard to imagine a story more counterromantic than "Defeat," from the 1940's. In it an escaping French soldier is helped by a schoolteacher, and says to her gratefully that a country is not defeated so long as its women are not. The same evening, from a hiding place, he sees the French girls turn out to attend an outdoor picnic and dance which the conquering Germans are conducting. In this tale again, the surrealist flight is cinematic; it foreshadows the bitter young soldier's discovery of the appeal of the conquerors: ". . . the German ranks had advanced bareheaded, in short-sleeved, summer shirts— young, blond-haired men with their arms linked, row on row, and their trousers immaculately creased; having slept all night in hotel beds, and their stomachs full, advancing singing . . . the bright-haired, blond demigods would march on singing across their dead . . . then would follow the glittering display: the rustproof tanks and guns, the chromiumed electric kitchens, the crematoriums."

Finally, in the penultimate story—"The Ballet of Central Park," a kind of fable—here is what complete ease with surrealism allows Kay Boyle to achieve: "It should be stated here that I am no relation to Hilary except inasmuch as all adults are related to all children. . . . I am perhaps that idle lady, twisted out of shape by the foundation undergarment she has chosen to trap the look of youth for a little longer, her feet crippled by the high-heeled sandals that grip her toes like a handful of cocktail sausages, who has strayed over from Fifth Avenue leading an evil-faced poodle, gray as a wasp's nest and as nervous . . . and I am equally the lady with the light orange hair and muscles knotted high on the calves of her shapely, still agile legs who taught Hilary ballet. . . . I am also, being adult, the police officer who apprehended Hilary except that Hilary could never be apprehended. She was beyond arrest or incarceration, for the walls of any prison would disappear if she laid the palm of her hand against the stone."

Kay Boyle's psychology is realistic and her situations credible, but surrealism is an authentic, unromanticized part of her vision of the world—a world of abrupt transformations from charm to anguish, anxiety to knowledge, delight to fear or—to borrow a phrase of her own from another source—"avidity for love . . . and . . . inexcusable despair."

No definitive assessment of Kay Boyle's achievement can be made without taking into account the novels and the poems, of course, but there is much that is moving and memorable in "Fifty Stories" and so much of technical interest that it should serve to get that assessment off to a strong start.

60 Years of Passion and Compassion

HUGH FORD

This collection brings together 25 essays, reviews and prefaces composed over six decades but mostly between the mid-1940's and the late 70's. Many appeared in The Nation and The New Republic, journals that accepted the writer's work when others didn't. As a supplement to her "Fifty Stories" (1980), "Words That Must Somehow Be Said" is invaluable. It is also a welcome confirmation of Miss Boyle's prolific and variegated career. Of her 14 novels, only a few are still in print, though once again available is the nonfiction work "Being Geniuses Together: 1920–1930," Robert McAlmon's expatriate memoir, to which she added chapters about her own experiences in Paris.

Many of the essays in the present volume afford unfaded, disturbing glimpses into our country's traumatic past and Miss Boyle's impassioned concerns, from the McCarthyism epidemic to the Vietnam War protests and the Attica prison riots. There is much autobiography here too, and a portrait emerges of the author as a bold and articulate defender of civil liberties and humane treatment of the neglected and defenseless. As the editor of this volume, the critic Elizabeth S. Bell, notes in an informative introduction, Miss Boyle's writing is consistently vivid and trenchant and, in the best pieces, compassionate and enduring.

In the first essay, "The Family," we get a sense of the writer's ancestry. Affectionately described are a general in Washington's army, a frontier doctor, a Kansas schoolteacher, an aunt who drew cartoons for the National Woman's Party and the author's mother, a stalwart and independent woman who had a profound influence on her daughter. From them Miss Boyle claims her pioneering spirit and devotion to free inquiry. In some evocative passages, they are revealed as moral touchstones guiding her deliberations.

The essays under the heading "On Writers and Writing" include early reviews of works by William Carlos Williams and Hart Crane (both appeared in transition magazine in the late 1920's). She celebrates Williams's essays in "In the American Grain" as an authentic rendering of America, unencum-

Reprinted by permission of The New York Times Book Review (August 25, 1985): 20.

bered by inheritance, an original depiction grounded in "chastity of fact." She dismisses Crane's poems in "White Buildings," however, as empty and dull, lacking the raw substance of life. In Katherine Mansfield's stories she discerns an "inadequacy to see in any other and wider terms the things she sensed so acutely," but in William Faulkner's 1938 novel, "The Unvanquished," she finds consummate skill and vision to effect both a personal and national passage out of violence.

Doubtless the imperatives she issued in "A Declaration for 1955" after she had borne the contumely of McCarthyism were reactions to the time, but her insistence that authors must not just speak their beliefs but also defend them, devoting themselves to altering society according to the "higher standards" of the individual, remains compelling. Among those who met the challenge to speak the "words that must somehow be said" she cites Dylan Thomas, Edward Dahlberg and James Baldwin.

In the book's final section, "On the Human Condition," Miss Boyle addresses the tragedy of this century: genocide. In a 1945 essay, she excoriates the beggarly conduct of André Gide, Sacha Guitry and Maurice Chevalier, who, during the Occupation, stood by while 11,000 Jews were incarcerated and deported. In 1949 she writes of two women traveling on the same train to Frankfurt. One is a civilian War Department employee who assuages her hatred of Germany ("a leper's colony") by spending weekends in Paris. The other is a German refugee, a Jew, who sustained herself in exile by remembering the words of Goethe: "freedom and life are deserved only by those who conquer them anew each day."

It was with some reluctance that Kay Boyle returned to live in Germany in 1948. Two years later came "The Smoking Mountain," a collection of stories describing that vanquished country. In the book's preface, a long, sharply observed report and commentary reprinted here, she set forth with sympathy and understanding the results of her "painstaking and almost completely loveless search for another face of Germany." She accepts the common finding of Goethe, Heine, Nietzsche and the novelist Theodor Plievier that Germans suffer from fatal dualities within themselves and that only when they finally acknowledge this will the national psyche be headed.

Her account of the trial of Heinrich Baab, a former Gestapo official accused of participating in over 50 murders, offers harrowing testimony about the difficulties facing a nation of bewildered and divided people. When a German jury finds Baab guilty and a German judge sentences him to hard labor for life, a young court guard Miss Boyle had noticed during the trial turns toward the press bench, his face "as clear as light with vindicated pride." "Until there has been a national upheaval, a clearing of our house by our own hands," a German friend told the author, "the twilight will remain."

If Kay Boyle defines the human condition in terms of war and its aftermath—the suffering and extinction of multitudes, violations of human dignity by totalitarian and democratic nations and relentless preparations for conflict under the guise of security—it is not because she has lost faith that man can prevail but because she believes he will. With the abolitionist John Brown, she holds that "a minority convinced of its rights, based on moral principles will, under a republican government, sooner or later become the majority." As this collection impressively attests, Kay Boyle has spent a lifetime speaking for the voiceless and acting for the inactive in pursuit of that goal.

Old Novel Offers Insights into Nazism

STEVE KETTMANN

This paperback reissue of Kay Boyle's potent and elegant 1936 novel about the people and passions that made Nazism a volatile force makes for a strong argument in favor of republishing important novels from the past.

The first surprise for a contemporary reader of "Death of a Man," which pluckily combines a romance with a political novel, is the ease with which Boyle's narrative voice remains neutral and her perceptions intelligent. In a rich and empathetic portrait, she introduces Dr. Prochaska, a "dark and hot-eyed" young Austrian who believes deeply in the cause of Nazism, although Boyle is far too skillful a writer to mention the party or its leader by name at this early point.

She repeatedly evokes the intensity in Prochaska's eye and the grace of the strong, lean hands with which he cares for the children in the isolation ward of a hospital in the Tyrolean Alps. She presents his love of the jagged mountains he climbs as neither more nor less understandable than his passion for the nighttime speeches from Germany he listens to on his radio, or the hope he finds in them of change for his out-of-work countrymen.

Boyle also gives the seemingly stiff Prochaska a taste for reckless love. Sitting high in the Alps and enjoying the afterglow of a vigorous climb, he sees a young couple climbing toward him. He spends the day with the amiable young Englishman and his sharp American wife. Not too many chapters later, Prochaska again finds himself face-to-face with the tall, ostentatious young woman, who sits at his table at the local *gasthaus* and tells him she has sent the Englishman away.

Boyle's subtle, complicated weaving of Prochaska's passion for the party, the Alps and Pendennis (the young American) give the book its rich narrative. Her strength lies not so much in fashioning a plot but in presenting an array of telling images that evoke an emotional pitch that stays with us.

"Dr. Prochaska felt the awful ecstatic urge, the terrible speechless movement of the mountains around them, the strange and absolute power, pure and perfect enough to draw his heart forth, trembling, from his breast."

Reprinted by permission of the *San Francisco Chronicle* (September 14, 1989).

Boyle's fresh, confident prose carries the narrative to a realm in which our conceptions about the obvious ignominy of anyone associated with Nazism lose much of their focus. This effect led contemporary reviewers of the book to charge Boyle with pro-Nazism, but that clearly is not her point.

A hard edge cuts through, of course. The name "Dachau" drifts into the narrative randomly, and a reader can be forgiven for feeling suddenly nauseous. Pendennis and Prochaska climb into the mountains at night to light burning swastikas, and they glory in the beauty of the sight. Later the apolitical Pendennis curses the men who have put out the fires.

For all that, at least from the distance of half a century, the novel feels mostly like a celebration. Boyle's prose overflows with excitement. Her two main characters plunge into a pursuit of what they find alone together. Her Austrian village vibrates with hope for a better future, hope that in this narrative remains largely unsullied by race hate or power lust.

Putting all this bubbly emotion into a historical moment at which we look back with horror may ask a lot of a reader, but Boyle's accomplishment is to make the big-jump relatively easy.

CRITICISM

♦

Kay Boyle

Richard C. Carpenter

In her autobiography, *The Passionate Years,* Caresse Crosby says of Kay Boyle: "Kay is built like a blade—to see her clearly you must look at her from one side and then from the other; both are exciting." This is an assessment which can be equally well applied to her writing, as can Mrs. Crosby's description: "neat as a needle . . . like a breeze or a bird's wing"—it is exciting, and it must be looked at from more than one angle to appreciate it thoroughly. After twenty-five years of writing short stories and novels, Miss Boyle manages to bring to her work the same vividness, the freshness of style, the subtle insights, and the craftsmanship that marked her first writing. Several of the tales in her most recent book, *The Smoking Mountain,* are as taut and clean as those which appeared in *First Lover and Other Stories* twenty years ago and as intense in their emotional currents as her first novel, *Plagued by the Nightingale,* which was published in 1931. The stories that appear from time to time in the *New Yorker* show no diminution of ability, and the chances are that reading one will bring an absorbing experience.

Yet Kay Boyle is singularly little known; even college English professors are as a rule only vaguely aware of her existence and may recall with some difficulty having read a story in one of the several anthologies in which her tales have appeared. Her some dozen novels and over a hundred short stories, while frequently praised and often reprinted, have not given her a wide reputation. Few people have encountered such fascinating tales as *Monday Night* or *The Bridegroom's Body,* both of them eminently worth reading. However, the fact remains that Miss Boyle has done much excellent work and should be better known.

Encouraged by her mother, she started to write early and had by the age of seventeen written "hundreds of poems, short stories, and a novel." Married at eighteen and settled abroad, presumably for a visit, but actually as a permanent expatriate as it turned out, she wrote stories throughout the twenties and had her first collection published at the Black Sun Press in Paris by Caresse and

Reprinted from *College English* 15, no. 2 (November 1953): 81–87, with the permission of the author.

Harry Crosby in 1929. This was republished in the United States as *Wedding Day and Other Stories*. In 1931 she started a full-fledged career of writing and, following her first novel, *Plagued by the Nightingale*, brought out four novels and two collections of short stories in the next five years. *Year before Last, Gentlemen, I Address You Privately*, and *My Next Bride*, all of them concerned with the pathos of love lost through weakness or circumstance, proved that she was a very subtle analyst of personality and established (together with *First Lover and Other Stories* and *The White Horse of Vienna*) her reputation as a stylist—an exquisite manipulator of the nuances of phrase and a craftsman with image and metaphor. By 1938 it appeared that she had laid claim to this title, for the blurbs on her books announced it, and the critics in general followed suit. While they praised her stylistic ability, they did, however, regret that her situations were not more realistic and that her people lived too much in the pale light of another world. At the same time they noted her uncanny immediacy and impact, for these tales are without doubt weirdly fascinating.

That she was an expatriate, using European backgrounds and characters largely, and that she soon came to be engrossed with political and social themes also were noticed—to her irritation, for she feels that she is writing about people, not places or politics. Still, such novels as *Death of a Man*, with its sympathetic analysis of the ideas and feelings of an Austrian Nazi; *Avalanche* and *A Frenchman Must Die*, "elegant potboilers"; and the short stories of this period show a preoccupation with the effect of political turmoil and war on quite ordinary people. Probably her weakest book, *His Human Majesty* (1949), is the result of her attempt to write on such a problem, the lives and loves of ski-troops, a task eminently unsuited to her kind of fiction.

A selection from her stories of the last twenty years or so, *Thirty Stories* (1946) affords ample evidence, nevertheless, that she is more than either a stylist or a writer mesmerized by the confusions and alarums of our weary world. It becomes clear, on reading through these stories, that her twice winning the O. Henry Memorial Prize for the best short story of the year, her constant appearance in such magazines as the *New Yorker* and *Harper's Bazaar*, and the recent inclusion of her novella *The Crazy Hunter* in Ludwig and Perry's *Nine Short Novels* (in the company of James, Kafka, and Mann) have been no mere flukes and are due to more solid virtues than are comprised in style or political consciousness, good though those may be.

Of course, it is undeniable that she is an able manipulator of language. She enjoys the play of words; she has a keen eye for the striking image; and she can fascinate with the bold trenchancy of her metaphors: "Here then was April holding them up, stabbing their hearts with hawthorn, scalping them with a flexible blade of wind," or "The waves came in and out there, as indolent as ladies, gathered up their skirts in their hands, and with a murmur, came tiptoeing in across the velvet sand." Especially is it true that she can create amazingly sharp, vivid pictures: "Prince and Star were black as seals and here they stood in the white unmelting world, the two black horses steaming against the hard, bright, crusted snow. The white boughs of the trees were forked full in the woods around, and the twigs of the underbrush were tubed in glass the length of the frozen falls."

Still, this mastery of style accounts for only one side of the blade that is Kay Boyle—the side that glitters and dazzles and, perhaps, blinds some readers to the more significant things she has to offer. Style is obviously integral to her work and makes it peculiarly her own; it undoubtedly helps heighten the intensity and immediacy which most readers recognize as the hallmark of Miss Boyle's writing. Dagger-sharp images and crackling metaphors do assist in raising the temperature of a story. Other qualities, however, seem to me to be more basic. First of all, a thorough acquaintance with the bulk of her work leads to an increasing appreciation of her mastery of her own kind of fictional technique. She has a most delicate touch in unfolding the lives of her characters, an exquisite sense of reticence and balance, all the while that the tale is trembling on the edge of pathos or sentimentality. Much of this effect she manages by carefully limiting the area of perception (something she may have learned from Chekhov or perhaps from Faulkner, whom she admires most highly), so that the reader becomes *aware* in the form of a gradual revelation, as do the principal characters. This contributes greatly to developing the "specification of reality," the sense of immediacy which James desired of fiction. When used, as Miss Boyle frequently does use it, with judicious foreshadowing, it creates a considerable current of tension without having much "happen" in the sense of the usual well-plotted story. We do not leisurely savor her stories but breathlessly turn pages, sure that these apparently innocuous events are somehow tremendously vital.

Beyond technique, Miss Boyle's basic themes are also productive of suspense and intensity. Her fiction world is not a happy one: she deals with disease, war, perversion, cowardice, frustration. Her people are complex souls undergoing a variety of torments, prevented either by their own weaknesses or by the devils of circumstance from living the rich and full lives which should be theirs. To make things worse, her people are not degraded but *potentially* fine and *potentially* happy. They are sensitive, courageous, artistic, profoundly emotional. We like them, usually, and would like to see them happy, but they are the beautiful and the damned. Miss Boyle achieves her characteristic force by showing us a vision of humanity in need of pity and understanding, a central idea that does not make for light reading but one which accounts for the realism and effectiveness we inescapably feel as we read through her work. While probably not the end result of a reasoned philosophy, it is a telling and significant attitude toward life that makes of her writing much more than a pretty toy or a tract. Miss Boyle is not simply *interested* in people; she is vitally *concerned* with people and profoundly moved to write about their struggles with themselves and with their dreams. She does not write just to tell a tale, to make money, to create a thing of beauty, even though these may sometimes be her motives; but, as she has said, she also writes "out of anger, out of compassion and grief . . . out of despair." This is truly the other side of the blade.

From her earliest work we can see Miss Boyle working out this idea. *Plagued by the Nightingale* and *Year before Last* explore the relations between people whose happiness is shadowed by disease; *Gentlemen, I Address You Privately* is an analysis of perverted love. *Plagued by the Nightingale* is the story of an American girl who has married into a French family cursed with a hereditary disease which cripples the legs of the men. The conflict grows out of the insistence of the family, particularly Papa, that the young couple have a child, even though everyone knows the risk. A silent but bitter struggle, beneath the surface of an idyllic family life, is waged, with the family using the lever of promised money to weaken the son's resistance. The family loses, eventually, but the girl loses as well, for she leaves her husband, and her love, at the end. The novel is almost a parable, with Bridget and Nicholas—youth, beauty, and love—defeated by age and corruption, symbolized by the nature of the disease, a "rotting of the bone" as it is called. The corruption comes closer to home in her second novel, *Year before Last,* since Martin, the hero, is handsome, brave, sensitive, deeply in love, as well as tuberculous. He is, perhaps, a bit too much of these things and a trifle impossible, but he and his inamorata, Hannah, reiterate for us that the beautiful *are* often the damned. As we watch them flee across the south of France, with the hemorrhages becoming more frequent and deadly, we find our feeling of pity and our sense of irony steadily increasing until the inevitable death at the conclusion.

An interesting aspect of these novels is that they ought to be merely depressing instead of enthralling. However, through the poetic use of language and the method of implication and reticence, Miss Boyle lifts the story. Besides, because the reader creates the emotional tone for himself, as he gradually becomes aware of the situation, the essential tragedy is not sharply emphasized. The tale unfolds slowly, flower-like, so that we are almost able—almost, but not quite, like the characters themselves—to close our eyes on the worm i' the bud. The enervation of some of her later work is undoubtedly due to a partial abandonment of this method of implication for that of stream of consciousness and interior monologue where we are brought directly and explicitly into contact with the people's thoughts and emotions, usually in italics. In her weaker writing Miss Boyle tells us too much; in her better we float on a placid, shimmering current, all the time aware of the cold, black rushing depths beneath.

Naturally, this method can be overdone, as it is in her third novel, *Gentlemen, I Address You Privately,* where we see everything through a glass most darkly, so much so that it is difficult to realize what the theme is. An analysis of the chiaroscuro, however, shows that all the characters are twisted in some way: the cast is composed of two homosexuals, two Lesbians, a prostitute, a fanatic, a sadist, and one fine woman starved for love. In general, love is perverted in this novel; the characters are lost souls, whirled through the darkness of their desires.

The tale comes to a flat and tasteless end, despite some tension in the last chapters, and its people are too much for us to swallow—possible perhaps, but hardly probable. Still, with all its frigidity and confusion, it somehow sticks in the mind, like a reflection in a distorting mirror, concentrating for us the pathos and irony of Miss Boyle's theme. It is, as well, the furthest advance she has made in the use of implication and memorable for that reason.

Throughout Miss Boyle's writings prior to the war we can see the same techniques, the same quivering emotion held in tight leash, the concern with the interrelations of personality, the same bitter brew. Though the short stories naturally play many variations, they show the same fundamental theme, not difficult to recognize once it has been analyzed.

In some stories the problem is pride, as in "Keep Your Pity," where the Wycherlys, impoverished Englishmen in the south of France, preserve appearances even beyond death. In others, such as "The White Horses of Vienna," it is the pathos of prejudice and misunderstanding. The young Jewish student-doctor, who has been called in to assist the injured Austrian Nazi, ought to be able to be a friend—he and the Austrian are really much alike, the Austrian with his worship of power and the Jew with his nostalgic idealism, his memory of the royal white horses of Vienna, "the relics of pride, the still unbroken vestiges of beauty bending their knees to the empty loge of royalty where there was no royalty any more." But of course they cannot be friends.

Other stories are tales of initiation, in which an innocent or unknowing character learns evil—as in "Black Boy," where a young white girl learns that she cannot have an innocent friendship with a black boy, at least not as far as her grandfather is concerned; or in *The Bridegroom's Body* (a novella), where Lady Glourie realizes that the young nurse who has come from the city has not been, as Lady Glourie suspected, in love with Lord Glourie or the farmer Panrandel but really with Lady Glourie herself. In "Natives Don't Cry" we see the beautifully low-keyed treatment of the real pathos in the old maid's life as the governess tries to pretend she is getting letters from her young man, when the mail was not delivered that day.

"Wedding Day," one of Miss Boyle's best, a light and delicate study of personal relations between brother and sister on her wedding day, does not force theme on our attention, but there is still the sense of loss, of youth left somewhere behind, forever. "Count Lothar's Heart" concerns itself with what has happened to a young man who has had a homosexual experience during the war and cannot get it out of his mind, his perversion symbolized by the swans of the Traunsee, emblems of passion. "One of Ours" studies through image and symbol the hidden feelings of a most proper Englishwoman who thinks a savage at an exposition is lusting after her—a projection of her desires, for he is really interested in the doll she is holding. The theme of distortion is carried out by her fascination with the savage's maleness as well as her fear of him.

It might be wondered whether or not Miss Boyle offers anything but utter blank and bitter pessimism with this constant iteration of the theme of a world out of joint. Indeed, it could be maintained that there is nothing else. A novel like *My Next Bride* (1934) leaves about as bad a taste in our mouths as anything we could find, with an American girl who deserves no evil falling into utter degradation through her love for another woman's husband. Perversely she becomes promiscuous rather than having her affair with Antony, making her pregnancy by some unknown especially fruitless. Probably the most unpleasant sequences Kay Boyle has ever written are to be found in the account of Victoria's attempts at abortion.

Yet the novel, *Monday Night* (1936), which has a protagonist who is repulsively dirty and possesses a nauseatingly mutilated ear, manages to distil something more positive from the flowers of evil. The contrast between the clean and the filthy, the innocent and the obscene, is implicit perhaps, but it is still there to provide a kind of counterpoint to the basic theme. In fact, this counterpoint may be seen running through many of her writings, indicating a corollary to the pessimism. A passage in "Count Lothar's Heart" symbolizes what this may be; speaking of the swans, she writes:

> Some of them had thrust the long stalks of their throats down into the deeper places before the falls and were seeking for refuse along the bottom. Nothing remained but the soft, flickering short peaks of their clean rumps and their leathery black elbows with the down blowing soft at the ebony bone. In such ecstasies of beauty were they seeking in the filth of lemon rinds and shells and garbage that had drifted down from the town, prodding the leaves and branches apart with their dark, lustful mouths.

Miss Boyle seems to be saying that the polarity between the beautiful and the ugly, the good and the bad, is central in our lives. Wilt, in *Monday Night*, disreputable and dirty, is yet a dreamer of beautiful dreams which he conveys to us in long monologues written in an incantatory style strongly reminiscent of Faulkner, who, Miss Boyle says, strongly influenced the book. Wilt ought to be a great writer, yet he is a seedy drunk. Miss Boyle is not telling us that he is going to triumph over himself; rather she is showing us that he cannot possibly do so: the fact that he and his friend never reach the goal they seek is the only logic that the underlying theme will permit the plot. Yet Wilt is somehow noble. He is giving himself to an ideal; the tale is almost an allegory, a *Pilgrim's Progress* of this modern world, where modern man fails of heaven as a goal but finds his soul in the quest itself. Here, as in other places, we can see Miss Boyle implying that devotion, integrity, and courage are the means by which we transcend our fate.

This implication is particularly evident in the tales since the war; dealing with social and political themes, they throw the contrast between what is and what ought to be into clearer light. In the backwash of a war-world, the need for undramatic devotion and integrity is particularly great. A number of tales since 1938 benefit from this larger context. There is less tendency toward attenuating the situation; the characters are often more believable, their suffering justified, their bravery less self-conscious, their defeat more real. It must be admitted that they transcend their fate but seldom. Many tales are vitiated by Miss Boyle's indiscriminate tenderness toward those who are the victims of war. Her best work in this type of writing is rather that which grows out of indignation, the failure of devotion and integrity. "Defeat," which won the O. Henry Memorial Prize in 1941, shows this indignation combined effectively with tenderness, the indignation coming from the failure of the French girls to resist the German blandishments of food and dance music, the tenderness for the men who realize their country is defeated only when its women are defeated.

Her most recent book, *The Smoking Mountain*, rings the changes on Miss Boyle's preoccupation with the war: there are some good stories in it and some that strain after sentiment. She is trying to show us the atmosphere of an occupied land in which all the old hatreds still smolder under the ashes of defeat. Probably the most interesting part of the book is the long, nonfiction Introduction, the account of Germans against German in the trial of a former Gestapo brute, a new kind of venture for her and one that may lead to more significant writing. A new venture is needed; to this reader it does not seem that Miss Boyle has lost any of her ability to perceive and convey human feelings and relations, there is no slackening of her mastery of prose style, and she has certainly not turned into a shallow optimist. Yet it would be a pleasant change to see a tale not tied to particular "conditions and conflicts," as she calls them, as universal as, let us say, the novelle *The Crazy Hunter* and *The Bridegroom's Body*, tales rich in background and symbol, powerfully motivated from within the characters themselves, subtly reproducing the conflicts of personality. To my mind, these two short novels are the cream of her writing, together with such stories as "The White Horses of Vienna," "Wedding Day," and "Natives Don't Cry." It is fortunate that Professors Ludwig and Perry have reprinted *The Crazy Hunter*, and it would be well if someone would do the same for *The Bridegroom's Body*, that eerie yet unforgettable re-creation of the swannery on the rain-drenched coast of England, with the magnificently vital yet tragically lonely Lady Glourie and the bitter irony of Miss Cafferty's love for her. Then more readers might be able to see that Miss Boyle not only can dazzle us with style but also can move us to a deeper understanding.

The Revolution of the Word

SANDRA WHIPPLE SPANIER

"It may appear to have been a time without much humor in the avant-garde literary movement, but it must be remembered that it was a time of the gravest crisis in letters, of furious schism and revolution in the arts. . . . This was a serious business, and if one laughed a good deal over café tables, one did not laugh very loudly on the printed page," writes Kay Boyle of the twenties (*BGT,* 214) [*Being Geniuses Together*]. In the twenties and early thirties, Paris resounded with highly charged talk about art, and to Kay Boyle, as to many others, art was both politics and religion. Looking back, she describes it as "a time of peril" in which "gravity was demanded of writers who fought against the sentence of death, of oblivion, passed on their work by critics and publishers, and on the life term offered as alternative, to be served in the ancient strongholds of the established conventional forms" (*BGT,* 214). The little magazines abounded with declarations, definitions, and manifestos, and in the ideological battles that raged between their covers moderation was no virtue.

One of the most colorful examples of the vehemence with which the pens were drawn appears in the second issue of *This Quarter.* In the July, 1925, issue of *Poetry: A Magazine of Verse* (a publication of twelve years' standing), editor Harriet Monroe had reviewed the first issue of *This Quarter,* politely expressing her reservations as to the need for yet another magazine succeeding to *The Little Review, Broom, Others,* "and other radicals even less stable whose fitfulness or early demise have been lamented from time to time in these pages." She ends the critique with cute condescension: "And perhaps in the next number they will show us the promised land!" *This Quarter* did not appreciate the indulgent remark. Its second issue reprinted the entire review, adding this preface:

> The episode is taken note of here because it is typical rather than exceptional of the kind of thing THIS QUARTER means to make war on: namely the insinu-

Reprinted from *Kay Boyle: Artist and Activist* (Carbondale: Southern Illinois University Press, 1986) 30–57, with the permission of the publisher.

ating school of criticism; the weary critic; the bald-headed critic; the judicial critic; the polite critic; the malicious critic; the thousand and one kinds of critic that ought to *shut up*. There is only one kind of critic worth having and that is the *judge* possessing judgement rather than judgements who *values* rather than *discounts* and who *kills* cleanly but does not *poison* and who either loves or despises. What cannot be either loved or despised is not vital enough to celebrate in print.[1]

In the third issue of *This Quarter*, Kay Boyle seconded the editors' pronouncement by placing "Miss Harriet Monroe" on her "Unrecommended List"—a choleric regular feature of the magazine in which various contributors listed their least favorite books, bars, hotels, and people.

Her ideology in those days is easy enough to piece together. She clearly—in fact, stridently—outlined her moral/aesthetic stance (the two were inseparable) in a number of articles. The fall 1928 issue of *transition* published responses by seventeen expatriate artists—Gertrude Stein, Robert McAlmon, and Harry Crosby, among others—to the question, "Why do Americans live in Europe?" In her feisty reply, Kay Boyle expressed her sense of alienation from her philistine homeland: "Americans I would permit to serve me, to conduct me rapidly and competently wherever I was going, but not for one moment to impose their achievements upon what is going on in my heart and in my soul. I am too proud and too young to need the grandeur of physical America which one accepts only at the price of one's own dignity." "Each citizen functions with pride in the American conspiracy against the individual," she declares, and with a proud jab at American softness and priggishness, warns her compatriots: "Cling, gentlemen, to the skyscraper by toefinger-eyelash, but do not come to Europe. Here nothing is done for you. You must write your own literature, you must walk up and down stairs, and you must drink like gentlemen."[2]

Of the artist, Kay Boyle demanded passion and originality. She lauded Eugene Jolas, editor of *transition*, who had written, "Follow the voice that booms in the deepest dream, deeper go, always deeper," calling him "a tireless stoker for a great wild fire" who "made a wondrous conflagration to warm cold nights and days." (The March, 1932, issue of *transition* had been solemnly subtitled "An International Workshop for Orphic Creation.") Of Gertrude Stein, who taught people "to fear the many-syllabled word and to mistrust the intellect," she writes: "It would be well if, for her might, economy, and devotion, she were sainted. I would be the first to bow the knee. Whether you will or whether you won't, each word she writes is a stone cast after you."[3] Nor was Kay Boyle's admiration of boldly original writers limited to her immediate contemporaries: in 1931 she wrote, "I have no religion except that of poetry, and in Poe, Whitman, and William Carlos Williams I recognize the apostles of America."[4]

She articulates her aesthetic values most completely in a memorial piece she wrote a few months after the death of her friend Harry Crosby. It begins: "To be living now, to be living, alive and full of the thing, to believe in the sun, the moon, or the stars, or in whatever is your belief, and to write of these things with an alertness sharp as a blade and as relentless, is a challenge that is a solemn privilege of the young." Harry Crosby stood "singularly alone" in her eyes in his "grave acknowledgement of that responsibility." "There was no one who ever lived more consistently in the thing that was happening then," she wrote, and she mused:

> Maybe it would be a good thing if history were never set down. It imposes a tradition of standards that has to do with the experiences of other people, and it makes criticism a literary right instead of a lonely deliberation of the heart. It puts judgment upon man before he is conceived even, and judgment on the life he has not begun to live. And if a man write down his poetry and his life, they are doomed before they are written by the poetry and the lives that have been done before.[5]

The stance was not original, of course. American writers had battled against a stale and inhibiting tradition the century before, and Emerson had already stated their case. For all their revolutionary talk, Kay Boyle and her contemporaries were more firmly grounded in a literary tradition than they perhaps recognized, descending in a straight line from American romantics like Poe and Whitman—not surprisingly, the very poets Boyle admired. What happened in the twenties was, after all, "a second flowering."[6] But Kay Boyle did not know of or did not recognize her antecedents. "You see," she explains, looking back, "I didn't have much of a formal education. I don't think I would have written all the books I did, over thirty books, had I realized that other people had already written everything there was to be said. I thought I had to tell people these things, because they hadn't been said before. That's why I felt compelled to write."[7]

Kay Boyle and her contemporaries plunged into their aesthetic revolution with religious zeal. Their mission was no less than to revive a desiccated English language:

> It is a sad time when the sap and the juice wither and dry in a language as when religion leaves the church and no longer resides in the symbols. But the English tongue was in for a long drought, and has been; parched and perished and written out as dry as sand. It has always been left to the poets to water the emotions, and when they sharpened their wits instead, it left the appetite high and dry.[8]

Many of Kay Boyle's poems, stories, and novels of that period are superb in their complex, innovative use of language and their authenticity of feeling.

All of them were conscientiously wrought as offerings to the Revolution of the Word in which she so fervently believed.

In the beginning Kay Boyle considered herself a poet. In her estimation, poetry was the highest form of literature. "There is prose everywhere, giving the shape and smell of a man, but there is not enough poetry."[9] While she believed that "the short story and novel form are adequate finger exercises," she declared, "I, for one, am working towards a broad and pure poetic form."[10] The *transition* advertisement soliciting contributions to her poetry anthology expresses her romantic exuberance and her devotion to the genre. The first volume of *Living Poetry*, it said, would appear in September, 1928, under the editorship of Archibald Craig and Kay Boyle, "*who deny* that romance went out to the slow music of sewing machines and motor cycles. And *who affirm* that poetry is going on with a hot foot in a true stride." They wished to print not only the "perfect poem," but "even more the personal adventure, the contemporary escapade," which "come into the poet's life and out of the poet's heart with the same intensity that ever they did in more gallant ages."[11]

Kay Boyle was first known for her poetry and had published a number of poems before her first piece of fiction, a short story entitled 'Passeres' Paris," appeared in the first issue of *This Quarter* (along with Hemingway's "Big Two-Hearted River"). She would receive a Guggenheim fellowship in 1934 to write an epic-length poem on the history of aviation (an abortive effort that resulted in a few published fragments). In the course of her career, she has published five volumes of poetry, the latest being *This Is Not a Letter and Other Poems* in 1985. And she still says that she prefers writing poetry because it is such a challenge.[12]

From the start, her poetic efforts were shaped by the belief that a poem should not simply convey a message in verse but should exist as an object of art on its own terms. Certainly, the idea was not her invention. Her friend Archibald MacLeish stated it clearly in "Ars Poetica" when he wrote, "A poem should not mean/But be." Samuel Beckett had written in *transition* that James Joyce was not writing *about* something, he was writing *something,* and Kay Boyle had been impressed enough by the piece to cite it in an interview some fifty years later as "a beautiful essay."[13] It is fair to assume that she espoused the aesthetics of her friend and mentor (and one of her "apostles of America"), William Carlos Williams, who declared that "the object of writing is to celebrate the triumph of sense" and that "in writing, as in art generally, sense is the form."[14]

Kay Boyle was also a close friend and long-time correspondent of Robert Carlton Brown. Inspired by a ticker tape machine, he had conceived of the "Reading Machine," a portable device that would liberate words from the convention of the printed page and revive "the optical end of the written word" by printing entire books on a single-line ribbon of paper to be unrolled beneath a magnifying glass.[15] His anthology of "readies"—pieces of poetry and prose stripped of such baggage as articles, pronouns, and connectives—was published by his Roving Eye Press in 1931 and included contributions by over forty of his literary friends, including Kay Boyle.

When she reviewed the *Readie Anthology* for *Contempo,* she cited as one of the best contributions a poem by Wambly Bald ("whose name in itself is an invention"): "*Dark a de rain a de cold a de bang a de bang the train like hell.*" It has "design, orphic sensation, and optical sequence," she wrote. Innovation was a primary virtue in the prevailing aesthetic judgment, and her demands of the artist were uncompromising: "There should be a fire of shame that scalds the neck and ears and face from off a man if he in vanity set down words in a way that they have been set down before."[16]

Kay Boyle, using pictorial language, was seeking to capture in her own poetry the essence of an instant. An early critic said that "to enjoy her poems one must accept the theory of poetry which rules out utilitarian language, the familiar sequence of cues to the intelligence by which common ideas are refurbished and represented; which instead seeks by a 'flaming collusion of rare words' to induct one without the aid of reason into a realm of pure poetic pleasure."[17]

When she was good, she was very good. In a 1926 poem entitled "Hunt," she writes:

> The buckhounds went on under the rain
> with the wet fern swinging lace over their
> eyes
> and their skins hanging like crumpled
> velvet.[18]

But as the same critic pointed out, "the weakness of the genre is that it is easier to run shallow than to run deep. If a phrase is not divinely right, it is nothing more than a silly waste."[19] The fresh image of the buckhounds is immediately followed by these lines:

> the bucks shod with leaves like silk sandals
> danced on chopsticks over the suey of red
> lizards
>> white stalks
>> and caterpillars

When the image fails, the effort seems precious. As a later critic put it, at times "her style pirouettes stiffly before a looking-glass."[20]

The subject matter of Kay Boyle's poetry is kaleidoscopic. One poem was written "In defense of homosexuality" (1925), and she attacked the simplistic military mind in "The Only Bird That Sang" (1929). ("The corporal died knowing that if Debs/Had been president there'd be a german general/In every maiden lady's bed," she wrote.)[21] In "A Statement for El Greco and William Carlos Williams" (1931), she pays homage to the artist who revitalizes our sense of our past. Other poems are intensely personal tributes. A number written in the late twenties are paeans to Ernest Walsh, although his name is rarely mentioned. They grieve for one who used to "Make sugars fly/up his cuffs after dinner find/potatoes hot in the dogs' ears"—for a "Young man who died one autumn."[22]

Kay Boyle was experimenting with form also. Her poems incorporate such varied devices as marginal glosses, parallel columns of dialogue, and prose paragraphs—sometimes printed in italics, alternating with lyrical refrains, or set apart with subtitles like "The Complaint in It," "The Story I Wanted to Tell You," or "The Spiritual for Nine Voices." Even her titles reflect an effort to define and extend the forms of poetry (as well as testify to how inextricably her art and personal life are meshed). Her first collection, *A Glad Day* (1938), includes "A Comeallye for Robert Carlton Brown," "A Confession to Eugene Jolas," "A Communication to Nancy Cunard," "A Christmas Carol for Emanuel Carnevali," and "A Valentine for Harry Crosby." It is hardly surprising that the book never became popular with "plain readers," but even critics felt the poems were too personal to be accessible to those outside her circle.

She did not much respect such evaluations, feeling the critics had not read carefully enough to grasp her universal themes, but Kay Boyle *was* continually frustrated by the elusiveness of a satisfactory form for her poetry. She wrote to William Carlos Williams: "Some kind of poetic form has to be found or I'll go crazy. I can't go on taking what you (and others) make possible and beautiful. I think I've got lots to say in poetry and no, no, no form. Lousy—loose—*no punch*—no shape—no agony of line like the back-side or a lovely thigh or whatnot."[23] But he was facing the same problem himself. In his response, a complete treatise on poetry (which he intended to publish in his revived magazine, *Contact II*), Williams agreed that "There is no workable poetic form extant among us today." In his own frustration he had turned to prose, he said, "since I didn't know what to do with poetry." He wrote: "Poetry can be a laboratory for metrics. It is lower on the literary scale. But it throws up jewels which may be cleaned and grouped."[24]

Kay Boyle's own prose writing would throw up far more jewels in the long run than would her experiments with poetry—although there are some to be found there. As early as 1932, *Contempo* called her "one of the best living short story writers."[25] It is primarily as a writer of fiction, especially as a first-rate short-story artist, that Kay Boyle gained her reputation and made her finest contributions not only to the aesthetic revolution of the twenties but to American literature of the twentieth century.

Perhaps *Wedding Day and Other Stories* (1930) cannot precisely be called Kay Boyle's "germinal" work of fiction. For one thing, it is not her first book; that was a slim volume unpretentiously called *Short Stories* (1929), published in a deluxe limited edition of 165 copies by the Crosbys' Black Sun Press. For another, it is not an organic composition. *Wedding Day* consists of the seven pieces in *Short Stories* plus six more. The stories were written over several years, and nine of the thirteen had been published previously in little magazines from 1927 to 1930. Nonetheless, *Wedding Day and Other Stories* is a significant book deserving a close look as a way in to a study of the author's entire canon: in these early stories she outlined and explored the themes central to nearly all she wrote for the next fifty years, and she did it with a skill that later she would at times be unable to match.

As the title suggests, the stories in *Wedding Day* concern love—generally lost or lacking, however. They are products of pain; it is perhaps significant that all were first published after the death of Ernest Walsh. Kay Boyle chose not to include in the book her first three published short stories—"Passeres' Paris," "Flight," and "Collation," which appeared in little magazines in 1925 and 1926—all rather mannered vignettes of artistic souls in exile. In fact, they have never been collected. Perhaps she felt the material was derivative, that her baptism by pain—the unfortunate requisite for many artists—gave her work substance. Soon after the book was published, she wrote: "There should be a lacking limb that grows to seize the pen and write only when man has passed through deep corridors of humility and death, and still survived."[26] If Kay Boyle's experimentation with language was not unique in that heyday of "orphic creation," the material in *Wedding Day* was her own—forged in her personal passage through "deep corridors" of loss and despair.

While her perspective is thoroughly romantic in the sense that she mistrusts the intellect, places her faith in intuition, and depicts the external world as a reflection or projection of the perceiver's consciousness, it most assuredly is not romantic in the sentimental sense one might expect of a book called *Wedding Day*. These are no ordinary love stories. A reviewer in 1932 noted that Kay Boyle's fiction deals with "the distress of human beings reaching for love and for each other, under the cloud of disease, or the foreknowledge of death. . . . The short stories particularly revive for us the painful brilliance of living. Here is poison—in the small doses in which arsenic is prescribed for anemia."[27] Still, love is clearly the author's primary concern. She finds it the one element essential to a meaningful human existence, and in the stories of *Wedding Day* she explores the tragedy of its unfulfillment, whether the barriers to contact be imposed by society, by one's own psyche, or by the biological inevitabilities of life itself.

Four stories of *Wedding Day*—"On the Run," "Portrait," "Vacation-Time," and "Spring Morning"—are complex, psychological studies of a young woman's responses to the death of her lover, who strongly resembles Ernest Walsh. In each of these stories, the man has coughed and hemorrhaged his way to death; it is obvious that the author was painfully familiar with the details of such a disease. Written in the years immediately following Walsh's death, the stories capture in white heat the agony, terror, and despair of her loss. They deal with the ultimate betrayer of love—death—the obstacle that could not be overcome even if people *were* always sensitive, honest, and strong.

It is in these four stories that Kay Boyle makes her most daring and perhaps most brilliant contributions to the Revolution of the Word. As she attempts to capture with absolute accuracy a state of consciousness or the precise course of an exchange, comparisons with the work of her friend James Joyce are hard to avoid. Margaret Atwood has said that Kay Boyle's is a "solid world solidly described, but it is also a world in which matter is merely a form of energy." Her writing approaches "the hallucinatory, or rather the moment of visionary realism when sensation heightens and time for an instant fixes and stops."[28] The stories are also important as her first working through of material and techniques she would use later in two novels exploring her life with Ernest Walsh and its devastating aftermath: *Year Before Last* (1932) and *My Next Bride* (1934).

In "On the Run" the situation is simple. A rootless young couple, drifting from one Alpine village to another, tries to conceal the man's consumptive disease from a suspicious hotelkeeper so they can settle down for some badly needed rest. As in many of Kay Boyle's works, the external landscape in this story takes on the shadings of the perceiving consciousness. As the couple's train pulls into Saint-André-les-Alpes, the objective is rendered subjectively by an unidentified but not unbiased narrative voice, and we know their stay will not be a pleasant one: "The crest of little alps was burning across the roofs of the town, with the dry crumbling finger of the church lifted and the sky gaping white and hot upon decay" (*WD*, 103).[29] We next see the ill man at the hotel ordering with feigned vigor pigs' feet grilled in batter in order to convince the *bonne* of "the natural beauty of his hunger" (*WD*, 103–4). But the fairly conventional narrative style is abruptly broken as the man speaks quickly and desperately to his companion in the English that the *bonne* does not understand: "Get her out of here he said I am going to cough Christ is this where the death will get me take the cigaret and when I cough walk around the room and sing or something so they won't hear me" (*WD*, 104).

Subtly, but with bitter irony, the author expresses her contempt for the bourgeois hypocrisy that makes a show of mourning yet gives to callousness the name of propriety. She describes the interview between the young woman and the proprietor, a middle-aged woman clad in the rich black costume of perpetual mourning: "The sweet sorrow of the crucifix faced them the rosary hanging like false-teeth on the bed-stead the sacred smile the Christ bled with artistry in the well-rounded arms of the Virgin. 'Madame,' she said without any hesitation, 'your husband cannot die here,' she said, 'we are not prepared for death' " (*WD*, 106).

When the young woman returns to her lover, he scolds her for leaving him for "a hundred years" and then says into the pillow, speaking to Saint

André, "I'm a sick man, I'm afraid. This time I'm afraid to go on." The story ends poignantly with a long, disjointed declamation by the woman that reveals her terror and love. As she packs their bags, she babbles to cover up the sound of his coughing. She is not whistling in the dark; she is shouting into it in desperation:

> You you afraid listen here packing the bags again the hairy-legged pointed ampoules as beautiful as earrings bottles of ergotine and striped pajamas we're going on somewhere else and have pigs' feet grilled and champagne and peaches with flames running on them this hole dries the guts in you do you remember Menton last February and every time you read Umbra the cabinay flushed may the Gods speak softly of us in days hereafter and the very small sausages for breakfast at the Ruhl

> > Saint-André-les-Alpes you're a perfectly ordinary pisspot
> > With a blue eye painted in the bottom of it
> > Fit only to be put in a cheap room under the bed
> > With education refinement and all the delicate bellyaches
> > Here's to bigger and better pigs' feet

The story ends: "Keep on keep on keep on he said maybe I'm going to bleed" (WD, 107).

On first reading, "Portrait" is a puzzling story, as Kay Boyle continues to explore what Jolas called the "night mind" and to experiment with the language of hallucination. The protagonist, again a young woman, waits alone in a dark hotel room for her lover to return from an evening out. They both know he is dying. The story is a bizarre dialogue between the woman and a voice in the dark that she calls "Tara." The author captures the woman's tension and fear while waiting in bed watching the room "through her eyelids," singing to herself a psalm-like lyric of her lover's return. "There would be a long time to wait and the voice of Tara would sit in the dark by the bed, fingers clasped lightly and elbows in black lace masks resting on the arms of the chair" (WD, 86). Tara speaks of death, of women and their lives without men, and asks her, "Someday if he does not come back to you what will you do?" The room takes on a strange animation: "when lights passed in the street the darkness stirred like a slow fan and the smooth mirrors were ruffled" (WD, 87). The woman imagines the joy of his return, and subject and object merge in her consciousness until the imagery loses contact with "reality:"

> He would come and he would sing in the room to you, holding his notes up in his fingers as though his song were a bouquet of flowers. Or dance in the room on his thin feet, picking gestures from the air and fitting them to his body. And the geranium leaves at the windows would lean in and clap their palms together. His breath would be new strange wax-cool odor shaped with the designs of his absence. His kisses would be lettuce leaves on your fingers. (WD, 88)

He would tell her fantastic stories to make her laugh and then "He would cough in his chest and sit a long time coughing and he would say 'Once I heard a man cough this way and in a few months he was dead.' And you knew there was no truth in that either" (*WD*, 89). And when Tara would assure her it was true, "you knew it was only that she wanted the blood up out of his veins and carried away in china vessels from the room" (*WD*, 89). In the final sentence of the story, Kay Boyle captures the young woman's rebellious refusal to acknowledge Tara's grim, serene pronouncements of reality and the fresh, if naive, relief that she knows will accompany her lover's return: "And you would beat the pillow and scream at her that his voice would be sudden cold glass in the hall, saying 'sacred Jesus . . .' he would bruise the points of your slippers because his boots were always longer than he remembered, he would come in and Tara would be your black silk gown over the chair, and the room would sit up in the light like a sleepy child" (*WD*, 89). The quality of nightmare vanishes in these lines and the simple objects in the room, personified into grotesque beings by the woman's loneliness and fear, return to their comprehensible states. It is a skillful and original exercise in capturing the complexities created when the imagination gets out of control and creates other, terrifying, worlds.

In *Wedding Day*, "Portrait" is followed by "Vacation-Time" and "Spring Morning," and the sequence corresponds to the events that have taken place in the young woman's life. The waking nightmare of "Portrait," half-amusing when dispelled, is triggered, of course, by the all-too-real fact that the lover's absence is soon to be permanent. And, as the author herself slipped into a two-month collapse a year and a half after Ernest Walsh's death, so does the protagonist of her stories. "I was walking around like a nut in the streets after the train had gone off, and the black was all running down my face from my eyes. I was going like a crazy-woman from one place to another thinking that tonight I must get into something deeper, the eyes full, the mouth full, to be sunk in it, to wallow like a sow" (*WD*, 91). So begins "Vacation-Time." In it Kay Boyle captures in hallucinatory, stream-of-consciousness prose the despair that engulfs the woman after her lover's death. She grasps for any contact, pouring out her soul to a stranger at a bar, babbling, "I am not able to sit home in intellectual quiet I am beginning to get tired of what is sensitive unable to acclimatize I am for the gay the biddy a great thing it is to roll home in the furnace of anybody's mouth blasting rust like wine all night and no sleep but the brain too going hot as a black bottom" (*WD*, 92). Like the author, she attempts to lose her grief in drink and promiscuity, yet she is haunted by the details of her lover's death. Like Walsh, he had died of consumption in Monte Carlo. Still at the bar, the woman carries on a bizarre mental dialogue with the district gendarmerie of Monte Carlo, trying to recall her lover's exact last words, and finally, on her third try, she is able to say clearly what had happened: "He did not draw himself up to his full height as a poet he sagged in the middle there was a bright fan of red velvet fluttering from his mouth and he was saying speak louder for Christ' sake the cocaine is ringing like hell in my head" (WD, 94). It is as haunting and devastating a scene as the one Emily Dickinson created when she obliterated the anticipated glory of death with a fly's buzz. The protagonist's rock-bottom despair is manifest as her mind returns to the present surroundings of the bar: "I looked into the bottom of my glass and I murmured to the soft blue clouds of gin I too I too should have spat my way to heaven with him" (WD, 94).

Raymond Duncan had refused to leave Kay Boyle's daughter with her when the colony went en masse to the South of France in the summer of 1928. "I actually felt the end of the world had come when they took Sharon to Nice," the author says.[30] The story's protagonist has just sent her little girl off to the South, too. As she is on her way to the Seine in a taxi, thinking, "I've got a heartful of misery to spill out I've got a long blue cape on that'll go down quick young feller," she tells herself, "And here is where you might have cheated, . . . just here you might have insisted upon love" (WD, 95). Yet in a passage that is either brutally honest or bitterly ironic, she regrets that she cannot feel the maternal love that might have been able to soothe her aching longing for her lover:

> Oh wonder-wonder mother-love why didn't I have a bit of you instead of this fierce agony which betrays me this decision of the soul which is decided for happiness and which results in complaint. Oh wonder-love which holds you by the throat until your breath is a red-white-and-blue celluloid rattle I will not have you warming your bottom on my heart. Oh wonder wonder mother-love how comfortable you would have made me instead of this thing scratching its thin back against a lamp-post. (WD, 95)

But the taxi-man will only take her home, not to the "dark Swanee Seine for which my heart was parched." Unable to drown her sorrows, she goes home alone, and we are left with a wrenching portrait of her grief. Beating on a mirror with her fists, biting her mouth until it is filled with blood, in an awful parody of her wish to have spat her way to heaven with her lover, she finally finds herself lying against the glass: "All night long I was lying against the mirror because it had a human face to it, lying with my arms around the mirror soothing the sad old face that was crying in the glass" (WD, 96).

The bitter irony of the title "Spring Morning" is apparent when the reader finally breaks into its difficult hallucinatory language—there are only two periods in the story for punctuation—and realizes that he or she is inside the consciousness of a woman awakening with "the latest corpse in the bed" with her (WD, 97). She is praying to the gods that she will find some sign in the room to give her a clue to his identity before he wakes up. The woman, whose lover has died, has found another human face with which to spend the night, but this one in the flesh is not much more comforting than the one in the mirror in "Vacation-Time." She says of her bedfellow that he is "as much a corpse as the one they lifted off the bed in his night-wear one morning and let fall into the coffin from a height that sent his arms wide open and his jaw dropping down and him grunting out loud" (WD, 97). Again, Kay Boyle will spare us no illusion that the death of a young poet is romantic. She introduces a third "corpse" to the story as well, slipping in a caustic commentary on a living poet, probably Ezra Pound, with whom This Quarter had had a falling out (the third issue retracted the second issue's dedication to him). The protagonist calls her night's companion "as much a corpse as the gentleman a timorous generation relies upon for brilliance Poetry he wrote is not to reveal the h'emotions but to protect them from abuse I have them does he add in the false bottom of me derby the rabbits to appear with pinker eyes the eggs with thinner crusts" (WD, 97–98).

From his canvases "turned to the wall showing their numbered backsides," the young woman is finally able to identify "this stranger who slept dreary as a hog." When she finds the signature, "Pruter 1928," she becomes bold and awakens him: "it is Hans Pruter whom I have done violence to up up Pruter my love roust yourself and be my noble crossing the yard and the underwear for a quart of Perrier" (WD, 98). Then she notices a "gentleman photographed and framed" on his dresser and remarks that they have a friend in common. "If I had money I would buy him," she says, painting her face at the glass. When Pruter jokes that the man was easily bought and that she would not be the first to purchase him, body and soul, she retorts that she would buy him outright "with the contract that he not compromise" (WD, 99). When Pruter remarks that she is making a "grand show" of her friend, she reveals her deep love for the man in the photograph: "I was putting the rouge on and the black on my eyes is it the poor bugger's fault I said that he is purpose and pride when everything else is rejected through a sewage of emotions" (WD, 99). A heartless banter ensues until Pruter complains that she lacks decency and that they have said nothing of real importance to each other. Her response is brutal: "Lean out of the bed said I and pass me the dictionary lean over the biddy said I and pass me the words withal" (WD, 101). Pruter longs for "a woman appealing to me mentally as well as," he says, but her heart is scarred closed. That her hardness masks desolation and a desperate need for love is revealed in the final paragraph.

I held my nose from the smell of Pruter rotting and still above sod a lively feeding ground I knew these hard iron rings of sorrow and contempt laid first one and then another in my throat I would survive but not the face photographed and framed. If I had money I would buy him I thought body and soul for the pleasure

This I would never escape or find words to whisper

I have waited so badly I have waited but so badly I have waited so badly I have waited so badly for you what are you going to do (WD, 101)

In a 1960 review of a book about Robert McAlmon, Kay Boyle identifies him as the man for whom she had "waited so badly." In response to her final questioning cry in the story, "What he did was to give me his typewriter, to keep, not to give back, so that I would write a book or two," she says.[31] As for Pruter's joke that "the man was easily bought," Kay Boyle explains that when McAlmon's wife, the poet Bryher, divorced him in 1927, her father, one of the richest men in England, settled such a generous sum on him that he became the butt of "scornful criticism," and was dubbed "Robert McAlimony."[32]

The remaining nine stories in *Wedding Day* are a catalogue of the ways in which love can fail. While the four drawn most directly from the author's relationship with Ernest Walsh explore the pain of love lost, the rest examine the anguish of love never gained. The obstacles to contact range from breakdowns in communication to repressive bourgeois proprieties to conflicting sexual preferences to the incest taboo. But whatever the cause, she consistently points to the thwarting of love as a fundamental tragedy of human existence.

From the first sentence of the title story, "Wedding Day," the reader senses that things are out of joint: "The red carpet that was to spurt like a hemorrhage from pillar to post was stacked in the corner." The wedding cake is ignored as it is carried into the pantry "with its beard lying white as hoarfrost on its bosom." "This was the last lunch," Kay Boyle writes, and the brother and sister "came in with their buttonholes drooping with violets and sat sadly down, sat down to eat" (*WD*, 25). Into the funereal atmosphere of this wedding day, she injects tension and bitterness. The son and mother argue as to whether the daughter will be given the family's prized copper saucepans, unused for twenty years. He mocks the decorum his mother cherishes when he commands her not to cry, pointing his finger directly at her nose "so that when she looked at him with dignity her eyes wavered and crossed" and "she sat looking proudly at him, erect as a needle staring through its one open eye" (*WD*, 26). As the mother and son bicker over who wanted the wedding in the first place, the bride-to-be is conspicuously silent. Finally, as he snatches away each slice of roast beef his mother carves until she whimpers her fear of getting none herself, the boy and her sister burst into laughter. He tosses his napkin over the chandelier and his sister follows him out of the room, leaving the mother alone "praying that this occasion at least pass off with dignity, with her heart not in her mouth but beating away in peace in its own bosom" (*WD*, 28).

Having delineated the tension between children and mother and suggested the exclusive camaraderie between brother and sister, the author shifts both mood and scene and describes in almost incantatory prose the pair's idyllic jaunt through the spring afternoon in the hours remaining before the wedding:

The sun was an imposition, an imposition, for they were another race stamping an easy trail through the wilderness of Paris, possessed of the same people, but of themselves like another race. No one else could by lifting of the head only be starting life over again, and it was a wonder the whole city of Paris did not hold its breath for them, for if anyone could have begun a new race, it was these two. (*WD*, 29)

The incestuous overtones are strong. "It isn't too late yet, you know," the brother insists as they stride through the streets, take a train into the *Bois*, and row to the middle of a pond. "Over them was the sky set like a tomb," and as tears flow down their cheeks, the slow rain begins to fall. Landscape and emotion correspond perfectly, external phenomena mirroring the characters' internal states. The rain underscores the pair's frustration and despair as they realize the intensity of their love and the impossibility of its fulfillment:

Everywhere, everywhere there were other countries to go to. And how were they to get from the boat with the chains that were on them, how uproot the willowing trees from their hearts, how strike the irons of spring that shackled them? What shame and shame that scorched a burning pathway to their dressing rooms! Their hearts were mourning for every Paris night and its half-hours before lunch when two straws crossed on the round table top on the marble anywhere meant I had a drink here and went on. (*WD*, 32)

The inevitable wedding itself forms the final segment of the story, and the lyrical spell binding the pair is broken the instant they set foot in the house again to find their mother "tying white satin bows under the chins of the potted plants" (*WD*, 32). The boy kicks down the hall the silver tray for the guests' calling cards, and his mother is wearily certain "that this outburst presaged a thousand mishaps that were yet to come" (*WD*, 33). The irony of the story lies not only in the reversal of expectations the title may have aroused in the reader but in the discrepancy between the different characters' perceptions of the same situation. The self-pitying matron worries only about the thousand little social mishaps possible when a major emotional disaster—the wedding itself—is imminent. But the guests arrive "in peace," and the brother delivers his sister to the altar. Yet the author captures magnificently the enormous gulf between the placid surface and the tumultuous inner reality as she takes the reader inside the bride's consciousness:

This was the end, the end, they thought. She turned her face to her brother and suddenly their hearts fled together and sobbed like ringdoves in their bosoms. This was the end, the end, the end, this was the end.
Down the room their feet fled in various ways, seeking an escape. To the edge of the carpet fled her feet, returned and followed reluctantly upon her brother's heels. Every piped note of the organ insisted that she go on. It isn't too late, he said. Too late, too late. The ring was given, the book was closed.

The desolate, the barren sky continued to fling down dripping handfuls of fresh rain. (*WD*, 33–34)

The mindless repetition of the phrase "the end" and the blind panic of the bride's imaginary flight have an intense psychological authenticity. The recurrence of the brother's phrase "It isn't too late" and its distortion in "Too late, too late," along with the continuing rain, are evidence of the skill with which Kay Boyle has woven motifs seamlessly into the fabric of the story.

"Wedding Day" ends with dancing. But in an ironic counterpoint to the flight she had imagined at the altar, the bride's feet "were fleeing in a hundred ways throughout the rooms, fluttering from the punch bowl to her bedroom and back again" (*WD*, 34). By repeating and transforming the flight image, the author underscores the fact that the bride henceforth will move within narrow limits. While the brother, limbered by the punch, dances about scattering calling cards, his mother, "in triumph on the arms of the General, danced lightly by," rejoicing that "no glass had yet been broken" (*WD*, 35). "What a real success, what a *real* success," is her only thought as her feet float "over the oriental prayer rugs, through the Persian forests of hemp, away and away" in another absurdly circumscribed "escape" that is yet another mockery of the escape to "other countries" that the pair had dreamed of that afternoon on the lake.

In its ironies and incongruities, "Wedding Day" is characteristic both in style and theme of Kay Boyle's work. She displays her ironic sense of humor in the son's cruel but not entirely unamusing taunting of his mother—an unsympathetically drawn embodiment of all the petty proprieties that keep people politely isolated from each other. But the author deals in dramatic as well as verbal irony, and the discrepancy between the way things seem and the way they are is at the heart of the story. Like "Vacation-Time" and "Spring Morning," the title "Wedding Day" arouses pleasant expectations which are promptly dashed. Within the story, too, there are gulfs between the different characters' views of the same events. In "Wedding Day" she juxtaposes a *real* loss of love with the surface gaiety of a wedding that celebrates no love at all, but which the mother terms "a *real* success." In Kay Boyle's world, what is real depends largely on one's perceptions, and the fact that different perceptions of the same situation result in disparate and often conflicting "realities" creates a disturbing world in which individuals collide and bounce off one another like atoms.

"Theme" is another story of thwarted love with incestuous overtones, exploring the fierce love of a mother for her son. Her emotions encompass the purest maternal tenderness, a fear of loneliness, nebulous sexual desires, and self-loathing. The mother is sitting in her kitchen awaiting her son's return from work. As in much of Kay Boyle's fiction, the action is psychological. The story lies in our realization of the pitiful contrast between the woman's rich inner life—her sharp intellect and passionate emotions—and the drab surface she actually presents to her son. All day she fantasizes. She imagines chatting brightly with her son across the dinner table about the Russian writers, "leaning over the table in the kitchen to him so that her breasts hung down in points . . . passing the bread over to him with her head on one side smiling" (WD, 39). Yet, as these rich thoughts occupy her, we see her cracking roasted chestnuts in her big teeth and drawing the worms out with the point of a pin: "She had a long face like a horse's face and she would sit eating the chestnuts slowly in her mouth with her long chin swinging back and forth under her face" (WD, 38). The contrast between her inner sensitivity and her bestial appearance is shocking, and we realize the tragedy of her existence when her son actually returns and she falls silent: "All day she had been talking to him but now there was nothing to say between them" (WD, 40). Because she is powerless to communicate with her son, he never has an inkling of the intelligence and love within her but sees only a crone with "full eyeballs tied with veins and the heavy old flesh hanging down on her jaws" (WD, 39).

The mother is painfully aware of the incongruity: "Ah, but if he knew what there was in her blood, she thought, he would be afraid to be in the room with her" (WD, 41). Yet these raging emotions are reduced to expression in whimpers and tears. When he announces he is going up to Chicago at the end of the month, she thinks, "I am a fierce woman. I am a fierce woman who is not afraid of solitude. I am a black wind, boy. I am lean and gaunt and strong as the wind." What she says aloud is, "I am an old old woman, what shall I do with myself when you leave me?" (WD, 41–42). The tragic gulf in understanding between the two is underscored when he charges, "You never wanted a son." The story ends: " 'Yes, yes,' she said. 'Yes, I wanted a son' " (WD, 44).

The exchange is intriguing. Is the son insensitive and blind to his mother's inarticulate but consuming love for him, or is his comment instead an acute one, revealing an insight that she wants not a son but a lover? In the first case, the failure of love may be blamed on the son, and we pity his unappreciated mother; in the second, the screw turns a notch and we suddenly sympathize with the son who has sensed some unhealthy sublimations in his mother's self-centered "love" for him and who has been deprived of pure maternal love. Kay Boyle herself postulates "Might not the son more likely be disturbed by guilt, by his inability to respond to, as well as being revolted by, his mother's love rather than being 'insensitive and blind'? I believe that is why he left, not for a moment because of his unawareness."[33] The reason for the gap in understanding between the mother and son is less important than the fact that it exists. What ultimately matters in Kay Boyle's work is the sad fact that human beings so often relate blindly with one another and that, instead of making contact, they skitter cold and lonely across the unpenetrated surfaces.

The bald facts of consanguinity are partly responsible for the failures of love in "Wedding Day," "Theme," and "Uncle Anne"—a story of a young girl's futile infatuation with her uncle, the black sheep of the family, who has impregnated the servant girl but who tells his favorite niece, "Whatever I have done is because I wanted always a thin wife with pink nostrils and little red apples in the points of her eyes" (*WD*, 84). In "Madame Tout Petit," Kay Boyle examines another obstacle to love: a conflict in sexual orientation. In bohemian Paris of the twenties, it would have been a familiar issue. Her poem, "In defense of homosexuality" (1925), and her full-length treatment of homosexual love in the novel *Gentlemen, I Address You Privately* (1933) indicate that she had more than a passing interest in the subject.

The narrator of "Madame Tout Petit" is a young woman who lives with her small daughter in an English boarding house. Through her we view the relationship between a lonely traveling salesman also boarding there and the proprietess, Madame Tout Petit, who does not love her husband but is infatuated with the salesman. On Friday evenings the traveler would come to the parlor and speak to the narrator of his lonely life on the road among men who laugh at limericks he finds "rather rum." Madame, smelling like a fresh rose and stitching at her embroidery, would listen "sweetly and sharply with her head" to their incomprehensible English, laughing "because the words collapsed before she could make any sense of them" (*WD*, 48). In the lulls of their conversation, Madame would quickly speak up, "brightly dropping her words through whatever his silence was suggesting," to complain of her husband's coarse ways. "I cannot tell you what took place in me," she says, recounting how her husband's hair was so curled and dandied on their wedding day that "the priest himself was slapping holy water on it to make it lie flat." The impossibility of communication between Madame and the traveler, already established by the language barrier between them, is wonderfully portrayed in their conversation, in which the import of each sentence slips past the other person until the exchange collapses in confusion:

> The priest himself. She shouted delicately with laughter. She looked at the traveling-man with her laughter scarring her face. *Bande de salauds.* Oh, rather, said the travelling-man. Oh, dear, dear, the Jesuits! He skipped across the room like a Nancy-boy. Madame Tout Petit's pure virtuous creed flamed in her face. I was speaking of my husband and the others, she said in confusion. He handed out cigars to them all to keep them from making jokes about marriage. I cannot tell you, she said, what took place in me. (*WD*, 49–50).

Later, as the salesman and narrator are rummaging through her grandmother's old dresses to find costumes for a dance that night, he produces a letter Madame Tout Petit had sent him, hinting at her unhappiness with her husband. The traveler, cynical and unmoved, comments that "her husband is rather a good sort," adding, "And I prefer her husband" (*WD*, 51). The narrator's account of the masquerade dance reveals, under the grotesque surface merriment, the painful clash of Madame's love for the salesman and his indifference toward her—and the pathetic loneliness of each:

> We were dancing together, and he would hop about on his feet with his legs doing the Charleston in the French way as if he could not afford to be ungraceful. And my old grandmother's shoulders had been fuller than his so that the sleeves slipping down he would keep putting back with his fingers. It is not a life, he said, it is not a life consisting of sleeping on a board. Madame Tout Petit clapped her hands and screamed with false delight. Oh, what a beautiful woman he is, screamed Madame Tout Petit, and her sorrow and her love for him were ready to fall in tears from her eyes. (*WD*, 52)

Even Madame now realizes the traveler's homosexuality; it is a measure of her desperation that she asks nevertheless if the narrator would intercede for her with "a word or two concerning the eternal constancy of a *femme honnête*:" "I can forgive him, she said, anything. And if he still refuses to respond, I shall ask the priest to employ me with charitable work in the parish. I shall succor the young, she said" (*WD*, 53). "*J'ai un cafard horrible*" is Madame Tout Petit's final statement. We can presume that while the homosexual traveling man's need for love will go unsatisfied in his life on the road among coarse hemen, Madame's longing for him will be channeled henceforth into charity work and sick headaches. They are two more individuals in Kay Boyle's world who cannot give away the love surging but dammed within them.

Madame Tout Petit—a woman who claims that on her wedding night "I pinned the curtains of the canopy from top to bottom with nursery pins and myself in the middle like a jelly-roll" (*WD*, 50)—represents a type that often infuriates the author, whose own introduction to France was made miserable by a mother-in-law horrified that she had not arrived clad in the requisite *tailleur gris*. The mother in "Wedding Day" is another example. The "lady," who is repressed by bourgeois morality and religion and who self-righteously attempts to inflict her inhibitions on others (usually younger members of her own sex), is a sort of villain in a number of Boyle's works, for proprieties that deny one's humanity in favor of sterile codes are yet another barrier between human beings in need of contact.

A prototype of this genteel monster may be found in "Summer," a vignette of sexual repression and frustrated desire. Like many of Kay Boyle's works, it is the unraveling of a psychological situation rather than a tale with a plot, and it contains some fine examples of her technical skill. It focuses on the thoughts and feelings of a presumably plain young woman caring for an old lady at a sanatarium. A young man, his eyes bright with disease, resides in the next room. The girl must suffer the old woman's constant denunciations of the man because he and a young lady are seen together setting off on long walks into the hills. The old woman rages that she is not too old "to still feel resentment against the abuses of decency, decency," and she demands to know what good anyone could be at in the hills all day. "A good brisk walk is another thing," she adds.

That night, as the girl is reading to her elderly charge, she hears the young man enter his room. A second set of footsteps follows. Inner and outer worlds merge as the author moves away from objective reality to try to capture in physical images the girl's state of consciousness. Her awareness of the events "a hand's breadth" away on the other side of the wall takes over her mind and finally shapes and animates her perception of the concrete objects in the old woman's bedroom:

> The voice of the young man was sounding as though heard over water, a deep swaying bell swinging down like a tool on metal. And the silence of his companion hung between the two rooms, stirring back and forth between them like a soft soft hammock hung under strong trees. Everything in the old lady's room was meticulous and sharp to the girl, neat and small corners and legs of furniture tossed up like little boats on the terrific water which went on under and about them sending them dancing like crazy men, sending the little white tufts of cotton flapping like burnt butterflies over the quilt. The girl sat reading out the words; and the great dancing orgy of silence wove and tore strongly in the room, tossed up the little grunts of the old lady's breath like corks on the smooth mouth of the horizon. (*WD*, 61–62)

After his companion has left the room, the young man's coughing fit begins. Kay Boyle describes it brilliantly through the metaphor of a fox, an image that she uses in several stories and in her novel *Year Before Last*—especially haunting when one realizes that her skill in recreating the torment of the dying is rooted in her own painful intimacy with the details of Ernest Walsh's disease and death. The girl listens to the "lean shriveled heart of the sound as it beat alone in the middle of the room." "And then it began to run in a frenzy in his room patting with quick hard paws on the glass of the windows. It was a trapped fox barking in a frenzy to get out of the room, and flinging down with its soft gasping belly on the young man's belly, its worn thin bark snapping its teeth at his chest" (*WD*, 63). In her heart, the girl calls to him, "But cry out, cry out, cry out, my love," until the sound dwindles down "in a point, even the sounds of the springs whistling like bats, and the point to become a long needle of pain in her" (*WD*, 63–64). The girl's desire is trapped inside her, and, as the man is held in the grip of his disease, so she is powerless to free herself from the repression the old woman personifies.

"Summer" is significant not only as an example of the author's continuing thematic concern with failed connections, but because she employs the protagonist to articulate her aesthetic stance. The book the girl is reading at the old woman's bedside is a conservative one: "The healthy school is played out in England," the girl was reading, "all that could be said has been said; the successors of Dickens, Thackeray, George Eliot have no ideal, and consequently no language" (*WD*, 59). Yet she would "wonder about language and if there were perhaps some now so new and so incomprehensible that it could serve only to wound them." Like her creator, the first signatory of the manifesto for the Revolution of the Word, the girl takes language seriously: "She wanted to believe in a language that burned black the tongue of the one who spoke and scarred the one who listened. She would demand nothing of it, but to serve it, and be humble before it" (*WD*, 60). The conformism that oppresses language parallels that which stifles a healthy acknowledgement of human needs and desires, and the girl's heart cries out in quiet desperation against both types.

While Kay Boyle's opinion of the "lady" generally borders on contempt, it would be a serious distortion not to emphasize her respect for woman. Two stories in *Wedding Day* are evidence of an understanding of very different types of women. "Episode in the Life of an Ancestor" and "Letters of a Lady" are, in Katherine Anne Porter's words, stories in which "an adult intelligence plays with destructive humor on the themes of sexual superstition and pretenses between men and women."[34] Sexism is one more obstacle to contact.

From her earliest short stories to her latest novel, *The Underground Woman,* she has written of the power of women. Often a strong woman of expansive spirit will play opposite a man made weak by egotism, narrow-mindedness, and petty possessiveness. Most of these men are nearly as pathetic for their limitations as they are despicable for their attempts at domestic tyranny. This is the theme of "Episode in the Life of an Ancestor," which she chose as the opening piece of both *Wedding Day* (1930) and her most recent collection, *Fifty Stories* (1980). The author apparently based the heroine of this story on her Grandmother Evans, a Kansas schoolteacher who at sixteen had married the superintendent of schools and later left him to go off to work in the Land Grant Office in Washington, D.C., taking her two young daughters with her.

"Episode in the Life of an Ancestor" explores an incident in the girlhood of the narrator's grandmother, one of the best horsewomen in Kansas. Her father was proud of "the feminine ways there were in her," especially the choir voice she used in church, but "It was no pride to him to hear it turned hard and thin in her mouth to quiet a frightened horse" (*WD*, 2). Yet the local people "were used to seeing her riding with a sunbonnet on her head—not in pants, but with wide skirts hullabalooing out behind her in the wind" (*WD*, 2). Kay Boyle will not reduce her heroine to the stereotype of tomboy. She contrasts the girl's competence in a wide range of skills with her father's narrow and selfish expectations of her. Although in truth he has little control over this bold spirit, he clings to the illusion that he can mold his daughter into the kind of woman who will serve his needs: "To her father it was a real sorrow that a needle and thread were never seen in her fingers. His wife was dead and it seemed to him that he must set flowing in his daughter the streams of gentleness and love that cooled the blood of true women. The idea was that she be sweetened by the honey of the ambitions he had for her" (*WD*, 3).

After she rides away one evening, "hammering off through the darkness with nobody knowing what was going on inside her or outside her, or what she was filled with" (*WD*, 6), the father roams the house, thinking of her future, wondering if she will marry the schoolmaster, the only gentleman in the countryside. In all his masculine glory, he is not self-sufficient, for he draws his strength and sustenance from her; his image of himself is a distorted reflection of what power he thinks he has in shaping her. Wandering into her room, he discovers peeping out from under her quilt a poetry book "with pictures engraved through it of a kind that brought the blood flying to his face." It is opened to a passage that begins, ". . . To the Nuptial Bowre/I led her blushing like the Morn" (*WD*, 9). (He does not recognize it—nor does the author identify it—as *Paradise Lost*.) Inside, he finds the schoolmaster's signature. "You fine example to the young, screamed the father's mind. You creeping out into the night to do what harm you can, creeping out and doing God knows what harm, God knows." And in his mind the schoolmaster's image balloons to monstrous proportions, the pores on the wings of his nose and the black hairs that grow between his eyes clearly visible.

The scene shifts to the young woman riding alone on the prairie in the quiet night. Suddenly, impatient with the tameness of the ride, she kicks the horse into fury in a passage that is unmistakably sexual—with the female in the role of mastery.

> Suddenly he felt this anger in the grandmother's knees that caught and swung him about in the wind. Without any regard for him at all, so that he was in a quiver of admiration and love for her, she jerked him up and back, rearing his wild head high, his front hoofs left clawing at the space that yapped under them. She urged him to such a frenzy of kicking that he was ready to faint with delight. Even had she wished to now she could never have calmed him, and she started putting him over bushes and barriers, setting his head to them and stretching him thin as a string to save the smooth nut of his belly from scraping, reeling him so close to the few pine trunks that streamed up like torrents that he leapt sideways to save his fair coat from ripping open on the spikes of them. It was a long way to travel back, but he never stopped until his hoofs thundered into the barn that had shrunk too small for him. There he stood in the darkness, wet and throbbing like a heart cut out of the body. (*WD*, 12)

When she strides into the room where her self-pitying father is wondering how he will ever know what had become of her, he wants to ask her what she had been up to, to say "that he had seen the schoolmaster walking out early in the evening up the road that led nowhere except out into the prairie." But the "grandmother" stalks over to the table and reclaims her book in silent anger (in this time warp, Kay Boyle gives her power and stature by conferring on her the more venerable title). The father is powerless to speak.

His thoughts turn again to the schoolmaster, but now his image of the man he had suspected of defiling his daughter shrivels and actually caves in before our eyes: "With this woman in the room with him he was beginning to see the poor little schoolmaster, the poor squat little periwinkle with his long nose always thrust away in a book. He began to remember that the horse his daughter had been out riding all night had once backed up on just such a little whippersnapper as was the schoolmaster and kicked his skull into a cocked hat" (*WD*, 14). The father must turn his eyes away from the sight of this woman who stands "with her eyes staring like a hawk's eyes straight into the oil lamp's blaze." The story ends: " 'What have you done to the schoolmaster?' he wanted to say to her. The words were right there in his mouth but he couldn't get them out" (*WD*, 14).

"Episode in the Life of an Ancestor" demonstrates Kay Boyle's skill in rendering the psychological states of her characters, as she simply presents without comment the protean images that fill their consciousnesses. The story also makes a statement about the nature of true power in a relationship between a woman and a man who would dominate her, exposing the brittle frailty of a rigid male ego when confronted by a woman's uncharted strength.

A self-proclaimed "crusading spirit," Boyle has little patience for emotional timidity, or even prudence, when it obstructs genuine passion. In "Polar Bears and Others," she takes a strong romantic stand. The story focuses on a young woman who feels threatened by her husband's interest in another woman, yet, interestingly, despises him for lacking the courage and conviction to pursue his heart's calling. The story begins in the tone of a fable. The first two paragraphs describe the plodding existence of polar bears who cannot adapt to the imitation-icicled caverns, false snows, and warm water pool of the zoo. The author's intention is obviously allegorical:

> They came from a country which is a small country because it is all alike, and they came from it with life only if their country and their ways be repeated for them. They came with their prejudiced bodies and their jaws gaping out for fish in empty water. They are like people who live in small countries and who go out of them with their small grudges strapped to their backs. In America, and in Russia, the big countries, there are little men but on them even there is a smell of romance. (And I believe in romance: that it should be snatched from the buttonhole where it has withered too long, so that reality can make a fresh thing of this poor faded flower.) (*WD*, 67–68)

The story then shifts into a first-person narrative. The protagonist's husband wishes to go the next day to have lunch with a woman passing through Le Havre to catch a boat back to America. "Because he stayed out in the garden with his thoughts I became afraid of this woman," she says. Her husband is disturbed because she will not come with him to lunch, and when he insists she must accompany him, she feels she could strike him in the face for this falseness. They go to bed with their backs to each other, and the narrator is bitter that she is something to be relinquished; yet she awakens the next morning feeling "a piercing gentleness for others which comes from life and not from innocence." "Innocence is obscene somehow, you know, but gentleness is the great wisdom of the emotions," she says (WD, 71). When the man decides to forego his trip, she is contemptuous:

> "I'll be something more than sacrifice and bitterness to you," I cried. "Go on, get out!"
> I knew when it was my turn I'd be off without a thought for him. "Listen," I said, "when it's my turn, I'll be off without a thought, so you'd better go now."

"Some other day maybe. Some other time," is his reply, and she retorts, "And maybe a tragedy would be as big as life, but you'd never see it" (WD, 72). She goes upstairs and screams in the empty room "thinking that perhaps here was a great love passing him by, and he not even going after it" (WD, 73).

The issue here is much larger than whether a man is going to have lunch with a woman not his wife. What Kay Boyle is speaking out against in this story is a rigid, narrow view of life that denies the emotions in favor of safe proprieties. She lacks respect for those "who must have a way prepared to dignity," those "who do not know what it is to go off and for yourselves be lost and lost and lost to all old dignities." "You do not know the humble way of beginning or of growing a new skin when the old one is ripped from your flesh," in the words of the young woman in her story (WD, 74).

In the author's view, dignity must be attained—through difficult confrontation with essentials, through loss of innocence, through pain—not simply maintained by preserving one's childish innocence intact. Such a dignity, guarded by remaining in one's own back garden, is no more than plodding provincialism, such as the polar bears exemplify. One can imagine Kay Boyle cheering Melville as he wrote to his friend Hawthorne, "I stand for the heart. To the dogs with the head!"[35] This stubborn romanticism would pervade and, in the opinion of some, taint much of her writing over the course of her career. Robert McAlmon had said she would be a good writer if she would not go so "Irish-twilighty" (BGT, 11). (He said the same of James Joyce regarding A Portrait of the Artist as a Young Man.) In her sixties, she admitted her romantic tendencies in the last line of Being Geniuses Together. After citing McAlmon's comment that she, come hell or high water, had to romanticize every situation, she concedes, "This may very well be true" (BGT, 332). From the very beginning, Kay Boyle believed that the heart's callings ought to prevail over convention and common sense, no matter what the consequences.

Finally, another story in which the barrier to love is internally imposed is "Bitte Nehmen Sie Die Blumen." The narrator, a woman with a baby living with a Frenchman named Peleser, has been scarred by the death of someone she had loved. The story is set in England in a company town where the men talk of rubber at the dinner table. The story revolves about the young woman's feelings for an Englishman living in the same boarding house, whose cool self-assurance both infuriates and infatuates her.[36] The woman is wary of love, and the author hints at what has jaded her: "I knew I had turned like an old maid now, when I met a man I wanted to wound him. I would think of the scars that death had put between my eyes, and I would think that even my love could not tell him of all that had dried up in me. Too much has happened that even my heart could not explain to you, I would think" (*WD*, 17–18). It would have been a familiar feeling for Kay Boyle at that time. This story first appeared in *transition* in December, 1927, a year after Walsh died; in *Being Geniuses Together,* she tells how she had closed off her heart to men after his death. Speaking of her friend in Stoke-on-Trent, Germaine Garrigou, Boyle recalls: "She would study Michael's photograph (which I kept at the bottom of a suitcase), and seek to learn his poems by heart, agreeing with me in a passionate whisper that I should never embrace another man and that I should wear black for the rest of my life" (*BGT,* 215).

Yet the narrator finds it impossible to stifle her feelings for this Englishman: "Everything in me was against him and I thought that I would not be beginning again but would get my mind off this man. And here I was ... thinking that for a turn of his body I would be leaving Peleser and making a new life with this man" (*WD*, 20). When she finds herself on the boarding house stairway with him, her conflicting emotions surge forth. She cracks nuts and drops the shells on the stairs, knowing how it will disturb his English sensibilities, and as he picks them up, her hostility explodes in a psychologically authentic passage that eschews the conventions of "realistic" writing:

> Listen I said you're perfectly safe all right seeing yourself always in situations where you can go upstairs and close your door and spend the evening deploring deeply deploring regretting lamenting unfortunate interviews but for God's sake don't begin doubting that you've got all the superiorities because then you'll be something else again. He said please, please, wearily with his hand lifted and I went past him up the stairs to my room it is impossible he said you insist upon too much what I said was. (*WD*, 23)

In her room the woman brushes back her hair, puts on extra lipstick and goes down to dinner in a sleeveless dress. As she cuts her meat, she will not lift her head to look over or around the vase of marigolds and ferns that blocks her view of him, sitting opposite her at the table. The story ends in a fine example of the banal charged with significance, reminiscent of scenes in Joyce's *Dubliners:*

> They were serving us spaghetti and I didn't know if he were cutting it up or twisting it on his fork when the pudding came on he put his head around the flowers. When he looked at me I felt that my flesh lit like a candle. I

looked at him as if I could never see enough of his face and I saw that he was humbled and that he was silenced by the sad proud humility of his heart. He was handing the menu to me and I didn't know if I were taking it in my fingers or letting it fall, and across it he had written Aber Gott Bitte Nehmen Sie Die Blumen . . . (WD, 24)

The story closes with this quiet illumination, a Joycean epiphany. It is about as close as Kay Boyle comes in this book to a happy ending, for one senses that the Englishman's request to please take away the flowers will be the gentle blow that will crumble the defenses keeping the woman from the human contact she so desperately needs. Among Boyle's characters, she is a lucky one. It is perhaps significant that she is so closely identified with the author, who herself passed through great pain *and* the "formal feeling" and finally was able to open her heart again to love. It is also noteworthy that the man who is so infuriatingly and indelibly English speaks the most significant line in the story—if the title is a fair indicator—in German, a neutral language for the pair. Perhaps this indicates that he is willing to abandon *his* defenses, his standoffish Englishness, and open himself completely to the possibility of real communication without barriers.

Wedding Day and Other Stories is hardly a budding writer's rough-edged first attempt in print. Contemporary reviewers were positive, although one paid the author a backhanded compliment at the expense of some of her coterie:

> *transition* was a brave venture and in that respect demanded and obtained one's sympathy—but it is a good thing for Miss Boyle and one or two other contributors that it is no longer able to confound their genius with (let us be kind) the high spirits of the mathematical sign writers. It was a cocktail with too much kick in it for most of us, and served only to hide from our muddled vision those works which deserved a more serious consideration.[37]

But the most insightful—and glowing—review was Katherine Anne Porter's, in which she termed Kay Boyle one of the strongest and most promising talents to have emerged from the shadows of James Joyce and Gertrude Stein. She says of Boyle, "She sums up the salient qualities of that movement: a fighting spirit, freshness of feeling, curiosity, the courage of her own attitude and idiom, a violently dedicated search for the meanings and methods of art," Yet Porter was the first to see, too, the concern for love at the core of Kay Boyle's work—the theme that is her *own* and that makes her work far more than just a fine example of a prevailing artistic movement: "Miss Boyle writes of love not as if it were a disease, or a menace, or a soothing syrup to vanity, or something to be peered at through a microscope, or the fruit of original sin, or a battle between the sexes, or a bawdy pastime. She writes as one who believes in love so fresh and clear it comes to the reader almost as a rediscovery in literature. It was high time someone rediscovered it."[38]

Wedding Day and Other Stories is a sampler of Kay Boyle at her best. Through these stories we gain insight into the method of her art. By probing the individual experience—most often drawn directly from autobiography in all its idiosyncratic detail—she extrapolates the larger patterns of human existence. By rendering with scrupulous honesty and precision the particular experience, she in turn gives voice and flesh to her universal themes. The finely wrought style that in time would lead some critics to pigeonhole her as a mere virtuoso is evident in its full range and power in these first works. Her reverence for the Word and her skill in manipulating it are demonstrated in her ability to capture an instant with the crystal clarity that matches William Carlos Williams' snapshot of a red wheelbarrow; in subjective descriptions of landscapes that are projections of a perceiving consciousness; in flowing, lyrical plays with the sounds of language; and in complex experiments in rendering streams of consciousness through the "language of hallucination." But besides contributing brilliantly to the Revolution of the Word, in these stories she introduces the theme that echoes through the entire body of her work for six decades: that love is a fundamental human need and that tragedy results when this vital force is thwarted, stifled, or destroyed.

Notes

1. " 'This Quarter' Gets Reviewed," *This Quarter,* 2 (1925): 305.
2. Kay Boyle, "Why Do Americans Live in Europe?" *transition,* no. 14 (Fall 1928): 103.
3. Kay Boyle and Laurence Vail, "Americans Abroad," *Contempo* 3 (15 March 1933): 4.
4. Stanley J. Kunitz, ed., "Kay Boyle," in *Authors Today and Yesterday* (New York: H. W. Wilson Company, 1933), 86.
5. Kay Boyle, "Homage to Harry Crosby," *transition,* no. 19–20 (June 1930): 221.
6. Malcolm Cowley entitled his study of the literature of the twenties *A Second Flowering: Works and Days of the Lost Generation* (New York: The Viking Press, 1974).
7. Tooker and Hofheins, 18.
8. Kay Boyle, "Writers Worth Reading," *Contempo* 2 (5 July 1932): 4.
9. Boyle, "Americans Abroad," 6.
10. Kunitz, 86.
11. Advertisement in *transition,* no. 13 (Summer 1928), n.p.
12. Boyle to Spanier, 22 January 1979.
13. Tooker and Hofheins, 24.
14. Editors' notes in *Contact* 5 (June 1923): n.p.
15. Hugh D. Ford, *Published in Paris: American and British Writers, Painters, and Publishers in Paris, 1920–1939* (New York: Macmillan, 1975), 306.
16. Boyle, "Writers Worth Reading," 4.
17. Evelyn Harter, "Kay Boyle: Experimenter," *The Bookman* 75 (June–July 1932): 252.
18. Kay Boyle, "Hunt," in *Collected Poems* (New York: Alfred A. Knopf, 1962), 82.
19. Harter, 252.
20. L. A. G. Strong, review of *Plagued by the Nightingale, Spectator* 147 (18 July 1931): 94.
21. Kay Boyle, "The Only Bird That Sang," in *Collected Poems,* 81.

22. Kay Boyle, "A Letter to Francis Picabia," in *A Glad Day* (Norfolk, Conn.: New Directions, 1938), 61–62.

23. Quoted by William Carlos Williams in a letter to Kay Boyle tentatively dated 1932, in *The Selected Letters of William Carlos Williams,* ed. John C. Thirlwall, (New York: McDowell, Obolensky, 1957), 129.

24. Thirlwall, 130.

25. "In This Issue," *Contempo* 2 (5 July 1932), 2.

26. Boyle, "Writers Worth Reading," 4.

27. Harter, 250.

28. Margaret Atwood, introduction to *Three Short Novels* (1958; rpt. New York: Penguin Books, 1982), ix.

29. Kay Boyle, *Wedding Day and Other Stories* (New York: Jonathan Cape and Harrison Smith, 1930). Cited in text as *WD.*

30. Boyle to Spanier, 4 June 1981.

31. Boyle, "Brighter Than Most," 1.

32. Boyle to Spanier, 30 May 1981. "We who loved him were impatient with this sort of abuse, for Bob gave all he had to others," she says. Indeed, he used part of the 14,000 pounds his father-in-law gave him in 1923 to start the Contact Publishing Company as a sorely needed outlet for artists who could not get their work published by commercial presses, and he brought out books by such writers as Mina Loy, Bryher, H.D., Marsden Hartley, Ernest Hemingway, William Carlos Williams, Mary Butts, Emanuel Carnevali, Robert Coates, Gertrude Stein, and Nathanael West. Besides publishing his first book, *Three Stories and Ten Poems,* McAlmon also financed Hemingway's first visit to Spain in 1923, only to be scorned for the entire trip because he did not share his companion's relish for bullfighting.

33. Boyle to Spanier, 12 June 1981.

34. Porter, 279.

35. Herman Melville to Nathaniel Hawthorne. 1(?) June 1851, in *The Letters of Herman Melville,* ed. Merrell R. Davis and William H. Gilman (New Haven and London: Yale University Press, 1960), 129.

36. In a letter of 18 July 1927, Boyle writes to Evelyn Scott from Stoke-on-Trent that she is thinking of leaving her "adorable daughter" there and "walking the continent" with an Englishman. She never did.

37. Richard Strachey, review of *Wedding Day and Other Stories, New Statesman and Nation,* 24 September 1932, 347.

38. Porter, 279.

My Next Bride:
Kay Boyle's Text of the Female Artist

Deborah Denenholz Morse

Kay Boyle's novel, *My Next Bride* (1934), concerns the moral development of its heroine, Victoria John, a young American artist who travels to Thirties Paris in search of Experience and Art, in retreat from American philistinism. The novel is thinly disguised autobiography. It details Boyle's own Left Bank experiences in Twenties Paris, experiences she recalled in the 1968 version of Robert McAlmon's 1938 memoirs, *Being Geniuses Together,* which Boyle edited, and in which chapters of her own recollections alternate with McAlmon's reminiscences. It is in this context that *My Next Bride* has received the contemporary critical appreciation of Boyle scholars like Sandra Spanier (Boyle's biographer) and writers such as Doris Grumbach, the author of the Afterword to the newly reissued Virago edition of the book.

While this historical and biographical context of Boyle's writings is central to an evaluation of the significance of her work, another important context for consideration of *My Next Bride* is as a female version of the *Künstlerroman,* the story of the artist's youthful apprenticeship. James Joyce, one of Boyle's companion expatriates in Paris, had written in 1916 what was to become the most famous modern *Künstlerroman* in the English language, *A Portrait of the Artist as a Young Man,* eighteen years before Boyle wrote her novel. In Joyce's book, Stephen Dedalus escaped the "nets" of Family, Church, and State to become a writer.

Many of the important portraits of the artist as a young woman that followed Joyce's book tell stories in which the heroine's need to be free of patriarchal dictates for women overshadows Stephen's need to escape institutional authority in order to create. The most galling confinement for the female artist, as defined by these texts, is the prison of gender. For example, two other books about a female artist written by British authors at precisely the same time as the American Boyle wrote *My Next Bride* are Antonia White's *Frost in May* (1933) and Vita Sackville-West's *All Passion Spent* (1931), novels that clearly illustrate this distinction between the male and female artist plot.

Reprinted with permission of *Twentieth Century Literature* 34, no. 3 (fall 1988): 334–46.

The novels offer overtly contrasting versions of the female artist plot that in fact are informed by a similar feminist ideology. White's book, a portrait of the artist as a young girl, traces the evolution of the artist's rebellious consciousness in Nanda Grey, as she comes of age in the conventional world of a Catholic girls' school. In contrast, Sackville-West's novel begins when Lady Slane is eighty-eight, just after the death of her husband. The rest of the book is concerned with the heroine's memories of her youthful aspirations to be a painter, and hence includes long sections which paint a portrait of the artist as a young girl. The book details the constriction of Lady Slane's private, artistic self by her marriage to a very public man, a man who becomes first Viceroy of India and then Prime Minister of England. The feminist ideology underlying both texts emphasizes the repression of the female artist by cultural expectations of womanhood, and the necessity of rebellion against those expectations in order to forge the identity of the female artist.

Boyle's vision of the nature of the female artist's rebellion as a liberation from masculinist values is akin to that embodied in other female artist plots. Her portrayal of the means of enacting that rebellion in order to create art—like White's and Sackville-West's—thus is radically different than Joyce's in *Portrait*. Stephen Dedalus, Joyce's artist-hero, always feels isolated and alienated, and moves toward his expatriation from Ireland in order "to encounter for the millionth time the reality of experience and to forge in the smithy of my soul the uncreated conscience of my race" (252–53).[1] Victoria John, Boyle's artist-heroine, begins her experience in expatriation from America, and moves toward community rather than isolation, toward engagement rather than alienation. In her exploration of Victoria's moral development, Boyle opposes her sense of the female artistic vision as necessarily grounded in social concerns to Joyce's embodiment of the male artistic vision as private, unique, and necessarily isolated.

Like other stories of the female artist's formative years, Boyle's novel focuses on the protagonist's realization of how society limits her sex, but her portrait of Victoria John's accretive self-knowledge is much less overtly polemical than many texts of the female artist: Sackville-West's or White's, for instance. It is only when two formal structures of *My Next Bride* are foregrounded that one can perceive that the subtext of this female *Künstlerroman* is a critique not only of male cultural values, but also of the early Joycean vision of the artist as separate from community, necessarily divided from political concerns. The first of these formal structures is the tripartite division of *My Next Bride*, a division that marks the stages of Victoria's artistic apprenticeship. The second is the prominence of metaphors of ravishment and nurturance, metaphors that suggest Boyle's awareness of feminist concerns and her sense of a male/female cultural opposition. The import of Boyle's novel, and the cultural lessons that Victoria John learns, lead both the reader and Victoria to see the artist's vision—and her mission—as political. Boyle ultimately prophesies a new role *within* society for the artist.

In Victoria's story, her progress to emotional and artistic maturity is marked by three stages, each of which is represented by a section of the book titled with the name of the figure who most influences Victoria at that point in her development. Each of these figures is also an artist, and is thus identified with Victoria, serving both as mentor and as the embodiment of an alternative experience for her. The first, Sorrel, is the *avant-garde* patriarch of a Left Bank commune in its demise. Victoria's willingness to serve Sorrel, whose ideology of the Rousseauistic natural man obscures his true moral corruption, marks the first stage of her development, in which she is willing to play female muse to the male artist. Based on Boyle's real-life experiences in 1928 in Raymond Duncan's colony at Neuilly, the depiction of Sorrel's ravages on his people indicts Duncan's immoral artistic vision, which vindicates the abuse of others for the glory of the male artist.

Sorrel's colony is a cooperative, happy community only in theory; in reality it is an autocracy that oversees exploitation of its less favored or weak members—including its children. Sorrel's commune once prospered under the auspices of his wife, the dancer Ida (based on Isadora Duncan); however, it has become decadent under Sorrel, whose own egotism coupled with the rule of his sensual wife Mathilde—controller of the colony's pursestrings—has brought spiritual and material ruin. Ida's former beneficent influence is indicated by a passage in which Victoria looks at a photograph of her that is inscribed "I would teach the whole world to dance," and thinks of the change that has come to the colony:

> Whatever they were, they had been that thing together, and when she was dead it left room for the other thing to come: the cobwebs across the corners, and the dishes piled up in their filth and waste in the kitchens; the cold slipping ice—white under the doors, marching strong as an army through the windows to the flesh and bone and marrow that survived in squalor there. (68)[2]

The image of Ida, posed "tall and lovely," and the declaration of the photograph's caption express her desire to nurture the world with her art. Against this image, Boyle juxtaposes a metaphorical "army" that ravishes the colony's inmates, invading the "flesh and bone and marrow that survived in squalor there" (68).

Victoria's realization of Sorrel's debased sense of values, demonstrated most painfully in his treatment of the commune's starving, ignored children, leads to her rejection of him and to her continued search for a more humane vision and a true community in which there is congruence between theory and practice. Instead of finding identity and purpose in the serene, natural communal life that well-heeled tourists come to revere, Victoria uncovers the greed and love of comfort behind Sorrel's rhetoric of the austere and the "natural." She finds him unwilling to accept moral responsibility even for his smallest acts of selfishness—implicitly asking permission to use communal money for treats, like a child, while the real children of the commune starve, eating "winter carrots and stewed turnips, cooked fast so that their hearts were hard and done to death in flour in the cold" (229).

Victoria's longing to believe in Sorrel as spiritual and artistic mentor leads her into complicity with the hypocrisy of his colony. As she tells Antony Lister (the wealthy, sensitive American expatriate who will be her second mentor), "Like any woman, I belong to the thing I have undertaken" (187). This longing, and her physical hunger, allow her to take Estelle's dish of ratatouille and "the hearts of things cooked delicate as a Chinese dish" (236) in the face of the children's starvation; the same desire to believe in Sorrel impels the myth of the harmonious colony that she weaves for the wealthy American customer, Mrs. Brookbank, in hopes of getting her money for Sorrel.

In Boyle's view, Sorrel's colony becomes a metaphor of the ravishment of both the body and the spirit. Many things impose the truth about Sorrel's moral bankruptcy on Victoria, even before the final "exposure" scene in which she stands by while Peri, a colony member abused for years by Sorrel, rises up to accuse his oppressor after Sorrel spends Mrs. Brookbank's money not on a printing press, but on a fancy American car. The most important of these revelations is her love for Antony, and his relentless search for identity and intense passion for the poetic vision of D. H. Lawrence, of Emily Dickinson. Unlike the egocentric Sorrel, Antony loves other people. As he tells Victoria about life with Fontana, "We like people more than anything else in life" (102). When Victoria speaks of her painting, Antony is so intent that "whatever he was was lost at once in the wonder for the thing somebody else might be" (102).

Victoria's experiences with the colony's children crystallize her discontent with Sorrel and force her to see the evil consequences of his hypocrisy. In one devastating scene, Victoria takes the children to a park for the first time in their lives. These children, who bear classical names like Hippolytus and Prosperine, have in truth no connection to Nature and are terrified of grass. Clad in togas like ancient Greek children—in accordance with Sorrel's aesthetic—the children are totally uncared for. One child, Bishinka, is in pain because, as Boyle's narrator ironically comments, the "ties on his sandals had been badly sewn" (267). Moreover, his "toenails had not been cut, had never been cut perhaps, and they were growing inward like great yellow sabres" (267). The children are described as "four little overtures to death, their feet whispering over the mosses an invitation to the grave" (268). In reaction to their plight, Victoria creates a story for them of the promised land, but the children in this colony supposedly dedicated to the creation of art are in truth so deprived that they have diminished imaginations; the sound of the story "was unfamiliar: they could not recognize their own faces unless they were Hippolytus, Athenia, Prosperine and Bishinka waiting in the common room for supper or lying down at night to sleep upon the floor" (269).

The next stage of Victoria's apprenticeship leads her to Antony, with whom she has a romantic, unconsummated love affair. Antony (based on the real-life Harry Crosby)[3] is a failed artist who has nearly given up his own painting; significantly, he offers his paints to Victoria. He also offers love and money—patronage—to her. Most importantly, Antony talks constantly of his wife, the sculptor Fontana—of their love of poetry and art; it is this talk, which brings Fontana (Caresse Crosby, to whom *My Next Bride* is dedicated) and Victoria together, that is his greatest legacy to both of these women. Although Antony is thus a mentor to Victoria, his vision is warped by his upbringing, which has been ruled by the values of the patriarchy. His father, Horace, insists that he quit painting, and reviles him for living on his wife's money while he pursues his art—although Fontana supports this unconventional situation. Significantly, it is only when Antony is alone with Fontana that he paints, while she sculpts. Together, they scrawl the words of D. H. Lawrence on the walls leading to their country house. But the conflicting claims of the materialistic patriarchy and of his own attraction to the spiritually redemptive beauty of art generate a destructive tension in Antony, an identity crisis that is ultimately consummated in suicide. As he writes to Fontana, in a letter she reads to Victoria:

"I am not" said the cable in Fontana's voice "gold, silver or copper, I am something waiting to be set to music . . . Mozart forgot me in his eighth year . . . hummed me over between Don Juan and the Magic Flute and forgot me going upstairs to bed in Salzburg . . . Anaconda Copper, Carro de Pasco, Seaboard Oil are passwords for departure . . . New York explodes inside me every time I step out the door . . . I can't do it . . . I can't do it . . . I can't do it." (287–88)

The self-destructive Antony cannot serve as a model artist for Victoria, although his kindness and true sense of questing mark a stage along the path of Victoria's apprenticeship. Unlike the egomaniacal Sorrel, there is no hypocrisy in Antony. Sorrel sees his hypothetical printing press—so easily abandoned for a shiny new car—as a vehicle to glorify himself, but when Antony tells Victoria that he wants "to print a book on the virgin passions of the soul" (135), he wants to glorify human nature. However, although Antony states that "I believe in the word now and in the transformations it can make" (135), he does not act upon a sense of social purpose other than the demands of his father and of American society that he make money. Antony's financial failure might logically issue in despair and suicide, since his losses on the stock market devalue him by the standards of patriarchal culture. While in her Afterword to the novel Doris Grumbach has called Antony's suicide "curious, melodramatic, almost unaccountable" (328), his choice to end his life might be traced to his futile efforts to be both himself and, as Fontana phrases it, "a good son to Horace" (288). Unable to find a role in which he remains comfortable, as he tells Victoria, "I saw there was no place anywhere that wrapped me close and held me fast for ever" (211). In any event, the real-life basis of this episode—the double suicide of Harry Crosby and his mistress—is surely just as inexplicable, just as strange.[4] Antony's suicide tragically fulfills the novel's epigraph, the declaration by Laurence Vail (Boyle's second husband) that "knife will be my next bride," the source of the book's enigmatic title.[5]

Nowhere in *My Next Bride* is Antony's crisis of identity and purpose more vividly illustrated than in the brilliant scene in which a poor street violinist refuses to take Antony's suit as a gift. Here, Boyle sets up a visual opposition between the most impoverished of art's practitioners and Antony: Antony tries to assume the identity of a poor worker, in his corduroys and labouring jacket, while the violinist will not take on the identity of a wealthy businessman, embodied in Antony's suit. The image of Antony's discarded suit, stretched "long and empty across the pieces of thin white ice that roofed the cobbles in the gutter, the loose limbs of it curved in weariness and the arms fallen open, the white shirt laid in at the neck, the jacket buttons buttoned, as if the man who wore it had lain down there and wasted to nothingness within," is eerily prophetic of Antony's suicide, the end of his assertion to Victoria that "one cannot be nothing" (210).

In his search for identity in relation to other human beings, Antony shares with Victoria and Fontana a longing to find social and spiritual values that will take precedence over material concerns. The reckless generosity with which Antony stuffs a great amount of money in Victoria's purse when he takes her home from a wild party, for instance, contrasts with the stingy grasping after money of Sorrel and Mathilde. The progress of this money through Victoria to the ones who need it most—the starving Russian noblewomen—serves as a kind of metaphor of the socialist beliefs of Boyle herself. And Victoria's gift of money, of freedom, to Miss Fira and Miss Grusha—who have been virtually imprisoned in one room for fifty years—continues a pattern of nurturing toward these two impoverished women that contradicts the alienation they have experienced since the Revolution. In the following scene, the images of release from pain are metaphors of a loosening of the specifically female strictures that have bound them to their place, to their outcast fate:

> She could not say put your hands down here on my knees, little women, let me take the pins out of your hair, let me draw the bones from your lace like taking splinters from your flesh. Whatever I do, I have enough left over, enough food, drink, love, time enough, enough to touch your hands and make you go to sleep quiet. You must believe in me for I am not afraid of anything the world can do. (154–55)

It is this fearless effort toward assuaging pain that, in Boyle's view, is not only the artist's but the human being's responsibility.

Similarly, when Antony sends food to Victoria, she shares it with Miss Fira and Miss Grusha. Later, Victoria cannot enjoy her lavish meal with Antony until they send delicacies to the Russian sisters. Finally, the Archibald MacLeish quotation that Antony sends with his first gift of food to Victoria ("Ah how the throat of a girl and a girl's arms are Bright in the riding sun and the young sky And the green year of our lives where the willows are—" [158]) conjoins nurturance with both human love and with art.

For a time Victoria allows her frustrated love for Antony to lead her into despair, following his pattern of experiential exploration. She is led to an orgiastic party with him, but goes to bed with someone else—she's not sure who—and winds up pregnant. Antony takes her home and leaves her money—but after that she's on her own. He leaves on his ill-fated trip to America, which he had postponed in order to be with her. Victoria's life spirals into physical and moral degradation after this, until Fontana rescues her from the colony's store and takes her home with her. From here, Victoria is taken care of by Fontana, who arranges a safe abortion for her and—with immense generosity of spirit—comforts Victoria at Antony's death.

The scene in which Fontana seeks out Victoria is particularly significant because Boyle places the metaphors of ravishment and nurturance in direct opposition. While Fontana speaks to her, Victoria—who is suffering agonies from the abortion pills she is taking—begins to feel unbearable pain, pain described explicitly as a ravisher of woman's body:

And now the wild bugles of pain were unwinding in her; they were crying high and shrill throughout her blood. They were stayless as arrogant riders, booted and spurred, riding ruthless over the country, the crops broken under as they passed and the slow quiet toil of the seasons ravaged. The elegant swordsmen had taken their swords from their scabbards and were turning them slowly in her flesh. (290)

Victoria expects the elegant Fontana to respond to her predicament with fastidious disapproval, to "pick up [her] skirts and go" (291). Instead, Fontana leads Victoria out to the filthy privy behind the colony shop (itself a metaphor of the nastiness behind Sorrel's facade of purity),[6] reassuring her: "I'll go with you . . . You might faint somewhere alone" (292). Like the poor woman "with shaking hands and warts around her nose" (283) who gives Victoria a clean handkerchief and five francs after she soils herself in public, the beautiful, rich Fontana responds to human misery with practical, unjudgmental succor.

The final stage of Victoria's apprenticeship begins with her recovery from despair under the care of Fontana. An integral part of this recovery is the inherently feminist realization that her frustrated desire to end an unwanted pregnancy safely and cheaply is a plight shared by many other women:

All the girls who had ever come into the place, the chambermaids from cheap hotels, and the girls from the Bon Marché and the nougat-stands in the travelling fairs, and the girls who must dance at Bobino or the Empire for a living, cheaply painted and cheaply paid; and all the others, the nameless ones *sans domicile fixe* and *sans profession,* with their heels walked sideways, like Victoria's, and their faces walked long and bony like horses' faces, all of them came forbidden and unbidden out of the darkness of the corners and gathered there around them. . . . And there must be something better than this, said Fontana drawing back from the sight of them in the place, there must be something better. . . . They were out the door, they were on the landing, and behind them in the silence of the *sage-femme's* rooms they could hear the dripping, the endless dripping of the life-blood as it left the bodies of those others; the unceasing drip of the stream as it left the wide, bare table and fell, drop by drop, to the planks beneath it, dripping and dripping on for ever like a finger tapping quickly on the floor. (302–03)

The long passage details Victoria's and Fontana's (and Boyle's) horrified reaction to the spectre of death faced by women undergoing abortion. While Stephen Dedalus's experiences lead him to affirm his own isolated, superior self, Victoria John's experiences lead her instead to an understanding of her identity with all womankind, of her body's kinship with those other female bodies. This realization of a commonality of experience is the basis of the nurturant social role Boyle envisions for the female artist. That Boyle is exploring the possibilities of this role is suggested by the fact that in *My Next Bride,* Victoria's pilgrimage to Paris is framed by the experiences of other female artists. Her inspiration as an artist comes from three women: her painting teacher, her mother, and her friend, the vaudeville performer, Mary de Lacey—who are themselves artists; she ends up in closest alliance with another female artist, the expatriate from wealthy New York society, Fontana, who is not only a devotee of literature and the arts, but is herself a talented sculptor. The book explores imagined possibilities for Victoria as artist—within Sorrel's colony, in love with Antony (who has abandoned his own painting), joined in mutual solace with Fontana after Antony's suicide.

In defining her artistic identity, Victoria learns from the experiences of these other artists, rejecting what is false (the hypocrisy of Sorrel), surviving the identity crises and the impulse to self-destruction that ended in suicide for Mary de Lacey and Antony, and ultimately being nourished by what is true—learning to have the strength of her Midwest art teacher, the conviction of her mother, and the commitment to beauty of Ida, Sorrel's dead wife, "a woman of poetic vision" (123). During her stay at the colony, Victoria is implicitly asked by Sorrel's sly, greedy mistress, Mathilde, to replace Ida as his muse, and while Victoria is under his influence, she paints the faces of old men, hoping that "perhaps something will happen to my own face" (77). Her developing moral awareness results in a clearer sense of identity, and her ultimate alliance is, significantly, with a sister artist, Fontana, whose words are the last of the novel, her voice "picking it up and putting it together and going on with it forever" (320). Victoria will be neither Sorrel's muse nor Antony's "next bride" (172) but, by the end of the novel, a woman who has suffered and matured, and has formed a moral vision that she will embody in her art.

This focus on the role of the female artist is especially prominent in the second chapter of the book, which opens with Victoria establishing herself in the room of a once grand Parisian home turned boardinghouse in which she has taken a room. The first thing she unpacks are three photographs, "the faces of three women separately framed" (12). The photographs are set on the chimney by Victoria and contemplated like religious icons. The first photography is of Victoria's art teacher, a silent, reclusive woman, a "stranger" who nevertheless inspired Victoria to travel East on foot "looking for whatever there is" (20). The second photograph is of Victoria's mother, a gentle woman with a "full, loving mouth," whose artistic efforts are beginnings that Victoria wants to complete in her own life: "Everything I do you began somewhere and didn't have time to finish—dancing alone to the sound of music before strangers until I could have died of shame for you, speaking of poetry and sculpture as simply as if the colored servants loved them best" (21).

The last photograph, from a newspaper article telling of her suicide, is of the "Australian songbird," Mary de Lacey. Riding the freight cars to Montreal with Lacey, Victoria learns of female comradeship, as "they went into each other's arms for warmth, and the words were better spoken and heard while the bodies kindled each other" (220).[7] From Lacey, who tells of her past experiences on the run from her abusive husband—three-year-old son and ailing mother in tow—she also learns of female courage, pain, and victimization. When Lacey's mother dies, the police find cyanide pills that Lacey planned to use herself if her husband found her, and the authorities require an autopsy. The pain of having her mother's body carved up is dramatized by the horror of the corpse being fed to the sharks in the harbor—an image that confirms the prophetic vision Lacey sees in the ink of the palm of her hand, a picture of sharks jumping, "fighting like mad over something or other. . . ." The hungry, whirling sharks that tear a woman's body—like the image of the bleeding women's bodies at the *sage-femme's*—serve as a metaphor of ravishment defining a vision of human existence against which the female artist must create both her moral self and her art.

Later in the book, when Victoria is almost delirious with pain and weakness while taking the abortion pills, she tries to quiet the imagined voice of Antony asking "that every one put down their weapons" by reciting Lacey's tough words as "truth": "You should keep your fears for the dark, alone, like your lovers" (278–79). However, although Lacey was twice Victoria's age when they knew one another, the young American girl cannot learn sustaining wisdom from the middle-aged Australian's cynical vision, because it lacks a belief in love. When Victoria tries to express her love to the older woman—"Lacey, you're good, bad, rain, wind, thunder, sun, everything"—Lacey replies, "Where did you get it? How much does it cost a yard?" (22). Moved by a Chopin piece played by Miss Fira, Victoria tries to defend her idealism to Lacey's photograph: "And what about the thing they can't get hold of? Victoria said suddenly, jumping up in passion. What about the trees growing in spite of them, pictures getting painted, words that will be there for ever, what about it, what about love anyway, she said" (26).

As Spanier states, "In Kay Boyle's view both love of another person and love of art are essential elements of existence" (79). The commitment to another human being, that intimate social and moral relation, is necessary to the artist's larger social and moral vision, the vision that will be embodied in her art. Amid all the human wreckage of the novel, it is Fontana's love and care that will not only ensure Victoria's psychic and physical survival, but will also validate that moral vision toward which Victoria has been moving during the novel. In her generosity to Miss Fira and Miss Grusha and in her care for the colony's children, Victoria has acted upon a belief in the redemptive power of human kindness in the face of cruelty and hypocrisy.

As a measure of Victoria's progress toward this vision, Boyle creates two comparable scenes of women together, one at the beginning of her novel and one at the end. In the first scene, when Victoria and Lacey embrace in the boxcar, their intimacy is imperfect because neither woman can fully accept the other's need for nurturance. Victoria told Lacey, addressing her picture after her death, "I never said some things to you, I never said love because of the shy sound it had beside you" (22). In the closing scene of the book, Boyle consciously echoes her previous words when she has Victoria say, " 'I like you,' . . . and she felt shy at saying anything so simply out" (313). Lacey insists that "I don't need anyone, don't kid yourself. I don't need anyone at all" (25). Fontana, in contrast, says, "You lie down, Victoria John, and I'll lie down beside you" (313).[8] Like the "sitting parent" who falls asleep with the little girl Felicia in her arms in the 1946 Boyle story, "Winter Night," Fontana recognizes our need for one another in our pain, and responds compassionately. Victoria, who "never cried" (320), is moved to weeping at Antony's death, crying for him, for all his lost possibilities. The women lying beside one another and the tears shed for another's pain are metaphors for a vision of life that contrasts absolutely with the terrifying vision of ravishment conjured by the starving children in Sorrel's colony, their toenails "growing inward like great yellow sabres," by Victoria's plundered body at the privy, by Lacey's mother's corpse mangled by sharks, and by the bleeding women at the *sage-femme's*.

The full measure of the final scene in *My Next Bride* can be appreciated only with the echo of a previous scene in the reader's mind: in that scene, Sorrel, justly excoriated by Peri, cries for himself, "alone, without anyone, in the dark" (311). In company with Fontana, Victoria has moved beyond the concentration on self that precludes Sorrel from weeping for anyone else, from true care for others. In the compassionate response of Fontana and Victoria— in life and in art—Boyle identifies the only possibility for our moral salvation. With the strength and awareness Victoria has gained in her journey toward self-knowledge, she has finally learned to cry, going beyond Lacey's cynical outlook or Antony's despair toward a vision of compassion for a world in pain. In creating that vision, Boyle has helped to shape a new kind of female *Künstlerroman* in which the expatriate hero of Joyce's text would indeed find himself on foreign terrain.[9]

Notes

1. James Joyce, *A Portrait of the Artist as a Young Man,* ed. Chester G. Anderson (New York: Viking Press, 1968).

2. All citations are from Kay Boyle, *My Next Bride* (New York/London: Penguin Books/Virago Press, 1986).

3. See Sandra Whipple Spanier, *Kay Boyle, Artist and Activist* (Carbondale: Southern Illinois Univ. Press, 1986), pp. 88–89. Spanier is the main source for the biographical references in my essay. See also Shari Benstock, *Women of the Left Bank: Paris, 1900–1940* (Austin, Tex.: Univ. of Texas Press, 1986).

4. For the story of Harry and Caresse Crosby, see Geoffrey Wolff's *Black Sun: the Brief Transit and Violent Eclipse of Harry Crosby* (New York: Random House, 1976).

5. The epigraph might explain Grumbach's assertion that Antony is based on Laurence Vail (323).

6. For an excellent discussion of Boyle's use of the privy as metaphor, see Spanier (p. 86).

7. On the homoerotic resonances of this passage, see Spanier, p. 89. She comments that in the flashback scene in which Victoria and Mary de Lacey had lain embracing on the floor of the boxcar, Lacey "had advised her friend, 'Don't fall for the skirts, Victoria, not till you've given the boys a trial. . . . You'll come to it anyway in the end.' "

8. Although Spanier discusses the erotic overtones of this scene (suggesting that while the knife of the epigraph may be seen as Antony's "next bride," the title might also apply to the developing relationship between Victoria and Fontana), she states: "It is only fair to note that Kay Boyle herself calls this interpretation of the title 'completely wrong': It applies only to Antony; in other words, death was his 'next bride' " (89). Spanier also points out the "striking repetition" between the flashback scene of Lacey and Victoria in the boxcar, and the final scene of Fontana and Victoria on the bed.

9. For a good account of the male *Künstlerroman* tradition see Maurice Beebe, *Ivory Towers and Sacred Founts: The Artist as Hero in Fiction from Goethe to Joyce* (New York: New York Univ. Press, 1964). Grace Stewart provides an original analysis of the subverting of this tradition by women writers in *A New Mythos: The Novel of the Artist as Heroine, 1877–1977* (St. Albans, Vt.: Eden Press, 1979). In her brilliant essay, "The Birth of the Artist as Heroine: (Re)production, the *Künstlerroman* Tradition, and the Fiction of Katherine Mansfield," Susan Gubar focuses on the "startling centrality of childbearing in the *Künstlerromane* of women" and concludes that "for the woman writer who seeks to uncover not only the fiction of male motherhood, but also the factious biological metaphor, the *Künstlerroman* conventions fashioned by men are insufficient" (26). Gubar analyzes how women writers "shaped the conventions of this genre to their own purposes" and "salvaged uniquely female images of creativity" (26–27). She discusses in particular detail how Mansfield supplants the male artist's progression "towards

the transcendence necessary to create art" by "coming to terms with the centrality of birth without mystifying it, by reconciling her writing with her rearing so that "she called into question the identification of artistry with autonomy" (26, 27). Gubar concludes that "finally, Mansfield's later stories . . . typify the redefinition of women as paradigmatic creators in the artist novels of feminist modernists like Dorothy Richardson, Willa Cather, and Virginia Woolf herself" (27). I am indebted to Gubar's essay for steering me to both Beebe and Stewart.

Tails You Lose: Kay Boyle's War Fiction

EDWARD M. UEHLING

In his famous introduction to the anthology *Men at War,* Hemingway observes that in combat "learning to suspend your imagination and live completely in the very second of the present minute with no before and no after is the greatest gift a soldier can acquire."[1] That statement has become, at least implicitly, the measure for all war fiction because the central figures in modern war novels have been revealed to us as they succeed and, more interestingly, fail to maintain such a perspective. Paul Bäumer (*All Quiet on the Western Front*), Frederic Henry, Billy Pilgrim, Paul Berlin (*Going after Cacciato*), and other such figures take on dramatic, moral intensity as they struggle with physical and psychological brutalities of war. Yet there are many stories of war—Vietnam has reminded us of that—and Kay Boyle's short fiction of World War II makes equally compelling statements about war and its consequences.

Harold Krebs, the shell-shocked veteran of Hemingway's "Soldier's Home," longs for "a world without consequences"; in such a story as "The Lost," Boyle captures what would terrify Krebs: a world of overwhelming consequences for "survivors" without homes to which they might return. It is Boyle's world of consequences that gives us the other side of the coin; however disquieting, it is one we must understand if we are to know the full cost of war. The social and political wisdom of Boyle's war fiction is all the more remarkable, though, for its skillful telling. Fiction written during or shortly after a war often struggles to find its moral and aesthetic center because the artist has not yet established sufficient distance (Vonnegut's *Slaughterhouse-Five* is more typical than Mailer's *The Naked and the Dead*). The relative speed with which Boyle could write about World War II and her control of difficult materials invite our closest critical attention.

But what, besides combat, is the proper material of war fiction? The nineteenth-century German historian Clausewitz understood "that war is simply a continuation of political intercourse"—an idea that helps us to consider the depth and complexity of its human components. Certainly his

Reprinted with permission of *Twentieth Century Literature* 34, no. 3 (fall 1988): 375–83.

perception of war as "another form of speech or writing"[2] expands our awareness of the tensions and consequences of war. It includes the before and after as well as Hemingway's "present minute": in short, the other side of the coin.

Such an interest in language forms the basis of the nearly overwhelming metaphor for war in the film *Apocalypse Now*. In *Heart of Darkness* (its source), when Marlow seeks Kurtz, he wants to hear the voice of the great man because he assumes a moral, reasonable order to the world is possible through communication. In fact, he thinks of Kurtz not as doing but discoursing. That faith dissolves when he discovers instead the atavistic figure who can only mutter "The horror! The horror!" The further dissolution of language is Marlow's, though, for when he returns to the presumed normalcy of society, he can offer only lies in explanation of what has happened.

Boyle exhibits a similar fascination with the possibilities and failures of language as she examines the people—soldiers and civilians; men, women, and children—of World War II Europe. I want to discuss two stories, "Army of Occupation" and "The Lost," although there are many others ("Hotel Behind the Lines," for instance) which similarly deal with this issue of language and are more overtly political, as well. But these two, both describing the aftermath of war, look from several angles at the gap between private thought and public utterance. In each story, as language fails, we see and hear more than the failure of moral courage: we discover a failure of human understanding and sympathy that suggests complete spiritual sterility.

"Army of Occupation" begins in Paris as a troop train prepares to return with American soldiers to occupied Germany "after a furlough spent . . . in pursuit of love."[3] The presence of American GIs so dominates the scene that there is no other sense of time or place: we are told, "it was not a French train" (439), and the MPs and GI ticket men stand, passing judgment on the French girls who have come to say goodbye. Whatever values emerge must come from the American soldiers on that train and the unnamed American correspondent who travels to meet her husband.

The intense drama of this brief story unfolds in a frightening counterpoint of voices and levels of meaning. As the woman boards the train, ignoring gapes from the men on the platform, we hear a chorus of voices from within. Drunken and terrible, it is described as a "sad, wild longing outcry—no longer recognizable as singing" (440). " 'Roll me over / in the clover,' wailed the voices in grief from behind the closed compartment doors, and far ahead, in almost unbearable sorrow, other voices cried out 'Reminds me of / The one I love' in drunken, unmelodious complaint" (441). We hear, but the woman is apart from this, perhaps by temperament: "the things that passed through her mind were different. She did not look toward the men, and she did not seem to hear them calling out" (440). From the outset, Boyle underscores the difference in sensibilities between the woman, whose "look of modesty, of shyness and vulnerability" (440) is reflected in the self-willed reality of her private thoughts, and the men, whose calls, whistles, and roaring are aggressively animalistic. The disparate voices of the story, motivated by fear, perverse longing, or disgust, are powerfully expressive but insular: no one hears or listens.

Stepping into one compartment of this soiled, discordant world, the woman faces three soldiers, each as distinctively ugly in speech as he is in physical presence and gesture. One, a sergeant, crudely waves and caresses a cognac bottle that hangs "between his spread knees" (441). The second, a big red-haired man, is educated enough to refer to Lochinvar and Morpheus but joins the sergeant in trying to coax her to drink from their bottles. The third, described as a farm boy, isolates himself and only occasionally blurts out contemptuous remarks about French war brides being no ladies, "then turn[s] his face to the dark of the window again" (443). From the moment she sets foot in the compartment, we witness a striking cluster of images that mock civilized, cultivated behavior. The sergeant's first "words" are not words at all but a baying wolf call. The big soldier apes polite conversation as he suggests that the woman is a commodity to be consumed: " 'Take a glance, gentlemen, at what they're passing around with coffee and leecures tonight' " (441). Indeed, throughout the confrontation of the story, he associates her with the bottle of cognac. Before the sergeant has grabbed the woman with encouragement from his big companion—" 'You take it first. I'll take what's left' " (448)— she belies her assertion that she is not afraid.

As a signal of her growing fear, the narrator distinguishes what the woman does say from what she thinks by italicized passages that indicate her attempt to impose a sense of calm: for instance, *"in thirteen hours now, a little less than thirteen"*; or, *"They can't do anything, not a single thing. In a little while he'll walk down the platform, looking in every window for me"* (448). Ironically, once inside the compartment, she does begin to hear the crude chorus, although it has grown less distinct, and even takes some comfort in the singing as she tries to think of her husband and not those with her.

At the same time, there are no instances of genuine communication as the two soldiers first attempt to seduce the terrified woman and then nearly succeed in forcing themselves on her. Their words, wholly artificial and perverse, distort the reality she internalizes and we would wish for. For instance, the sergeant attempts to evoke pity from the woman by showing her a certificate that verifies his attendance four days earlier at the funeral of his infant son by an English war bride. But as his comrade drunkenly observes, " 'Does it occur to you that the lady is bored with all this kind of talk? Does it occur to you that beauty incarnate doesn't give a snap of her dainty fingers for your relatives?' " (445). By resorting to speaking about her as though she were not present, the two demonstrate their crude intention and the inadequacy of any response she might offer to halt its progress. At this moment, the third soldier, from whom one might hope for moral outrage, can muster only disgust for everyone unlike himself: "with the cap tipped low on his brows, [he] turned away from the rushing darkness of the night outside and looked at them bleakly, almost reproachfully, again" (446). He issues another brief, unintentionally ironic condemnation of French war brides (and really all women); " 'I found out too much just in time. . . .' He looked at them in something like hesitation a moment, as if there were more to say and as if he were about to say it, and then turned back to the fleeting darkness. . . . 'Roll me over / In the clover,' came the faint, sad chorus of crying down the corridor" (446).

Yet we have not experienced the utter failure of language until a blue-eyed corporal enters the compartment, ostensibly to offer his seat in another car to the woman, but really to make a childish bid for her favor. A brief sampling of his declarations reveals him as foolish, not gallant: " 'You're American. You're wonderful.' " Or, " 'You're beautiful. You're like all the girls at home who don't come over' " (449). And his last words: " 'My God, you're beautiful. I love you. I respect you' " (452). Although we are told "his ears [were] deaf to everything except what she might say" (449), she says nothing to him until the increasing threat of physical violence drives her to attempt to accept the offer of his seat. Instead, the corporal literally takes the woman's place, is essentially raped with the ubiquitous bottle in her place.

While the "farm boy [sleeps] in peace against the cold, dark window glass" (452), the sergeant knocks the corporal senseless with a bottle. As he lies "as if in sleep," the sergeant prepares for another blow, when the woman cries out: " 'Don't touch him! Don't you dare to hit him again!' " (452). The story closes with an ironic juxtaposition of inadequate voices and silences. The woman's own private voice fairly races in an effort

> to save from annihilation the actual flesh and bone of all that remained of decency. "*They're other people on this train, like people you know, like people you see in the street. . . . They're Wacs, and brothers, and sons, and husbands . . . they're people singing. . . . People who understand words, if I can get to them . . .*" (452–53)

But interspersed with these silent pleas are the voices of the chorus, "far, unheeding, calling out in nostalgia" (453) and also the narrator's careful words which describe the woman's furious exit from the compartment. To the woman's final spoken words—"Get out of my way!"—the sergeant makes a noteworthy response: "And he did not speak, but, half smiling still as she flung by him, he lifted his hand and stroked her soft, dark hair" (453). The story's final words suggest that what she runs from may be no worse than what she runs to—"toward the sound of the sad, sweet, distant voices in the rushing train" (453). What is real? The loneliness of those voices, as well as the tenderness perversely evoked by their description? Or simply their message—"Roll me over / In the clover."

The paradox of Boyle relying on words for her art when developing this idea of failed language is perhaps even more pronounced in "The Lost." This is a story of children displaced by the war and the American woman who manages a Children's Center from which they may be officially relocated. As in "Army of Occupation," setting reinforces a distorted pattern of historical connections. Once a massive baronial manor house in Bavaria, the Center conveys to the arriving America Relief Team "the chill of winter and silence and death that stood like a presence in its feudal halls" (515). But that is only one past reality of the place: during the war, it served as a Selection Camp for genetic and racial losers who were dutifully recorded, photographed, and sent to labor or extermination. From their neatly alphabetized records, their pictures haunt us: "It was the eyes of these men and women, who were there no longer, which looked now at the Americans, and beyond them, upon some indescribable vista of hopelessness and pain" (515). Against such a background, the American presence seems more orderly than useful—a source of food and playground equipment, but not of restored identity.

The story's most powerful representation of "hopelessness and pain" comes through its many voices. Three figures, called "boys" by the narrator, are addressed as "men" by the American woman. Orphans and mascots of various U.S. Infantry units, they are neither civilians nor children. How to name or understand them is more difficult still because of their speech and what it implies. The oldest, Janos, is fifteen, once was Czechoslovakian, calls himself Johnny Madden, and speaks with the accent of the black sergeant from Tennessee, Charlie Madden, by whom he hopes to be adopted. The other two are younger, perhaps fourteen and twelve, and remain unnamed. The fourteen-year-old, filled with cynicism, looks for an angle or a private deal and refuses to recross the threshold of the Center and the child's world it suggests. "His accent might have come straight from Brooklyn," we are told, "except that it had come from somewhere else before that, and, as he spoke, he folded his arms upon his breast, and spat casually" (517). The youngest, whose grandfather is eventually located in Naples, is able at least superficially to rejoin the world of swings and sandboxes, but his voice parrots that of the GIs with whom he has lived.

During their initial interview, the woman discourages hope of adoption in the practiced litany of a middle-level bureaucrat:

> "And probably when the G.I.s made you those promises they thought they would be able to keep them. . . . I've talked to some of these men, I've had letters from them, and I know they believed they would be able to keep the promises. But there were other kinds too. There were some kinds who didn't care what happened to you men afterward. . . . They wanted you to learn how to drink and smoke and gamble and shoot crap and use the kind of language they used—"

The twelve-year-old's reply betrays his misunderstanding: " 'I begin shooting crap in Naples,' the small boy said in his high, eager voice. 'I clean up seven bucks the first night there.' " For once her composure is punctured: " 'Look, kid . . . if Italy's your country, perhaps you ought to pack up and go back there' " (520). The play of language in this exchange is remarkable. Her irritation leads her to replace "men" with "kid," a term nearer to the truth but still without sympathy or even recognition of individuality. Moreover, both speakers' use of "crap" to describe the game of dice, "craps," suggests that neither the woman nor the child fits in this strange world of war; it further hints at the ineffectuality of such talk/"crap." The woman evokes a startling reply from the boy: " 'I ain't no Eyetie no more,' he said and he did not raise his eyes to look at her because of the tears that were standing in them 'I'm American. I wanna go home where my outfit's gone' " (521).

Janos has watched the sunlight reflect blankly upon her glasses and has listened to her as "neither woman nor American, perhaps not human being even, but a voice—disembodied, quiet, direct—which might be coming now to the words they had been waiting to hear her say" (520). The words will never come; instead, this scene introduces a terrifying isolation as these characters continually fail to go beyond expressiveness toward communication.

In fact, throughout "The Lost," people rarely look at or hear each other. That failure develops most obviously through numerous images of dark and lightness. For instance, the second hayloft scene, in which Janos brings table scraps to the second boy, contains many plays on light and dark that underscore shifts in language and its ultimate inadequacy. Janos crosses the stable door "in the darkness" and finds the boy framed by the window through which there are "stars shining clearly . . . and Janos could hear his [the other's] voice speaking out across the hay-sweet dark" (528). The words are even harder and more defensive now: " 'My God-damned lighter's gone dry as a witch's tit,' the boy said. 'I've got to get me to a PX and get me some lighter fluid' " (528–29). Perhaps for him there is already no other possibility of light than that of the now empty Zippo. His sweater, we are told, "showed dark against the starry square of night" (529). It might be argued that his language makes him darker than the night; certainly the contrast of his fierce despair with Janos' insistent hope for a future sense of place rings clearly in Boyle's representation of their voices. Offering a nearly empty bottle of schnapps to his older companion, the outsider says, " 'Have a swig, kid,' " echoing the woman's retort. Then there is more tough talk: " 'I've got to get me to a man's-size town where there's a PX quick,' the boy was saying in the darkness" (529). To Janos' innocuous reply, the other begins laughing and Boyle writes, "He lay . . . beyond Janos in the darkness" (529).

For the sixth time in this scene darkness is mentioned as Janos recalls Sergeant Madden's instruction on the naming and placing of stars. Two qualities of his declaration are noteworthy. First, the reference to stars and thus to light and hope is linked to the one trustworthy figure in Janos' world. Although we do not hear his buddy's words, they obviously have remained with Janos as proof of the order represented by Madden. Equally revealing, Janos conveys all of this as though he is speaking to himself or at least without expecting that his words can become part of a real communication in the darkened loft. We discover that such words, with their implicit faith in happy endings, can elicit only the briefest acknowledgment of pain before the facade of the Brooklyn accent resurfaces: " 'Oh, Christ' " the other boy mutters as he curses a system where rank has privilege, a system that will always exclude him. Another spasm of ironic laughter jerks from him and he dismisses Janos' hope: " 'You listen, kid, . . . The cards is stacked against us' " (530).

Hearing these American dialects apart from the sources that should accompany them makes us wince, particularly because the topics addressed would be painful even to adults. All three children speak of their parents' deaths matter-of-factly; their voices would be utterly detached except that they are eager to prove that they may go "home to America" because their parents have not survived. The unconscious mimicry of their voices echoes their empty lives.

Finally only Janos remains, writing every night to Madden, who has taught him to fix things, and practicing the mechanical skills that he hopes to use in Madden's garage. But the final image of darkness, Charlie Madden's race, catches him. It is, as the woman explains, "the color question."

> Janos stood there listening to the words she said, and, as he listened, the woman again ceased being woman, ceased being human being even, and it was merely a voice in the shed that spoke quietly and bitterly of the separate lives that must be lived by people of different colors, as she had on that first day spoken of the hopes that might never come to anything at all. (532)

Yet the final sorrow of this unresolved story is not that Janos cannot live with a black man in Tennessee. It is the manner in which he rejects even the compromise of living with another family in America. "Neatly and inaccurately" he composes the polite lie to Madden and disappears without a trace: "Yesstidy I talk to the US consil Charlie and what do ya think now? Seems my fammillys jus as good as they ever waz so Charlie I make up my mynd sudden to go back whar they waz waiting for me Im shure ya thinks its for the best Charlie so I says so long" (534).

Earlier, Janos' writing every night might be regarded as a form of light in the darkness. But the effect of his final letter is quite different. Here its flawed form and substance underscore the displacement of meaningful language by an English that intends to protect both sender and recipient but does not connect; an English that is distorted, false, occupying yet lost. Either way, heads or tails, the world of Boyle's war stories is an unforgiving, lonely place.

Notes

1.   Ernest Hemingway, ed., *Men at War: The Best War Stories of All Time* (New York: Crown, 1942), p. xxvii.

2.   Carl von Clausewitz, *On War,* quoted here from p. 1 of W. J. T. Mitchell, ed., *The Politics of Interpretation* (Chicago: Univ. of Chicago Press, 1983).

3.   Kay Boyle, *Fifty Stories* (New York: Penguin Books, 1981), p. 439. Subsequent references to "Army of Occupation" and "The Lost" appear parenthetically within the text.

Call Forth a Good Day:
The Nonfiction of Kay Boyle

Elizabeth S. Bell

Noted as a stylist and awarded distinguished recognition for her short fiction, Kay Boyle, in her prodigious writing during the 1930s, earned for her fiction and poetry an enthusiastic and discriminating following. Her later reputation, born perhaps from her reporting of post-World War II Europe and nurtured in the caldron of McCarthy's 1950s, encompasses another element of Boyle's concept of what a writer should be, for Kay Boyle is now additionally recognized as an articulate spokesperson for a variety of political and social issues, a voice of society's conscience, and—not coincidentally—a crafter of the essay as well. Rather than being a separate manifestation of Boyle's writing, the political activism of her recent career is a direct development of the concerns she expressed in her earlier poetry and fiction. Her essays, spanning almost sixty years of this century, reveal the connections that unite her work and chronicle the growth of her artistic vision.

Boyle's essays about literature or writing or writers themselves, those written in Europe before World War II as well as those written after her return to the United States in the 1940s, demonstrate convincingly the growth of Boyle's commitment to and development of the full scope of literature as a profound form of communication between writer and audience and culture. She began with the aesthetic conviction that the writer must draw from deep engagement with his or her themes, but as she saw and experienced the turmoil of the Spanish Civil War, World War II, and the metaphorical McCarthy-era war, she became convinced that writers must become committed crusaders, speaking for those who have no voice and addressing the injustices of contemporary life. While she earlier called for writers to be deeply concerned, she now wants both deep concern and the courage to articulate for a less sensitive world the truth that must be said.

During the late 1920s as neophyte writer in the ferment of Europe's artistic community, Boyle wrote two significant reviews for *transition*, one dis-

Reprinted with permission of *Twentieth Century Literature* 34, no. 3 (fall 1988): 384–91.

cussing favorably William Carlos Williams' *In the American Grain* (1925) and the other dealing negatively with Hart Crane's early poetry. The underlying concern she expressed in these essays revolves around the writer's responsibility for accuracy, both that of image or archetype—as she articulated in both essays—and that of language—as she argued more specifically in the Crane essay.

The earlier essay, "In the American Grain" (1927), focuses on Williams' attempt in his book of the same name to redefine the American literary heritage. He returned, Boyle tells us, to the documents, court letters, diaries of the past to recapture an unbiased version of life as it was, without the overlay of "borrowed interpretations" based on a perhaps more attractive false image too often attached to any systematic account of the past available in our century (28).[1] In the process, Williams discovered an authenticity—"sound and color and smell" (29)—that Boyle finds invigorating. Just as Boyle, Eugene Jolas, and their contemporaries in Paris were decrying the limp and inarticulate poetic diction of the late Victorian and Edwardian ages and calling for a Revolution of the Word to inject vitality and meaning into twentieth-century literary language, so Boyle here rejects with Williams the pallid and lifeless portrayal of the American heritage that was contained within "the national American mind" (28).

Her 1928 review, "Mr. Crane and His Grandmother," provides a conjunction of the issues concerning image and language, for Boyle faults Crane on both counts in his poetry. In an extension of her theme from the Williams essay, Boyle's most telling difficulty with Crane comes from the cavalier portrait he painted of his grandmother in "My Grandmother's Love Letters" (*White Buildings,* 1926). She resents the "gently pitying laughter" he granted to his grandmother as he led her through "much of what she would not understand," for Boyle finds the woman "a better bet than he" (83). Boyle abhors Crane's patronizingly chauvinistic portrayal, for it denies real acquaintance with the woman herself and illustrates a profound lack of understanding on Crane's part of the reality of her life—by extension that of all women within the American experience. For Boyle, whose own fiction demonstrates a strong autobiographical thread and an unswerving drive toward recreating in fictional context the real and true, Crane's lack of insight indicates a serious flaw in his poetic vision. In contrast, Boyle's earlier review of William Carlos Williams' *In the American Grain* commends his nod of recognition to the "Pocahuntus tradition" which speaks authentically of the female American experience as the alternate tradition to the "Pilgrim or the Indian polished to bronze" (27).

Yet for Boyle, Crane's writing is ultimately unsuccessful because it lacks vitality and humor; in fact she finds that he uses words to observe truth, finding them useful in "hiding a human fear" (32). She contrasts his poetry with a graphic and visually explicit passage about wild boar hunting from Robert McAlmon and, instead of McAlmon's crisp and clear language, shows Crane's poem to be clouded in essentially incomprehensible images. His meaning is not communicated to his audience because it is not unwrapped in the vital, vigorous language the twentieth century demands.

In attacking Crane's use of highly abstract images, Boyle by definition clarifies her own stance in the matter. In many ways her attack on his imprecise poetic imagery extends the concern she expresses in her review of Williams' work. She craves accuracy of language in much the same sense and with very much the same fervor with which she rejoices in Williams' call for precision in historical image; for her the two demands are, in fact, tightly interwoven. In a later decade, the 1960s, Boyle refers to herself and her earlier compatriots in Europe as resistance fighters in a particular context: "The resistance was against the established English language, and the fight was for the recognition of a New American tongue" (38). In the 1928 Crane essay, she was actively engaged in the validation of this new tongue, particularly in poetic language, and she found Hart Crane's latest book of poetry to be a throwback to a tradition better left behind.

In book reviews produced during the 1930s and very early 1940s, Boyle returns to these two themes, faulting for example Katherine Mansfield for belonging to an older world and Elizabeth Bowen for lacking connection to the real world. Yet she blends her concerns for the writer's precision with a growing demand for passionate commitment to one's themes in the literature one produces. In Mansfield's case, Boyle finds a "lovely, proud, appealing woman" whose best stories and tragic life had kept her immune from a true evaluation of her work. Many of the stories she produced, with only a handful of sparkling exceptions, are shallow and lifeless, "not enough, for what the intent must have been, not love and comprehension for the persecuted young or old, or satire bitter enough for those she would condemn" (54). The passion is lacking, and more sadly, Boyle believed Mansfield knew it. Instead of the issues of life and death, she is confined, according to Boyle, to a world of "irritable and irritating themes" (54). Bowen, too, suffers from a lack of deep commitment, creating a "singularly immature and ungrateful theme" (48). In her earlier books, Bowen's collective protagonist—regardless of name or occupation—seems to Boyle to be too much a victim, too little aware or assertive to engage in meaningful action, too pallid to contain significant insight. Boyle's review contains hope for Bowen's latest effort, *Bowen's Court,* for in her opinion it represents "a truly heroic effort to connect with reality at last," perhaps indicating the birth of a deeper commitment or perception on Bowen's part (50).

One writer of this period, the years immediately before World War II, whom Boyle finds to be noteworthy is William Faulkner. Her 1938 review of *The Unvanquished,* "Tattered Banners," praises his "hot devotion to man's courage" and his passion and "fury to reproduce exactly not the recognizable picture but the unmistakable experience" (55). She finds Faulkner's commitment to his themes to be not just the province of *The Unvanquished* or any given of his novels, but of his work in its entirety. He is a risk-taker who explores his themes with insight and conviction, making him "the most absorbing writer of our time" (56). In fact, Faulkner matches Boyle's description of the ideal writer, for he combines precision of image and language with that deep commitment to his themes she believes to be so necessary.

These early essays follow standard formats, concentrating on an individual writer and perhaps specific works of that writer. The prose is clear, the point of view definite, and the persona reasoned. As models of their kind, stylistically and philosophically well-honed, these early essays allow Boyle to deal with writers within the context of their own canons. She looks for internal significance and themes, demanding of the writers a dedication to their individual visions and themes. The revolution she supports during this time is an aesthetic and conceptual one: re-visioning language, reconceptualizing reality, making poetry and literature vital in this twentieth-century world. While her own fiction of this period deals with more political subjects, she does not demand that kind of commitment to social change of her contemporaries.

By the mid-1940s, however, Boyle's world had dramatically changed. From her special vantage point as a newly returned exile of sorts, she observed statewide reactions to the cataclysm in Europe. Her 1944 essay, "The Battle of the Sequins," conveys with almost Swiftian satire the outrage she felt at the societal nonchalance she saw: In the midst of a world gone mad in war, with death and dying everywhere one looked, the scuffle of well-dressed customers for a department store's sale-priced pieces of spangle takes on for some more meaning than the real life-and-death battle going on throughout Europe. The essay's persona magnifies the irony involved by reporting in matter-of-fact tones the grabbing and shoving of the women at the sales counter, while recognizing that moving among them are the ghostly faces of dying soldiers and victims of the war, complete with battlefield and jungle landscapes. The women in the store are cautioned not to look too closely—a needless warning—for "you will see something you do not wish to see" (157). The unexpected juxtaposition of such a trivial setting as a department store with the profoundly moving issues in this essay heightens its ironic effect and demonstrates a new willingness on Boyle's part to experiment with essay form for the sake of communicating a vivid message. Furthermore, although the essay does not deal directly with either literature or writers, it signals a new element in Boyle's philosophy that she would soon attach to her literary essays. After all, Boyle and her generation had witnessed a world-wide loss of innocence: in the post-Holocaust age Boyle knows that no one, especially not the writers, can afford to be as complacent as they had been in the age that existed before.

Boyle's subsequent essay, "Farewell to New York" (1947), marks a turning point in her literary commentary. Although the focus of this essay—

spoken in the voice of "the Spaniard"—is predominantly socio/political, Boyle uses it to introduce the writer's role in world events. The Spaniard tells her that when a political man is exiled from his country, "he is maimed and mute," but a writer in exile can retreat into "a spiritual terrain of silence which is native to him, and which he can turn to in any country where he is" (74). Because the writer can create this native soil, the writer by nature is not compelled to be silent. Boyle closes the essay by addressing her friend personally, from the perspective of a later, wiser time, to tell him that she feels guilt because so many who had been given the opportunity to speak out "a long time ago" had remained silent or non-committal or deliberately isolationist (76). She calls these writers by name—Pound (in 1937 before his involvement in World War II Italy), Waugh, Eliot—and allows their own comments to speak volumes for them.

In technique this essay experiments with time, point of view, persona. Unlike Boyle's earlier literary commentary, it ignores aesthetic concerns directed toward a particular writer's work; unlike later essays it accuses without providing a model of appropriate behavior. Yet the essay establishes Boyle's guiding principle: it no longer will suffice for her to write—even as passionately as she has always done—of deep commitment and precision of language, the aesthetic concerns of a less traumatized world, without adding to those issues a call for involvement on the part of those—the writers—who have access to the pages of world thought. Boyle's philosophy does not so much change its course as that it adds societal cogency and purpose to the elements of commitment, passion, and precision that she has always valued.

In "Farewell to Europe" (1953) Boyle explains the personal necessity she felt of returning to America to speak out against McCarthyism. One of her earliest concerns, as explored rather impersonally in her 1927 essay about Williams, is the nature of one's American identity. In 1953, she felt this concern to be even more immediate and its impact far more personal. Her own background, as she tells us, contains many strong voices raised in defense of individual freedom and its corollary, individual responsibility. Yet in the essay she must also chronicle a growing disbelief in American democracy on the part of many Europeans of her acquaintance, for they had heard too loudly and too long the strident voice of "McCartair," the McCarthy who would change the lives and fortunes of many Americans before his day in the sun ended (96). Boyle tells of her friends who advise her to stay in Europe where she will be freer to speak out than in the suddenly repressed and oppressive America. It is Boyle's recognition of the irony of this situation and her commitment to the values of the democratic country of her heritage that compel her to return to America, against the wishes and better judgment of her friends, to "speak out with those of the other America clearly and loudly enough so that even Europe will hear" (98). Her emphatic defense of American individual freedom coupled with her realization that such defense was not immediately forthcoming leads her to establish a central metaphor that recurs in her essays for the next several decades: the writer's "voice" and the related need for "speaking out."

In "A Declaration for 1955" (1955), she turns her passion for commitment into a clarion call for all writers in America, for democracy demands "that one take part in it" (63). Wiser and more determined in 1955 than she had been earlier, Boyle recognizes the enormity of McCarthyism's threat, whether in the voice of McCarthy himself or in the apathy of those afraid to speak, and she calls for the Artist to live up to his or her moral responsibility for changing the world. Recalling that Thomas Mann—who would appear in several of her post-World War II essays—placed the moral and ethical responsibility for any given age on its writers, she urges the Artist to become crusader: "The transforming of the contemporary scene is what I now ask of all American writers" (65).

By 1964, McCarthy had long been discredited, but the silence he engendered was still deafening. For Boyle it was no longer sufficient for just the Artist to speak out, but the young must be given the courage and the insight to do so as well. Boyle writes to teachers of writing in the NEA Journal (1964) that learning "how to release reluctant students to speech" must be a major consideration for them (86). In a later essay, "The Long Walk at San Francisco State" (1970), Boyle identifies a writer/teacher/Artist who has done just that—Sonia Sanchez, who urged the students in her creative writing class to use their own language to describe their own worlds, to write "poetry that would have meaning to others in their community, and that is probably one of the things that good writing does" (83). Inherent in the essays of this period is a growing awareness on Boyle's part that those who have traditionally remained silent or been rendered voiceless must be empowered to speak for themselves and for their counterparts. The writers of this period whom she praises are those who have with courage and clarity addressed the issues of contemporary life: James Baldwin, Edward Dahlberg, Dylan Thomas, Emanuel Carnevali, and others.

In many ways these essays, particularly the later ones with their heavy emphasis on socio/political action and concern for justice, complete a circle, uniting the Boyle of the activist late twentieth century with the young Boyle of the 1920s. She herself makes this connection in "The Triumph of Principles" (1972) in which she reminds us, "I remember the days in Paris when we who were writers or painters or composers wrote pamphlets and distributed them in the streets and cafés. I remember when we signed manifestos and read them aloud on street corners, following without any humility whatsoever in the traditions of Pascal, Voltaire, Chateaubriand, Victor Hugo, Zola, so that the world would know exactly where we stood, for we considered ourselves a portion of the contemporary conscience, and we had no pity on the compromiser or the poor in spirit of our time" (190).

The young Boyle wanted writers to express with accuracy and passion the truth that is around them. The mature Boyle can no longer satisfy herself with accurate portrayals of the past or with language to capture the present. She wants nothing less than to spark the voices that will shape the future, and those with the courage to do so must write, must produce a language and a forum for those who find themselves without political power or presence. For herself and with great faith in the integrity of the Artist, Boyle can say with conviction, "It is a good day when the writers speak out loudly and clearly" (191).

Note

1. Kay Boyle, *Words That Must Somehow Be Said: Selected Essays of Kay Boyle, 1927–1984,* ed. and with an introduction by Elizabeth S. Bell (San Francisco: North Point Press, 1985). All references to the essays in this collection will appear parenthetically in the text.

Introduction to the 1989 reprint
of *Death of a Man*

BURTON HATLEN

When Kay Boyle's *Death of a Man* was first published in 1936, most reviewers read the novel as expressing pro-Nazi sympathies. Mark Van Doren, writing in *The Nation,* said that the book tries to "hypnotize the reader into a state of what may be called mystical fascism." In *The New Republic,* Otis Ferguson characterized "Miss Boyle's case for the Nazi spirit" as an instance of "special pleading." As Ferguson read the novel, "Those who plot in the wine cellars and keep the swastikas burning on the mountains at night are the outstanding characters; the author's sympathy and understanding are theirs." The *Times Literary Supplement* spoke of "the glamour which Miss Boyle casts over the National Socialist movement," and the anonymous reviewer in *Time* described the novel as a "Nazi idyll."

This array of reviewer's comments must startle anyone who knows anything about Boyle's life, for her politics have been consistently Left. Boyle's political awareness developed early: her mother and grandmother were both active in the women's rights movement. In one of her inter-chapters in *Being Geniuses Together,* Boyle describes how the Sacco-Vanzetti case dramatized for her the oppressive structure of American society. During World War II, Boyle wrote two *Saturday Evening Post* serials and many other works designed to bolster American morale in the struggle against Nazism, and after the war she published two novels which warned against the danger of a lingering Fascism in Europe (*The Seagull on the Step*) and in American culture itself (*Generation without Farewell*). In the 1950s Boyle was blacklisted for her presumed "Communist" sympathies, and in the 1960s she became an important figure in the civil rights and anti-war protest movements. Given this political record, it is hard to imagine Boyle writing a pro-Nazi novel.

Is it possible that during the 1930s Boyle persuaded herself that Nazism represented a "radical" political movement? Possible, but hardly likely. It

Reprinted from *Death of a Man* (New York: New Directions, 1989): v–xii, with the permission of the author.

seems more likely that the reviewers quoted above were wrong, when they read the novel as advocating the Nazi cause. In the end, I believe, the novel does make a judgment of the Nazi movement—and a negative judgment, too. But even more important, Boyle never makes the mistake of assuming that a human being can be summed up under a single rubric, such as "Nazi"; and the early reviewers, I would suggest, misread the sympathetic under-standing which the novelist extends to some of her Nazi characters as an indi-cation of a sympathy for Nazism itself.

Further, *Death of a Man* is less interested in the virtues and vices of Nazism as such than it is in the effects of the will to power on the lives of human beings, and especially on the relations between men and women. In this respect, *Death of a Man* represents a natural extension of the themes of Boyle's previous novels, all of which were born out of a recognition that power and sexuality are intertwined. *Plagued by the Nightingale* explores the tyrannies of nation, culture, and family, which distort and finally destroy the love between a French man and an American woman. The portrait of Eve Raeburn, the Ethel Moorhead character in *Year Before Last,* is a memorable study of maternal-erotic possessiveness; the portrait of Sorrel, the Raymond Duncan character in *My Next Bride,* provides an equally subtle analysis of the male will to control; and *Gentlemen, I Address You Privately* offers a courageous explo-ration of the power dynamics of a same-gender erotic relationship. So, too, I suggest, *Death of a Man* explores the ways in which the personal becomes political and the political becomes personal, as Boyle elucidates what might be called the sexual politics of Nazism, a movement which the novel sees as an extreme manifestation of what current feminist theory calls "patriarchy."

If many early readers saw *Death of a Man* as a pro-Nazi novel, one pri-mary reason is that the central male character, Dr. Prochaska, is an undeni-ably sympathetic character, and his commitment to the Nazi movement inclines us to see that movement in a positive light. In the opening chapters, Boyle develops a contrast between the vigorous, athletic Prochaska, who climbs about the Austrian Alps with absolute confidence, and the limp, cyni-cal, effete Englishman whom Pendennis, the female protagonist, has recently married. Further, Prochaska is characterized not only by animal magnetism but by artistic sensitivity; for example, he speaks of Mozart with warm admi-ration. We also learn that Prochaska's warmth and charm have won him the devotion of the nuns with whom he works and the children he cares for. A lean, athletic Nazi, even a Nazi who loves Mozart—this we might have expected. But a Nazi who can charm a lay sister and who romps with a three-year-old diphtheria victim through a hospital ward—this comes as a surprise. Boyle refuses to let us hate this man. And if we cannot hate Prochaska, how can we hate the movement to which he has dedicated his life?

To place Prochaska's politics in perspective, we should also recognize that in the Austria of this novel there were only two political alternatives:

Hitler or Dollfuss. And we must also recognize that Dollfuss's pro-Mussolini regime represented, not an alternative to Fascism, but simply another kind of Fascism. We see in the novel no Left-wing or even Centrist option; and indeed there were no such alternatives in the Austria of the mid-1930s, for in 1934 the Dollfuss government had effectively destroyed the Left opposition in a military assault on the working class district in Vienna. (This attack is briefly mentioned in Boyle's novel.) Given the choice between Hitler and Dollfuss, we can understand Prochaska's preference for Hitler. For as the novel makes clear, the economic situation in Austria was desperate, and the Nazis promised both bread and social change. In contrast, the Dollfuss government represented only a final attempt of the Austrian aristocracy to retain its privileges.

Prochaska is not the only Nazi that we meet in *Death of a Man*. In particular, we see a good bit of Praxlmann, the local party boss. Praxlmann is at times a ludicrous figure, as when he laments the destruction of his beergarden by a bomb thrown into the yard of a neighboring, anti-Nazi newspaper, and then tossed over the wall into the beer-garden by an alert nightwatchman. But more often Praxlmann is a frightening presence. Boyle describes his "eye" as "shrewd and vicious," and his general demeanor as "violent and strong." Praxlmann's brutality is particularly apparent in his treatment of the women in his life: his wife, his daughter Cilli, and his wife's niece Hella. Praxlmann demands absolute obedience not only from family but also from the party faithful, including Prochaska. A will to power, and especially a will to power over women—these are, Boyle's portrait of Praxlmann thus suggests, another characteristic of the Nazi movement. And ultimately this will to power incarnates itself in the figure of the patriarch, who treats both real daughters and spiritual sons like Prochaska as so many possessions.

To the oppressively masculine world of the Praxlmann *Gasthaus*, Boyle opposes the beautifully sketched world of the *Infektionhaus*, the hospital for contagious diseases where Prochaska works. The *Infektionhaus* is a world of women and children, for Prochaska himself is apparently the only adult male who enters this region. Boyle begins her description of the *Infektionhaus* with a resonant image of birds flying in the open window and through the children's ward. The birds evoke a wild, untrammeled life which moves through the hospital but is never captured by the institutional structure. This world of freedom and spontaneity is available at a terrible price: only the diseased are allowed to enter. But, with a twist that may owe something to Mann's *The Magic Mountain,* Boyle suggests that perhaps only women and children, and only the sick among them at that, are able to break the shackles of social convention long enough to experience, even momentarily, the wild, free life within them.

When we look at Prochaska through the lens of the woman-centered world of the hospital, he becomes a more ambiguous figure than he may first seem. He moves through the hospital as an alien presence, with "a look of hot-eyed resolution, singularly incongruous in this apparently aimless and langourously drifting tide of pain." "All his life," we learn, Prochaska "had been fearful of becoming as soft as other people were," and in the hospital he can daily demonstrate that he is not "soft." The language here suggests another, darker side to our Nazi hero. Prochaska, his vigor and charm notwithstanding, has been so blinded by his male ego and his political obsession that his human responses have been suppressed. Prochaska's character is the product of a particular society and a particular social moment, both of which have taught him to aspire toward a "manly" self-confidence which is simultaneously energizing and crippling, since it causes him to resist the self-surrender which love demands. In the course of the novel, we will watch how the power of love works upon Prochaska, to draw out his human potential. But this transformation remains only partial, and at the crucial moment he is unable to make a total commitment to love.

Against the figure of Prochaska, Boyle plays off her female protagonist, Pendennis, who is also both liberated and crippled by the culture which has shaped her. Pendennis is a late variation on the James/Fitzgerald theme of "the American girl abroad." Like earlier versions of the American girl, Pendennis is a fiercely independent person. Tearing up a letter from her father, she says, "That's what I do with orders! Every one I've ever had in my life, that's what happened to it and he ought to know it by this time." But Pendennis, unlike earlier versions of the American girl, is no innocent: rather she is flamboyantly erotic—and flamboyantly neurotic. As soon as she meets Prochaska, she directs erotic signals at him, totally ignoring her new husband. That there is something predatory about her is also clear during this first meeting, in the course of which Prochaska has a momentary vision of Pendennis as "a hard, bitter, cold-eyed old woman, a tight fisted witch, unasking and ungiving."

The reasons for Pendennis's neurotic behavior are also clear in the novel: she too, even more dramatically than Prochaska, is a victim of patriarchy. Pendennis's life has been haunted by her father, who never appears in the novel, but who sends her periodic letters that drive her into wild rages or panicked flights. Like Prochaska's spiritual father, Praxlmann, Pendennis's father embodies "violence and strength," a will to master: "He used to make me do everything I didn't want to do. That's why he stays put together when everyone else falls in pieces." Pendennis has deeply identified with her father. "When I'm fifty," she tells Prochaska, "I'll look like him." And a little later, she says, "My father made a man of me."

Pendennis's impulse to identify with her father suggests that her culture has given her no usable models of how to live as a woman. The status of women in American society is established most forcefully in an extended flashback, in which Pendennis tells Prochaska about her twin brother Gerald, whose attempt to emulate his father's hard masculinity caused the death of their mother. This story, perhaps the most powerful passage in the novel, tells

us all we need to know about the fate of women within the American version
of patriarchy. Pendennis, because of her upbringing, is caught between a
model of the female as hapless victim and a model of the male as manipulator
and oppressor. In the absence of usable female role models, Pendennis lives by
pure whim, but these random impulses can only briefly conceal the vacuum
where her self should be. At several points in the novel Pendennis thinks of
herself as "nobody, nothing," and it is her American upbringing which has
taught her to see herself as "nothing."

In the encounter of Prochaska and Pendennis we are witnessing, Boyle
suggests, a meeting between Old World and New, Europe and America. Prochaska has been born in a place where every object tells him he is "something
really of value, of quality, either to his family or to history or to himself." In
contrast, nothing tells Pendennis who she is; or perhaps everything around
her tells her she is nothing. But despite the difference between the sense of
order and tradition which controls Prochaska's behavior and the wild struggle
of wills which characterizes Pendennis's America, both cultures represent
equally tyrannical forms of patriarchy. Violent, strong fathers attempt to rule
the destinies of both these young people. And in falling in love, both are
rebelling against their fathers. The result is a clear antithesis: patriarchy versus sexual love.

Pendennis fully recognizes the implications of her love for Prochaska.
She has no hesitation about repudiating her family and all it represents in an
attempt to create a new world of love. But Prochaska cannot bring himself to
reject so quickly his "father" Praxlmann, or his abstract love of "Austria."
Because his feelings for Pendennis run counter to his political commitments,
Prochaska experiences his love for her as an implacable destiny. When Pendennis offers herself to him, Prochaska feels, in language that echoes the
idiom of D. H. Lawrence, a "keen and powerful tide of blissful torment
[sweep] through his blood." A loss of will, an ecstatic melting-away of the
self: such is the form which love takes, at least for people like Prochaska,
obsessed as he is with issues of power and control.

Granted, the opposition between political commitment and love is not
absolute, for both can cause a sense of ecstasy. Prochaska and Pendennis share
a moment of political ecstasy, as they watch their swastika bonfire blaze in the
night. But Pendennis surrenders to the quasi-erotic appeal of Nazism only for
a moment, and her critique of this kind of ecstasy becomes Boyle's critique of
it too. Even before she and Prochaska descend from the mountain, Pendennis
begins to recognize that the moment of ecstasy she experienced while lighting the bonfire has been purchased at the price of her selfhood. The lovers, in
flight from the Austrian police, take refuge in a mountain cabin. There Pendennis looks at herself in a mirror and thinks to herself, "I'm nothing,
nobody. . . . I am whichever way he's going. I'm not even me." And as soon as
the lovers descend the mountain, Pendennis begins to defend herself against
this threatened annihilation, by challenging Prochaska to choose between her

and the party. Both erotic and political ecstasy may entail a loss of rational control, but Pendennis knows the difference between the two, and she knows that one nourishes the self while the other destroys it.

Prochaska is at first unwilling to make the choice which Pendennis demands of him, and as a result he loses her. Nevertheless, he too has a moment of recognition. The occasion is a trip into the mountains to meet a courier from Germany, who is carrying money and messages for the Austrian Nazis. The courier launches into an ecstatic description of Hitler's speech on the 1934 purge of the Brownshirt faction in the German Nazi party. Suddenly, Prochaska finds himself repelled by all this frenzy, which seems to him, as he looks about at the inhuman serenity of his beloved mountains, merely silly. The young courier is, Prochaska realizes, "drunk, stupefied on the thought of death and the rapture of his own fearlessness to meet it." But Prochaska's recognition of the death-wish in Nazism comes too late to allow him to break the chains of history. He finally opts for Pendennis over the party, but his faith in her proves too weak. When he cannot find Pendennis in Vienna, he decides that she is, after all, merely a selfish, faithless human being. So Prochaska gives up the search, and in the final pages of the novel the trains carrying the two ex-lovers pass (literally) in the night.

Death of a Man seems to me a remarkably prescient and courageous novel. The courage here lies in Boyle's willingness to go beyond stereotypes of gender, nationality, and politics, in creating a male character who is both erotically attractive *and* deeply political, and who is erotically attractive for the very qualities—physical vigor, passionate devotion to a cause, a capacity for ecstatic self-surrender—which have led him to commit himself to the Nazi movement. In Pendennis, Boyle has created a female character who is, in her alienation from her own culture and her uncertainty as to her identity, deeply neurotic, but whose very neuroses dramatize for us the destructive consequences of specifically American forms of patriarchy. (After World War II, Boyle would explore this theme at much greater length in *Generation without Farewell*.) In flight from the sense of herself as "nothing," Pendennis seizes upon the Nazi doctor, who at least "believes in something." Her love is thus itself twisted, neurotic. Conversely, Prochaska is the product of a culture which equates eros with weakness, and so he is unable to make the final commitment to Pendennis that might have allowed this love to survive.

Nevertheless, the love between them allows Pendennis to glimpse an alternative to "nothing," while it also liberates Prochaska to recognize the death-frenzy within Nazism. As this dialectic works itself out, we come to an understanding of the destructive effects of patriarchy upon both these young people. Their struggle to escape the patriarchal control exercised over them by the Fathers (Praxlmann, Pendennis's father) and by the patriarchal values within their own minds ends, finally, in ironic confusion. Nevertheless, their willingness to commit themselves to this struggle affirms the possibility of love, and both lovers are irreversibly changed by this experience. As read from the feminist perspective which I have here proposed, *Death of a Man* seems—despite the complaints of early reviewers, who often saw the book as a collection of lyric fragments—an integrated work of art, in which every detail works toward a subtle, complex effect. Fifty years after its initial publication, *Death of a Man* deserves a new generation of readers, both for the delicacy of its arts and the power of its political and psychological insights.

Revolution, the Woman, and the Word: Kay Boyle

Suzanne Clark

Women's experimental writing had an especially problematic relationship to modernist experiments with poetic language because the women were part of the culture of modernism, representing attachments to everyday life that were not literary. Even though it may now seem that modernist men and women were inventing a kind of *écriture féminine,* challenging paternal conventions by a maternal authority, the men and women of modernism repressed the specific innovations of women writers because they denied these feminine connections. Kay Boyle's early work put the old categories into motion and marked out a new literary space of intense descriptive prose. Yet her impact on literary history has not seemed so powerful as her writing would warrant. In 1928, Boyle signed the manifesto for *transition* calling for "The Revolution of the Poetic Word."[1] Other signers included Hart Crane, Harry and Caresse Crosby, and Eugene Jolas. The "Proclamation" asserted, among other things, that "the literary creator has the right to disintegrate the primal matter of words" and that "we are not concerned with the propagation of sociological ideas except to emancipate the creative elements from the present ideology."

It must be admitted that Boyle's rewriting of the new word was a different matter from the poetics of someone such as Hart Crane, a difference she in fact had signaled herself in a critique of his obsession with the primacy of words, in "Mr. Crane and His Grandmother."[2] Although she shows herself to be in the tradition of Baudelaire and Rimbaud as well, Boyle prefers the American renewals of William Carlos Williams and Marianne Moore. Her innovations in prose style qualify her as a revolutionary of lyric language.[3] In her early works, such as "Episode in the Life of an Ancestor," "Wedding Day," or "On the Run," she swerves her narratives into a language of illumination and intensity that disorders story sequence and the familiar forms of remembering.[4] She experiments in a way that recalls the hallucinatory surrealism of

Reprinted from *Sentimental Modernism: Women Writers and the Revolution of the Word* (Bloomington: Indiana University Press, 1991): 127–54, with the permission of the author.

Rimbaud's prose and fulfills the aspiration of the poetic revolution for "the projection of a metamorphosis of reality." But what does this powerful disintegration of conventional writing have to do with writing as a woman?

The strong old forms of the sentimental novel were part of what this modernist poetics—and she too—rejected. And yet, for the modernists, the cultural image of women and writing was deeply involved with that past. A shattering of language seemed to be at odds with writing like a woman, and challenging the image of woman seemed itself feminist and sentimental. Like other modernist women who felt they had to separate themselves from that conventional past, Boyle herself has taken pains to dissociate her work from the older tradition of women's writing and from the politics of feminism. Nevertheless, her reworking of the relationship between time and place, narration and description, also makes the connection between the time of poetic revolution and the place of the woman. I am going to suggest that Boyle shows us how the transition was made, from a representation of woman as the author of conventional romance to the function of woman as a disruptive, disturbing—and so revolutionary—difference in the rhetoric of fiction.

Julia Kristeva, herself a woman who has complicated relationships with revolution and women's writing, may help us to see how time operates in Boyle's work. In her essay "Women's Time," Kristeva redefined Nietzsche's idea of monumental or mythic time, a kind of temporality that is left out of rational discursive history.[5] Kristeva defines "women's time" as "repetition" and "eternity," in contrast with the linear movements of history. Women's time is characterized by

> the eternal recurrence of a biological rhythm which conforms to that of nature and imposes a temporality whose sterotyping may shock, but whose regularity and unison with what is experienced as extrasubjective time, cosmic time, occasion vertiginous visions and unnameable jouissance. (191)

If the order of production defines the time of history, it is the order of reproduction which seems to define this other kind of time, time which is so bound to the monumental, and the regional, that it is almost a kind of space. The cyclic and monumental forms of time associated with female subjectivity are far from the linear times of progress and project. But we must proceed very carefully, with Kristeva as with Boyle, for it would be wrong to suggest that either of them advocates a splitting away of a woman's order from human history.

In her *Revolution in Poetic Language*, when Kristeva associates certain innovations in avant-garde poetics inaugurated by writers in the tradition after Mallarmé with a breaking open of the possibilities of language, she is ambiguous about how women writers might participate in that fracturing.[6] If language itself oppresses, the language itself must be broken in order that marginal subjects, such as women, may be able to speak. And the woman, as marginal subject, is in a position of privilege to do this. But Kristeva's theoretical practice, like Boyle's prose, has been at odds with the discourse of feminism. Let us be careful not to see her antifeminism or Boyle's as simply old-fashioned modernism (let the paradoxical vocabulary resonate for us), for it is attached to some of the most unsettling and promising aspects of modernist experiments with subjectivity.

Boyle, in her practice, resists the binary coding of opposites which would make clear gendered structures for her stories, working instead at multiple and complex borders. Her early work practices this resistance to extremism in the midst of the 1920s modernist extremism about gender. She defies the ideological either/or which would either deny the existence of gender difference in the name of equality or, in a move which Catharine Stimpson calls the "modern counterreformation in support of patriarchal law," claim gender difference, as D. H. Lawrence does, for example, to be the final truth.[7]

If Boyle refuses to write polemically, in behalf of an alternative woman's reality, she also refuses to omit gendered, female elements from her writing. Working within a culture of gendered extremism, she softly moves to put the contradictions into motion. The word *soft* has a certain significance; in an age which favored the tough over the tender, Boyle uses it so frequently it is almost a stylistic marker. A certain radical fluidity characterizes the forward movement of her narration. Hers is not a strikingly avant-garde text, not even at its most experimental, in the sense that such a text by its mode of presentation challenges the reader's ability to read, or breaks flagrantly with the bourgeois norms of realistic prose. But she makes visible the movement of what is left unspoken by the controlling enigmas of realism. So the luminous otherness of her work might well pass unremarked, since it is "soft," since it is neither an embrace nor a refusal of modernism's radical gendered Other.

Boyle's work resists certain categories, traps of ideology, and this includes the categorical oppositions of male and female. It would be too easy to imagine that time could be divided and separated into the two orders: the male order of linear plots, the female order of cycle and reproduction. But, as Julia Kristeva has argued, women's time cannot escape history, and the question for women today is, "What can be our place in the symbolic contract?"[8] Given that our language sacrifices the specific moment as it sacrifices the individual's bodied, material relations to others, Boyle like Kristeva is interested in an aesthetic practice which would make the excluded felt and known. The attention to structures based on linear time and productivity has left us separated from reproduction, from the maternal, from the moral and ethical representations once provided by religion—that is, from cyclical and monumental forms of time. Radical feminists of the seventies, recognizing this, began to talk about a separate female utopia, as if women's time and space could be wholly separated and alternative to the linear forms which organize modern culture. Language does not bridge the gap between individuals because they are identical or identically subjected, inscribed within it, but makes the connection across difference, metaphorically.

II

Kay Boyle's work might be thought of as revolutionary, then, not only because of the shattering of syntax which connects her experimental writing to the avant-garde. She makes the metaphorical connection between individuals, across difference. Her writing subverts the male plot, linear time, by a recursive, anaphoric temporality. And perceptions flow with the voice of the speaker across the boundaries of subject-object, rewriting the romantic identifications with exterior images which Ruskin criticized as the "pathetic fallacy." Boyle uses the fluidity of poetic forms to wash out the one-track temporality of male discourse and to undermine the singularity of gender ideology by a multiple sympathy. She unsettles the stabilities of identity. Women's time enters into history, making it less singular, undoing its regularities.

Three of her early stories will serve as examples of how Boyle's writing might participate in such a project. What kind of narrative time is operating in the story called "Episode in the Life of an Ancestor"? What kind of story is an "episode"? Is it singular or plural? A kind of turning point, or a repeated event?

In the story, a young woman defies her father's conventional desires for her to act like a submissive woman. The masterful way she treats their horses is like the mastery she exercises over her father and a would-be suitor, the schoolmaster. But the conflict between the father and daughter is framed by the long view of history. This is the story of an ancestor, very close to that of Boyle's own grandmother as a young woman.[9] The whole shimmers ambiguously between the backward long vision of memory and the immediacy of a present moment: "But at a time when the Indian fires made a wall that blossomed and withered at night on three sides of the sky, this grandmother was known as one of the best horsewomen in Kansas" (17–18).

The point of view also shifts to produce discontinuities in the linear structure of the plot. It is her father's egoistic will to dominate which provides the conflict in the story: "Her father was proud of the feminine ways there were in her. . . . It was no pride to him to hear [her voice] turned hard and thin in her mouth to quiet a horse's ears when some fright had set them to fluttering on the beak of its head" (17). The daughter/grandmother, however, is not drawn into the conflict. Her perceptions involve the repeated, habitual, physical world, and her mode is exclamatory, even joyful: "What a feast of splatters when she would come out from a long time in the kitchen and walk in upon the beasts who were stamping and sick with impatience for her in the barn" (19). From the daughter's point of view, sympathy is a strong recognition of difference, and her "way with horses" is mastery without egotism. Her point of view flows into the animal sensations of the horse:

> This was tame idle sport, suited to ladies, this romping in the milkweed cotton across the miles of pie-crust. Suddenly he felt this anger in the grandmother's knees that caught and swung him about in the wind. Without any regard for him at all, so that he was in a quiver of admiration and love for her, she jerked him up and back, rearing his wild head high, his front hoofs left clawing at the space that yapped under them. (23)

The wildness of the horse seems to represent some kind of primeval vigor and sexuality that might remind us of D. H. Lawrence. It is, however, an energy both shared and directed by the woman. Against this energy, the father's will appears as unreal imaginings: he longs for "the streams of gentleness and love that cooled the blood of true women" (18). He doesn't know what is going on inside her or outside her. As he sees it, she goes off into the unknown for her ride into a night "black as a pocket." The ironic folds in the fabric of their relationship turn about the schoolmaster, a "quiet enough thought" by comparison to the woman and the horses until the father imagines him in the sexualized landscape of her midnight ride. Then his rage produces a paranoid close-up of the schoolmaster's face in his mind's eye—the detail of hairs and pores—in a failure of sympathy which wildly reverses itself again at the end with his unspoken cry: "What have you done with the schoolmaster?" (14). The father's fantasies are chairbound and disconnected from life. In the end, he cannot even put them into words.

The grandmother has hot blood, a heat that spreads and permeates the vocabulary of the story in a membranous action. The woman is woven into the fabric of the moment as she is into the words of the text, part of the whole cloth of experience. This displacement of human energy onto the surrounding objects of perception makes the descriptions seem luminous, surreal—not imaginary but strongly imagined. The grandmother's intensity spreads into the landscape with its contrasts of soft and hard, white and red, domestic flax and wild fire: "soft white flowering goldenrod," "Indian fires burning hard and bright as peonies" (20). The deep valleys and gulfs and the blossoming prairies form a topology of pocketing and hollows. The father registers how the daughter is a very figure of thereness: "When she came into the room she was there in front of him in the same way that the roses on the floor were woven straight across the rug" (23). He, on the other hand, is the very figure of absence, speechless, longing nostalgically for someone "of his own time to talk to" (23). On the recommendation, apparently, of the schoolmaster, the woman has been reading the passage from *Paradise Lost* about the creation of Eve. Milton's lines expose Boyle's poetic figure, the mutuality of flesh and landscape, and the spousal emotion. But this revelation of poetic influence offends the father, perhaps as much as the sexuality implied in the passage.

Like Milton, her father takes an accusatory stance toward the woman's sexuality. However, the daughter's refusal to be feminine his way, "the cooking and the sewing ways that would be a comfort to him" (20), undoes his ego-centered plot, an undoing which opens possibilities for the woman to be heroic in more multiple ways. Instead of a single hero dominating a single plot in time, Boyle produces the double figure of the daughter grandmother and a narrative which circles back from a lifetime to an episode. Instead of a hero who would make the woman over in his own image she produces a heroine who moves through mastery—of the horses, the schoolmaster, even her father—to a sympathy which is not identification with a male voice. The story is contained by long-distance temporality, as if written on a tapestry, a legendary mode which mimics the male heroic modes only to name them "episode." Female desire reshapes the forms of narrative as well as the forms of description: the woman is a hero who changes the forms of the heroic.

But in "Wedding Day," Boyle does not shrink from showing us female power of a less attractive kind, allied with the bourgeois projects of family and possessions, and the literary mode of "realistic" representation. In this story, it is the mother who works to dominate, through organizing the details of the daughter's wedding day which will initiate her all-too-energetic children, the too-loving brother and sister, into the empty exchanges of proper social relations. The wedding will initiate—and separate—them. It is the mother who makes the violent cut that institutes order—as if she were founding the very system of culture by preventing the incest of brother and sister—but the gesture is also absurd and grotesque. So it finds its image in the "roast of beef" that "made them kin again" as "she sliced the thin scarlet ribbons of it into the platter" (26).

Not that the mother has, exactly, forced this marriage; she says it was not her idea, and her son defends his sister's choice—whose choice it was is confused. The issue is more primitive; the mother's negativity is on the side of the cut, the ceremonial structure, against any outbursts of trouble or love. She opposes her son with a prayer for "dignity," but they find her, returning from a last excursion together, on her knees tying "white satin bows under the chins of the potted plants" (28).

She must maintain the objects of family life as intact mirrors—so it is that she counts the wedding "a real success, . . . a *real* success" when "no glass had yet been broken." Of course, it is the bride at the wedding who is "broken," but that happens beyond the precincts of the "real" which the mother so carefully maintains. Thus, from the point of view of the mother, the story has a happy ending; if she were the author of it, the incestuous energy of the brother and sister's love would be repressed.

Just as the brother and sister threaten the social order and its objects with their desire, the descriptive intensity of Boyle's style violates the decorum of the ceremony with a contradiction and violence that threatens to flood out the containing devices of concrete objects. What are these images doing at a wedding?

The red carpet was to "spurt like a hemorrhage." "No one paid any attention" to the wedding cake, "with its beard lying white as hoar frost on its bosom." What is this negativity? There is the "thunderous NO" of the mother, who refuses to give the copper pans to her daughter as the spirit of a family inheritance might suggest. The mother must keep the pans orderly and unused, the "pride of the kitchen," "six bulls—eyes reflecting her thin face." She wishes, indeed, for the orderly household objects to serve as mirrors for the son and daughter as well, representations of the selves she would have them take on.

The young people challenge the civilizing project. These two are Nietzschean creatures, with "yellow manes," "shaggy as lions," "like another race." Like a refrain, the brother keeps repeating, "It isn't too late." But what else might they do except enter into the schemes laid out for them? Something, this story suggests, as it exceeds and overwhelms the bourgeois "real" of the mother: "in their young days they should have been saddled and strapped with necessity so that they could not have escaped. . . . With their yellow heads back they were stamping a new trail, but in such ignorance, for they had no idea of it" (27).

The necessity of youth, of freedom, of a new race encounters the violence of April, like Eliot's April the "cruelest month," bringing the death, here, of childhood. "Here then was April holding them up, stabbing their hearts with hawthorne, scalping them with a flexible blade of wind" (26). "Over them was the sky set like a tomb, the strange unearthly sky that might at any moment crack into spring" (28). The brother and sister take a ride in a boat together. If the boat ride were solitary, it would be an easy allegory; the wedding would represent the shackling of the poetic spirit. However, they are two; what is between them we are less likely to see as a visitation of the romantic imagination than as incestuous desire. Neither they nor we know if they should act on what they feel. "And who was there to tell them, for the trees they had come to in the woods gave them no sign" (27).

The signs of the story produce not a judgment about how the plot should have gone but a negativity that opens up the forms of the wedding and the story to something else, something which like the sister and brother does not wholly fit in the bourgeois "real," something full of energy, destructive and exuberant. At the end the daughter's "feet were fleeing in a hundred ways throughout the rooms, . . . like white butterflies escaping by a miracle the destructive feet of whatever partner held her in his arms" (29). The wedding, far from locking her exclusively to one person, has propelled her into an anonymity of social exchange. The brother's antagonism scatters the calling cards around the rooms. An exotic, almost romantic, energy inhabits the mother's performance as she dances, undermining her decorum, and destroying the very syntax of the sentence: "Over the Oriental prayer rugs, through the Persia forests of hemp, away and away" (30).

In "Wedding Day," Boyle reveals the hidden violence of the social contract and releases the energy of exposure to work on the forms of prose. At the same time, she does not wholly cast the mother as executioner, the daughter as victim. Rather, she exposes the sacrificial violence of the wedding itself, and the relentless secularity of its bourgeois forms. Boyle resists a "women's writing" which would trap her in an oppositional category identified with the bourgeoisie; she neither endorses nor combats but rather eludes capture in the mother's forms.

Boyle's elusiveness produces an unsettling. She is always in favor of something which illuminates the landscape with significance—call it love, something which bends the narrative plot away from its resolutions, which turns the eye inescapably to the detail, apparently decorative, but now repeating anaphorically the interestedness of the subject who writes. These are stories not about isolated selves but about the mutual imbrications of relationships among people, and so they do not disguise the complexity of perspectives which our feelings for each other are likely to generate.

Even a story as purely focused as "On the Run" shows the contrary motions of resolution coming up against one another and that language of significance breaking closures, keeping the time itself open. The situation is close to autobiography: two lovers, like Boyle herself with Ernest Walsh, are wandering across the south of Europe, unable to find a place for the sick man to rest—thrown out of hotels because he is dying. In "On the Run," memory is left permeable—fragile, undecided, unpunctuated, determined only by the universal timelessness of death that thus seems everywhere. David Daiches says that Boyle's stories are like parables, with "a special kind of permanence" about them.[10] In our culture, this sense of permanence may be identified with women's time, appearing as a contrary narrative that works across the linear, historical plot. This is especially visible in "On the Run," where the history is known, and the story exists nevertheless not in a past but in a recurring present, like a parable.

The young couple must deal with a woman who orders them to leave rather than helping them. It is not just a person but social convention itself which opposes them. The proprietress of the hotel is, in fact, in mourning. She seems to know all about death:

> Bereaved in the full sallow of her cheeks bereaved and the tombstones rising politely polished with discreet sorrow bereaved and remembered with bubbles of jet frosted on her bosoms and mourned under waves of hemmed watered crepe. I have mourned people for years and years this is the way it is done. (105)

She seems also to possess a kind of knowledge about religious conventions of sacrifice: there was her "rosary hanging like false teeth," and "the Christ bled with artistry" on her crucifix. But her knowledge has all been projected onto the objects, reduced and transformed to fetishes. So what she says is: "Your husband cannot die here. . . . we are not prepared for death" (106). Here is the terrible irony, that the sick man must keep on going. Like the mother in "Wedding Day," the proprietress does not seem to know what women are supposed to hold in custody: the value of relationship, the cycles of time, of the generations, of biological time. And like the mother, she has translated all of it into the social symbolic.

Thus women's time must return through the narrative of the story. Boyle's writing stops the forward pressing of historical time, like the train stopped at "Saint-Andre-les-Alpes," and sidetracks it into sensuous, loaded detail: "As the train stopped a soft pink tide of pigs rose out of the station-yard and ran in under the wheels of the wagon. The crest of little alps was burning across the roofs of the town, with the dry crumbling linger of the church lifted and the sky gaping white and hot upon decay" (103). She strips the sick man's words of their history to let them fly out as if prophetic, repeated, stripping them even of punctuation: "Get her out of here he said I am going to cough Christ is this where the death will get me take the cigaret and when I cough walk arouna the room and sing or something so they won't hear me" (104). There is no period after his words.

The conflict with the proprietress does not appear as a single plot with a conclusion but as the anaphoric structure of enduring betrayal. The message of betrayal is repeated three times, each introduced by the phrase "The bonne came back to say." It is a sacramental structure. At the end, too, the man's words seem to escape the symbolic conventions of the story and sound in the mind like stream of consciousness, recurring. This is anamnesis, a resurrection of the past and not just memory: "Keep on keep on keep on he said maybe I'm going to bleed" (107). Such a resurrection takes place in the process of a narrative dialectic between the linear time of history that is past and the personal time of remembrance, anamnesis. Anamnesis is the form of recollection which Plato associated with eros—and with access to eternal truth. It is the word for the "remembrance" of Christian communion. And it is the unforgetting of the past which Freud advocated, the healing memory of pain which psychoanalysis could effect. This time which Boyle produces is associated, as well, with what Julia Kristeva calls "women's time."

This resurrection—and not just recollection—of a moment of pain and love inserts difference into the history. The position of difference which we may associate with women's time here is different from the polarized opposition which some of Boyle's characters, like the mother and the proprietress, seem to inhabit. This alternate version of narrative, with its descriptive intensity overwhelming the forward movement of plot, opens language up to the surreal, the hallucinatory. Narrative time gives way to descriptive space.

The energy is not in the story, or the forward movement of plot, but rather in the metaphorical connections among people and places—in relationship. Even though these connections shift and develop through time, so that it looks as though there is an elaboration of plot, the motive force of the story is not erotic in the masculine mode. That is, the displacement of desire does not take the form of an adventure. The energy here is moral, even if the situations are unconventional.

Let us look a little more closely at this descriptive language which so many of Boyle's readers have noted—which Margaret Atwood cites as one of her most striking attributes.[11] Sandra Whipple Spanier associates it on the one hand with a Joycean project and on the other with the romantic perspective in Boyle: she "depicts the external world as a reflection or projection of the perceiver's consciousness."[12] Like Joyce, Boyle writes a "lyric" novel, which decenters the lyric subjectivity, the image of an ego. Boyle opens language to the pressure of the unspeakable; her words are saturated with the residues of what cannot be said but can be mutually felt. In doing this, she changes the way we might think about the so-called pathetic fallacy.

Boyle rewrites the romantic reflexivity, shattering the mirror relationship of self and nature under the pressure of a point of view that flows everywhere and comes from no single or stationary ego, or subjectivity. In this, she eludes the very categories of romantic, unified selfhood, of the "true and false appearances" with which Ruskin had thought through his influential critique of the "pathetic fallacy."[13] Ruskin, let us recall, had argued that it is "only the second order of poets" who delight in the kind of description produced by violent feeling, a "falseness in all our impressions of external things" which "fancies a life" in foam or leaf instead of maintaining distinctions. Ruskin's "great poet" masters feeling:

> But it is still a grander condition when the intellect also rises, till it is strong enough to assert its rule against, or together with, the utmost efforts of the passions; and the whole man stands in an iron glow, white hot, perhaps, but still strong, and in no wise evaporating; even if he melts, losing none of his weight.[14]

The whole man arises in the imaginary as if forged in the steel mills, the image of reason. This nineteenth-century vision of the strong ego, the rational individual, has retained its heavy influence in twentieth-century criticism, visible in the work of critics such as John Crowe Ransom and Yvor Winters, and visible in the great fear of a "sentimental" softening which permeates criticism.

Boyle's practice, like Joyce's, breaks open this paranoid logic of the subject. In the place of individual heroic figures, she has the multiple connections of relationships; against the center of a linear plot she brings a counternarrative to bear. Words do not simply mirror subjects; the luminosity of her language tracks the energy of a freed desire to make connections. Hers is the logic of a poetic revolution which makes room for the woman, as for others. In this it is not simply experimental, and indeed, the chief characteristics I have observed here are to be found, in slightly different forms, in her later, apparently more conventional work.

Boyle works to rewrite the extreme imagination of reason which erases woman from the place of the subject or installs her as the singular Other of male discourse. Hers is instead a lyric refiguring of the story which produces more multiple possibilities. It might simply be called the logic of sympathy.

Freud introduces the sentimental into the heart of rational discourse, and that is the formula of modernism, but he also strengthens the rhetoric of countersentimentality, which forbade not only happy endings but also love stories. Boyle's fiction allows this anamnesis of the sentimental to overwhelm the tragic plot, so that her insistent interruption of forgetting produces a certain politics of solidarity not with family ideology but with women's lives.

The struggle of narratives appears in fiction by men and by women. Ernest Hemingway's *A Farewell to Arms* is like much fiction written in the painful aftermath of World War I, seized by the desire for some kind of return to human relationships. As Sandra Spanier has convincingly argued, critics have lost sight of the context of Hemingway's work. Catherine has the qualities Hemingway most admired, attributes usually associated with his male heroes.[15] Her death because of childbirth in the novel should not, then, be attributed to a cynicism about love on the part of Hemingway. The novel is an example not of countersentimentality but of the increasing impossibility felt by writers of producing an anamnesis of love and of maternal themes which would not be contained by a more tragic plot: it is an example of Hemingway's sentimentality. And it is an example of the deep longing to escape the tragic plot which would permeate modernism from Proust's *madeleine* to Eliot's rose garden, and emerge as the dominant chord of postmodernism, whether as carnival or as nostalgia.

This struggle with love and desire appears in literature at the time when the efficiency of the machinery for regulating and organizing human labor had been ratcheted up several notches, first by the military in the war, and then by the Taylorization of industry and the invention of the assembly line. As the forces of work become more and more demanding, it becomes increasingly important that work contradicts the domestic plot which it pretends to support—work drives the family underground. That is, the separation from the maternal leads to not a *paternal* role but a rejection of the whole enterprise—the father absents himself, and the family, not just the woman, is repressed. The military attitude was surely no more antifemale than the industrial, though the military has been more forthright about its stance: "If we wanted you to have a wife, we'd have issued you one" was a Marine Corps commonplace as late as the war in Vietnam.

The important place of irony in modernist literature is related to this repression of the domestic. The wife that used to make it all possible is now a hindrance; technology takes over the wifely work, as Barbara Ehrenreich and Deirdre English have detailed in *For Her Own Good*.[16] Sandra Gilbert has argued that women's culture and men's culture separated dramatically before the 1920s because of the First World War, when women found themselves newly powerful and men found themselves disillusioned.[17] Paul Fussell's *The Great War and Modern Memory* greatly influenced Gilbert's notion of the war's impact.[18] He argues that the horror-filled and nightmarish experience of the infantryman grounds a sense of reality which patriotic optimism denied. Irony is the only possible point of view. Gilbert goes on to conclude that women's experience was excluded from a literature with such assumptions. But our ability to read even Hemingway is severely affected as well.

The dialectic of love and tragedy, the personal and the public which generated male modernism hardened into a critical party line which excluded not only women but attitudes that seemed feminine, or sentimental. Fussell, says Ian Hamilton in a 1989 review of his book on World War II, is so driven by his own terrible years as an infantryman in World War II that he rejects all but the ironic stance and "his hostility to America's 'unironic' temper, to its earnestness and sentimentality, is of such depth and ferocity that it leads him to over-value almost any piece of writing that is not actively soporific or mendacious."[19] This suggests that, while Fussell has helped us to interpret modernism, it is because he represents the modernist attitude, and the obsession with the repetition of military horror which reproduces it. The ironic stance is thus more than irony; in the form of this horror it has seized the imaginary and come to seem the only credible stance for the whole of this century's literature.

Yet neither Freud's sense of tragedy nor the postwar bitterness of disillusionment provides an alternative to the overdetermination of a single narrative plot and the domination of an image of separation and loss extended as linear time. And even though the story seems to entail growing up to face reality, it involves denial of the human bonds which situate the maternal real. It is a plot writers have struggled to rewrite, and the struggle between irony and American sentimentality does not belong to women writers alone. The dominance of a thematized irony has meant exploring alternatives to the alienated individual who spins off into war and into the free-market economy, free as well from any complicated or novel-length human connections. The pain of these explorations surfaces as the recollection of feeling in style. In that respect, Kay Boyle is both innovative and paradigmatic in her writing. Her attention to the issues of women places her closer to the borders of the problem. Far from giving us the sentimental as an escapism, she makes us recognize how a love story might be closest to the real problem.

III

The "revolution of the word" appears to precipitate a crisis of the family by rejecting domestic claims along with domestic, genteel fiction. Thus the themes of free love appear and reappear, and challenges to the old codes of a social Puritanism make up an important part of what seems revolutionary, from Emma Goldman through Henry Miller. D. H. Lawrence and James Joyce both celebrate sexuality at the same time that they open up family structures to intensities of disequilibrium, so that the carnivalesque of style which undermines conventional prose also undermines conventions of sexuality and family relations. The family order of mothers, fathers, daughters, sons seems not the origin of emotional freedom but the very structure which oppresses. Freud's narrative sequence dominates narrative form, directing plot toward separation. At the same time, the family romance provides the fictional matrix, so that the more the discourse is about escaping the maternal, the more it is contained by the maternality thus conjured, which operates as an unconscious eternal return of the same. The conflicts generated by this internalizing of narrative mark modernist fiction and modernist life with extreme violence.

Writing inside this extremity, Kay Boyle nonetheless seems to discover a style which opens up the crises of the family. That is, she puts the sentimental narrative back into play, not as a mode of mastering the plot and rescuing it for family values but as a discourse which softens and disputes the forms of revolution. Nothing, at the end, could be more like having it all than the multiplicity of loves for which she manages to find a place. Yet this protean inventiveness is not quite comic; it has, in fact, its own irony. She does not deny violence and pain, and she resists the narrative closures which might provide a contemplative or satirical distance.

The first pair of novels she published operate like a counterpoint opening up the impossibilities of love in a culture dominated by bourgeois manipulations. The descriptive voice—speaking the American speech as Williams heard it, as an empirical, democratic voice which believes in perception—establishes a strangeness relative to its setting in European bourgeois culture. This descriptive empiricism separates patriarchy from the ordinary American observer. In *Plagued by the Nightingale* and *Year before Last,* Boyle writes the kind of closely observed love story that a French sensibility might recognize, but this does not mean that the style is European, not at all. The negativity and questioning evoked by the revolution of the word are directed against the European patriarchal orthodoxy instead of the middle-class gentility of American culture, where, Boyle claims, it is merely derivative and translated.[20] Thus Boyle's modernist critique of the domestic and the genteel is very different from that of Eliot or Pound, who are critical of American culture but, like James as well, identify with European conservative attitudes.

Furthermore, the narrator representing the ordinary American free individual is a woman. Such a point of view is already well connected to themes of feminism, independence, and even free love in American literary traditions, and after Daisy Miller and Edna St. Vincent Millay, readers may have almost expected Boyle to present such a female narrator. But Boyle separates her critique of the bourgeois family from the conventions of free love, with its rebellions against the connectedness of individuals and its unholy alliance with Mill's rationalistic feminism. This sensuous narrative voice lodges its critique in the body, the figure, the symptom—not accepting the family romance in any of its formulas. The narrator rebels against the bourgeois family's manipulative economy, for example, by deciding to do exactly what the family apparently desires: have a baby. There is no retreat from the sexuality of the maternal.

In *Plagued by the Nightingale* Boyle critiques a classic French bourgeois family. Two newlyweds arrive for a summer with the family and find themselves trapped, Nicolas the victim of the family's disease, and both without escape from its "safe" imprisonment. Family imperatives are diseased, crippling in themselves, and parallel the crippling illness imposed by the family genes on the young husband. The new American wife, Bridget, who tries to learn both French and the family language, finds herself at odds even with her husband, who fights and is ever more entangled.

European patriarchy constructs domesticity as a feminine world, "a world of women who lived without avarice or despise . . . a woman's world built strongly about the men's fortune and the men's fortitude" (69), and Maman's forceful management extends to the village, where she organizes the people to fight a fire. It is the men who have the disease, who act like children—Jean, with his fortune, is forever dissolving in tears—but it is the men, too, who police the bourgeois standards: there is "Papa's intense feeling about immoral literature" and Oncle Robert, who presses past Maman's defenses to discover the glass ring left on her cabinet, and leaves a judgmental remark with the others about Bridget's earrings. Nicolas feels the disease is the family's, that they never should have had him knowing the crippling heritage, that they are responsible for him now. His rage is murderous—"imagine the joy of slowly killing Maman . . . ripping Papa up the middle!" (50)—but the family's desire is always for more children, for babies, and the family desire is inexorable.

The story is told from the point of view of Bridget, who does not speak French and who comes from an American family which let its members go off as individuals. Thus the book is written as if outside language and culture, in objects and gestures and places, without judgments. The bourgeois feminine world is "strange." Bridget enters it first to last as a body, as the object of the family gaze and the design for more babies. When she goes for a swim, her legs are bare, but the others cover themselves in bathing dresses, and Bridget sees Annick, the daughter who would be a nun, look at her with "half-revulsion for her exposed legs and arms" (13). She is a female body, the object of reproductive desire but also of revulsion.

The family plots revolve around the family's own reproduction. Charlotte has married the first cousin, Jean, brought his fortune next door, and produced five children. The three girls—Annick, Marthe, Julie—are in long-term pursuit of the young doctor, Luc, who visits each year and seems ready to be ensnared by the family. And Nicolas has brought home the American bride, who must now produce a child. The men's control of the fortune is all directed toward managing the family's reproductive will. Papa promises fifty thousand francs to the couple if they have a child, while Jean and Oncle Robert refuse to lend them any money to make an escape. If it is a feminine world, the women's only power rests in maintaining themselves in this time of reproduction, apart from history and change. When Charlotte's body becomes repulsive in her last pregnancy, as she grows more horribly sick, her breath foul, her tongue white and swollen, her revolting body confined to her dark bedroom, the family's ruthlessness becomes more apparent: they delay the necessary surgery too long and she dies. The woman is the sacrificial body, and woman's work is having children.

What Bridget's American point of view brings to this family plot is not a male alternative—not escape, not adventure. Instead she finds some mutual attraction and encourages Luc's resistance until he decides not to marry into the family: "What was the nightingale's small liberty to the deep wide exemption she had given Luc, she thought" (334). She agrees with Nicolas, that she brought him back to "the heart of his family and now it is up to me to get him out" (211). She listens without denial to his proposals that she have a child with another man, to avoid the disease. At last she resolves to have a child. Whether Nicolas will be the father is left decidedly open. Thus the reproductive realm of "women's time" comes to operate not as the defining center of the bourgeois family but as a maternal irony that recognizes the family's deadly exploitation of Charlotte's body—and Bridget's enduring ability to escape family regulation altogether by the freedom to make love with someone else. This maternal, female irony is not the utopian vision of total escape associated with advocates of free love—it is the irony always available to the oppressed, to colonized, domesticated peoples (including America) as to women.

As the novels work out the implications of sensuous style on an external scale, on the level of culture as well as experience, one of the chief consequences is that style works to elaborate a borderline individuality, not isolated but rather metaphorically related to others, to place, and to context, woven into the tapestry. The experimentalism in linguistic point of view that crosses boundaries and denies isolation works not only in Boyle's early stories, where condensation and stream of consciousness make the form private, intense, and lyrical. Comparing the short story "On the Run" with her second novel, *Year before Last*—written after the death of Ernest Walsh—may suggest how the shift from internal to external focus operates.

The scene represented in "On the Run" appears again in *Year before Last*, greatly changed. Instead of concentrating all the times when hotels rejected the dying man into a single, symbolic moment, the scene is one added chapter in a painful series. The novel externalizes the private experience, extending it across many spaces: the northern town, the southern chateau, the restaurants, train stations, hotels, Saint-André, St. Jean-les-Pins. The question is not whether Hannah and Martin will love each other—there is no courtship, only consequences. Nor is it whether or not he will die: he is living on a pension, on externally funded time. He has, in a sense, already been killed in the war:

> There's nothing to me, said Martin. I'm not here at all. My boots were found on a tree-top, sticking up to scare the crows from their direction. My clothes, he said, and he touched his cloak, are now hung on a peg and stuffed with straw to make them human. Touch me, Lady Vanta, said Martin softly leaning forward. Touch me. That was the night I died. (182)

What changes as the story develops is, instead, the relationship with the other woman, the relationship between Hannah and Eve (was she always already other?). It is not allegorically simple; the two women are like sisters, rivals, and like mother-daughter. Eve is a difficult, strong—and "virginal"—woman who owns the magazine which Martin is at work editing. "But there was Eve as well, between them there on their first morning together: the woman who could go to prison for a thing. . . . She was a brave woman, thought Hannah" (5).

The question between the women is whether the erotic young love of Hannah and Martin has any moral force. Hannah has left her husband, Dilly, to be with Martin, and Martin's alliance with Hannah has caused Eve to leave him, withdrawing not only her financial support but also her magazine.

> Now if I were a brave and a simple woman, thought Hannah . . . I would see sin and virtue and be able to distinguish between them. I only believe in sin when I see the fury on Eve's face, and I must be the sinner. When I see the look she has now with him I know there can be no virtue in having come between these two. (67)

The two women are reconciled at the end, at the scene of Martin's death: "Hannah, Hannah, my darling, Eve cried out like a woman gone mad. Hannah, will you save him! Can you save him, Hannah, Hannah, my lamb?" (219). The women seem to occupy two points of a Freudian family triangle. This is not to argue, however, that Eve represents the maternal and Hannah the erotic in a straightforward psychological allegory: Hannah cares for Martin as she did for her husband in a motherly way, starching the collars of his shirts, administering his medicines. Eve, on the other hand, is cruel and jealous and flirtatious.

Nonetheless, the elements of plot are a familiar triangle: they are the endlessly recombining elements of the family drama, and like the soap opera, they have no necessary conclusion but death. That is, the forms that structure this work are continuous with the forms that structure the texts of mass culture—the best sellers and romances for women as well as the soaps.

That does not mean that we should be critical of such forms. Like the experimental structure of the short stories, the relational plot lets Boyle overthrow the hero-centered formula of fiction. Tania Modleski's argument in *Loving with a Vengeance* for the interest of women's mass culture texts will perhaps help us to carry on this discussion in a way that continues to take these forms seriously.[21] That women's plots are easy to recognize should not make them any more trivial than masculine plots with more action and less moral agonizing. Modleski suggests that the pleasure women take in the soap opera might be something feminists would want to build on rather than reject, because the apparent limitlessness of the text has the effect of "decentering" the classic (masculine) heroic self or ego: "soap operas may not be an entirely negative influence on the viewer; they may also have the force of a *negation,* a negation of the typical (and masculine) modes of pleasure in our society" (105).

I am arguing as well that another kind of plot needs to be put into dialectical relationship with the linear plot of action and adventure. In *Year before Last,* Boyle writes a love story, refusing to make it carry some other significance about the tragedy of desire. Words, almost a good in themselves like the colors aroused by paint or the light of perception, take up the energy of a desire for connection. Another kind of temporality is installed. Boyle's style performs the drama, making precise the metaphorical nature of subjectivity. Thus objects—like words—become acts: they dramatize not only the self but the way the self connects to others, to the world. Take, for example, Eve's dresses:

> She had taken a room on the other side of the hall. And there were her frocks shaking out on their hangers. Five pairs of elegant shoes were out of her bags already and set along the wall, waiting, with their toes turned in. Waiting for tangoes, waiting for rhumbas, waiting till Martin could go stepping out again. I've been taking dancing lessons to fill in the time.
> The time, said Eve and the word gaped wide before them. (209)

It is as if the motive force for action were not lodged in a singular "I" but rather was dispersed into all the environment. The point is to resist "the time" of inexorable death. The law of cause and effect seems beside the point, and morality is not a matter of rules and consequences. But the acts of individuals are not wholly irrational either; they take place as a function of context, as a matter of what can be described rather than analyzed. *Year before Last* coheres around the intensity of lost love, and the tragedy that not heroism but the loss of a connectedness brings. The metaphor of relationship proves to be the figure of a moral law.

Boyle's early fiction seems experimental but not political, and as her later fiction becomes less experimental, it also seems more involved in the context of history, more firmly embedded in historical time. Superficially, her career seems to follow an evolution of writing away from the personal and toward more public forms. But this is misleading. Contrary to this appearance, her early work already establishes the basic moral principle, the metaphor of intersubjectivity. Furthermore, I believe that her later work becomes more difficult and less accessible in a way that is significant for feminism. As the novels become "clearer," and more clearly lodged in a sense of political history that defies dominant positions, they also become more rhetorically challenging to familiar (family) ideologies of human relationship and more clearly *different* from familiar male narratives.

Boyle's soft revolution defies convention by describing the intensity of relationships that should not be "interesting," like the relationships of women to one another, or that should not be seen sympathetically, like the love of an American woman for a Nazi doctor in *Death of a Man*, or the pain of a prisoner of war returning to Germany in *Generation without Farewell*. She does not give us predictable American attitudes or relationships. Jaeger, the protagonist of *Generation without Farewell*, is a man who identifies with women. But more than that, couldn't we say that the narrator, winking at us over the heads of these characters, is a woman? Nancy Miller's *The Heroine's Text* explored how male narrators looked at the reader through the texts of their heroines, so that the story is still governed by a male exchange.[22] It would be interesting if we could show that Boyle institutes a female narrator who does the same. But if so, how do we explain this femininity in a narrator looking into a phallogocentric culture? Isn't this move out of the hands of the author?

Boyle works this by identifying her female narrators with other oppressed subjects and subjects of colonization. Jaeger, displaced, is a returned German prisoner of war, working in ersatz-wool clothes and second-hand shoes, identifying with the Jews and with the resistance. And is the female narrator, looking past him at her readers, not in a similar position? The character who at once represents his German culture and yet resists it resembles the American Kay Boyle, and the resistance of women. Thus there is an exploration of the complexities of complicity, of loss of power, of subversion. But this figure—Jaeger—is a difficult hero. Who is to identify with him? What reader will be able to read such a point of view? When Boyle lodges subversion in this kind of resistance, a negativity which depends upon the response of readers, and does not direct it, she makes her text vulnerable to the other readings of history which surround her. And indeed, she has suffered.

Boyle is a modernist writer, but not in the mainstream of American modernism. Description in her work is different from both journalistic reporting of historical events and a certain line of modernist metafiction. In her work description is infused by an ideology of democratic appeal—call it sentimentality—which *represents* the problem of the feminine, thematizes it. Yet her description also problematizes the woman in language at the level of the signifier, forcing language back upon itself into internal reflection and disrupting its paternal functioning. Alice Jardine's comparison of American and French writers can perhaps help to clarify Boyle's position. In *Gynesis,* Jardine argues that modernity operates differently for the two traditions.

> The American interpretive response to twentieth-century crises in legitimation has not been one of exploding paternal identity, concepts, and narrative to get at their feminine core, through a rearrangement of *techne* and *physis,* a radical rearrangement of gender. . . . The writing subject and his sentence both remain integral unto themselves—and very male—by shoring up textual barriers against the "Nature" that threatens them (Burrough's "virus") or by deriding and dismembering that body, which, if explored, would disturb their satire as technique (Barthelme's Mother and Julie). . . . [The American version of *gynesis*] seems to exist here only at the level of *representation.* (236)[23]

But, as Jardine points out, the insertion of female voices into this dichotomy reveals new possibilities for feminists to take advantage of the interrogations modernity has inaugurated. Boyle's work identifies the narrator with other suppressed voices—challenging male modernity at the level of representation—and at the same time puts the gendered subject under question at the level of the signifier, a practice which differentiates her work from American modern and postmodern texts. What Jardine means by "modernity" begins with the period which includes American modernism but is really most of all what we call postmodern. Boyle needs to be seen within this cosmopolitan modernity, as a writer who has written after modernism from the beginning, and a writer who has directed European sensibilities and American speech to a practice American interpreters cannot quite recognize, inserting the question of the woman into *style.* Nonetheless, the confusion or even the disregard of Boyle's readers may signal for us how difficult such work must be, and how the revolution of modernism has not finished.

In a speech titled "Writers in Metaphysical Revolt," Boyle tries to specify the nature of the literary revolution of which she was a part. It is democratic. It involves putting the voice of the people into writing. She sees herself, like William Carlos Williams, like William Faulkner, as part of a particularly American project: "There was . . . before the twenties, no lively, wholly American, grandly experimental, and furiously disrespectful school of writing, so we had to invent that school" (3). American culture, however, is not necessarily receptive to the disrespectful, especially when the woman furiously subverts the panaceas of family respectability. What Boyle submits to the experimental cauldron of her prose is the most threatening of cultural forms, the very plot of the family romance.

Forty years after those novels of the late twenties and early thirties, Boyle wrote a closely autobiographical novel from inside the events of the late sixties in San Francisco: the protests against the Vietnam War, the jailing of protesters, the concurrent struggle for civil rights engaging black Americans, and the darkness of the Hell's Angels and the cult of Charlie Manson. *The Underground Woman* thematizes a politics grounded in personal attachments and confronts the pain of a family order which comes apart on the level of representation. Boyle might well remind us here of Emma Goldman's voice telling of the same descent into the other world of prisons, outrage fueled by the same maternal sympathy. The political is personal. "Believe that our separate lives are of no importance? . . . Is anybody ever prepared for that? Isn't that the thing they always forgot to make convincing in church or school or whenever we asked for advice?" (55). And the fiction is rhetorical, filled with argument for a moral stance. By its overt advocacy it is kin to Harriet Beecher Stowe and the old traditions of women's prose. Its appeals are sentimental. It is hard to read, and for different reasons than *The Waste Land* was hard.

In *The Underground Woman*, Boyle tells the horror story of a mother whose daughter is taken away by a cult, juxtaposed with the more public story of the woman's protests against Vietnam. Athena, the Kay Boyle character in the book, is a professor of mythology—an interpreter of ideologies, not a writer. The members of the cult invade Athena's house, propelled by the fury of "Pete the Redeemer" who had declared, "I hate the world, and I'll hate it until it's completely destroyed" (119). There are different orders of destruction in the book: the cancer that killed Athena's husband, the cult that takes her daughter, the government that goes on with the war. But Athena is not propelled by hate. The mother's solidarity with another protesting mother, Calliope (Joan Baez's mother was the model), is absolutely dependent on their moral commitments. When they go for a climb up Angel Island on a free day, they find disengagement from the antiwar effort very difficult, almost immoral.

> "This is the one day in our lives we can have away from everyone!"
> "We can start by rejoicing that we're free" and at once the shadow of guilt fell on their hearts. (257)

The guilty freedom seems escapist. Deer follow them, and Boyle turns to one of the most conventional of sentimental emblems to express the commitments that mobilize their fellow feeling. In spite of the two women's shared experiences in jail, in the free pleasures of the hike there is a veil between them. "Yet if one of these deer, just one, should be felled by an illicit hunter, Athena pictured how she and Calliope would turn as one person, inseparable in its passionate defense" (259).

Is this use of sentimental rhetoric something we should criticize in Boyle? A sort of need for irony may be generated in us by these emotional appeals, even though they ground the argument through history for all humanitarian appeals. As readers, we are well trained in modernism. It is extremely difficult to talk about a feminine rhetorical *tradition* as "sentimental" which connects the political fiction of Boyle to the political autobiography of Emma Goldman without seeming to denigrate both writers. The tradition comes into view always already discounted. And yet Boyle's appeal is to a convention so familiar that postwar Americans would think of it as the "Bambi" appeal—this is public rhetoric, not a less accessible literary imagery. Boyle extends the pain and love of experiences between mother and daughter, man and wife, woman and woman, across the limits of family into the politics of protest against the war. This fiction is rhetorical. We have great difficulty reading this kind of work. Boyle herself thought it had problems. We have been brainwashed by antifeminist constraints to think of it in literary terms that narrow and reduce literature itself.

And what appears strongly in *The Underground Woman* is the solidarity of women in the very scene of oppression. In the jail they learn to question the isolation of individuals: "they were learning that night that they were not, and had never been, a hundred women lying on their cots in the dark, isolated, and thus lost, in their own identities, women now who were neither black nor white nor Chicano, but all with interchangeable skins. The attack upon one girl in the darkness of her cell was an attack on their flesh . . ." (113). At the same time, no social form can be adequate to the revolution, and the potential for evil influence is great. In spite of Pete the Redeemer's promises, "the commune was not for an instant a revolutionary place," and "the redemption he offers is fame and fortune, these words of promise given his followers like a Bank of America card or a Master-Charge plate" (116). Freedom finds its act in resistance to the story, "there isn't any *story*" (184).

The plot of the book moves from one form of imprisonment—the jailing of protesters—to another—the malign influence of the commune—and returns to another jailing. There is no progress. Martha, an alcoholic prisoner who hoped to reform, returns at the same time as the protesters, with her eye black, her face a "wreck." The conclusion is a return, not only to the "barren walls" of jail but to the recognitions of personal loves and personal losses: "Sybil and Paula would write, but Melanie and Rory were gone forever, somewhere far, far away. *Oh, reality, hold me close, hold me close* the underground woman asked in silence of the barren walls" (264).

The "reality" which Boyle as underground woman here faces is configured as the bare walls of jail. This "reality" is metaphorically connected to the reality of oppressive state societies addressed by a literature of subversion since Dostoyevsky's *Notes from the Underground.* The prison metaphor is also a fact of life, a part of contemporary history which Boyle recalls in her essay on her imprisonment, "Report from Lock-up." She sees a connection between the unfortunate women she finds in prison and twentieth-century history, from the prison memoirs of Emma Goldman's old friend Alexander Berkman, to the Birdman of Alcatraz, the Chinese once imprisoned on Angel Island, and the Native Americans who took Alcatraz back for a time. Imprisonment is a feminist tradition: she cites Alice Paul (whom her mother had brought home to lunch) and Doris Stevens's report of the force-feeding of Paul in a psychiatric ward.[24] The prison metaphor is a modern matrix, calling up a kind of new mythology. The new commonplaces of twentieth-century literature are these scenes of violence and despair, in prisons, in confrontations with the police. In *The Underground Woman*, Boyle invokes these images and at the same time she juxtaposes them to the other set of commonplaces, the interior scenes of family relations, the domestic, the sentimental. She finds the violence at home. *Home.* The horror stories of European culture are relocated inside American institutions and inside the experience of the ordinary American individual—that is, of course, inside the woman.

IV

The solidarity of women in Kay Boyle comes out of family feeling but also defies the family romance. Boyle makes us see the alternatives within canonical modernism—she is, or ought to be, part of the modernist canon. She practices the revolution of the word in a way that should be visible from a postmodern point of view. She writes, that is, in full recognition of both the possibilities of style and a need to recuperate love as the final metaphor, the best subversion. She allows the antiplot to emerge into rhetoric only in later works, particularly in *The Underground Woman* and then explicitly in essays. But she maintains the political commitments that the modernist revolution seemed to imply in the beginning. Her childhood experience with feminism joins with a perspective about the place of the intellectual that most American modernists shared with Europeans in the time of the expatriates:

> It is *always* the intellectuals, however we may shrink from the chilling sound of that word, and, above all, it is *always* the writers who must bear the full weight of moral responsibility. Frenchmen will tell you that the decision to speak out is the vocation and life-long peril by which the intellectual must live. . . . American intellectuals . . . prepared and oriented our revolution: the only revolution in history . . . which did not destroy the intellectuals who had prepared it, but which carried them to power. (190)

This resistance to the fatalities of irony is not an antimodernism. It is inherent in modernism as part of the struggle—the sentimental *within* modernism: what, in fact, makes the literature so powerful. Boyle's relationship to modernism is that of a second generation which has really absorbed the implications of the first. Like young women growing up right now, seventy years later, Boyle heard *Tender Buttons* from her feminist mother. The family in Boyle is divided into a patriarchal order of violence and oppression—or failure—and a maternal order of subversive pleasure and morality. In her essay "The Family," Boyle describes her extraordinary mother, who was responsible for her most important education and introduced her not only to the words of Stein but to a virtual honor roll of the revolution:

> George Moore, Dreiser, Shaw, Isadora Duncan, Caruso, Roman Rolland, George Santayana, Oswald Garrison Villard, Mary Garden, James Joyce, John Cooper Powys, Alice Paul, Alfred Stieglitz, Norman Angell, Susan B. Anthony, Mozart, Upton Sinclair, Margaret Anderson, Jane Heap, Bach, Eugene Debs, Jules Massenet, Cezanne, Monet, Picasso. . . . (6)

Her mother was in fact friends with some: Alice Paul, Alfred Stieglitz, Mary Garden, John Cooper Powys. Boyle attributes her mother's involvements to simple human motives such as "her wish to help a beautiful and talented young woman," Marie Lawall, on whose behalf her mother contacted Mary Garden. But the mother's knowledge is mysterious.

> I do not know how . . . she realized it was important to take me to the Armory Show in New York in 1913 to see Marcel Duchamps' "Nude Descending a Staircase" and Brancusi's "Mlle. Pogany" and his "Bird in Space." . . . Isolated as Mother was from the literary scene, I also cannot explain her understanding of the urgent need to send word of support to Margaret Anderson, who was threatened with arrest for publishing in the *Little Review* chapters of Joyce's banned *Ulysses*. (8)

But it was probably the very isolation of women that propelled her, "an unending loneliness."

The first experience Boyle had of the solidarity of women was with the alliance of her mother and herself against the men in the family, an alliance connected specifically with the modernist revolution:

> It was difficult to speak at the dinner table at night of the acts of moral courage achieved by total strangers, inasmuch as the men of the family spoke of more familiar things. It was because of instances such as these that Mother and I became part of a conspiracy of silence and discretion, one that involved a great many people, some of whom lived in other countries, a conspiracy to bring to life another reality in which one could put one's faith and it would never be betrayed. (8)

The "moral courage" to present "another reality" is joined to social action: "There was another complicity in her life, and that was her covert alliance with the underprivileged, the lost, the poor" (8). In Boyle's mother, as in Boyle's fiction, the revolution of the word is joined to a moral revolution, a conspiracy on behalf of "another reality."

Boyle's modernism implies a political practice. In her 1947 essay "Farewell to New York," she remains critical of writers who failed to support the Spanish struggle against Franco in 1939: "if I feel guilt . . . it is because there are writers and poets to whom the invitation to speak was given, a long time ago, and they gave their answers" (76). She cites Pound, Evelyn Waugh, and T. S. Eliot. In 1953, she wrote "Farewell to Europe," juxtaposing the voices of Europeans who counseled staying away from an America transfixed by McCarthyism, and her decision to return: "This is one of the times in history when one must go back and speak out with those of the other America clearly and loudly enough so that even Europe will hear" (98). This reflects her conviction that it is an American voice, an American speech, which is revolutionary. Nothing about the disillusionment of the twenties challenged that assumption so violently as the McCarthyism of the fifties must have done. Boyle and her husband, Joseph Franckenstein, were victims, the subjects of a loyalty hearing. The *New Yorker* dropped Boyle as a writer. Her writing was blacklisted—for a decade she could not publish anywhere. If she spoke for the "other America," that voice was indeed not to be allowed.

If we read Boyle as a daughter of feminism and modernism, we will begin to understand the particularly contemporary complexity of her project. At the same time that she rejects patriarchy, she asserts continuity with women; at the same time that she destroys narrative continuities, she softly moves to enlarge the province of sensuous perception so that the perception itself is imbued with emotion and the experience of commitment. These are texts like a body of pleasure but also an embodiment of moral perspective, texts like Emma Goldman.

Boyle is one modernist who does not revolt against the maternal tradition, whose maternal tradition *is* modernism and the promise of moral progress. She is in the lineage of strong women such as Emma Goldman and Gertrude Stein. She reminds us that there is such a lineage. She is decidedly not in the lineage of submissive women who subsume their own moral certitudes to the "realities" of jails and Mastercards or to the masters of the house. Boyle's work upsets the hierarchical order and reminds us again and again of women's time as a space of freedom and love.

In *The Underground Woman,* Boyle violates the sense of direction implied by Freudian narratives. She deplores the isolation of individuals, she sees the loss of her daughter as tragic, and she claims that bonds of compassion are the foundation of political action. The book is not about justice, or violations of law or even of principle. It advocates a return to the maternal enclosure of human relationship—even though this solidarity has to be located within the barren walls of prison. This is not, in other words, the substitution of a woman's story leading to togetherness instead of the male story leading to separation; it is a recollection of another order which ruptures the story and stops the movement of separation, which drives language itself to turn aside. That opening up of language to the pressure of emotion is both modernist and womanly.

Whether or not a writing which practices this kind of revolution may be powerful enough to work larger changes in literary culture remains, however, an open question. This writer offers us an artistic practice which can say things that could not be said otherwise. As her readers, it is up to us now to find ways to speak about Kay Boyle's words and the revolution of the woman.

Notes

1. For an account, see Sandra Whipple Spanier, *Kay Boyle: Artist and Activist* (Carbondale and Edwardsville: Southern Illinois UP, 1986) 25–26.

2. Kay Boyle, *Words That Must Somehow Be Said,* ed. Elizabeth S. Bell (San Francisco: North Point Press, 1985) 31–34.

3. For a convincing discussion of Boyle's experimental writing, her collection of stories in *Wedding Day and Other Stories,* and her contribution to the "revolution of the word," see Spanier, *Kay Boyle* 30–56.

4. These stories appear in *Wedding Day and Other Stories* (New York: Jonathan Cape and Harrison Smith, 1930). "Episode" and "Wedding Day" also appear in *Fifty Stories* (New York: Doubleday, 1980), and "On the Run" was reprinted in the special issue on Kay Boyle of *Twentieth Century Literature* (Fall 1988). References are to the most recent editions.

5. This essay, published originally in French as "Le temps des femmes" in *33/44: Cahiers de recherche des sciences des textes et documents,* no. 5 (Winter 1979), first appeared in English, translated by Alice Jardine and Harry Blake, in *Signs: Journal of Women in Culture and Society* 7 (1981), and has been reprinted a number of times. My references are to the text in *The Kristeva Reader,* ed. Toril Moi (New York: Columbia UP, 1986) 187–213.

6. Julia Kristeva, *Revolution in Poetic Language,* trans. Margaret Waller (New York: Columbia UP, 1984).

7. Catharine R. Stimpson, "Stein and the Transposition of Gender," *The Poetics of Gender,* ed. Nancy Miller (New York: Columbia UP, 1986) 2.

8. "Women's Time" 199.

9. She writes in "The Family," in *Words That Must Somehow Be Said,* that her own grandmother was a strong woman who worked in the Land Grant Division of the federal government and lived a life of independence: "I knew she ran, and danced, and sang before the horses in the beginning of the day because she wasn't afraid of the Indians or of anything else in life" (23). Boyle does not know "where Grandma Evans had found the courage to leave Kansas and a grandfather I was never to see and to move with her two young daughters to Washington D.C." (23).

10. In the Introduction to Boyle, *Fifty Stories* 14.

11. See Atwood's introduction to Boyle's *Three Short Novels* (New York: Penguin, 1982) ix.

12. *Kay Boyle* 36.

13. See John Ruskin, "Of the Pathetic Fallacy," *Critical Theory since Plato,* ed. Hazard Adams (New York: Harcourt Brace Jovanovich, 1971).

14. "Pathetic Fallacy" 619.

15. Spanier's argument about Catherine as a heroic figure is set out in "Catherine Barkley and the Hemingway Code: Ritual and Survival in *A Farewell to Arms,*" *Modern Critical Interpretations: "A Farewell to Arms,"* ed. Harold Bloom (New Haven and New York: Chelsea House, 1987) 131–48. Spanier goes on in another article to situate the novel in the context of

the aftermath of the Great War, and to argue that critical interpretations have often missed the significance of love and the personal to Hemingway in that novel because they have lost sight of the context: "Hemingway's Unknown Soldier: Catherine Barkley, the Critics, and the Great War," *New Essays on "A Farewell to Arms,"* ed. Scott Donaldson (Cambridge: Cambridge UP, forthcoming 1990).

16. Barbara Ehrenreich and Deirdre English, *For Her Own Good: 150 Years of the Experts' Advice to Women* (Garden City: Anchor Books, 1979).

17. Sandra Gilbert, "Soldier's Heart: Literary Men, Literary Women, and the Great War," *Signs* 8.3 (Spring 1983): 422–50.

18. Paul Fussell, *The Great War and Modern Memory* (London and New York: Oxford UP, 1975).

19. *London Review of Books* (September 28, 1989): 6.

20. See the speech "Writers in Metaphysical Revolt," *Proceedings of the Conference of College Teachers of English of Texas* 36 (September 1971): 6–12.

21. Tania Modleski, *Loving with a Vengeance: Mass-Produced Fantasies for Women* (New York: Methuen, 1982).

22. Nancy Miller, *The Heroine's Text: Readings in the French and English Novel, 1722–1782* (New York: Columbia UP, 1980).

23. Alice Jardine, *Gynesis: Configurations of Woman and Modernity* (Ithaca: Cornell UP, 1985).

24. An elaboration of the subject of imprisonment appears in "A Day on Alcatraz with the Indians," "The Crime of Attica," and "Report from Lock-up," *Words That Must Somehow Be Said* 104–51.

Entering the World of Politics

Marilyn Elkins

The best epitaph a man can gain is to have accomplished daring deeds of valor against the enmity of fiends during his lifetime. (*The Seafarer*)

In the forties, Kay Boyle expanded the physical scope of her fictional worlds. While many of her novels continued to feature women, her heroines were now involved in social and political issues. This entry into the realm of national politics seems a natural outgrowth, for as Margaret Higonnet points out, the female author often perceives that "political discourse and familial order lie in a continuum" ("Civil Wars" 93). As a resident of Europe, being as Glenway Wescott states always "more completely abroad than the rest of us [American expatriates]" (quoted in Ford 224), Boyle also understood the political implications of events in that sphere with greater clarity than her American contemporaries. Living in Austria (1933–1936) and in Megeve in the French Alps (1938–1941), she witnessed the more subtle ways in which Europeans' daily personal lives were being transformed. This knowledge gives her writing about the European conflict an immediacy of detail that escaped her American counterparts.

While Hemingway and Steinbeck were focusing on the civil war in Spain and the dust bowls in America, Boyle looked at additional ramifications surrounding her treatment of Nazism in *Death of a Man*. This time, however, she concentrated on a less apparent political threat to freedom in the twentieth century: the appeal of Nazi Germany's ideology to the inhabitants of the countries that Germany had defeated. Four of Boyle's novels treat the theme of coexisting with the enemy, looking at the psychological and practical effects of both collaboration and resistance: *Primer for Combat* (1942), *Avalanche* (1994), *A Frenchman Must Die* (1946), and *1939* (1948). Each of these novels also questions prevalent assumptions about gender, race, and nation as they control and explain individual behavior in war torn countries.

Reprinted from *Metamorphosizing the Novel: Kay Boyle's Narrative Innovations* (New York: Peter Lang, 1993): 109–46, with the permission of the author.

Yet these works, especially *Avalanche* and *A Frenchman Must Die,* have attracted considerable critical censure. In his first review as Clifton Fadiman's replacement as literary critic for the *New Yorker,* Edmund Wilson called *Avalanche* "nothing but a piece of pure rubbish," adding that it "is simply the usual kind of thing that is turned out by women writers for the popular magazines" (66). Reviewing the book for *Time and Tide,* Walter Allen says that not even Boyle's "distinguished style can make up for the perfunctoriness of the characterization and the sentimentality of the story."

Perhaps these male critics responded so negatively because Boyle permitted her heroines' active participation in wartime activities that everyone, including the more prominent writers of the period, assumed belonged exclusively to males.[1] Constituting Boyle's most overtly political writing, these novels also repudiate earlier claims that Boyle writes about characters who are divorced from the reality of the public world. She adopted the popular adventure genre to gain wider exposure for the ideas that she expounds in these works. The writing, while it is innovative in its assignment of the hero's role to a female, lacks the subtlety of her other novels that treat the war in Europe. Having found, however, that the popular acceptance of the form allowed her to reach a larger audience, Boyle returned to it in two later novels: *The Seagull on the Step* (1955) and *The Underground Woman* (1975), interesting as a rare example of a novel that focuses on an older woman as heroine. Both novels are "feminine" adaptations of the adventure tale.

The less commercial novels, *Primer for Combat* and *1939,* successfully present both the attractions and evils of fascism in a realistic and complex manner; they also analyze the appeal of Nazism for the idealist. In these works Boyle treats the psychological impact of compromise. Looking at the tension created when inhabitants of a defeated country are forced to choose between the practical and the ideal, Boyle also analyzes how a nation's emphasis on success influences political decisions.

This political concern and its balanced treatment seem a natural outgrowth of Boyle's earlier background. In support of her beliefs, Katherine Boyle ran for a seat on the Cincinnati Board of Education on the Farmer Labor ticket. And Boyle's grandfather's "winning, gracious tyranny" gave her an early example of the attractive form that some oppression can take. She instinctively rebelled against such oppressive authority, recognizing the enslavement that lurked just beneath its apparently benevolent, but inherently selfish, aims (*BGT* 16). This early personal experience probably helped Boyle present the attractive.personal qualities of such despots and their political movements with greater clarity and force. It must also have helped her avoid the oversimplification that denies such attractions exist.

Primer for Combat treats the period from June 20 through October 2, 1940 in occupied France. Written in the form of her journal entries, it covers the life of Phyl, an American woman living in France with Benchley, her American husband, their children, and Phyl's teen-age brother. An interesting mixture of the personal and fictionalized, the novel's main character exchanges letters with Nancy Cunard and makes references to living and dead *literati* that Boyle knew personally. Long before Ishmael Reed and E. L. Doctorow would experiment with including living and dead historical personages in their fictional works, Boyle combines the fictional and the real, giving this work a sense of intimacy and immediacy.[2]

In addition, she continues to valorize her own experience as a woman living outside the confines of patriarchal rule. Until Wolfgang defects from the beliefs that have established the relationship between the two lovers, the first-person narrator gives Phyl no disapproval for her adulterous relationship with him. Her matter-of-fact rendering of the rather unusual triangle makes the novel an important breakthrough in terms of women's narrative forms. It gives a woman approval for abandoning a man who no longer shares her ideological and political beliefs without placing blame or judgment on her actions.

A complicated metafiction that uses intertextual references as part of Phyl's reading and rumination, the novel includes important philosophical reflections upon the armistice.[3] It looks at such issues as women's roles during political upheavals, the human inclination to accept the easier route, and the effects of such conflicts upon the human spirit. It also pays tribute to individuals who are able to retain their sense of individual worth in the midst of political contingencies, treating them as important exemplars. The novel suggests that women would wield governmental power more efficiently and humanely than men.

By far the most important character, Phyl, as the novel's narrator, sets the novel's tone and establishes her own honesty and independence of thought in the novel's opening pages. In contrast to her husband's "coolest, soundest, and most objective familiarity with the past and present imaginable" (159), she establishes herself as a compassionate person who has the necessary self-knowledge to recognize that her passions sometimes mislead her into hasty actions. But Boyle clearly indicates that Phyl's instincts are always with the individual's worth and importance within the larger world in which he or she acts. An inveterate reader who questions what she reads by measuring its truth against the reality that surrounds her, Phyl is an important American heroine, unusually well-read and introspective in ways that are generally assumed to characterize male personae.

The novel's important portrayal of Phyl's strong character makes a woman's reaction to occupation the novel's primary subject matter: its center is the story of Phyl's growth. A *Bildungsroman* for an adult woman, the plot forces Phyl to evaluate the importance of personal love when it encounters deep-rooted philosophical and political differences in the beloved. This development provides a personal microcosm for the larger implications of questions of loyalty that surround the French armistice.

In the journal's opening pages, Phyl admits that she possesses "a woman's narrowing of experience, so that in a war she must have had a lover, and in a town made a purchase before either war or town has significance for her" (12). And throughout the novel's early chapters, the war is menacing for her only in terms of its effect upon Wolfgang, an Austrian skier who has joined the French Foreign Legion rather than serve in a concentration camp for foreigners with German papers (the French considered all Austrian citizens as German citizens after the Anschluss). Married to the French Corrine, he and Phyl have begun their affair because of Phyl's personal needs. When she makes this realization, she describes her reaction as a

> cold, determined need to be a part of what is to become of us all [that] possessed me . . . I had gone down to the *gendarmerie* with Benchley . . . when he talked to Leroi, the captain of the Pontcharra gendarmes, about enlisting with the French. I had not wanted his age to be against him; a great disaster was on us all, and I did not want other women to shed my tears for me. And now I can say that Wolfgang became, through accident, the name for the separation. (150)

Since Benchley, an American historian, remains exempt from the army, Phyl can participate vicariously only through taking a lover who will be directly affected. Admitting "I'm no good for anything but action, I haven't the endurance for anything else" (247), she becomes involved with Wolfgang as a way of taking action. Yet she is always firmly aware of her limitations, acknowledging that "what disposition may be made of the Legion under the armistice terms . . . is so personal and small a portion of the whole that I object to its unworthiness" (17). The gaps in the text suggest that if women were allowed more active roles, Phyl would have been less susceptible to this personal collaboration.

Mistakenly, Phyl thinks that Wolfgang shares her passionate resistance to Nazism. She eventually realizes, however, that she has placed her faith in a man who has no principles. When she learns that he is more interested in his own survival than in defeating the Germans, she recognizes that she has allowed her passion to mislead her assessment of his character. But like all Boyle heroines, she refuses to see herself as victim, saying that she has "not the patience to remain with a self whom I can no longer bear" (245). Instead she insists "it is as myself that I have at last, slowly, blindly, stupidly, but at last recognized the choice" (246). Now that Wolfgang has chosen the "clever, the worldly, the shrewd way out . . . I've nothing more to say" (247). Her resentment of the limitations placed on her own participation fuels her attraction for a man who appears more politically active than her husband.[4]

Boyle also uses Lucia's character to stress the unfairness of patriarchal assumptions of power and political action. "[S]mall and slight as a child" (11), she longs to join the battle and is braver and more independent than many of the male characters. When her young friend St. Cyr leaves to join his soldiers, she feels "a savage rage with life that she couldn't be a boy or man and be doing what they had to do far better than they themselves could do it" (16). Yet, Lucia certainly seems more battle worthy than St. Cyr. Home on leave from the Army, he looks "even more childish and foolish than ever in his smart little uniform" for whom "war never meant this in military school . . . His pistol was loaded, and his face was hot as if from illness; he looked too young and too uneasy to be allowed to go" (16). His melodramatic departure contrasts sharply with that of Lucia who valiantly leaves for the south of France on a bicycle, planning to avoid foreign control at all costs.

Clearly, Lucia receives strong approval from the narrator. Her friendship with Phyl offers the novel's strongest emotional link between two people, continuing Boyle's emphasis on the importance of female bonding. The two women also contrast favorably with the novel's more traditionally portrayed women. Lacking Lucia's independence and self-sufficiency, Matilde clings to Phyl, continually asking for her assistance. Matilde uses whatever method is available to keep her weak, artistic husband unaware of the difficulty he causes her, helping him avoid the knowledge of his own insufficiency. Boyle stresses the contradictions in Matilde with her physical description: her face is "very grande dame, and strong-looking, and noble, in contrast to the weak, eager penniless hands" (4). Matilde circumvents the patriarchy, working from within the system to get what she wants. She learned this method from her family, fighting "against the obstinate old man who berates her for her profligacy and . . . against the old woman who clings to life hand in hand with him and who, when she can, slips ten or twenty francs without his knowing it" to Matilde (5).

The novel's other female characters also present more self-sufficiency than the males. Wolfgang's wife, Corrine, a goddaughter of Petain, manages to get to Africa and rescue Wolfgang from the Foreign Legion. Because she left her first husband for him, Corrine's insistence upon remaining married to Wolfgang at any cost seems more pride than love. She refuses to "look into people's faces and say it all came to nothing in the end. To say I was a fool . . . never" (128). She knows Wolfgang's weakness for other women and his desire to be liked and tells Phyl that he "would write anything to any woman to get him out of where he was" (129).

Once a French patriot, Corrine has begun to admire the Germans, saying that "France was defeated because she was profoundly ready to accept the German ideal, the German demigod as redemption, to honor . . . the flesh of Wagner's implacable heroic man" (102). Her response causes Phyl to question the altering of Corrine's mind as either a "sort of genuflection to success" or the "kind of thing the betrayed must repeat to one another to persuade themselves that they have been subjugated . . . by a superior . . . race" (102).

But Corrine is not so weak as Wolfgang, who finally decides to come back to France and collaboration rather than risk death trying to escape. Unable to bear disapproval, he "can have affiliation only with the successful cause" (76). Commenting upon "his incurable preoccupation with applause,"

Phyl records his fears about the disdain he receives as an outcast in the French Foreign Legion. A handsome, muscular blond "who must have a woman on each arm and the approbation of men as well (even the approbation of the husbands of those women on his arm, if possible)" (15), Wolfgang emerges as charming, but unprincipled. Phyl finally realizes that his need to be liked, "not for what he is but for what each person he respected would wish him to be" renders him scarcely more substantial than "the unconfused and perfect athlete who understands one thing only: the exact moment to spring from the board . . . and who waits for that and nothing else besides" (240). As a result, the reader approves Phyl's decision to end their affair upon his return to France.

The reader's reaction to Benchley is, however, more complicated. He knows about Phyl's relationship with Wolfgang, telling her "I'll do what you want to help him—money, if that will do it—but I'll never understand it. A Don Juan, a cheap lady-killer, an Austrian yodeler" (20). But in spite of his generous acceptance of Phyl's decisions, he is ultimately rather ridiculous. Phyl's description of the movie he plans to make about a boot disparages his aesthetics and his ineffectiveness. The entire project sounds pretentious, and Benchley's lack of decisiveness becomes apparent when Phyl describes his difficulty in choosing "the right boot to be cast in the role" (19).

Yet his love for nature is a "thing that cannot be exhausted and cannot go bitter as design and ambition and emulation can" (178). He nurtures his children and helps Phyl get her brother home to America and Wolfgang out of the Legion. She decides that he had known how to take the couple's past "with the naturalness and the fierceness of the man to whom the country, not cities, belongs" (177), but he also seems unprincipled when he is compared to the novel's real hero. And Phyl must have a relationship with a man who has a serious commitment to freedom, one that does not depend upon extraneous circumstances.

That man is not Wolfgang, but the Austrian Sepp, who "will not (as Wolfgang does) ask that things be done for him" (193–194) or ignore the necessity for positive action as Benchley does. Sepp has refused to return to his homeland despite letters from his family and friends asking him "to come back and accept what has to be" (222). But Sepp wants only to reach a de Gaulle recruiting office to continue his resistance to Hitler. And Phyl helps him establish a plan to reach that goal. Although the two do not discuss their feelings for each other, their emotions seem apparent within the subtext of the novel as Sepp receives more and more approval in Phyl's diary. The conversations that she records reveal his dauntless devotion to anti-Fascism and his love for Shakespeare, his family, and freedom. When Sepp gives Phyl his sister's red ladybird pincushion that he has used as a talisman in the concentration camp, Benchley fills Sepp's cup with wine, saying "Have some more love potion . . . This is very Tristan and Isolde" (311).

Seen as products of the patriarchal system, many of the novel's men have become dangerous because of this system's insistence upon surface appearances that deny inner reality and humanity. Phyl describes the Gestapo officers as "those to whom imagination, and thus daring, and thus a spirited temper, and thus a vision, and thus love, have not been given" (207). She reasons that such men "having been thus punished . . . must punish in return" (208). And she looks at the way such character has been formed when she tries to understand St. Cyr's transformation from French patriot to collaborator:

> This is the way it happens to men, in their youth, and once they are taken with it there can be no recovery. It can begin: "You belong to Saint-Cyr [a religious order where Lyautey, a French fascist, studied in his youth]! You are not free!" and the next words will be spoken in St. Cyr's voice saying: "We didn't lift our arms very high. Just enough to conform," and the next confession one more final still. (65)

The individual who has not been trained to question authority falls victim to its capriciousness. Such preoccupation with outer ritual leads to "the magnificently trained and dedicated flesh" that Corrine describes as the German army (101). And it leaves few people to ask the necessary questions raised by Phyl:"What of the foundations, the premise, the end?" (101).

Reflecting Boyle's political ideology, Phyl describes these programs as "even more monstrous" because they prepare men for death on such a grand scale (101). She connects this machine-like approach to war with the French authoritative opinion on absorbing foreigners, describing "the absolute futility of any human appeal in the face of the official machine" (162). And she realizes that St. Cyr has succumbed to the new doctrine to " 'colonize' the Frenchman on his native soil" (136). She sees this dream as "the dream of all disciplinarians . . . who can ignore German ideology because of their envy of Germany's social sense, her taste for collective effort, and her devotion to the state" (136).

The novel uses frequent analogies, presenting the plight of humans against actual war machines, to portray human vulnerability to such ideological systems. Matilde's husband describes his flight under a bombing attack as

> "just running foolishly along, exposed to the machine's exactly calculating eye, and they're up there knowing how futile every move is that you make. You've remained human still, through some mistake in judgment, and they've become superhuman in a diabolic way." (170)

The description captures the vulnerability and helplessness of man against such odds. This idea of the machine as invincible is also apparent in the admiration that Schuwald and Corrine evidence for the German army, even though they have suffered defeat at its hands. Schuwald's supposed-to-be-funny anecdote of the brave Sengalese soldiers who are destroyed by a tank amuses only himself and Corrine; the reader, like Benchley and Phyl, is horrified at Schuwald's lack of feeling.

In contrast with the efficient, machine-like German army, the French forces seem only too human. Naturally rebellious, these men resist authority of any kind. They feel that they have been betrayed by the army chiefs and government, and when they are given ammunition for their guns, declare "Who's talking about shooting the Germans? It's the captain and the lieutenant we want to put away" (9). Lafond, the town mayor, maintains that the men who really love their country in France are "not wearing officer's uniforms, and they're not in the Chamber of Deputies," but are in prison (9). The returning French soldiers who pass through Pontcharra take time to find milk for their adopted pets and make jokes about the campaign slogans that they used in the fall.

Finally the reader must concur with Lafond who argues that "the Fascists have won it. Not a nation, but a class" (33), for more and more of the French succumb to the appeal of the German forces amongst them. And the women appear vulnerable for other reasons than the need to have supported a winning team. Paul, Quincy's friend, suggests that "if you're one kind of woman any kind of uniform looks all right to you after a certain time" and you succumb to the need to wear your new dress and partake in the chocolates being offered by the German soldiers (188).

Yet Boyle sees women's limited participation in government as at least partially responsible for France's downfall. She suggests that French "women had had their part in everything. . . . and they'd been good lawyers, and doctors, and artists, and musicians. . . . The only thing they haven't had their part in is the French government" (190–191). She implies that the lack of female participation is responsible for both France's inefficient armies and the signing of the armistice.[5]

The novel's self-conscious use of stories and story telling helps illustrate the role of rumor in war. Repeating oft-heard stories, Boyle allows the reader to choose an ending, emphasizing the shifting reality of truth itself. In this passage about the role of the press, she emphasizes the ever present difficulty of knowing the truth:

> The French press makes little of the RAF raid on Berlin last night, saying that the English bombed several nonmilitary objectives but caused no damage, but we learn from the English broadcast the possible important effects, and from the Swiss the understatement which lies between the two. (252)

The novel's method often mimics that of the media it describes. Boyle presents various versions of the French defeat and armistice, showing how each character interprets his own truth and tries to put these "down exactly and entirely, every word of it, without judgment here" (239), affording the reader the opportunity to find truth of his or her own. As a result, the novel has added density; the character's stories reverberate against the passages from Mozart, Hegel, Lawrence of Arabia, and Nietzsche that are placed in Phyl's diary without judgment or comment.

The juxtapositions between the stories and the borrowed writing from philosophers make the reader reevaluate both. For example, after Boyle includes St. Cyr's comment that "we didn't lift our arms very high. . . . And then we decided we were making fools of ourselves. After all, the Italians didn't win the war" (63), she makes no comment on his inability to see that he fails to ask the necessary question: Should a defeated French soldier give a Nazi salute? And then she includes a passage from Lyautey with its instructions to "act by way of example, of the respect you show for your own ideals, of your staunchness, of your self-denial" (65). The connection of small gestures with bigger ideals remains for the reader to discover and interpret. Consequently, the novel continues to call attention to the writing process and the relationship between reality and writing.

Primer for Combat presents the inhabitants' various views, reaching no authorial consensus about a singular French vision of the occupation.[6] And the novel maintains psychological tension through Boyle's careful depiction of Phyl's struggle to discover the truth about herself, her lover, and the strange new world they inhabit.

The book provides a concrete criticism of twentieth-century society. It gives a non-doctrinaire presentation of society's failure to nurture the individual's sense of dignity and self worth. The novel also offers an unusually complex portrait of an intelligent woman, one who looks at that society and tries to understand what truths can be discovered by combining her careful, open observations with philosophical reading.

1939 also contains highly unresolved discourse.[7] Giving equal time to each of the novel's lovers, Boyle divides the book into two sections that present Corrine's and Ferdl's versions of their response to war and its impact upon the community created by their illicit love. This equal allotment of physical space for the two stories reflects Boyle's presupposition that the psychological bravery war demands of women is as great as that it demands of men. And through the novel's form, Boyle also subtly reinforces the idea that a woman's experience of war is equally important.

The novel covers the twenty-four hour period just following Ferdl Eder's reporting for induction into the French army. Its immediate action details Corrine's response to Ferdl's departure and his growing discovery that he will not be allowed to serve with the army, but will be placed in a concentration camp for foreigners. As the couple go routinely through the first twenty-four hours of their separation, Boyle juxtaposes their immediate actions with their ruminations about their relationship. These flashbacks provide the exposition for their present situations as the novel breaks linear time, thus allowing for more complicated temporal inversions and the inclusion of memories.

Corrine's section presents her version of the couple's love affair in interior monologues that alternate with descriptions of her rather mundane physical activities. Another of Boyle's love relationships that defy society's conventions established for love and marriage, the couple has been living together since Corrine left her husband, a French military officer, to join Ferdl, an Austrian ski instructor. Four years younger than she, he has remained in the French alps following the Anschluss. Both sections of the novel contain frequent shifts in voice and time and, as in *Primer*, much of the discovery of truth is left to the reader. Within the individual sections, Boyle also changes perspective frequently. As a result, the reader often receives the lovers' perceptions of themselves and their relationship almost simultaneously with other characters' contradictory impressions. This technique underscores one of the novel's major themes: the difficulty of assessing people's interior qualities based on their outward appearance.

In Corrine's section, the people in the small village clearly envy her for "what was shameless and complete declaration of passion, what was beauty too elegant and reckless for these mountains and this village, what was figurehead for Romance naive enough to split your sides with ridicule" (12). Boyle's frequent use of such undercutting keeps the reader maneuvering between the narrator's lyrical accounts of the lovers' emotions and the cynicism that registers how unrealistic such feelings are. It also deflates the novel's occasional inflated language, freeing Boyle's writing from empty abstractions. Forced to reevaluate the relationship between the myth of the couple and their actuality and the myth of patriotism and its reality, the reader assumes the burden of deciphering the true perspective.

Corrine's pride and independence emerge almost immediately. Her "rich, wavy hair springing up from her scalp in pride," her "hollow cheeks," "boy-like shoulders . . . recklessly modelled face . . . uncorseted, narrow body . . . quick and lithe" that takes her "supple-limbed to a flagrant, adulterous bed," and her "painted mouth . . . delicate-boned, unpowdered nose . . . fearless, impatient eye" combine to "defy priest, mayor, and peasant" (13). The villagers' ambivalence toward her is apparent: they hate her for an instant and then forgive her "because of the side of her face turned austere and lovely as an Etruscan woman's against the backdrop of the village" (17). And her actions reinforce her arrogant appearance. She refuses the villagers' attempts to offer her sympathy, jerking "her head in brief, immune dismissal" (15) at the clerks' references to her being alone and their hints that Ferdl will not be returning. But she feels less complacent than she appears; her fears for Ferdl's safety dominate her thoughts.

Combined with the village women's reaction to Corrine, her impression of their response to Ferdl underscores their sublimated sexuality. They respond sexually to his handsome, physical appearance. Corrine's remembrances of Ferdl concentrate on his masculine pride and physical attractiveness, both of which have made him legendary in the village:

> no one else having found yet the name for that puritan glacier of pride which chilled the vocabulary of desire on their tongues and left their throats (the mothers and wives and virgins out of school) choked with what (your blood standing as cold as the shop's pane between their mouths and your mouth) could not be decently said. (24)

Just as the language stresses the hypocritical puritanism of the town women's response to Ferdl's physical beauty, it also stresses how envious the village is of the couple's illicit relationship. Compared to the pairings of the peasants and local couples, their involvement seems more vital and alive. And it confuses the villagers since it goes against their moral beliefs, but is clearly more intense and attractive than their own relationships. Because the novel's married couples lack the passionate intensity of Corrine and Ferdl, marriage emerges as an example of patriarchal rules that stifle passion and love.

Attacking marriage through Corrine's conversation with the peasant who makes his living by castrating animals, Boyle has him say "That's my calling, cutting the instinct out of beasts like they say the marriage ceremony cuts it out of man" (47). Although he is married with eleven children of his own, he is only slightly more tolerant of Corrine's adultery than the village women are. Like them, he assumes that now Corrine will "take your thirty years and your painted mouth and your shameless eye back to where they came from; you, French, or just pretending to be French, but just as much a foreigner as he was because you took up with a foreigner like him" (51). He wants her to leave so that peace and purity can be restored to the Sabbath and the mountains.

Yet Corrine has never seemed human to the village inhabitants. They have been unable to decide what she is because "they had not read about her in a book or seen her on a moving-picture screen" and they seem incapable of bringing "in without instruction the verdict on this daily re-enacted drama of infidelity" (29). The couple has lived publicly "and without shame" with "the tremulous, wild delight of what they were to each other held cool and even in their eyes" (29). They have become a legend, their hearts "passionate, unblemished sign giving permanence to what other men have only dreamed about or written books to, or at best known in their flesh just once and for a little while a long time back" (30).

Unlike the town women, Corrine doesn't go to church or bear children, and she sleeps with a foreigner. But now, underscoring the leveling effect of war, Corrine has become like one of them, a woman bereft of her man and defenseless against the war and its machines. Once Ferdl joins the other men to take "his part in that gradual, ordered disappearance in which husbands, lovers, brothers, sons, are blotted out first, for a little while from life and then perhaps forever" (35), she also becomes "bereaved in the same way" and is no longer considered a painted stranger in their midst (35). Like them, she must learn to be self sufficient and can no longer depend upon men for protection or physical necessities. Her fierce independence makes her refuse this acceptance; it comes too late to seem genuine.

One of the novel's major themes is the necessity for women's self-reliance. Because they disrupt the usual division of labor—often allowing women to enter industries that were formerly considered to be masculine—wars make women more aware of society's arbitrary definitions of gender roles. This concept is particularly true when women prove exceptionally capable of entering formerly male provinces. The novel offers a clear demonstration of this unsettling effect, for its women appear more capable than their men, especially the ones who remain in the village during the war. The butcher's wife bemoans the mayor's inefficiency, insisting that "if he's a good mayor you can go to him and he'll stand by you" (31), but he fails to see "to the means of transporting and slaughtering livestock when the men are mobilized and the women and children are alone" (31). Forsaking the male promise of protection, the few remaining men leave the women to "look out for ourselves, all of us" (31). The women insist that the priest, doctor, and mayor "stand with their hands out for what we have to put in them, too much before and now a little bit more that the men aren't here to see what's going on" (33). Even Tarboux, the village's pharmacist who adopts Godlike proportions for the local peasants, seems useless and futile when compared to the women.

In order to survive, the women assume masculine roles. The butcher's wife is compelled to slaughter pigs just as she's seen her husband do: she will "get the habit quick enough" (33–34). At first, the women imitate the men because they have no other vision of how things should be. Corrine even takes "a man's nourishment at man-established intervals," saying that since she has "no mayor . . . no priest . . . I exhort a man's history to repeat or defy the errors of the unsubmissive, turning—weak as a woman—to the chronicle of man" (56).

But from the beginning, the women entertain less idealistic views of war and its consequences than those held by the men. Corrine tries to dissuade Ferdl from fighting for his adopted country. The wife and daughter of a soldier, she tells him "let the officers, the fathers, if they must, the husbands, the brothers, die. This is their show, not yours; let war and all the gentlemen costumed and decorated and castrated for it cease if it means this time you have to go" (25). Her ancestors fought with Napoleon, but she feels that France is "mine, not Ferdl's to go to war for . . . My father not his dead at Verdun and no son except what there is of male in me to bear on" (27). She also sees clearly the inhumanity that comes with the military authority of officers, referring to her husband as "Captain Straight-from-the-Barracks-Wear-Your-Medals-Where-They-Show Audal" and "Captain Keep-Them-Down-with a-Gentlemanly-Well-Groomed-Hand-But-Throttle-Them-If-You-Have-to Audal" (40). And she is unintimidated by such empty pomp, slapping her husband twice across the face when he treats Ferdl like a servant.

Ironically, Audal has misinformed her about the army's plans for foreigners so he manages to punish the lovers through Ferdl's incarceration. Her belief that "this time men without passports, whatever their countries had been or were now" would be allowed to serve comes from false information that she has received from her husband (80), and the reader assumes that his letter has deliberately misrepresented the truth as his revenge for their adulterous behavior.

At the end of her section of the novel, however, Corrine mistakenly believes that Ferdl will be allowed to enlist. She denies the message that Tarboux brings her; he insists that Ferdl will not be allowed to fight and is proven right by the novel's conclusion. His claim that in a Fascist country foreigners would "have been shot the first week to save the food and the vital space" (71) does little to answer Corrine's charge that since Ferdl is an enemy alien for the French government, "he doesn't count as a man any more" (68). While Tarboux insists that in France "we have a rather sardonic respect for life because we haven't acquired the habit of seeing it collectively . . . we as a nation see its isolated dignity" (72), Ferdl's treatment belies Tarboux's claim.

The Austrian emerges as "the outcast of human dignity as well" (77). And he gets imprisoned "like a criminal" for volunteering to give the French "the only thing that history's left him . . . his skin" (79). Reminding the reader of the fragility of the individual against systems that deny their individuality, Tarboux concludes that even the legendary Ferdl will "be lost to official memory the way his identity is already lost," unless someone "puts the question" about his whereabouts to the proper authorities (81). By raising these considerations, Boyle continues her insistence on the necessity for questioning society's authority and arbitrary systems that are allowed to rule over the individual, making him or her powerless to act.

And the second half of the novel presents the individuality of Ferdl's predicament clearly, giving other versions of the public legend of Ferdl and Corrine and demonstrating that the worst of Tarboux's assumptions are correct. It also uses the first half as a kind of intertextual reference for the reader, one that he or she is now forced to revise. For example, Ferdl's best qualities, his "habit of pride and reticence taken young" endanger him in this section. They inhibit his attempt to join the French army since he refuses to "give them none of the history of this sort of honeymoon he was taking with his own identity, hauling and hacking and skiing his own way to redemption" (85). And when the reader encounters Ferdl's account of his struggle to build his home in the French alps, then Corrine's earlier claim that for Ferdl "this house, only this house, is Ferdl's nation" (54) becomes true in a way that was not clear before. These details reinforce Boyle's careful delineation of the complicated conflicts that arise when individual senses of nationality come up against national doctrines and prejudices.

Ferdl's section also reinforces the connection between national policies and the family unit. In Ferdl's imaginary dialogues with his family, Boyle presents their calloused insistence on his being what the family has expected, ignoring his individuality. The father insists that "my son was to have been what I was before him . . . he was to have lived by the faculties of his mind . . . not by the muscular development of his legs" (92). His father castigates him for the sacrifices that his family has made and his own indifference, insisting that Ferdl has given up everything for a woman. His sarcastic description of his son as "that flesh and blood and bone we conceived twenty-six or seven years ago and put our hopes in and our schillings aside for . . . stooping down before foreign women fastening their skis on their feet for the price they pay him" (95) demonstrates that his real concerns are not for his son, but for his family's name and his own pride.

When Ferdl's young sister Luise speaks, Boyle uses her description of the doll's house that the two children have shared to underscore the roles that men and women must play because of society's expectations:

> the water . . . turned the wheel inside the doll's house . . . so that every two minutes the wooden man opened the door on the first floor and ran the length of the balcony and then jerked himself around . . . and as soon as he was gone . . . the wooden woman downstairs opened the front door right away. She'd run out to the pump by the toy birdhouse and fill the bucket and carry it back to the chalet and jerk herself inside the door . . . (100)

The mechanical actions symbolize the governmental and familial mechanisms that govern the individual's freedom. Caught in the pattern imposed by their creation, the wooden man and woman cannot alter their actions. These figures duplicate the actions required of real men and women who have been caught up in a system that they cannot control and in which they are no longer seen as individuals capable of independent thought and behavior.

Ferdl's imagined conversation with Luise also continues Boyle's elaborations on truth's inaccessibility. Luise proclaims that "they [the parents] got the story word by word out of him . . . And by the time they got the story out of him there was nothing left, no truth" (104). And the reader begins to get still another version of the couple's love affair, one in which Corrine is portrayed as an evil temptress who is "protestant, married, and the betrayed husband still giving her the protection of his name" (93). Luise understands that her parents have had to invent their own version of their son to justify their rejection of him:

"They were the first to make something else except a son out of him; only they've told themselves another story; they've saved themselves to themselves by another explanation now that he didn't come back to fight when there was war." (105)

And the passage resonates for the reader as a comment on the necessity of rationalizations in war, the need to justify one's actions through placing the blame on others for one's own shortcomings.

Only Luise can admit that family has no right to dictate behavior to its members without considering their individual desires. When her parents ask her to entreat Ferdl to return, thinking that he will come back to Austria now "that tourists with money in their pockets were pouring in the way they did before the frontier was closed" (106–107), she refuses. She recognizes the power of the individual saying that "I knew he would come back when he wanted and how he wanted, and this would be the thing that nobody else could ask him to do" (107). For Luise allows herself to see other people's truth; unlike her parents, she does not assume that only economic factors motivate behavior. She insists that "they wrote like that to him because he was nothing to them any more . . . because youth is nothing, absolutely nothing to the old" (107), underscoring the age's calloused approach to war's effect on the young. She insists that Ferdl left "for something else he wanted and we didn't know how to give him and his country didn't know how to give him, or else he wouldn't have had to go and he wouldn't have had to stay away" (109–110), emphasizing a common Boyle theme that the individual has a worth that cannot be measured in monetary terms. Reaffirming her belief in the family unit as a microcosm of the larger political world, Boyle shows how this principle of prosperity at all costs gets reflected in national policies as well.

Luise's version of the love story also enables the reader to recognize the lovers' common values, making their love seem more grounded in reality than in its earlier versions. For money also means little to Corrine who has left "the house in Biarritz and the flat in Paris over the trees and water of the Bois, left the monogrammed linen and silver . . . for a blond lad in jumper's trousers and a jersey" who is a "warbling, yodelling, gold-plated figure streaming fast down mile after precipitous mile of snow" (77). The lovers' insistence on creating their own world in which money and outside opinions do not matter emerges as an act of bravery and daring. Consequently, their current separation resonates with more emotion than it had when only the townspeople's and Corrine's version were available.

The lovers' attempt to ignore the outside world proves dangerous as well, making them particularly vulnerable. Their adulterous relationship converts them into targets for hostility and envy which they fail to see. Just as Corrine makes the mistake of believing her husband's claim that Ferdl will be allowed to serve, Ferdl focuses on her and cannot see the reality of his own situation clearly. He "might have begun seeing it then, except that he was still thinking of getting across the street to the cafe where she was sitting waiting without a hat on and her mouth painted and her eyes seeing nothing else" (111), but, like Corrine, he has been blinded by love, a failure that precludes his escaping the *gendarme* who is escorting him to the concentration camp. Corrine is, therefore, "abruptly blotted out as they turned their backs on her," and the train leaves to take Ferdl to the camp (113).

Boyle also uses Ferdl's interior monologues to show his growing awareness of his political situation. In one of the novel's most poignant passages, he holds imaginary conversations with Frenchmen he has befriended and who he feels can vouch for his good intentions toward his adopted country. These doctors and banker's sons inevitably turn away as each of Ferdl's daydreams gets interrupted by his gradual awareness that these people can no longer be depended upon to help him. Emphasizing the ways in which friendships and the individual's sense of self are altered by national policies and politics, Ferdl thinks "by some error in conjecture there seems to be war after all, and I don't know what part I'm cast for. I don't know the proper lines to speak because I don't know yet what role they're going to let me play" (124). Yet he seems bound by the prejudices that have produced the slogans on the walls: "Tous les Autrichiens sont des sales Nazis!" (124). And when he tells the *gendarme* that he wants to train the chausser troops, the Frenchman thinks "A Boche showing Frenchmen how to ski!" (128) and is offended by his arrogance, ignoring Ferdl's skills as a skiing instructor and his French degree in physical culture.

Boyle gives the difficulty that comes with deserting one's family and homeland because of political constraints vivid treatment. Because he wants to meet his mother once more in Italy, Ferdl has applied for a German passport. His sense of being unlimited by geographical boundaries is important to him, symbolizing his need "to be free and be alive . . . the single portrait of himself that must remain unaltered, and that no woman . . . ever came into it at all" (143). But just as he has difficulty choosing to fight his brothers and friends, he struggles with the idea of giving up his identity as an Austrian. He can only see his mother in Italy if he uses the German passport, and he longs to see her. He also clings to the idea that he is "an Austrian still; in spite of the Anschluss" (147). But he realizes that once he lets "them touch the passport of Germany and put their validation on it," he will become a German by virtue of "stamps, the undecipherable signatures of functionaries" (147–148).

So the passport becomes an international bribe that he cannot afford emotionally or psychologically. Finally, he admits that the rules for Tarboux's game of cards also apply to his current situation. He realizes that "you can't ask for two cards, you can't do it . . . That's one of the rules you can't change in the game" (153). Because of Ferdl's thorough questioning of the warring claims on his allegiance, the reader sees the difficulty that he has to overcome before he destroys his newly acquired German passport.

The continued metaphor of war and life as a game played by difficult and sometimes arbitrary rules gives the book a sense of irony and cynicism that contradicts usual assumptions about war being fought for glory and honor. In her portrayal of Ferdl's difficult situation and his indifferent treatment by his adopted country, Boyle stresses that such concerns often lie within the hands of bureaucrats who have no sense of justice or fair play. Balancing Ferdl's argument that "countries don't go, people don't disappear as long as they're living . . . and only death after all wipes families and peoples out" against Tarboux's claim that "nothing ever as grand and final as death can do it, but one small disciplined detail following another effaces the names of countries, of people, families, individuals from the textbooks and from the variously tinted maps" (133), the reader is forced to consider the complexity of each individual's response.

This novel offers an unusually perceptive account of the European situation in 1939, one that emphasizes the special difficulties involved when wars are fought by people whose geographical borders make them neighbors. Given their relative national isolation, Americans often find this an especially difficult problem to comprehend. *1939* allows Americans to look at the emotional complexity of national loyalty in wars between countries who have little geographical separation, a perspective that is unusual for Americans.

Avalanche and *A Frenchman Must Die*—also focused on the European conflict—lack the subtlety of *1939* and *Primer*. This change in her own writing was deliberate. Boyle wrote the two novels quickly for serialization; she wanted to get out an important message about France, her adopted country, to the American reading public. Writing for the audience of the *Saturday Evening Post,* Boyle wanted "to reach as great a number of Americans as possible"; she maintains that she was not writing literature and doesn't "need a critic to point that out" (quoted by Spanier *Artist* 163).

Ironically, *Avalanche* brought Kay Boyle her first large reading audience.[8] Yet its critical reception damaged Boyle's career as a serious writer, particularly because of Edmund Wilson's scathing review. The review set off a controversy that seems to receive its most even-handed treatment in Elizabeth Bullock's response in the *Chicago Sun's Book Week* column (2). Declaring the book a "honey" of an espionage tale, Bullock castigates Wilson for missing "the frankly stated intention of author and publisher."[9] Comparing Boyle's novel to works by Graham Greene and labeling it as "literary adventure," Bullock argues that as such the novel succeeds. Certainly the book relies upon complicated plot devices, but as Bullock points out, the critics seem to be responding more to their own prescription that Boyle "write for Art, for the chosen few" (2). She suggests that such reviewers are saying: "We don't want you to display versatility. When you step out of character like that, it upsets our world, which is inflexible and fitted out with a dandy assortment of pigeonholes" (2).[10] Apparently to Wilson, Boyle's biggest sin is that she disappointed his expectations based upon the stylistic accomplishment of her earlier writing; he makes frequent references to her earlier, more "avant-garde" writing.

Yet *Avalanche* is successful. When it is looked at as one of the earliest versions of a liberated woman's adventure tale, it becomes an important innovation. For women who grew up reading Nancy Drew mysteries with their young, courageous female sleuth, the protonarrative that Boyle constructs may not seem so unusual. But a narrator's approval of an active adult woman who fights against evil forces in a 1944 novel is unusual. The heroine does get her man, an idealized bronze God—making Wilson's claim that the novel overemphasizes romance absolutely true. But the nature of the heroine, the "Girl" as Wilson disparagingly calls her, may in fact be responsible for his over-reaction. Certainly her character makes Fenton an important female role model and establishes the novel as innovative.

Unlike passive heroines of the romantic novel who await their rescue by a male savior, Fenton is an independent young woman who forsakes her French-American family and the safety of America to return to occupied France, her adopted country. She wears "knickerbockers" and "heavy, nailed boots" (46) and "no rouge on her mouth" (47). When she finally encounters her lover, she looks "without equivocation" into his eyes (135). An expert skier who knows the countryside and its inhabitants well, Fenton's involvement in the Resistance does not seem as incredible as Wilson indicates. Her physical courage and physical strength seem a result of her childhood in the mountains of the Haut Savoie.

The narrator never treats Fenton as object, but rather introduces her by describing the qualities of her mind. She has been schooling "herself to quick, cool judgment of face and voice" (5). The caution she displays in identifying herself and her mission is admirable; she thinks "Wait and listen, wait and listen. Do not speak the name of any man or destination, no matter how hot and urgent the words are that want to be said" (6). While many of the locals provide de Vaudois, the Nazi spy, with information he should not have, Fenton says nothing. She even foregoes asking Jacqueminot, the mountain guide who shares their car, for news of her beloved Bastineau, displaying uncharacteristic restraint for a female romantic character. When she realizes that she has unwittingly caused Jacqueminot's death, she volunteers "not to live here as a woman" but "as Jacqueminot did . . . If I could take his place, it might be some sort of retribution" (208).

With her loyalty and determination, Fenton provides the ethical force that drives the plot. Ignoring old Chatelard's warning about the dangers of the mountain, she insists that she "can climb as well as a man" (131). She successfully disguises her interest in the excursion (a chance to ascertain information about Bastineau's death) as pity for de Vaudois. With the creation of Fenton, Boyle transfers many heroic attributes to a female character.

The relationship between the two united lovers is also unprecedented for an adventure tale. Bastineau does not send Fenton away to protect her from involvement in danger. Instead, he tells her "You're in this now with the rest of us," giving her instructions to find out what de Vaudois knows. And the lovers' planned rendezvous is organized primarily to let Bastineau know what she has been able to discover about the gestapo agent's plans. In contrast to the marriages that rescue a woman from poverty, theirs will be one in which the husband has "no roof over my head, no money, nothing to call my own" (208). They marry so that she can work with Bastineau in the Resistance. The novel's *Deus ex Machina* ending with Bastineau's last minute rescue of Fenton seems utterly contrived, but it comes after the heroine risks her life to save a man. Assuming that she will now die, she covers her face, thinking "I am a coward, I cannot take it with the eyes uncovered as the hostages do" (201); her expectations for her own brave behavior within the relationship make it an unusual pairing of equals.

Certainly, no reader can misread Boyle's message about the bravery of the French Resistance and their continued struggle against those who have chosen collaboration. Once one accepts the book as an adventure tale, it becomes one with which women readers can identify without leaving all the brave actions to males. No passive flower of femininity, Fenton is an important role model for women in relationships and in wartime as well. While the novel's complicated plot renders its actions rather unbelievable, at least the feats of heroism and daring are shared equally among the novel's lovers, making it innovative in terms of its treatment of gender issues within the adventure story genre. As Higonnet points out, "gender is not an extractable feature of literary texts but an aspect of the relationships among characters and in turn therefore of plot" ("Civil Wars" 81). Boyle's gender characterization of Fenton marks out a sexual territory, shaping the war narrative as much as the events of the war.

The heroine of *A Frenchman Must Die* continues this new tradition. Even more daring than Fenton, the French double-agent Danielle Monnet continually bests the novel's half-American Resistance fighter, Guy Mitchie. Like Mitchie himself, the reader is shocked to find that the words spoken by the person who set up the roadblock belong to a woman. Her voice sounds "soft, clear, and casual, and unmistakenly Parisian." Dressed in a "man's jacket with a zipper up the front," "trousers that might have been jodhpurs or might have been competition ski trousers strapped neatly inside the climbing boots," and a "motorcyclist's leather helmet," Danielle orders the men to allow her to inspect their cargo (25). She appears "scarcely more than . . . a tall, slender, rather arrogant girl who stood with her hands in her trousers' pockets [placed there because she holds a revolver inside her right pocket], narrowing her eyes at them" (26). Her lips, too, "are unpainted," and she carries a G. I. torch in her other pocket. Her eyes are "cool and fearless," and her voice contains "the edge of contempt" (27).

She dismisses the hero as "tres amusant" in his ill-fitting suit and demands that the other resistance fighter Forelli come out of hiding. She responds to the hero's suggestion that she has been seeking a man based on "a matter of the heart," as "oh, that, . . . the heart . . . If that's what you'd call it" with a brief laugh (32). When she mounts her motorcycle with a "casual and long" stride, she touches "it with that degree of pride which is permitted by tradition . . . only to the male; that singular gratification in the feel and the shape of metal mechanized and rendered animate by its potential speed" (33). When Mitchie offers to drive, annoyed that "she, whose role should be the incompetent one of a girl whose throat is white and whose lips are soft, should be this other thing as well" (34), she refuses, quietly saying "I like to drive . . . Get up in back and hang on hard . . . I'm going to take it fast" (34).

And she does take it fast, too fast for the hero whose forced kiss she wipes from her mouth with her hand, telling him that only he will remember the kiss, and her voice, "above the sound of the motor was quiet, even, cool" (35). She springs forward on the motorcycle, swinging sharply to the curve, before his shots can reach her. As a result of her quick action, Mitchie must walk and lose valuable time in his pursuit of Pliny, an ex-collaborationist who is slowly having all former Resistance fighters killed.[11]

But in spite of his being made to look foolish by a woman, Guy Mitchie is brave and appealing. Tall and handsome, he has distinguished himself in his fight against the collaborators, returning from the safety of America to fight in 1939. His mother, a French woman who married her American husband during his World War I French military service, has trained their son to love her country, and she seems to have given him a great admiration for women. Boyle uses stream-of-consciousness to show the effect of the mother's patriotism on her son and his reasons for being in France. But in spite of his strong mother, Mitchie smugly assumes that women are unable to fight in the resistance. Danielle's actions demonstrate that Mitchie is wrong.

That Danielle's tough exterior hides sensitive feelings and emotions seems to be his first lesson. When he encounters her again, she has destroyed the milk for the quarter and feels remorse that the children must now go hungry. But Mitchie still sees her as "determined on the thing she wanted, reality or dream" (71), and mistakenly thinks that she is chasing a man for romantic purposes. Convinced that his maleness gives him the right to tell her what to do, he says "If you're chasing some poor unfortunate man, my girl, you're going the wrong way about it. No man likes that kind of thing" (72).

When Mitchie blurts out a comment about her beauty, she responds by saying "It's funny, hearing you say that. Funny because nothing like that seems to be of any importance—it hasn't mattered for so long that one simply doesn't think of it . . . like you taking the time to kiss me on the road last night" (73). This heroine obviously has more important thoughts than those of romance usually attributed to females in adventure tales. And like Fenton and Bastineau, these two lovers also look "without equivocation into each other's eyes" (74).

Mitchie immediately tries to assume the role of male protector saying "I want to believe that because we are working together it will not be necessary for you to do any of the foolish, desperate things a woman working alone might have to do" (180). He then "puts his arm in protection in seigniory now through the girl's arm, holding her fast as if against the implacable and impersonal current of a tide" (181).

She allows him this action only after ascertaining that he is indeed the legendary Guy Mitchie. But even now, "the shoulder that pressed against his arm was lean as a boy's, and the straight back that advanced before him was boy-like, and insolently, nonchalantly young" (184). Boyle refuses to give her heroine the typical sexual swoon in which the heroine suddenly becomes softer and more "feminine" that usually culminates such fictional versions of romance and intrigue. Instead, she reiterates Fenton's attributes that stress her assertive, rather masculine character.

Both of Boyle's French Resistance heroines, Fenton and Danielle, seem almost too brave and, therefore, unbelievable. But they would seem just as questionably above normal mortals if they were male. The plots they enact are contrived, designed Boyle readily admitted to keep her serial readers continuing to turn the pages (Spanier *Artist* 162). Written to get her political ideas to a wider audience and for money to support her large family, these works compare favorably with much of Fitzgerald's fiction written for *The Saturday Evening Post* and motivated solely by his financial needs.[12] Yet critics no longer suggest that his more serious work should be held in less regard as a result of his work—to use Wilson's term—"turned out . . . for the popular magazines." Instead, they discuss his stories' success within their genre. By comparison, the treatment accorded to Boyle's serialized fiction seems unfair.

Boyle's adoption of this genre was bold: she risked her literary reputation by placing a woman so firmly at the center of a standard male war story. Unlike most other action tales of combat and intrigue, Boyle's version rescues women from their usual marginal roles as passive observers. She ignores the gender code of war that frequently insists women defer to male power in return for protection. She writes from the female subject position, valorizing male actions only as they are observed by female characters.

Boyle returned to versions of this genre at two other points in her career: in writing *Seagull on the Step* (1955) and *The Underground Woman* (1975). These works, however, seem less innovative than the two novels just discussed. Unfortunately, the more overtly polemical Boyle's works became, the less inventive they seem. In these novels, Boyle returned to the adventure genre because she felt her ideology was too important to risk being misunderstood by an unliterary audience. She seems, however, to forego her usual literary taste when she tries to oversimplify. When they are evaluated as protonarratives, these works do not offer women a greater range of possibilities for exemplifying caring through effective action. By the standards established in my opening chapter, *The Seagull on the Steps* and *The Underground Woman* fail to explore uncharted territory and are only minimally innovative.

Boyle's decision seems deliberate, however, and should not be attributed to an inability to write more complexly. As Boyle matured she came to view writing that was not directed toward political change as mere aesthetics. Both of these novels were written with the specific idea of improving the world. Outlining *Seagull* to her agent, she said that she wanted to "explain France now as *Avalanche* explained France in the year I wrote it" in "*Saturday Evening Post* terms" (quoted in Spanier *Artist* 183).

This adventure genre adaptation depends partly upon an overly contrived murder-mystery formula as well. Mary Farrant, a young woman who has been living in Paris with an American diplomat, is the novel's assertive heroine. Like Fenton and Danielle, this young expatriate woman is an active participant in her political arena; she is not concerned with the artistic worlds of Bridget and Victoria. In response to a challenge published in a local newspaper, Mary goes to the South of France looking for Michel Vaillant, an eponymously named former resistance fighter. Once there, she meets with a series of accidents designed to discourage her, but she retains her conviction that the people of France and the United States can continue their friendship, despite the hostility that surrounds the U. S. occupation of Europe.

Unlike Boyle's earlier heroines, however, Mary faints and swoons, often depending upon last-minute male rescuers for her survival. She seems to have fallen for the unlikeable Peter Cornish because he is convenient; when she replaces him with Vaillant, the substitution seems predictable and contrived. Boyle closes the novel with the two men jousting for Mary's favors; this use of a woman as the spoils of victory is a capitulation to a romantic convention that seems out of character for Boyle—and for the fictional Mary.

The book also inserts heavy-handed symbolism which insures that the audience does not miss Boyle's message. The bus Mary rides is described as "France on four wheels" (32). The Algerian, Marrakech serves as a representative of the French colonies; Mary seems to symbolize "the wheat fields of Ohio" (239) and America's naive—but well-intended—national character. Peter Cornish, as an American diplomat, represents the American who drives a large car, just speaks louder when no one understands his English, and is, generally, an insensitive boor. Vaillant is "new France": he dreams of uniting the good factions in France and America to forge a stronghold against communism and corruption.

Boyle's sincerity seems to get in the way of her critical judgment, and her writing is flat. This is also true of *The Underground Woman*, another book undertaken to explain a political situation to the American public, written when Boyle was in her seventies. The novel's heroine is named Athena, and—for the reader who may have missed the name's symbolism—she explains that "I was also the wrong one to be designated as a goddess of war" (205). She is, as Spanier points out, a thinly disguised Kay Boyle (203). While Boyle has reduced her age by twenty years and her number of children by three, the details of the character's life and her own are highly similar. A widow, Athena teaches at San Francisco State, lives in a Victorian house in a transitional neighborhood, owns a large collection of white earrings, and has a daughter who is involved in a diabolical commune.[13]

Despite its account of the activist sixties, its portrayal of older women as revolutionaries (although Boyle's reducing the age of the autobiographical representation of herself by twenty years makes praising this innovation somewhat problematic), and its depiction of the solidarity of women, the narrative scarcely qualifies as innovative. Working at organizing resisters to the Vietnam war, Athena frequently points out the irony of her name. She renames the folk singer mother and daughter combo, based on Joan Baez and her mother, "Callisto" and "Calliope"; describes the loss of her daughter with over-emphasized allusions to Demeter and Persephone; and insists that "mythology transcends the individual and contains the life stories of all men and women" (195).[14]

The novel's plot is thin. In Boyle's works, the lack of narrative action is usually more than adequately compensated for by psychological depth and lyrical language; her earlier adaptations of the adventure tale contain moments of great excitement. This is not, however, true of *The Underground Woman*. Sentenced to a ten-day incarceration, Athena makes friends with the long-term prisoners and her fellow protestors and raises the consciousness of the inmates by planting flowers, embroidering the men's underwear with "peace" and "love," and organizing a strike. The novel never seems to address the very real differences between the lives of the regular inmates and the lives of the protestors who have chosen to be imprisoned as a political statement, probably because Boyle wants to emphasize their sisterhood.

Once she is released from prison, Athena is held captive in her own home by her daughter and members of a Charles-Manson-like commune. She contemplates, briefly, an affair with a black man who helps her evict the members of the commune. Eventually Athena's protests get her arrested again, and the novel closes with her return to prison. But her proselytizing about the necessity for political involvement stifles any momentum that the skimpy plot provides. As an argument against the Vietnam war, the novel seems ineffective; its plot merely provides Athena with the opportunity to make speeches about civil liberty.

Suzanne Clark posits that the novel is underrated because of its frequent "argument for a moral stance" and its similarities in rhetorical appeal to that of Harriet Beecher Stowe's *Uncle Tom's Cabin*. The thesis of Clark's argument—that Boyle's use of sentimental rhetoric makes her writing unacceptable to today's critics because we have been "well trained in modernism" (148)—may well be true.[15] Clark argues that in this novel as Boyle "rejects the patriarchy, she asserts continuity with women"; she praises Boyle for doing this *"softly"* [emphasis added] (151), making much of Boyle's softness as a feminine opposition to male-gendered modernism.

But the novel lacks immediacy in language and detail. It is not dialogic; it never permits the polyphony of voices of *Primer* or *1939;* it never trusts its readers to fill in gaps, but insists on offering explanations. It uses too-familiar images—from the deer discussed by Clark (148) to the novel's central image of prison to its representation of Tallulah's language—in a way that borders on cliche. While it engenders our approval for Athena's beliefs, it does not engage our emotions as fully as other political novels written by women about this period. Alice Walker's *Meridian,* Marge Piercy's *Woman on the Edge of Time,* and Elizabeth Spencer's recent *The Night Travelers* come immediately to mind as more engaging examples of, to use Clark's term, "rhetorical fiction."

This novel is not a protonarrative that affirms powerful women; it concludes with both Martha, an habitual offender, and Athena returning to prison. While the community of women sing about "liberation inspiration," Martha, who "could not toe the line as a lady was supposed to" (264), looks away. This scene seems to reinforce the lack of real connection between the regular inmates and Boyle's community of protestors, as it illustrates the futility of the women's actions.

Both *The Seagull on the Steps* and *The Underground Woman* seem less successful attempts at using the narrative structure of the adventure genre to reach large audiences, a technique that had helped Boyle with her important concerns in the forties. They were not commercially successful, nor do they bear close scrutiny for their style. But placing too much emphasis on them prohibits a fair assessment of Boyle's career as a chronicler of war or as an innovator of narrative form. Each of her European novels about World War II offers a perspective that differs greatly from that of most American writers of the period. In *Primer for Combat* and *1939,* her use of polyphonic voices makes the works resonate with a dialogic impact that is highly inventive. By presenting these differing voices, Boyle forces her readers to ask important questions about the relationship between individual and national loyalties. She invites a searching look at society's institutions as they are manifest both in individual sexual relationships and in national political policies.

While her more commercial novels handle these issues with less subtlety, they still reinforce Boyle's belief in the individual's simultaneous need for connection and individuation, whether in romantic, familial, communal, or national allegiances. They reiterate her insistence that the public and private are connected and raise important issues about the false assumptions underlying stereotypical representations of gender, racial, and national characteristics. All of these works erase the frequent misconception that war is men's work, reserved for male participants through action or imaginative writing. By their appropriation of war as subject matter, these novels defy the system that relegates men to active participants and women to weaponless spectators. And they all suggest that more active participation by women in the political arena would ensure a fairer, more democratic and humane universe.

War texts often contain elaborately constructed dialogue that makes claims about the ultimate worth of war. Because both sexes are affected by political actions, the texts that describe them belong to both. Boyle is a feminist pioneer in her refusal to accept the more prevalent dualistic vision of women as chroniclers of peace and men as portrayers of war. But her claims as chronicler of war do not rest solely upon her reversals of gender expectations. As Edward Uehling points out about Boyle's short fiction, through "her control of difficult materials," she was able to find war's "moral and aesthetic center," and as a result much of her war fiction invites our closest critical attention (375–376). This claim is equally true of her longer fiction written in the forties.

As Boyle continued in her writing and political career, she came to believe even more firmly in women's responsibility to fight against gender, racial, and national prejudices and to make such fights a matter of public statement and action. She expanded these arenas beyond the boundaries of gender, nationality, race, and age, focusing on the continued necessity for the writer to sound "the inarticulate whispers of the concerned people of his time" ("The Vanishing Short Story?" 115). But she directed much of the energy that might have gone into writing fiction about such matters into direct political action and the more apparently polemical writing of essays.

Notes

1. Maureen Honey points out that the Office of War Information established a Magazine Bureau to encourage authors "to write stories which would make war work sound attractive to women readers," telling editors "to publish fiction designed to weaken prejudice against working women" (39), yet these stories were also designed to "maintain traditional values within a context of radical changes in women's roles" (37). They were intended to encourage women's entering the male-dominated work force during wartime emergency only; women were expected to leave these jobs at the war's end to permit returning male soldiers easier access to employment. *Avalanche* and *A Frenchman Must Die* do not fit the paradigms of such "propaganda . . . falsifying the meaning of women's war work," to use Honey's terms (37), for they assign resistance combat roles to women characters. Fenton and Danielle go into battle, and while this part of the plot is never directly attacked by Boyle's reviewers, I am suggesting that they found this active female participation disquieting at some subliminal level.

Writing about the battlefield has traditionally been a male's prerogative. In his preface to *Men at War: The Best War Stories of All Time* (1942), Hemingway states that his sons can now possess "the book" that contains "*the* truth about war as near as we can come by it," since these "best" stories show what "*other*" men that we are a part of had gone through" [emphasis added] (xxvii, xi). That Hemingway felt threatened by any invasion of such male territory is evident in his response to Willa Cather's front line scene in *One of Ours*. Writing to Edmund Wilson, he dismisses this scene as a "Catherized" version of the Battle scene in *Birth of a Nation*. He says that the "poor woman had to get her war experience somewhere" (Wilson 118). His language suggests that men consider stories about war as their gender's speciality, a no-woman's land that can be infiltrated neither by woman's experience nor imagination. Boyle enters this world and exacerbates her entry by including women warriors.

2.   The novel is not exactly a roman a clef, but as Spanier stresses, "she [Phyl] speaks for Kay Boyle herself" (*Artist* 159). Boyle wrote McAlmon that "Joseph, by the way, is Sepp von Horneck in my book . . . That will give you a pretty accurate idea of what he's like" (3 Nov. 1942. Kay Boyle Collection. University of Delaware Library). The character of Wolfgang seems to be based upon a friend of Franckenstein's with whom Boyle had a brief affair; he is referred to simply as Kurt in letters written to her mother during this period (Kay Boyle to Katherine Evans Boyle. 1939. Kay Boyle Collection. Morris Library, Southern Illinois University).

3.   This novel is described as "a fascinating historical record set down by a sensitive and articulate eyewitness" (Spanier *Artist* 160) or as "part love story" and "part parajournalistic reportage of momentous happenings in contemporary history" (Gado 126). Its polyphonic technique and resonance are generally overlooked.

4.   In a letter to Robert McAlmon, Boyle complains that Laurence should get involved in the war "not from any high falutin' ideas of patriotism, etc., but because it's a thing that's going on and it can't very well be ignored. Laurence and I really parted on the day war was declared in France—our differences were absolutely defined then—and increased from that moment on" (18 Feb. 1943. Kay Boyle Collection. University of Delaware Library). Boyle's insistence on participating in the public life of her time is certainly reflected in Phyl's reaction to—and frustration with—her husband's inactive nature.

5.   The concept that women should be given more government responsibility remained with Boyle throughout her writing career. In 1970 when she was working on the lengthy history of Germany and German women that was never published, she said she hoped "to be able to demonstrate that if individual women had had more political power, and German women *en masse* more power as human beings, the history of Germany might have been a very different matter" (Boyle to Nelle. 31 October 1976. Kay Boyle Collection, University of Delaware Library).

6.   As a result Gado's description of the novel as merely surveying "a small town's society as a microcosm of the French nation" (157) seems particularly unfair. The multiplicity of voices without the more usual resolution to a "correct" vision makes this novel a good example of what Bakhtin describes as a polyphonic novel: "a plurality of independent and unmerged voices and consciousness, with equal rights and each with its own world . . . (that) are not merged in the unity of the event" (6).

7.   Boyle actually began *1939* before working on *Avalanche* and *A Frenchman Must Die*, but it was not published until 1948 by Faber and Faber (Spanier 164). Spanier suggests that Boyle shelved the book because she doubted it would sell. But perhaps Boyle's concerns may have also been motivated by her strong need to defend her adopted country to Americans, and she realized that *1939*, with its rather unsympathetic portrayal of France's xenophobia, would not help her meet that goal. (In *His Human Majesty*, completed in 1949, Boyle shows that this xenophobic reaction is not limited to the French, but is a hazard that all countries faced with war must avoid.) Her difficulty in finding a publisher for the short, uncommercial novel and her need for money may also have been factors.

8.   Boyle believes that this is the first novel to be written about the French Resistance (Spanier 160). Its early response to this war may, in fact, have also weighed against its acceptance. For as Susan Schweik argues, Hemingway describes a canon of war writing that is composed almost exclusively of material that was withheld until after the war (239). According to Hemingway "the good and true books finally start to come out" only after fighting has ceased and authors no longer need worry about censorship and trauma (xv). Interestingly Simone de Beauvoir, a writer who is more readily accepted by feminists than is Boyle, also wrote a novel about the resistance, *The Blood of Others* (1948). Her narrative centers on a male protagonist, giving Jean a gendered conflict that requires him to choose between his father's political action and his mother's pacifism, assigning the two options their more traditional gender associations.

9.   While the book seems designed to explain the role of the French Resistance fighters and to defend the French nation against charges of universal collaboration, Boyle appears to have intended it to be a fairly accurate description of Resistance fighting. She insists that many of the novel's details are accurate; she based them upon stories that she had been told by Marcel Duchamp and Mary Reynolds, the Monsieur et Madame Rose Selavy to whom she dedicates the book. Reynolds had been an active member of the Resistance before a narrow escape over the Pyrenees. Boyle shared the proceeds of the book with the couple (Spanier 237).

10.   Bullock continues to say that "[i]t would be interesting to know what Kay Boyle's critics might have said of G. K. Chesterton's mystery stories, H. G. Wells' pseudo-scientific tales, or, for that matter, much of Robert Louis Stevenson, if they'd reviewed them when they first came out" (2). Jauss' observation that works that disrupt the reader's horizon of expectation may at first be undervalued seems particularly relevant here (26).

11.   Boyle's introductory note to *A Frenchman Must Die* explains that Georges Mandel and Maurice Sarraut, leading political figures in France, were the victims of such retaliation. As further proof of her novel's "accuracy," she cites the trial of Petain in which "all the jurors received letters threatening them with death" if they found Petain guilty (preface). De Beauvoir's Resistance novel also delineates the way in which such violence leads to violence, looking at how the Resistance tactics caused German reprisals, often at random against French citizens who had not been involved in active Resistance fighting.

12.   Boyle wanted these books to help Americans who thought France "had lain down on the job" understand "how all that was simple, and good, and admirable in France had been betrayed" (quoted in Spanier *Artist* 163).

13.   For a fuller explanation of other similarities see Spanier (201–205).

14.   Boyle has explained that in choosing Athena's name she was "saying metaphorically that her father and his generation had given her a name and a destiny which she rejected. I exaggerated Athena's intellectualism so that the development, the final rejection of the myth and quotation, by which she has lived, have more impact" (Boyle to Bessie Breuer. 14 Feb. 1972. Kay Boyle Collection. Morris Library, Southern Illinois University).

15.   I do not, however, consider this novel sentimental, nor would I evaluate the two other novels on which Clark focuses her discussion of Boyle, *Plagued by the Nightingale* and *Year Before Last,* as sentimental. They combine their protonarratives with freshness of language, insight, and female possibility; *Underground Woman* does not. I realize that I am "the product of the dynamics of a system" that Barbara Herrnstein Smith characterizes in her book *Contingencies of Value: Alternative Perspectives for Critical Theory* as impossible to escape: "because we are neither omniscient nor immortal and do have particular interests, we will, at any given moment, be viewing it (a work) from *some* perspective. It is from such a perspective that we estimate the value of a work and also from such a perspective that we estimate its probable value for others" (16). I want to suggest here that Clark's reading is more favorable because she approves the feminist rhetorical arguments that Boyle's text is making and is, therefore, less critical of its method or of what its narrative says about the effectiveness of women's action. Approving this text's depiction of woman as victim and woman as prisoner is problematic for me, despite its positive portrayal of women's nurturing and bonding.

Works Cited

Boyle, Kay. *Avalanche.* New York: Simon and Schuster, 1942.

——. and Robert McAlmon. *Being Geniuses Together 1920–1930.* 1968. San Francisco: North Point P, 1984.

——. *A Frenchman Must Die.* New York: Simon and Schuster, 1946.

————. *1939*. London: Faber and Faber, 1948.

————. *Primer for Combat*. New York: Simon and Schuster, 1942.

————. *The Seagull on the Steps*. New York: Knopf, 1955.

————. "The Vanishing Short Story?" *Story* 36 (July–Aug. 1963): 108–119.

————. *The Underground Woman*. Garden City, NJ: Doubleday, 1975.

Bullock, Elizabeth. "*Avalanche:* The Book Versus the Critics." *Chicago Sun Book Week* 23 Jan. 1944: 2.

Clark, Suzanne. *Sentimental Modernism: Women Writers and the Revolution of the Word*. Bloomington: Indiana UP, 1991.

Ford, Hugh. *Four Lives in Paris*. San Francisco: North Point P, 1987.

Gado, Frank. "Kay Boyle: From the Aesthetics of Exile to the Polemics of Return." Diss. Duke U, 1968.

Higonnet, Margaret R. "Civil Wars and Sexual Territories." *Arms and the Woman*. Eds. Helen M. Cooper et. al. Chapel Hill, NC: U of North Carolina P, 1989. 80–96.

Honey, Maureen. "New Roles for Women and the Feminine Mystique: Popular Fiction of the 1940's." *American Studies* 24.1 (Spring 1983): 37–52.

Schweik, Susan. "A Needle with Mama's Voice: Mitsuye Yamada's *Camp Notes* and the American Canon of War Poetry." *Arms and the Woman*. Eds. Helen M. Cooper et. al. Chapel Hill, NC: U of North Carolina P, 1989. 225–43.

Smith, Barbara Herrnstein. *Contingencies of Value: Alternative Perspectives for Critical Theory*. Cambridge: Harvard UP, 1988.

Spanier, Sandra Whipple. *Kay Boyle: Artist and Activist*. 1986. New York: Paragon, 1988.

Uehling, Edward M. "Tails, You Lose: Kay Boyle's War Fiction." *Twentieth Century Literature*. 34.3 (Fall 1988): 375–83.

Wilson, Edmund. "Kay Boyle and *The Saturday Evening Post*." *The New Yorker* 15 Jan. 1944: 66–70.

Abortion, Identity Formation, and the Expatriate Woman Writer: H.D. and Kay Boyle in the Twenties

Donna Hollenberg

In memoirs written later in life, when they were self-assured, H.D. and Kay Boyle speak of their respective decisions to leave America for the "freedom" of England and France as if their youthful expatriation were simply liberation from outmoded literary conventions and inhibiting roles as women. H.D. wrote, referring to the anomaly of being a woman writer in the male literary world of America in 1911, "We had no signposts, at that time" ("Compassionate" 12). In fact, in both cases their anxiety over the conflict between conventional femininity and literary ambition increased soon after arrival abroad. For although expatriation was ultimately crucial to each woman's artistic development, Europe during World War I and its aftermath also proved a place of personal suffering.

Both women were seriously ill and emotionally troubled in connection with pregnancies during the early part of their sojourns abroad: H.D. lost her first child, stillborn in 1915, and almost died of pneumonia in England during her second, illegitimate pregnancy in 1918–1919 (during which her brother and father died). Although she and her daughter survived, a continuing conflict about creativity and procreativity may have contributed to a third pregnancy and her decision to have an abortion in 1928, a year after her mother's death, a choice that exacerbated her psychological pain (Guest 194, 195).[1] Kay Boyle, in addition to bearing a daughter out of wedlock in France in 1927, after the death of her lover before their child was born, underwent two abortions in the twenties. The first, in 1921, at the beginning of her first marriage, before she went abroad with her husband, seems to have been relatively benign ("Kay" 17–22).[2] The second, during a period of collapse in 1928–1929, when she was separated from her daughter, coincided with the contraction of spinal meningitis (*Being* 317).[3]

Reprinted with permission of *Twentieth Century Literature* 40, no. 4 (winter 1994): 499–517.

Expatriated, bereaved, and separated from their families, both women regressed emotionally during these crises. They reverted to an earlier mode of psychological functioning, a state of mind that H.D. later called the " 'jelly-fish' experience of double ego" (*Tribute* 116), referring to an unnerving heightening of perception after her daughter's birth, and that Kay Boyle described as a "total disintegration of whatever I was or was not" (*Being* 317), referring to the period of depression and promiscuity before her second abortion. However, perhaps because their emotional adaptation had falsified them in the first place, this regression led to a penetrating exploration, in their early fiction, of psychological and social patterns that contributed to the repetition of the very gender roles they chafed against.

Both writers record their painfully acquired maternal subjectivity in psychologically specific ways, and they learn to read their personal circumstances as part of larger cultural power structures. In particular, such *bildungsromans* as H.D.'s *Asphodel, Paint It Today,* and *Palimpsest* and Kay Boyle's *Plagued by the Nightingale, Year Before Last,* and *My Next Bride* embody a psychological drama of underlying, problem-ridden mother-daughter attachment that combines with a social drama of exile, with conflicting longings for freedom, and with yearnings for a maternal home. In addition, H.D. in her short story "Two Americans," written shortly after her abortion, uses geographical and racial metaphors to recast her anxiety about motherhood and authorship in cultural terms. Because of their protagonists' position between cultures, the meanings of "home" and "abroad" become overdetermined and ambiguous in these texts. Each is alternatively oppressive and desirable, so that they cancel each other out as areas outside the self, revealing, instead, an inner region that has been repressed (Gilbert).[4]

Such feminist theorists as Jessica Benjamin, Nancy Chodorow, and Luce Irigaray have analyzed the effects of gender polarity on the formation of identity. For these theorists the view of female development prevalent in general psychoanalytic discourse, in which differentiation from an objectified mother is necessary for successful initiation into heterosexual adulthood, does not adequately analyze the effect of maternal subjectivity, or its lack, on the developing child. Benjamin's investigation of the interplay between love and power considers domination and submission to be the result of a breakdown in equal and mutual human relationships rather than of inevitable aggressive instincts in human nature. Benjamin blames this unbalance on the division of labor, which empowers the male as a subjective agent and sees the female as immanent and unchangeable. She calls attention to the child's need to articulate the mother's independent existence as a factor in the formation of her/his identity, which, she argues, results optimally from mutual recognition, from both attunement and separateness, rather than simply from separation. Chodorow, too, stresses the importance of analyzing maternal subjectivity. In her discussion of the reproduction of mothering, she stresses the differing consequences of women's mothering for girls and for boys. Because girls are the same gender as the mother, she argues, they tend not to develop firm ego boundaries, never separate completely from the mother, and hence are less cut off from pre-oedipal modes of experience. Irigaray claims that because the pre-oedipal relation between mother and daughter is less repressed, women's selves remain more fluid, interrelational, and less split off from bodily experience than men's, a situation that is not yet fully represented in existing (phallocentric) discourse.

These early works of H.D. and Kay Boyle, written in the context of extreme, even transgressive, maternity, move toward filling in this gap in representation. Here Shari Benstock's point concerning numerous white American women writers is relevant: that because such women were already "expatriated in patria," living abroad enabled them to externalize in their writing the internalized exile they felt at home (25). Instead of providing an escape from gender roles, expatriation resulted in clarification, so that they could "write out" their sense of exclusion from internalized patriarchal law and self-definition. I would add that, because they were unable to reconcile their artistic ambitions with the conventions of motherhood they had internalized, H.D. and Boyle delineated a threshold of conflicted female affiliation that was crucial in the development of their mature vision.[5]

Like many other women writers, in their early fiction H.D. and Kay Boyle write about fears of self-loss through immersion in the roles of marriage and motherhood. Such fears drive H.D.'s fictionalized autobiographies *Asphodel* and *Paint It Today*, written in the early 1920s, both of which return obsessively to the period 1911–1920, years marked not only by her expatriation but by the attenuation of her friendship with Frances Gregg, the failure of her engagement to Ezra Pound, the failure of her marriage to Richard Aldington after the stillbirth of their first child, her near death during the second, successful pregnancy, and finally, her rescue by Bryher (Winifred Ellerman), the younger woman writer who would become a lifelong friend. As in H.D.'s life, in both novels the heroines' fear of the incompatibility between their literary ambition and the social institutions of marriage and motherhood threatens their integrity. In both, trauma connected with pregnancy causes them to regress.

Since a woman reexperiences her self as a cared-for child when she becomes a mother, her identification with her own mother often revives issues from her childhood that have remained unresolved (Nadelson). As I have written elsewhere, trauma in pregnancy bound up this identification in H.D.'s case, increasing her need to reconcile motherly virtue with intellectual achievement. In these early novels she invented competing imaginative strategies to accomplish this reconciliation, both of which revealed instead the social and emotional constraints that inhibited it. In *Asphodel,* H.D.'s heroine, Hermione, associates writing with virgin birth, thus tacitly acknowledging the power and safety of the patriarchy by excluding men who would make her feel vulnerable. Her affair with Cyril Vane, who takes her to his country home in Cornwall to rest and write poetry after the stillbirth of her first child and the failure of her marriage, is depicted as an idealized compensation for her extreme emotional distress. Her second conception in this magical setting, amid the remains of Druid goddess worship, has a marked parthenogenetic quality: she thinks about her compelling wish to develop her own genius and welcomes a swallow flying outside her open window as an omen of God's will. A symbol of artistic annunciation, this swallow is associated less with biological conception than with her need to incorporate an omnipotent idealization of herself.

In *Paint It Today* H.D. divorces mothering from heterosexual subordination, replacing it with a lesbian love that enhances the heroine's sense of integrity by enabling her to mother herself. After Midget's friendship with Josepha has been marred by the latter's marriage and motherhood, to which Midget responds with intense anxiety, her rededication to writing takes the form of a more satisfying lesbian relationship with an alter-ego, Althea. This relationship culminates in a veiled allusion to the welcoming of a child, described as an embryonic being, part self, part other, that suggests a desire for personal integration and ownership of her (pro)creativity.

In both novels the voyage away from proper turn-of-the-century Philadelphia to cultural centers in Europe exacerbates the heroines' conflicts. The distance from home enables them to recognize evidences of sexism that riddle the splendor of the historic shrines they visit, but instead of whetting their ambition and anger this new insight provokes more fear and guilt. For example, in *Asphodel*, when Hermione visits the birthplace of Joan of Arc, she considers the risks that her own unconventional ambitions could incur. Like herself, Joan of Arc had "visions"; for this she was burned at the stake as a witch and a heretic, a punishment that Hermione describes in terms of gender roles: "They had trapped her, a girl who was a boy and they would always do that. . . . This was the warning" (9). And her initial rebellion against the institution of motherhood, evident in an irreverent meditation on the story of the Madonna and Child, becomes fraught with guilt as she remembers her own mother, whose conventional life makes her feel ashamed by comparison: "Such a good little Eugenia with a bustle and her hair caught with a diamond arrow. . . . I'm not good" (23).

Similarly, in *Paint It Today* the tension between home and abroad, neither of which satisfies, echoes and intensifies the heroine's sense of self-division. Midget's attempt to escape the stifling effect of rigidly defined sex roles by remaining in Europe with her friend Josepha is thwarted by the latter's mother, who insists that her daughter return to America, a step that leads to Josepha's marriage and motherhood. Midget's own mother's approval of this plan provokes a matricidal fantasy that only increases her guilt, as self-expression becomes associated with devastating hurt and reprisal. Moreover, although Midget does stay abroad, war erupts soon after her own marriage, and she feels estranged from her soldier-husband, who returns from France "with the smell of gas in his breath . . . the stench of death in his clothes" (46). Marital unhappiness, anxiety at the news of her friend's pregnancy, and disillusionment with a culture that could produce world war, cause Midget to develop a new trick of seeing, a mode of perception that transforms the horror of her world to "snow and ash" at great personal cost. This ability to distance herself, reminiscent of the strategy of repression H.D. employed in her Imagist poetry, provides Midget with a means of artistic survival that soon proves unsatisfying.

H.D. gives this conflict over creativity and procreativity resonance in *Palimpsest,* where she takes an archaeological concept as the principle of coherence for three related stories which, taken together, represent a critique of female identity formation in a patriarchy. (A palimpsest is a "parchment from which one writing has been [imperfectly] erased to make room for another" [title page]). Under this rubric H.D. connects "Hipparchia," a story set in "War Rome" (the ancient city she associated with London), seventy-five years before Christ's birth; "Murex," set in "War and Post-war London," the place and period of her pregnancies; and "Secret Name," set in the timeless modernist locale of "Excavator's Egypt." Thus, as Susan Friedman has pointed out, the historical, the personal, and the mythical intersect, and travel through space and time becomes a central metaphor for a woman artist's coming to understand herself ("Exile").

The concept of a palimpsest also allows H.D. to layer the psychological issues that concern her. By presenting the three stories as related "scrapings," she combines the heterosexual romance plot with an underlying story of problematic mother-daughter attachment. "Hipparchia," the story of a woman whose attempts to separate from her mother complicate her relationships with men and with her work, shows the uneasy conjoinment of the two plots; in "Murex," where a woman's poetry encodes maternal loss, the intersecting plots produce artistic inhibition; and "Secret Name," where the heroine is awakened to a buried source of creative power within herself during a visit to the tomb of a dead Egyptian king, implies that integration and artistic independence are contingent upon modifying the androcentric romantic myths that influence women's sense of possibility. In all three, the need to ground creativity in a revised story of female development, and an awareness of the connection between the personal and the political, are central to a cohesive sense of self.

The connection between maternal subjectivity, expatriation, and broader cultural hierarchies of power is most poignantly depicted, however, in a short story that H.D. wrote after her abortion in the late twenties, in which issues of gender, nationality, and race intersect. Not surprisingly, H.D.'s abortion intensified the conflict between motherhood and authorship, described above, making her struggle for psychological integration and artistic expression increasingly desperate. As she indicates in her short poem "Gift," her "ardent / yet chill and formal" poetics was becoming increasingly untenable (*Collected*

338). Yet she lacked the positive inner imagery necessary to effect an imaginative breakthrough. In "Two Americans" she resorts to racial stereotypes, in which blacks become the repository of libidinal longings, to clarify her conception of herself as a woman artist in ways which also express her sense of having transgressed gender roles.

It is important to say, here, that H.D.'s use of racial stereotypes to serve her own needs was unconscious and even contradicted her intention. I agree with Susan Friedman that the gender issues H.D. struggled with led her to critique other aspects of the social structure that were inhumane and oppressive. She did indeed identify with all marginal people—Jews, blacks, Indians, homosexuals—who were similarly falsified by racial or sexual stereotypes ("Modernism"). However, I would add that the nature of that identification, at this particularly low point in her life, also led her to participate in a version of "romantic racism" that was prevalent in white Modernist writing. As Aldon Nielsen describes it, this discourse, often admiring in tone, proposes the nonwhite "as an unconstrained libido acting out the sexual and social fantasies of the white subconscious" (11).

More specifically, race became a significant marker of H.D.'s conflict when H.D. met Paul Robeson, whose artistic success in London in the late twenties had made him an international celebrity. She admired Robeson's attempts to portray the dignity and humanity of his race in recitals of Negro spirituals and his ambition to act in films that would controvert the racial stereotypes that were perpetuated by both the American and British film industries (Schlosser). She and her companions, Kenneth Macpherson and Bryher, invited Robeson and his wife Essie to their home in Switzerland to make the experimental film *Borderline* in 1930, in which they wanted to show the connection between white racism, a psychological phenomenon growing out of the deplorable history of race relations, and other noxious psychic states (Friedberg 132). In particular, they connected white racism with unhealthy repression of the sexual instincts, with "neurotic-erotic suppression" (H.D. "Borderline" 32). In the film Robeson plays the role of Pete, a black man living peacefully in a mid-European "borderline town" until the arrival of his mulatto sweetheart, Adah (played by Essie), ignites an interracial tangle with a degenerate white couple, Astrid and Thorne (played by H.D. and Gavin Arthur). The "dipsomaniac" Thorne deserts Astrid to have an affair with Adah, which drives Astrid into a jealous rage. The town is disrupted, and Pete and his sweetheart leave unhappily (Duberman Chap. 8).

In an essay accompanying the film, H.D. draws on racial stereotypes to denounce both racism and sexism, stereotypes that reappear in "Two Americans." Pete is described as an exemplary creature of the natural environment in stark contrast to the enervated white man, and it is Adah's suspicious sexuality that drives the plot (Nielsen 88). Thorne acts out his (sexual) "cravings" with Adah, a woman on the "other" side of the social/racial border, who complies. His deserted wife Astrid, "the white-cerebral," finds recourse in an "intemperate fury" that whips her into a state of "dementia" in which she very nearly stabs herself and her husband with a dagger. Astrid's words, "It has all happened because these people are *black*," reveal how much rage between the sexes is concealed behind the ideal of the pure, "cerebral" white woman, who feels robbed by her husband's attraction to the body of another woman for sexual satisfaction, an avenue not openly available to her (H.D. "Borderline" 46).

That H.D. took the role of this self-destructive woman, whose racism also serves an inimical cultural ideal of womanhood, is particularly poignant given her own sense of loss after the abortion. As if in grim self-parody, she is listed in the cast as "Helga Doorn," a pseudonym she chose because of its affinities with Ibsen's melodramatic women (she mentions Hedda Gabler in her essay), whose desperation and debasement similarly reflected widespread discontent. Thus racial fantasies become a vehicle for critiquing the sexual double standard.

Issues of nationality, race, and gender appear to intersect more benignly in "Two Americans," a story based on an informal gathering that may have taken place during the Robesons' visit with H.D. and her friends. A close reading, however, reveals a level of unintegrated anxiety beneath its surface detachment that appears related to H.D.'s abortion. Here H.D. explores the psychological ground between two expatriates—a white American woman poet Raymonde Ransome (based on herself) and a celebrated black American male singer, Saul Howard (Paul Robeson)—who are brought together by Daniel Kinoull (Kenneth Macpherson), the British director in whose film they are working. The story's impetus is Raymonde's troubled response to Saul's easy friendship with Daniel as a fellow artist, despite his racial difference, a camaraderie she cannot share. Though, like Saul, Raymonde admires Daniel's work, her earlier sexual intimacy with the film director has given her feelings of personal defeat that she cannot account for satisfactorily. Her relationship with Daniel has become a burden: he is like a "steel pin," or a "silver thorn" in her side, which she must rid herself of in order to write more freely ("Two" 95). Saul appears to have successfully used his role as artist to overcome the psychological setbacks of being a black American, so she uses his example to bring the dimensions of her own difference "home" to her.

Henry Louis Gates's point that race is the "ultimate trope of difference," because it is so arbitrarily applied in a racist, sexist society clarifies the meaning of this identification. Because the polarity between black and white persists in culture independent of any significant biological reality (unlike that between masculinity and femininity), the use of racial metaphors in this text allows H.D. to perceive truths about gender that ultimately explode the parallel with race. Again she describes Paul Robeson's presence in mythic terms which float upon the same pool of racial fantasies that are evident in *Borderline*. Again, these fantasies place her protagonist in a double bind. For though her artist-heroine's identification with the celebrated African-American singer is partially self-affirming, in that it confirms her own artistry, her womanhood is still subject to an inimical cultural ideal.

For despite the fact that they are both marginal Americans, Raymonde sees Saul's self-acceptance in terms which ally him with a pagan tradition more conducive to free artistic expression and sexuality than her own Puritan one. He is a dark fertility god, able to inspire the whole company with his talent: "He was no black Christ. He was an earlier, less complicated symbol. He was Dionysus as Nietzsche so valiantly struggled to define him" (94). Unlike her own "crippled song-wing," which was too "shrill," his song "flowed toward all the world, effortless, full of benign power, without intellectual gap or cross-purpose of hyper-critical consciousness to blight it" (94). She would like to be the Apollonian counterpart to his Dionysus, but despite her efforts she can't make this self-representation stick because of guilt connected with her being a woman.

H.D.'s concealment of the causes of Raymonde's "cross-purpose of hyper-critical consciousness" provides clues to her own psychological concerns even as it undermines the story's coherence. Raymonde attributes her "crippled" emotional condition both to an obligation to protect Daniel, who after the war "brought back [her] faith" (we're not told in what), and to war memories that continue to haunt her. Though H.D. does not make the factual content of these memories explicit, she depicts the lingering emotional affect, the monstrous guilt and pain that are the cause of Raymonde's anxiety. Like H.D., Raymonde is suffering from "a certain sort of monster," a deeply punitive sense of self:

'Thou shalt kill' reversed commandments for her. She had taken that ever-so-great War too seriously. She had recalled 'thou shalt kill' far, far too personally; it had become for her an actual blood-Minotaur or a sort of blood lust incarnate. (112)

Though these veiled references to killing make the narrative obscure, knowledge of H.D.'s life and earlier, autobiographical fiction accords them psychological credibility and importance. For although in this story she does not fully express her feelings about the transgressive decision to abort, she does inscribe her guilt in the form of her heroine's clouded memory of an earlier wartime death. The narrator's observation that Raymonde had taken " 'thou shalt kill' . . . far too personally" conflates H.D.'s abortion with her earlier stillbirth during the war in a way which forgives her agency in the later decision. This conflation makes further emotional sense when we recall that H.D.'s anguish after that stillbirth was increased because she had been ambivalent about the pregnancy. In *Asphodel* she fictionalized her negative feelings explicitly, depicting her heroine's pregnancy as a "deadly crucifixion" and comparing her ordeal in labor with that of a soldier in battle (113). Thus, though it is not explicitly acknowledged in the text, Raymonde's comparison of herself with an "other" (black male) American artist is implicitly in the service of defending an impugned womanhood.

H.D.'s deep-seated anxiety about her womanhood is operative at a second point in the story when problems of gender role again supersede racial difference or national affinity. For Raymonde identifies with Saul Howard against his light-skinned wife, Paula, whose criticism of her husband, Raymonde suspects, results from feeling overshadowed by his fame, though it takes the form of an apparent racial slur. (Paula accuses her husband of being "lazy.") Dismounting her own suspicion that maybe Saul is lazy, Raymonde infers that Paula's criticism of him is related to her attempts to be "Paris and chic," but different "from that tribe who had given jazz to Europe" (101). Though Paula's behavior threatens her racial integrity, it insures her the sexual attention usually accorded a beautiful (white) woman, attention she needs to shore up her self-image as the mere wife of a famous artist. Paula's willingness to sacrifice racial integrity for social gain is an exchange that Raymonde considers anathema.

Finally, Raymonde's inability to identify with *either* Saul or Paula eradicates the parallel between gender and race that has occluded the deeper sources of Raymonde's anxiety, and she is driven into psychological retreat. Though she feels a rivalry with Paula for both Saul and Daniel, Raymonde prefers to detach herself from sexual competition. Instead she allies herself with Gareth (Bryher), whose asexual, "schoolgirlish" interest in Saul is less threatening to Raymonde's fragile artist-identity. Unlike the black singer, whose sexuality coincides with his artistic goals, or his light-skinned wife, who trades on hers, she adopts the asexual mask of "scribe and priestess" to avoid guilt or compromise.

In the mid-thirties, analysis with Freud was a key factor in enabling H.D. to move from this self-protecting emotional stance to a more positive utilization of her maternal subjectivity in her art, a process that has been described more fully elsewhere.[6] Although beyond the scope of this paper, it is noteworthy that H.D. glanced back at the period around her abortion and her friendship with the Robesons in the first section of her last long poem, *Hermetic Definition*. Here the speaker's ability to mediate between opposites in the universe (her connection with Hermes) is dramatized by employing the trimesters of pregnancy as a central trope. Again, infatuation with a young black man is instrumental.

Problematic maternity as a catalyst in the development of authentic, cohesive selfhood, viewed from an expatriated perspective, is also evident in three of Kay Boyle's first four novels, *Plagued By the Nightingale* (1931), *Year Before Last* (1932), and *My Next Bride* (1934). Based on traumatic events in Boyle's life, these novels cover the period between 1923, when she and her French husband, Richard Brault, arrived in France, and 1929, when she began a new life with her second husband, Laurence Vail. In this interval she separated from Brault during a serious illness, conducted a doomed love affair with the dying poet Ernest Walsh, gave birth, out of wedlock, to her daughter Sharon, and joined Raymond Duncan's "artists' colony," where, according to her account in *Being Geniuses Together,* she became increasingly depressed and self-destructive. As in H.D.'s novels, fears of self-loss through traditional female roles determine the atmosphere of these three works, although the heroines of most of Boyle's novels are not fledgling artists but simply bohemian young women in search of definition. Again, troubled motherhood and abortion combine with expatriation to cause self-division and regression. In Boyle this combination leads not only to insight into the way female self-denial is socially constructed, as it does in H.D., but to a more outer-directed thematic focus on her later work, and to political activism upon her return to America.

In Boyle's novels the initial equating of America with convention and entrapment and Europe with freedom and independence is reversed, illuminating both as geographical metaphors for inner struggle. Her heroines come from American families who have instilled a spirit of adventure and individuality that they are inexplicably unable to realize. They experience painful interpersonal relationships in terms of European cultural decadence and class warfare, thus externalizing an inner conflict that has oppressed them. In *Plagued By the Nightingale,* although her own American family has inculcated individualism, Bridget finds the security offered by the inbred, tightly knit family of her French husband, Nicolas, reassuring despite its price. She welcomes the prescribed world of his Papa, Maman, and sisters, although she recognizes the literally paralyzing control they have over her young husband, who is heir to the family bone disease as well as its fortune. Desiring freedom and independence on one hand, she is afraid of being alone on the other. In the end she succumbs to the family's pressure to become pregnant despite her husband's unwillingness to inflict his disease on future generations and his resentment at having to produce an heir in order to receive money from his father. Willing to accept his family's proviso because she can think of no other way to "make a fortune" and get away, she denies her own tears at the unacknowledged exploitation of her body (90).

Extreme self-abnegation as a condition of motherhood becomes more explicit in the fate of Bridget's favorite sister-in-law, Charlotte, the epitome of womanly graciousness and warmth. Pregnant with her sixth child at the age of thirty-two, Charlotte is unable to imagine any other existence: "One more won't matter," she replies to her brother's worried remonstrance. "It's my life, isn't it?" (128). When she falls ill with a disease resulting from her incestuous union with her husband, a first cousin, and the family tries to deny the seriousness of her illness, she expresses her growing distress as a longing for the nightingale that has disappeared from the ancient acacia tree outside her window. A powerful symbol of violation and enforced silence through its association with the myth of Philomel, and, ultimately, of the transformative power of sisterhood and song, the nightingale here becomes associated with Charlotte's death.

The bird also becomes associated with Bridget's failure to help Charlotte or to learn from her experience. To cheer her up, Bridget buys Charlotte a nightingale in a wooden cage, but it will not sing. When she discusses this problem with Luc, the young doctor who the family has assumed will marry one of Nicolas's sisters, Bridget suggests letting the bird go as a solution. Luc's reply mirrors Bridget's existential dilemma: "You can't just *give* freedom. It's a much more complicated thing than taking it away" (158). Indeed, Bridget's own desire for freedom is played out through her relationship with Luc, whom she manages to free from the grim prospect of marrying into the family. Eliciting his offer of love and then rejecting it, she gives him more freedom from the social script than either she or the nightingale has. Despite her insight, she is unable to extend this freedom to herself.

The emotionally flat ending of the novel becomes explicable when we consider that although Boyle began the novel during her marriage to Richard Brault, father of the first child she aborted, she did not complete it until after the birth of her daughter Sharon, who was conceived out of wedlock during a love affair with Ernest Walsh after she had separated from Brault. In a recent interview, in which she defends these early choices, Boyle poignantly remembers "the passing of the little thing," although she disavows guilt over the abortion, and she is adamant about having wanted Walsh's child, despite its illegitimacy. Perhaps the "very deep feeling" she recalls (198), which she associates with the birth of her daughter, was charged with the memory of her earlier loss, and these mixed feelings were displaced onto her first novel, resulting in the novel's ambiguity.

Her next novel, *Year Before Last,* chronicles her love affair with Walsh, omitting any reference to the pregnancy. On the surface a paean to free love and the pure life of the spirit, to bohemianism versus bourgeois philistinism, this novel contains a subtext of moral masochism that may also be a function of the author's internal conflict. Boyle's heroine, Hannah, whose palindromic name underscores her lack of self-definition, is an American woman in an unhappy marriage to a conventional Frenchman, who falls madly in love with a tubercular young Irish poet and editor, Martin, as if commitment to his spiritual force will give her the courage she needs to live her own life. As the novel opens, they are living in a deserted French château with barely enough to eat, having abandoned their respective domestic obligations: she, her husband, Dilly, who has sent her to southern France to recuperate from a lung ailment, and he, his aunt Eve, a glamorous suffragette who bankrolls his literary magazine. The novel follows their life together during the year before Martin's death, as they move from village to village, looking for an inn that will permit them to stay, so that he can recover and put out his magazine. The intensity and instability of their lives, and their sense of homelessness in the face of those who fear contamination, could be read as a metaphor for the plight of pure art and love in an inhospitable world.

Indeed, Sandra Spanier has interpreted the novel as an assertion of the unassailable, transcendent power of love (Chap. 3). While I agree that this is its dominant thematic line, I would add that Boyle's idealism is undercut by her depiction of the lovers' ambivalent relationship with Eve, Martin's Scottish aunt, who functions as a mother-figure to both of them. In the psychological dynamics of this ménage-à-trois, Boyle shows the masochism underlying Hannah's social alienation, the sense of fragmentation marked by gender polarity and a diffuse sense of guilt. Eve—the character is based on Walsh's older friend Ethel Moorhead, who was a feminist activist and an artist in her own right—could have been depicted as a strong role model for Hannah. In *Being Geniuses Together* Boyle describes her attraction to Moorhead's independence and commitment to poetry as well as the older woman's jealousy of her affair with Walsh (174–80). However, in the novel the narrator stresses the two women's competition for Martin's love, which makes such an alliance impossible. Compared with Eve, who "knew her way and had it," Hannah is a self-effacing presence, "a hesitant wife as frail as a thread . . . who was lingering now, on the outskirts, cringing, and waiting to be bid to go or come" (*Year* 154).

In fact, the parts played by Hannah and Eve resemble the splitting of the erotic and the maternal in conventional representations of femininity, to which Boyle may have resorted imaginatively because of psychological stress. As Suzanne Clark has suggested, Boyle seems to be questioning "whether the erotic young love of Hannah and Martin has any moral force" compared with the stronger older woman's chaste dedication to their common artistic project (143). Boyle, however, accords Hannah's love for Martin the superior power. At the end of the novel, having fought with Eve about ownership of the magazine, Martin cries out for Hannah's presence. Further, Eve overcomes her animosity toward the younger woman when, desperate for Hannah to save the dying man, she suggests that the three of them start over.

A comparison of Eve's role in the novel with that of Ethel Moorhead in the lives of Boyle and Ernest Walsh confirms the sense that Boyle's punitive characterization of Hannah as weaker than Eve is related to internal conflict over her abortion and illegitimate pregnancy. In *Being Geniuses Together,* where Boyle includes her pregnancy, she not only describes Moorhead's deathbed quarrel with Walsh over the magazine, she also delineates her reconciliation with Moorhead, which occurred under quite different circumstances—after Walsh's death, when she offered to support Boyle and the baby. Boyle's description of her response to Moorhead's offer suggests a role reversal that is a product of intense relief at the older woman's acceptance:

When I put my arms around her, all strength seemed to leave her, to drain from some fatal wound that could never be staunched and that she wanted no hand to touch, no eye to see. She slipped to her knees, and I kneeled with her, holding her in my arms still, rocking and cradling her now as if she were my little child. (191)

Boyle's depiction of the women's affiliation and equivalency here suggests that her omission of the pregnancy from the earlier plot served a struggle with issues of desire and power that devolved from her history of transgressive maternity.

If moral masochism as a result of psychic fragmentation is the subtext of *Year Before Last,* it is the starting point of Boyle's last novel based on her life in the twenties. A much more disillusioned book, *My Next Bride* overtly connects the heroine's painfully acquired maternal subjectivity with her ultimate recognition that expatriation does not provide escape from the inequity of gender roles. The young artist Victoria, whose name reflects her American-Puritan background, comes to Paris with a naive hope of finding love and self-definition abroad: "She was fresh from somewhere else and she did not know yet how it could be. . . . [Hers] was a voice speaking out of a bodily, a national ease that had never been betrayed" (9).

In the novel's first two sections, which chronicle this betrayal, Victoria allies herself unsuccessfully with two fellow male expatriates. Out of a combination of idealism and poverty, she joins an artists' commune run by Sorrel (based on Raymond Duncan), who seems to share her longing for the simple America of the pioneers who lived a life attuned to nature. When she is not working in the colony's store selling scarves and tunics, she paints pictures of the lives of saints, of "angry, good, old men," who she hopes will give her own face definition and strength. But her belief in Sorrel's mission becomes eroded as she sees the inequities and abuse within the group, particularly the way the children are treated, and it is exploded when Sorrel buys an expensive American car for himself with group money from the sale of goods in the shop, instead of the printing press he has always said they needed.

Victoria meets a more subtly corrosive influence than Sorrel, however, when Antony Lister (based on Harry Crosby) appears in the shop. A bohemian American artist like herself, he seems to be a person with a solid identity, who is very much in love with his wealthy artist-wife, Fontana (based on Caresse Crosby, to whom the book is dedicated). But as Victoria comes to know him better, and they fall in love themselves, his own spiritual crisis becomes apparent. The black sheep of a materialistic Boston family, who do not understand his artistic aspirations, Antony is torn between his allegiance to them and his longing for the redemptive beauty of art. He tries to drown his confusion in drink and sex, and ultimately returns to America, where he commits suicide, an act that yields the novel's epigraph, "Knife will be my next bride." One night in a bar, Antony expresses his personal crisis in terms of yearning for a lost, radical Puritan America, in which social and spiritual values took precedence over material concerns:

Every day I'm in Europe . . . I can see the map of America in my head and the mountain-ranges. I think of State lines and I hear the people talking as well as I hear you and me. Nobody over there sees it or hears it the way I do. . . . They can't hear what is going on the way you and I hear it sitting here in a bar kissing the rock of Plymouth, the stone breasts, the iron mouth of Plymouth, because I'm for Plymouth, I'm for the Puritan women and for the ancestors who were not afraid of beginning there. (162)

This puritanism, part of what Victoria also defines as essential to her self-concept as an American, leads them both to disaster. For by denying Victoria natural access to her sexuality, it sets her up for self-destructive rebellion: she becomes involved in a mindless course of drunken partying that leaves her feeling dirty and dazed. Waking up one day to find herself pregnant, she goes to the vaudeville dancer at the colony to give her pills to "bring it off," and is nearly destroyed physically as well as psychologically. When she collapses in the Metro, her revival is described in terms of national apostasy. As she stands in the street watching the waiters prepare for the Americans who would soon gather for breakfast on the terrace of a nearby café, Victoria realizes that she has nothing left to say to America: "she said America's that way, over there, and her teeth were knocking together. Listen, America, she said, and her nose was running. America, listen, listen, she said, but there was nothing more to say" (283–84).

Her revival is also depicted in terms of rescue by another woman, Anthony's glamorous wife Fontana, who helps Victoria to get the abortion she seeks. Victoria's relationship with Fontana, to whom she confesses the shame and pain of her inadvertent pregnancy, is crucial to Victoria's survival and to the beginning of self-acceptance at a more fundamental level. For it is in Fontana's company, in the presence of a treacherous *sage-femme*, that Victoria sees the specter of death faced by all the poor women who undergo illegal abortion:

and all the others, the nameless ones *sans domicile fixe* and *sans profession,* with their heels walked sideways, like Victoria's, and their faces walked long and bony like horses' faces, all of them came forbidden and unbidden out of the darkness of the corners and gathered there around them. . . . There must be something better somewhere else, the thing that was brimming in her eyes was saying. They were out the door, they were on the landing, and behind them in the silence of the *sage-femme's* room they could hear the dripping, the endless dripping of the life-blood as it left the bodies of those others; the unceasing drip of the stream as it left the wide, bare table and fell, drop by drop, to the planks beneath it, dripping and dropping on for ever like a finger tapping quickly on the floor. (302–03)

Unlike Antony, she comes to realize that neither repatriation nor expatriation will solve her need to be whole because she has been alienated from her own body.

In fact, Victoria's alliance with Fontana, around the pain and agony of the abortion, represents a kind of intrapsychic "rematriation" on the part of Kay Boyle, the beginning of a clearer sense of female kinship that is a turning point in her career. For this alliance develops a motif that has been implicit earlier: the commonality of the heroine's plight with that of other women and her desire for connection (Morse).[7] To sustain her journey abroad, Victoria has carried with her pictures from home of three women who have served as flawed sources of inspiration: her cold, unyielding art teacher, "who had never given a word of herself away," her loving mother, who lacked the courage to finish what she started, and her vulnerable friend Lacey, a singer who committed suicide rather than return to an abusive husband, whose cynicism prevented her from recognizing Victoria's offer of love (20–25). One of the last scenes, in which Victoria and Fontana fall asleep in each other's arms, mirrors an earlier memory of Lacey, but this time Victoria is the needy one. She survives her identity crisis and impulse to self-destruction by taking the comfort that the older woman offers. As Deborah Morse has pointed out, the cultural lesson that Victoria learns leads Boyle to prophesy "a new role *within* society for the artist" (336). In the thirties she became more concerned with communication than with self-expression, more directed toward the social world (Spanier Chap. 4).

H.D. also ultimately integrated her experiences in childbirth with her poetic practice in ways commensurate with the problems and promise of her early prose, although, unlike Boyle, she never articulated the experience of abortion in either fiction or poetry. This lack of overt representation may reflect an ambivalence that contributed to the lasting power that the trope of childbirth had for her. For both writers, expatriation provided the psychic space in which to explore the impingement of gender roles upon their lives and aspirations. In these early works, they portrayed the effect of inadequate maternal role models upon their developing identity as artists, articulating a tension between motherhood and authorship that they could no longer repress. Driven inward by painful experiences in childbirth in the twenties, H.D. and Kay Boyle delineated elements of maternal subjectivity that became the underpinning of their mature vision.

Notes

1. Guest quotes from a letter in 1928 to H.D. from Kenneth Macpherson, her lover and the probable father of the child, in which he urges H.D. to come to Berlin to have an abortion in the following words: "Brave, handsome, beautiful, sad, noble, furry dignified kitten, hurry up and come and have that star or starfish or star maiden or whatever it is removed. . . . Just get on that train and tell itself its troubles are almost over, and tell itself it must be a NAICE woman from now on."

2. This autobiographical piece was based on an interview with Boyle when she was very old and frail. In it Boyle describes both of her abortions and the birth of her first child in

the context of contemporary pro-choice politics. In her account of the first abortion, she credits the woman doctor in New York who risked her professional career to perform abortions for working women.

3. It is noteworthy that, although she also describes this abortion in "Kay," Boyle is more frank about her emotional pain in this earlier memoir, which she wrote in the late sixties.

4. Gilbert argues that a whole tradition of women writers, including Elizabeth Barrett Browning, use metaphors of the healing and making whole of a wounded woman/land to articulate the reality and fantasy of their own revitalization.

5. I am indebted to Marianne Hirsch's argument that female modernist writers were in a liminal position between maternal/female and paternal/male affiliations.

6. See especially Hollenberg, Friedman, and Kloepfer.

7. Morse distinguishes between Boyle's *kunstlerroman* and those of her male contemporaries, on the basis of this desire for connection.

Works Cited

Benjamin, Jessica. *The Bonds of Love: Psychoanalysis, Feminism, and the Problem of Domination.* New York: Pantheon, 1988.

Benstock, Shari. "Expatriate Modernism: Writing on the Cultural Rim." In Broe, ed.

Bonavoglia, Anna, ed. *The Choices We Made: Twenty-five Women and Men Speak Out About Abortion.* New York: Random, 1991.

Boyle, Kay. "Kay Boyle." In Bonavoglia, ed. 17–22.

———. *My Next Bride.* New York: Virago: 1986.

———. *Plagued By the Nightingale.* New York: Penguin, 1981.

———. *Year Before Last.* New York: Penguin, 1960.

——— and Robert McAlmon. *Being Geniuses Together 1920–1930.* San Francisco: North Point, 1984.

Broe, Mary Lynn, and Angela Ingram, eds. *Women's Writing in Exile.* Chapel Hill: U of North Carolina P, 1989.

Chodorow, Nancy. *The Reproduction of Mothering: Psychoanalysis and the Sociology of Gender.* Berkeley: U of California P, 1978.

Clark, Suzanne. *Sentimental Modernism: Women Writers and the Revolution of the Word.* Bloomington: Indiana UP, 1991.

Duberman, Martin B. *Paul Robeson.* New York: Knopf, 1988.

Friedberg, Anne. "Approaching Borderline." *Millennium Film Journal* 7–9 (Fall/Winter 1980–1981).

Friedman, Susan. "Exile in the American Grain: H.D.'s Diaspora." In Broe, ed. 87–111.

———. *Penelope's Web: Gender, Modernity, H.D.'s Fiction.* New York: Cambridge, Mass.: Cambridge UP, 1990.

———. "Modernism of the 'Scattered Remnant': Race and Politics in the Development of H.D.'s Modernist Vision." In King, ed. 91–116.

Gates, Henry Louis. "Writing 'Race' and the Difference It Makes." In *"Race," Writing and Difference.* Ed. Henry Louis Gates. Chicago: U of Chicago P, 1986. 1–20.

Gilbert, Sandra. "From *Patria* to *Matria*: Elizabeth Barrett Browning's Risorgimento." *PMLA* 99 (1984): 194–211.

Guest, Barbara. *Herself Defined: The Poet H.D. and Her World.* New York: Doubleday, 1984.

H.D. (Hilda Dolittle). *Asphodel.* Ed. Robert Spoo. Durham, N.C.: Duke UP, 1992.

———. "The Borderline Pamphlet." *Sagetrieb* 6.2 (Fall 1987): 32.

———. *Collected Poems 1912–1944.* Ed. Louis L. Martz. New York: New Directions, 1983.

————. "Compassionate Friendship." 1955 memoir. Unpubl. Ms. New Haven: Yale U Beinecke Library.

————. *Hermetic Definition.* New York: New Directions, 1972.

————. *Paint It Today.* Ed. Cassandra Laity. New York: New York UP, 1992.

————. *Palimpsest.* Carbondale, Ill.: Southern Illinois UP, 1968.

————. *Tribute to Freud.* Boston: Godine, 1974.

————. *The Usual Star.* Dijon: Darantière, 1934.

————. "Two Americans." In *The Usual Star.*

Hirsch, Marianne. *The Mother/Daughter Plot: Narrative, Psychoanalysis, Feminism.* Bloomington: Indiana UP, 1989.

Hollenberg, Donna Krolik. *H.D.: The Poetics of Childbirth and Creativity.* Boston: Northeastern UP, 1991.

Irigaray, Luce. *This Sex Which Is Not One.* Trans. Catherine Porter. Ithaca, N.Y.: Cornell UP, 1985.

King, Michael, ed. *H.D.: Woman and Poet.* Orono, Me.: National Poetry Foundation, 1986.

Kloepfer, Deborah Kelly. *The Unspeakable Mother: Forbidden Discourse in Jean Rhys and H.D.* Ithaca, N.Y.: Cornell UP, 1989.

Morse, Deborah. "*My Next Bride:* Kay Boyle's Text of the Female Artist." *Twentieth Century Literature* 35.3 (Fall 1988).

Nadelson, Carol. " 'Normal' and 'Special' Aspects of Pregnancy: A Psychological Approach." In Notman and Nadelson, eds. Vol. 1, Chap. 6.

Nielsen, Aldon. *Reading Race: White American Poets and the Racial Discourse in the Twentieth Century.* Athens: U of Georgia P, 1988.

Notman, Malkah, and Carol Nadelson, eds. *The Woman Patient: Medical and Psychological Interfaces.* New York: Plenum, 1978.

Schlosser, Anatol. "Paul Robeson in Films: An Iconoclast's Quest for a Role." In *Paul Robeson: the Great Forerunner.* Ed. Editors of *Freedomways.* New York: Dodd, 1978. 71–85.

Spanier, Sandra Whipple. *Kay Boyle, Artist and Activist.* New York: Paragon, 1988.

Kay Boyle, Always a Poet

LINDA WAGNER-MARTIN

Kay Boyle's most intensive period of poetry writing covered both the high modernist (1920s) and proletarian (1930s) years. When she defined herself as a serious poet during the early 1920s, modern poetry was dominated by the spare tenets of Imagism, with Ezra Pound, T. S. Eliot, and Amy Lowell insisting on the suggestive and the laconic. Later in the 1920s, under the influence of American poets Lola Ridge, Waldo Frank, Ernest Walsh, Horace Gregory, William Carlos Williams, and the many other avant-garde writers she came to know both in the States (as Ridge's assistant in the offices of *Broom*) and in France, married to Frenchman Richard Brault, Boyle wrote poetry that was a realistic and even militant means of reaching the common reader. In less than a decade, she wrote both lyric portraits in the Imagist poems "Morning," "Shore," and "Portrait" (from "Three Poems"), as well as the long-lined and multi-part suites that often spoke of personal loss ("Summer," "For an American," "Harbor Song").[1]

From the start, however, Boyle wrote distinctive poems. Her Imagist poems were never starkly impersonal—as were many of that mode. "Portrait" opens with the metaphor, "Richard is a gold beach," and includes the striking image of "The sharp elbows of his mind / Through his threadbare face."[2] Short and metaphoric though they were, even Boyle's earliest poems bordered on prose poetry. Regardless of how she arranged lines on a page, her work showed her willingness to recreate a sense of language as voiced.

It is that voiced expression that creates refrains—useful repetitions to achieve tone and nuance—even in Boyle's most formal poems. The sentence "I have wanted other things more than lovers"[3] opens her first published poem, which appeared in 1922 in *Poetry*. (Somewhat romantic, and unfortunately titled "Monody to the Sound of Zithers," the poem was not included in any of her later collections.) It has some good phrases ("To learn by heart things beautiful and slow," "layers of river-mist on river"); it shows the young Boyle attempting to become a part of what she had referred to in a 1919 letter to *Poetry* as "a torrent" of the modern. There she had defined avant-garde

This essay was written specifically for this volume and is published here for the first time by permission of the author.

art as led by Sherwood Anderson, Amy Lowell, Picasso, and Brancusi, artists she called "our explanation, the story which the future generations shall read of us."[4]

Encouraged by her feminist grandmother and her perspicacious mother (who read to dinner guests from both Gertrude Stein and Kay Boyle), Boyle—at only seventeen—spoke authoritatively about what she saw occurring in the arts. She knew she was to become a writer, and like so many of the modernists (for example, Ernest Hemingway, John Dos Passos, e. e. cummings, H.D., William Faulkner, James Joyce), she started as a poet. By 1925, however, her language suggests that traditional poetic form had become restrictive. Challenging the modernists' vers libre, she instead shaped her poetic language into short paragraphs. Part IV of "Harbor Song," a poem published in the February 1925 issue of *Poetry*, is entitled "Negroes on the Frozen Quay." The images Boyle juxtaposes with the title draw from the Surreal as well as the Imagist and resemble Gertrude Stein's effects in her word portraits from *Tender Buttons*:

IV. NEGROES ON THE FROZEN QUAY

Blue-beaked fingers plucking at stray plumes of sun . . .
    lids are smooth burnished cups pouring dark wines
    across the bladed air. Words in their mouths are cool
    and luminous as silver grapes, as cold camellias gathered
    new from loam, and offered tentatively, one by one.[5]

The tension Boyle creates between light and dark, heat and "bladed air," works best in the section's long concluding sentence, in which language mimics a hesitant yet sonorous black speech. Later in the poem, she echoes that rhythm in a closing section that describes the sea as day breaks, using ellipses rather than line breaks to control the reader's pace:

Dawn curves his cold body seaward . . . dawn of cool
    orchid flowers slowly widening . . . drifting pale
    shadowed lids across his mouth.

In her repetition of light-dark imagery, and her anthropomorphization of Dawn to recall the negroes described earlier, Boyle tries to force unity from the disparate images so characteristic of fragmented modernist writing.

Imagism as a movement was comparatively short-lived, in part because creating cohesive wholes from slips and bits of imagery was almost impossible. In her eight-part poem "Summer," also published in 1925, Boyle tries to catch the elements of the season in language she hopes will be melodic. Heavily adjectival, her descriptions weave a dense pattern of images that seem too disparate for any real unity. Again, it is the voice of the poet that attempts to hold the sections together: "I press through the enclosing darkness to the window"; "The dry tongue of my sheet turns me slowly, tentatively."[6]

Published in the first issue of the little magazine *This Quarter*, "Summer" is not so different from Boyle's first published prose ("Passeres' Paris"), which also appeared in that issue. In that story, too, dense paragraphs describe the character of Miss Thrasher, a tourist trying to absorb French culture from her boardinghouse dining room. Again, physical details are asked to carry the weight of the accuracy—sometimes obscuring the direction of the writing. "The small fragile nails pressed on the platter edge, releasing the white flakes of cheese from the paper. On the second, three peewits of white in the iris nail. She examined it lying pallid on the pearl handle of the knife. Letters."[7] As with some of the disjunctions within "Summer" and "Harbor Song," the reader is not always sure what Boyle's emphases and repetitions are meant to convey.

Boyle's breakthrough to some of her best poetry came in 1926. She had learned the craft of choosing, and arranging, exact words; she was comfortable with designing form to suit theme; and she had found an appropriate subject matter for her work. Both "For an American" and "To America" are written in the prose-paragraphs common to her early poetry (although when she reprinted these poems in book form, she set them in separate, explicit lines, with first words capitalized). Published in the 1927 issue of *This Quarter*, both are dedicated to Ernest Walsh. While the young writer's death is superimposed on the poems, the larger question that fueled much of Boyle's best poetry is here suggested in the titles: from the perspective of the 1920s avant-garde, who *were* "Americans," and what *was* their role, as expatriates, in the creation of American art?

In both poems Boyle casts Walsh as a prototypical American artist (as in the metaphor "rich dark banners flying under the plow"),[8] linking his brilliance as both writer and person with the best American spirit of discovery. She forces a fusion of images, from scenes of the land lying in "strong furrows" to a recounting of the quasi-religious—"the miracle, the hot road, the long slow heat of the sea"—to a glimpse of the poet's soul as it is crushed in death ("hot wine red in the veins and . . . the heart, the heart in the breast shriveling like a burning flower"). As Boyle describes it, the spirit of America/Walsh/poet is urgent—sometimes lyrical, sometimes destructive, but always passionate.

In the midst of these intentionally hard images, she places the fourth part of "For an American," a cool evocation of life in New England. The five-stanza poem opens:

> The white houses of New England, the immaculate
> waters; the cool dark avenues are stalks of ferns

carrying your blood, your chaste blood in their timber,
in the still petals of sea that lie among the hills. . . .

Matching the man's traits with those of this stable, hardy landscape offers the reader another definition of Americanism, "ringing and deep as a deep bell." Never exotic, these pristine surroundings are also powerful, and they too lament the poet's loss. Boyle closes the poem with a stunning sense of intimacy, a tone that unfortunately is lost in later revisions:

> Only the sweet
> wood, fresh as the flesh of apples, remembers sap in
> the body and the long touch of your hands.

In these early versions of "To America" and "For an American," grief is the dominant tone. The lines and passages that Boyle cuts in her later collections recount that grief, and loss, repeatedly. The stanzas of "For an American," which begin "Death is a hand under the chin lifting the eyes" and "Here I sit quiet and blind in the sun," make clear that, at the time of their initial composition, Walsh's death was Boyle's primary theme.

Perhaps that origin explains why the spirit of America as she draws it in these poems is so lushly sensual. In "To America," she writes,

> . . . He will be a full
> swinging river that has always flowed for you, he will
> be rhythmic beasts crossing you, his footsteps will be
> wild vallies thundering down your hills.[9]

In a stanza removed from the later version, Boyle evokes the image of anger— at Walsh's loss, at the loss of the expatriate writer who leaves the hostile environment—as she explicitly equates the poet's character with his country:

> Every street is a way to his anger and every stone is a
> rebuke to you saying A wind has died down in an old
> country Now let there be bells filled with a hard wine
> of sound. O silence was a sly lover who had no way
> with him, coming with soft flesh to be gathered and
> folded and smoothed out like worn cloth in the hands.

Closing with the movingly austere line, "He will be a long time in your blood," this poem too is revised and cut for book publication (the "rhythmic beasts" segment in the first passage above is deleted, as is the entire second passage). In nearly every case, the poem's eroticism is lessened.

Another great loss in these revisions is the first poem in the "For an American" suite. In this segment that opens "Land is a white bee-comb, silky as flax / Running with warm light . . .",[10] Boyle suggests the power of Native American expression in the body, voice, and power of the male protagonist, set in a primitive water/land setting. Moving swiftly to express her anger at Walsh's death, she equates the violent force of the Indian's dance with the frontier's "burnt ground and devastation . . . soil closed like a fist about the roots of flowers." The remarkable passage ends with one of Boyle's striking image fragments: "Violence and dry-rot; under grapes gone to powder in / their thin silks."

I

Writing in 1926 and 1927, after living abroad for five years, Boyle (like countless of her expatriate American friends, including Walsh) was questioning her role as misplaced American artist/writer and defining herself as a "resistance fighter." When she reminisced about her New York years in the early 1920s, working in the *Broom* office, she described the mood of many young American artists:

> Every resistance fighter in the underground literary movement of the 1920s came at one time or another to the basement office that Lola [Ridge] kept functioning on practically no funds at all. Williams, Marianne Moore, Bodenheim, Louis Ginzberg, John Dos Passos, Kenneth Burke, Jean Toomer, Slater Brown, Waldo Frank. . . . The resistance was against the established English language, and the fight was for the recognition of a new American tongue.[11]

Metaphors of frontiers and Native Americans were part and parcel of this evocative image; and in her struggle with Walsh to find funds to publish *This Quarter,* a magazine that would never make a profit, Boyle was reminded again of the battle the avant-garde (or even the modestly new) would continuously face.

A few years later, when novelist Robert Cantwell reviewed Boyle's first novel, *Plagued by the Nightingales,* for the *Nation,* he spoke about her choice of the mixed English-French language as a metaphor for the position of the American writer who chose to live abroad:

> [T]he predicament of the exile, more or less isolated in a society he can only partially understand, and unable to communicate with those around him, perhaps corresponds to the predicament of the individual in American society more closely than we ordinarily acknowledge.[12]

Cantwell, who was to write the powerful proletarian novel *The Land of Plenty*—a lament for the loss of community in the States—saw that in America "the diversity of specialized experiences and the absence of unifying traditions have created barriers to communication almost as great as those supplied by the lack of a common language."[13] Boyle's novel, *Plagued by the Nightingale,* is in no way proletarian fiction, but she does present the separation of people (French and American, male and female) as a permanent condition. As her poetry showed so well, Boyle recognized that the battle to reach others—whether as readers or as friends—was ongoing.

Susan Stanford Friedman has recently described what expatriation meant for H.D., another American woman modernist. In so doing, she narrates as well key moves in Kay Boyle's development. Although Friedman thinks H.D.'s fascination with being American was more visible in her fiction than in her poetry, her subject in both became increasingly "her Americanness and the Americanness of her expatriation."[14] Rather than reading H.D.'s work as autobiographical, Friedman points out that the woman persona in her fiction is often "an American woman."[15]

In another way, too, according to Friedman, H.D.'s exploration of expatriation—and, implicitly, of American identity—"fostered the development of international, geographic metaphors for psychic states of mind."[16] Some of this reliance on metaphors of place is evident in Boyle's writing. In a 1928 poem, for example, "The United States" (dedicated to that most American poet, William Carlos Williams), Boyle draws on the intrinsic difference between countries. A central image is "the Indian, the silent ways of the old man you were asking; / Days with the sun worn thin as a 'coon's cap, deep creeks where salmon took the falls." (*CP,* 37).[17]

Placing Williams as an American (amid references to his English grandmother), Boyle sets her amply descriptive poem in the United States of her memory. The America that she announces as "Not a land, or like other lands" is once more her subject—"the birch moon drifting cold as Maine water," "the owls crying softly in the rain." After the 23-line paean to the States, she ends the poem with a coda that focuses on both her expatriation and her memories:

> But to go back, to go back to another country, to go back
> And to say from here I can see it;
> Here and here a leaf opening, here the cherry-gum dripping,
> Here a stream broken through, here and here a horse run wild. (*CP,* 37)

Similarly, in another 1928 poem she continues the dialogue with her fellow poets about national characteristics. "A Confession to Eugene Jolas" contrasts the States with France, Russia, and Italy and begins a scrutiny of the way individual languages become part of such characteristics. Her 1927 poems "A Letter to Francis Picabia" (which opens "There is one country / and no shame to it" [*CP,* 24]) and "A Christmas Carol for Emanuel Carnevali" both use imagery of place to describe the poems' dedicatees and to continue Boyle's pervasive recounting of her grief for Walsh. Her combination of both themes and sensual images is illustrated in the following stanza from part II of the poem to Carnevali, an intimate of Walsh's who was himself both poet and convalescent:

> Italy, contained in you
> As richly as in the skin of a grape,
> I would find on your tongue some flavor
> On your lips some word of him.
> Italy
> Like opening a window upon a garden
> Which need not be pruned, pathed, swept, or weeded,
> A land sown with miracles
> Before which the snow parts into spring,
> A coast you walk drawing
> The warm sea back on your shoulders
> The sun down over your brows. (*CP,* 30)

II

As the poems to Williams, Jonas, Carnevali, and others also show, much of Boyle's poetry was occasional poetry. Written with a compassionate friend in mind, each poem is less about the friend or the friend's concerns than it is the kind of discourse that Boyle might have had with the friend. With Carnevali, she would have lamented Walsh's death (as well as his own terminal illness). With Jolas, she would have wondered at the international flavor of the Parisian literary world, so well exemplified in Jolas's magazine *transition.* With Williams, she would have continued their long-running dialogue about what it means to be an American. The pose of the occasional poet was, of course, thoroughly unfashionable in the twentieth-century world: Boyle's use of these titles, less ironic statements than codes of meaning among friends, was another means of proving herself an unconventional modern.

"A Valentine for Harry Crosby," "A Glad Day for Laurence Vail," "A Comeallye for Robert Carlton Brown," "A Landscape for Wyn Henderson," "A Waterfront for Allan Ross Macdougall," "A Complaint for Mary and Marcel," "Angels for Djuna Barnes," "A Statement for El Greco and William Carlos Williams," "A Poem of Gratitude" for Caresse Crosby—if the recipient's name is not included as part of the title proper, it appears as a dedication. Some of the descriptive titles are ironic (her "valentine" for Harry Crosby was written after his suicide, for example, and asks the reader—while mourning his loss—to question the traditions that bind living lovers); others ("A Landscape," "A Watercolor") use a subtle synesthesia to link written words with the aesthetics of painting.

Boyle's pretense of writing certain kinds of dedicatory poems also allowed her great variety in poetic form. She relied on the shape and traditions suggested in the named form, but she continued her general use of long, speech-inflected, lines, at times intermixing prose passages with more standard poetry. As her 1928 essay on Hart Crane shows, Boyle was aware of negative criticism about modern poems in the States, and she spoke directly to the issue of critics who claimed that the modern poem "is no more than clever prose broken up into short lines."[18]

For Boyle, the length of lines per se was no longer an interesting issue; in her own writing, and that of her friends, the poem arranged in multiple parts had become second nature. That some of those contrasting parts might be written as prose was seen as a given, as is clear from a number of works by other writers that were published in the same magazines that Boyle's work also appeared in frequently. Boyle's own "A Landscape for Wyn Henderson" uses italicized prose sections set in the midst of formal lyric lines to tell an ostensible story ("My love lies here a place grown tired . . ." [CP, 51]). "A Waterfront for Allan Ross Macdougall" dispenses with italics but uses headings, "The Tragedy" and "The Comedy," to introduce the margin-to-margin lines of the narratives embedded in the poem proper. "A Complaint for Mary and Marcel" aligns two print columns side by side for two pages to represent the Duchamps's voices set against the voice of the poet, which leads to more pages of prose poetry headed "The Story I Wanted to Tell You." That poem concludes with a formal lyric (which itself has an embedded prose section) entitled "Your Love Song," which Boyle names "The sweet high declaration. . . . It may be sung without rehearsal any night / At bars or café tables. . . ." (CP, 65).

Of the many mixed-genre poems Boyle published during the late 1920s and 1930s, the best known is her "A Communication to Nancy Cunard," her so-called Scottsboro poem. Published in 1937, the multisectioned work incorporates prose from news accounts, defendants' statements, factual observations, and lyric language to chart the 1931 trial of nine young blacks who were charged with raping two white women in the freight car in which they were all riding. Boyle draws on all her effective techniques: prose sections ("So here goes and I shall try faithfully as possible to tell you as I understand if not mistaken that Olen Montgomery, who was part blind then, kept saying because of the dark there was inside the boxcar and outside it: 'It sure don't seem to me we're getting anywhere'" [CP, 68])[19] surrounded by Boyle's own lyric voice ("These are not words set down for the rejected" [CP, 66]). The poem shows her ability to use repetition of phrases for ironic effect, to connect all parts of the poem (not "getting anywheres" refers as much to the situation of American justice as to the blind boy's comment above). Particularly effective near the heart of the poem is the appearance of the divided page, so that phonetically spelled testimony from Haywood Patterson, one of the charged blacks, is set opposite the pathetic voice of Victoria Price, one of the alleged victims:

THE TESTIMONY

Haywood Patterson:	Victoria Price:
"So here goes an I shell try	
Faitfully an I possibly can	
Reference to myself in particularly	"I
And concerning the other boys	cain't
personal pride.	remember."
And life time upto now.	
You must be patiene with me	
and remember	
Much of my English is not of	"I
much interest	cain't
And that I am continually	remember."
Stopping and searching for the	
word. (CP, 67–68)	

Boyle's artistry is particularly evident when she breaks into the assumed objectivity of reportage by closing the long work with two formal poem sections, "The Spiritual for Nine Voices," a melange of black speech (spelled conventionally for greater reader impact), and "The Sentence," a long-lined lament for the boys' deaths. The latter opens, "Hear how it goes, the wheels of it traveling fast on the rails," the "long high wail" of the train waking listeners to the realization that such trains—supposedly symbols of technological progress—actually pass "in no direction, to no destination, / Carrying people caught in the boxcars" (CP, 69).

Here Boyle reaches her most explicit political statement, saying directly that justice does not exist for "people with this in common: People that no one had use for, had nothing to give to, no place to offer. . . . The loose hands hang down, and swing with the swing of the train in the darkness, / Holding nothing but poverty, syphilis white as a handful of dust, taking nothing as baggage" (CP, 69–70).

III

Perhaps "A Communication to Nancy Cunard" is often anthologized because it is both highly effective and less autobiographical than some of Boyle's earlier work. In some ways, however, it is an anomaly. Boyle was not living in the States, and although the genteel poverty of the artist was a way of life for her, she had not lived through the depression. It is important to remember, however, that although she lived in Europe through much of the 1920s and 1930s, Boyle's aesthetic and intellectual community was largely American. Even after the height of American expatriation, she was surrounded by people who were newly arrived from the States or who were in the process of going and coming across the Atlantic. Besides, what was happening in America, the land of the dream and all its promise, was international news. If it had not already been so, the Communist Party would no doubt have seen to it that information about the evident failure of capitalism made headlines the world over. The Scottsboro trial was one of the reasons the party could make such inroads in American political life during the 1930s, particularly in Harlem.

So it was in the context of the American depression that Boyle continued to write poetry and to see a different set of uses for her art. Like her friends Lola Ridge and Genevieve Taggard, as well as Stanley Burnshaw, William Carlos Williams, Muriel Rukeyser, Kenneth Fearing, and a host of others, Boyle believed that language could change lives. She had customarily lived in cultures where writers had political power (see her poem "World Tour," written for her daughter Sharon). By the 1930s, Boyle's investigation of what America was, and what it meant to be American, took on a more obviously political flavor. The minds and hearts of many American intellectuals during the depression were filled with details of tragedies of the country's poor. The abstract notion of "class struggle" had become concrete: the homeless lurking in city doorways, the hungry standing in seemingly endless breadlines, the farmers quietly hungry in the midst of failing fields. Although Boyle is seldom included in discussions of proletarian writers, her sympathies with the issues of 1930s America is evident in "A Communication for Nancy Cunard."

It is clear that much of Boyle's later poetry also springs from a wider cultural impulse, blending the private with a more outward-looking (and often political) discourse. Charlotte Nekola writes of poetry from the 1930s:

> Poetry was a weapon of class struggle: this was the main message of literary radicalism. Its focus was to be social, public, and mass—not private. Bourgeois poetry, radical critics said, suffered from an excess of private despair and hid in language too highly wrought and too obscure for a mass audience. It led readers to mere escapism. . . . Revolutionary poetry should speak directly, address experience, and incite collective social action.[20]

Boyle's poetic career follows this move from the realm of the bourgeois—when her early love relationships provided much of the content for her art—closer to that of the revolutionary, when she silenced her own voice in order to let the common idiom of her subjects reach an audience. Perhaps her title for this poem, "A *Communication* for Nancy Cunard" [emphasis added] rather than a *poem,* suggests the shift.

By the 1960s, in fact, Kay Boyle was known more for her political poetry rather than for more aesthetically based poems. When her collection

Testament for My Students and Other Poems was published in 1970, no one was surprised that the title poem was a commemoration of her politically active students at San Francisco State University. Drawing on the same techniques she had used in her proletarian poems, Boyle memorialized students by name, told their narratives, and wove separate strands of story through a lyric text that was as effective poetically as it was accurate historically. That the word "testament" has replaced both "communication" and "poem" is also indicative of the importance the seasoned poet found in her life as educator, writer, and—still—"resistance fighter."

The poem begins directly, as it will conclude, with an apostrophe to the students, lovingly termed "sweet emissaries":

> Each year you came jogging or loping down that hall
> Bearded or not, sweet emissaries from Arizona
> Montana, Illinois, Mass., beneath the light silk hair
> Or the dark, or the natural crown, skulls crushable, ribs breakable. (*CP,* 126)

Boyle describes the students in long-lined sequences, linking them with their "brothers and sisters" who are fellow writers: "such brothers as Baudelaire / Melville, Poe, sometimes Shakespeare, Genet, Rimbaud; or sisters / Like Dickinson, Bronte, Austin . . . / Or Gertrude Stein telling you over and over how Americans were doggedly made" (*CP,* 26). The unanticipated center of the poem is one of Boyle's astutely shaped prose sections, describing the offensive and self-praising introduction of a black scholar by a white academic. Titled "The Ungarbled Story That Unfolded Before Me," this long narrative makes clear how racism and classism corrupt supposedly impartial, objective scholarship. The very place students come for insight is itself blind.

The poem's ending blends the individual students' behavior and language with their calls for wisdom from the hallowed writers. The last section begins

> You were not afraid of death, sweet emissaries from Arizona
> Montana, Mass., and Illinois; or of mace, or of handcuffs or clubs
> And there's one thing more: you bore the terrible knowledge
> That colonized men and poets wear their sharpest pain on the surface
> Of their flesh, like an open sore (*CP,* 130)

Obviously political in its talk about protests, the poem goes beyond its ostensible historicizing. Boyle confronts not only academe, but the writers the students sought, saying that those writers—in her imagination—were "turned suddenly to stone. Their tongues were hacked from their throats / By bayonets, and the blows came steadily, savagely, on the exquisite / Brittleness of bone" (*CP,* 130). The conclusion of the poem ameliorates this bitterness, however, and shows the older poet to be wrong in this assessment. The indomitable students, shouting through the blood in their mouths, continue proclaiming that Rimbaud, Whitman, Poe, and Baudelaire are still their heroes.

IV

Reading Boyle's fiction provides another way to demonstrate that for Boyle, like her mentor William Carlos Williams, writing was writing; and the techniques of one form were fair game for any other kind of writing, depending on the poet's need, urgency, and perspective.[21] So far as her poetry is concerned, even the small amount of her work that is included in the 1985 *Collected Poems of Kay Boyle* shows the deft skill with which she struggled against conventional modernist forms, as she moved toward the voice that she wanted to be recognized as that of Kay Boyle, poet. There also remain the many uncollected poems, among them the prose-poem versions of "To America" and "For an American," which seem to be more effective than the later collected versions.

A rich vein of poetry also suffuses much of Boyle's short fiction and novels. It seems clear in retrospect that she considered herself a poet at all periods of her life: she wrote poems consistently, and she read poetry throughout her long life. Perhaps most important, she incorporated much of her fiction and non-fiction prose into her poems to achieve the kind of metaphoric density that poetry customarily demands.

Notes

1. The personal loss was the terrible death from tuberculosis in 1926 of Ernest Walsh, her lover and the editor of *This Quarter,* the magazine that published much of her writing. In addition to the versions in Kay Boyle, *Collected Poems of Kay Boyle* (Port Townsend, Wash.: Copper Canyon Press, 1991), see "Portrait," in "Three Poems," *Poetry* 29 (February 1927): 250–52; "Summer," *This Quarter* 1, no. 1 (1925): 40–42; "For an American," *This Quarter* 1, no. 3, (1927): 111–15; and "Harbor Song," *Poetry* 25 (February 1925): 252–53.

2. "Portrait," *Poetry* 29 (February 1927): 250.

3. "Monody to the Sound of Zithers," *Poetry* 21, (December 1922): 125; subsequent quotations from this poem are on the same page.

4. Kay Boyle, letter to the editor, *Poetry* 19 (November 1921): 104–6.

5. "Negroes on the Frozen Quay" is the fourth section of "Harbor Song," 253; subsequent quotations from this poem are on same page.

6. "Summer," 41, 42.

7. "Passeres' Paris," *This Quarter* 1, no. 1 (1925): 140.

8. "For an American," 111; subsequent quotations from this poem are on pp. 111–15.

9. "To America," *This Quarter* 1, no. 3 (1927): 109; subsequent quotations from this poem are on pp. 109–10.

10. "For an American," 111.

11. Kay Boyle, preface to "The Autobiography of Emanuel Carnevali," in *Words That Must Somehow Be Said: Selected Essays of Kay Boyle, 1927–1984*, ed. Elizabeth S. Bell (San Francisco: North Point Press, 1985), 37–38.

12. Robert Cantwell, "American Exile," *Nation* 135 (20 July 1932): 61.

13. Cantwell, 61.

14. Susan Stanford Friedman, "Exile in the American Grain: H.D.'s Diaspora," in *Women's Writing in Exile,* ed. Mary Lynn Broe and Angela Ingram (Chapel Hill: University of North Carolina Press, 1989), 101.

15. Friedman, 101.

16. Friedman, 101.

17. Quotations from Kay Boyle's poems in the *Collected Poems* of Kay Boyle are cited in the text using the abbreviation *CP.*

18. Kay Boyle, "Mr. Crane and His Grandmother," *Words That Somehow Must Be Said,* p. 33.

19. This is a significant dedication because, though wealthy, Nancy Cunard had endured prejudicial treatment in the States because her lover was black.

20. Charlotte Nekola, "World's Moving: Women, Poetry and the Literary Politics of the 1930s," *Writing Red, An Anthology of American Women Writers, 1930–1940,* ed. Charlotte Nekola and Paula Rabinowitz (New York: Feminist Press, 1987), 129; see also the following excellent recent treatments of women's proletarian writing: Constance Coiner, *Better Red, The Writing and Resistance of Tillie Olsen and Meridel Le Sueur* (New York: Oxford University Press, 1995); Barbara Foley, *Radical Representations, Politics and Form in U.S. Proletarian Fiction, 1929–1941* (Durham, N.C.: Duke University Press, 1993); and Paula Rabinowitz, *Labor and Desire: Women's Revolutionary Fiction in Depression America* (Chapel Hill: University of North Carolina Press, 1991). See also these more general studies: Daniel Aaron, *Writers on the Left: Episodes in American Literary Communism* (New York: Harcourt, Brace, 1961); and Cary Nelson, *Repression and Recovery: Modern American Poetry and the Politics of Cultural Memory, 1910–1945* (Madison: University of Wisconsin Press, 1989).

21. The essential books for information about Boyle's oeuvre are Sandra Whipple Spanier, *Kay Boyle, Artist and Activist* (Carbondale: Southern Illinois University Press, 1986); Marilyn Elkins, *Metamorphosizing the Novel: Kay Boyle's Narrative Innovations* (New York: Peter Lang, 1993); and, to a lesser degree, Joan Mellen, *Kay Boyle: Author of Herself* (New York: Farrar, Straus and Giroux, 1994).

Female Roles and National Identity in Kay Boyle's *Plagued by the Nightingale* and Edith Wharton's *Madame de Treymes*

Dianne Chambers

Kay Boyle admits in *Being Geniuses Together* that moving to Paris "in the late twenties" and having French citizenship due to her marriage to the Frenchman Richard Brault might "seem to disqualify me as a member of the lost generation or as an expatriate." However she goes on to claim, "But I was there, in whatever guise, and even if a bit late."[1] Written from the vantage point of over forty years later, Boyle's chapters detailing her life in Paris and the French provinces make an intriguing counterpoint to Robert McAlmon's original record of the personal and literary lives of the numerous American expatriates to France in the 1920s. Texts such as Boyle's revision of McAlmon's memoirs offer alternative accounts of the conventional expatriation narrative first shaped by the masculine modernist perspectives of such writers as Ernest Hemingway, F. Scott Fitzgerald, and Ezra Pound.[2]

Another such revision of the expatriation story can be found in the fiction and nonfiction of Edith Wharton who first leased an apartment and began spending winters in Paris in 1907. Wharton's version of French culture and American artists, having been shaped by another class, generation, and value system, provides a view that differs in many ways from that of Boyle's. Nevertheless, placing the lives and work of these two writers side by side reveals certain powerful commonalities. For Wharton and Boyle, living and writing in France in the 1920s granted them a personal and professional freedom neither of them believed was possible in their native America.[3] To Wharton, life in France meant immersion in a rich and venerable aesthetic tradition and personal friendship with a network of artists and writers who valued her intellectual capabilities and admired her work.[4] To Boyle, becoming an expatriate meant living among like-minded writers determined to remake literature and reject the very traditions Wharton valued so highly.[5]

This essay was written specifically for this volume and is published here for the first time by permission of the author.

Despite their radically differing experiences, expatriation shaped their memoirs and informed their fiction in always significant and, sometimes, parallel ways.

Indeed, much of their work struggles to define national difference and American identity. It is as if distance from the place called America only heightened the need to define what it means to be an American against the backdrop of European space and culture. Initially, the writings of Boyle and Wharton seem to parallel expatriate narratives of the encounter between the American and the European made familiar by writers as diverse as Nathaniel Hawthorne, Henry James, and Hemingway. Nevertheless, Wharton and Boyle offer a significantly different perspective in at least two important ways. First, their work enacts the story of international cultural conflict in gendered terms. Second, this struggle is presented from a female point of view. As women expatriates, Wharton and Boyle were forced not only to negotiate cultural differences at large but also to engage with very different cultural conceptions of female roles. As writers in a place seen as especially conducive to the creation of art, Wharton and Boyle used their art to explore the ways in which gender, culture, and nationality impinged on the lives of women expatriates in the first third of the twentieth century.

Explorations of the gendered nature of the expatriate experience occur in both their fiction and nonfiction. Wharton's *French Ways and Their Meaning* offers useful commentary on her earliest ideas about French culture as represented in the short novel, *Madame de Treymes*.[6] Boyle's autobiographical revision of Robert McAlmon's memoir, *Being Geniuses Together 1920–1930*, provides an important historical context for readers of her autobiographical novel, *Plagued by the Nightingale*.[7] Although the two authors saw their relationship to the expatriate movement and its emphasis on modernism and experimentation in very different ways, they both accepted the axiom of 1920s expatriate writers—that one could write more freely and produce better work abroad. However, they also found that culture (both French and American) intersected with gender in particular ways for women. Thus their efforts to define what it meant to be an American living abroad of necessity took into account cultural attitudes toward women and their roles. In *Madame de Treymes* and *Plagued by the Nightingale* the struggle to understand French culture and define one's American identity centers specifically on conceptions of motherhood. These works demonstrate that women occupy a powerful position in French society. Yet, female behavior is rigidly controlled and the exercise of the power is carefully contained. The consequences of this cultural paradox inform the work of the two writers.

Admittedly, Edith Wharton and Kay Boyle saw their places in the American literary tradition in opposing ways. Although Wharton's writings display many modernist traits, she liked to refer to herself as a kind of literary relic.[8] In a 1925 letter to Fitzgerald, she claims: "I feel that to your generation, which has taken a flying leap into the future, I must represent the literary equivalent of tufted furniture and gas chandeliers."[9] She had little patience for the high modernists, Joyce and Eliot. In a 1923 letter to the art critic Bernard Berenson, she calls *Ulysses* a "turgid welter of pornography . . . & unformed and unimportant drivel." She goes on to claim that "until the raw ingredients of a pudding *make* a pudding, I shall never believe that the raw material of sensation & thought can make a work of art without the cook's intervening. The same applies to Eliot."[10]

Boyle, however, wanted nothing more than to become a part of the great literary experiment she believed was taking place among the expatriates. In an interview, Studs Terkel claimed, "We think of Kay Boyle as the golden girl of the Twenties in Paris, and the artists who were there. She knew Joyce, you name them, Duchamp, Beckett, she was there, this girl out of Cincinnati, and she was writing."[11] In *Being Geniuses Together,* Boyle articulates her resolve: "I wanted to find work in a bookshop (Sylvia Beach's), or with a publishing company (Robert McAlmon's), and give my daily allegiance to the words that others were able to set down."[12] She describes exchanging letters with William Carlos Williams and Emanuel Carnevali, lunching with James and Nora Joyce and Brancusi, working for *transition* with Eugene Jolas, and spending evenings wandering the Left Bank with Robert McAlmon. Indeed, Boyle defined herself as a member of a revolution directed specifically at "the ancient strongholds of the established literary conventions" represented by American writers like Wharton.[13] As late as 1984, in the afterword to the new edition of *Being Geniuses Together,* Boyle argues, "The revolt that *Being Geniuses Together* bears witness to was against all literary pretentiousness, against weary dreary rhetoric, against all the outworn literary and academic conventions. 'Down with Henry James! Down with Edith Wharton! . . .' the self-exiled revolutionaries cried out. . . . There was no grandly experimental, furiously disrespectful school of writing in America, and we were going to create it."[14]

Despite their opposing views on modernism, Wharton and Boyle agreed that expatriation to the European center of the modernist movement, France, situated the writer in a culture more sympathetic to aesthetics and the arts than that of America at the time. For Wharton, French culture offers a kind of refinement of the senses essential to an artist. She argues in *French Ways and Their Meaning* that French sensibilities require "splendour on occasion, and beauty and fulness of experience always. . . . [F]ood must be exquisitely cooked, emotion eloquently expressed, desire emotionally heightened, every experience must be transmuted into terms of beauty before it touches their imagination."[15]

Boyle believed France provided a political climate which made space for the artist. She describes the trip she and her husband made to France in 1923 as not only "a search for individual freedom" but also a "search for what we believed could be the true meaning of democracy."[16] But it quickly becomes clear from Boyle's account that politics was inextricably linked to aesthetics. She argues, "In a country that did not put its socialists in jail, as Eugene Debs was jailed in America, and did not harass its writers, as Upton Sinclair was harassed, I was going to write a novel in the quiet and peace of alien Brittany."[17]

But while French culture clearly afforded these writers the aesthetic, political, and imaginative freedom in which to practice their professions, it remained an alien land. Differences in European attitudes and sensitivities represented a kind of liberation to the expatriates precisely because they were differences. Taking up life in a country not one's own clearly sets the stage for a clash between cultures. Indeed, Wharton and Boyle examine in some detail the interplay between French and American culture. As expatriates, they were forced to negotiate cultural tensions inherent in the meeting between conventions of a relatively new—even upstart—society and the old traditions of Europe. They had to develop a double sightedness that would enable them to explain France to Americans and at the same time to give an accounting to France of themselves as Americans.

Wharton understood the benefits and challenges inherent in a meeting between two cultures. She notes in *French Ways and Their Meanings*, "It is obvious that any two intelligent races are bound to have a lot to learn from each other." But she also articulates the difficulty in formulating an adequate strategy for seeing across the cultural divide:

> Race differences strike so deep that when one has triumphantly pulled up a specimen for examination one finds only the crown in one's hand, and the tough root still clenched in some crevice of prehistory. And as to race-resemblances, they are so often most misleading when they seem most instructive that any attempt to catch the likeness of another people by painting ourselves is never quite successful.[18]

For Wharton, any chance for two cultures to come to know one another must come through the mediating gaze of the seasoned traveler who has spent much time in both countries. She argues, "It takes an outsider familiar with both races to explain away what may be called the corned-beef-hash differences, and bring out the underlying resemblances."[19]

Perhaps the key term in Wharton's instruction is "outsider" because it hints at the way the mediator is not clearly situated in one place. Wharton's advice at least implicitly raises the question of what happens to an American abroad. Does one, in a sense, have to become an outsider to both cultures to mediate the cultural divide? To what extent does immersion in an alien culture disconnect one from one's native place and transform one's experience of Americanness? To what extent does the expatriate experience both reinforce and call into question national identity, ask the mediator to both celebrate and critique the American character?[20]

Indeed, both Wharton and Boyle express a sense of not entirely belonging anywhere.[21] Wharton tells Sara Norton, "One's friends are delightful;

but *we* are none of us Americans, we don't think or feel as Americans do, we are the wretched exotics produced in a European glasshouse, the most deplace & useless class on earth!"[22] Boyle expresses a similar cultural rootlessness when she describes in *Being Geniuses Together* the reasons she and Richard Brault went to France:

> We were determined to be free, and yet that freedom did not have a specific name to it. . . . We were going to work hard and save enough money to go to France and spend a few weeks with Richard's family. . . . But we had no intention of accepting them on their merits, for our judgment on them had already been irrevocably passed. We knew what we were about, and perhaps the clarity of our vision would reveal something fresh and new to them—they who had handed us the unspeakable horror of a world war and its aftermath and made no apologies about it.[23]

Having rejected most of what France had to offer, Boyle in the next sentence makes clear that America offers little reason for optimism, either, as long as it continues to imprison socialists and writers. This disconnection from any geographical place becomes the ground for Wharton's and Boyle's cultural analysis of the traditions which undergird French society. Working within a space fixed neither in America nor Europe, both writers explicitly address the conflicted forces of tradition in French postwar society in relation to their native country's own values. Wharton and Boyle are particularly interested in the way this tradition appears to police relationships between men and women, establish a gender hierarchy, and govern gender roles.

Wharton's *French Ways and Their Meanings*, written in the closing years of the war and published in 1919, had been at least in part a kind of war effort, an attempt to explain a foreign culture to a group of Americans who had previously had little experience with European customs and traditions.[24] America's entry into the war brought American soldiers onto French soil and exposed the fighting young men to a culture they had heretofore only read about.[25]

The experience of these men, the increased interaction between Europe and America in the postwar years, and the general threat to national integrity and geographical boundaries during warfare created an opportunity and established, in Wharton's mind, a need to explore the intersection of the two cultures. She notes: "The world since 1914 has been like a house on fire. All the lodgers are on the stairs, in dishabille. . . . [O]ne gets glimpses . . . that a life-time of ordinary intercourse would not offer." Seizing what she sees as a unique opportunity to explain France to Americans, Wharton singles out as "typically 'French' . . . the qualities of taste, reverence, continuity, and intellectual honesty."[26] But what distinguished France from America most in Wharton's eyes was the admirable respect France showed toward tradition and custom developed and adhered to over time. In Wharton's view, French civilization offered a mature perspective and rich experience to "a people . . . still, intellectually and artistically, in search of itself." She argues:

> The French are the most human of the human race, the most completely detached from the lingering spell of the ancient shadowy world in which trees and animals talked to each other, and began the education of the fumbling beast that was to deviate into Man. They have used their longer experience and their keener senses for the joy and enlightenment of the races still agrope for self-expression.[27]

In Wharton's estimation, French culture represented a vastly superior milieu for the intellectual and aesthetic life she yearned to lead.[28] One major reason for her celebration of French culture was that it offered women a vital and clearly delineated place in a society sanctioned by years of custom.[29]

Wharton devotes an entire chapter in *French Ways and Their Meanings* to the new Frenchwoman who indeed "has always been there" and whose traits the war has only developed further rather than altered. According to Wharton, this Frenchwoman was "as different as possible from the average American woman." Benefiting from the continuing experience of "real living," which "has its roots in . . . close and constant and interesting and important relations between men and women," the French wife is an intelligent business partner and a stimulating companion in marriage. Unlike her American counterpart, the French wife is accorded an "extraordinary social freedom" that allows her to be "less concerned with trifles, and less afraid of strong feelings, passions, and risks." She "is distinctly more grown up than her American sister; and she is so because she plays a much larger and more interesting part in men's lives."[30]

Wharton makes clear that the social power of the Frenchwoman is connected to her status as a married woman and mother. She admits that a French girl spends "her girlhood in seclusion" but wonders how it can matter, "provided she is free to emerge from it at the moment when she is fitted to become a real factor in social life." She also recognizes that "the French wife has less legal independence than the American or English wife" but goes on to note that the "practical fact" vastly outweighs "the technical situation." Despite her lesser legal standing, the Frenchwoman takes an active role in her husband's social and business enterprises, moving beyond the "theoretical restrictions to the heart of reality" to "become her husband's associate, because, for her children's sake, if not for her, her heart is in his job."[31]

French women wield a great deal of social power, but even the admiring Wharton admits the oblique quality of that influence. She notes that "where interesting and entertaining men are habitually present the women are not expected to talk much." She also asserts that the Frenchwoman "does not teach man, but . . . inspires him." Nevertheless, in contemporary culture, Wharton claims "the Frenchwoman rules French life, and she rules it under a triple crown, as a business woman, as a mother, and above all as an artist."[32]

Boyle paints a more chilling picture of the veneration of tradition and female authority in *Being Geniuses Together*. Arriving in June 1923 at Le Havre, Boyle describes meeting the Brault family for the first time. The mother and two sisters are dressed in "identical grey suits," the only acceptable garment for the upperclass traveling woman. Boyle describes Richard's mother: "Maman's shoulders were stooped in her grey jacket, weary yet cautiously alert under the weight of eternal and aggressive authority that was her lot."[33] Feeling immediately and irrevocably out of place in her cheerful summer dress of blue challis with red flowers, Kay rides off in the family limousine "in tight-throated silence," her French becoming "more and more inadequate" as the miles pass.[34]

Boyle's description of her entry into the world of the upperclass French family underscores the tradition of female authority but also details the way in which that power is circumscribed. Boyle's mother-in-law's concern is not with what Kay reads or her aspirations to be an artist and a free-thinking woman but with the lack of the appropriate grey suit and hat. Maman and customs officials alike ignore the incendiary modernist material carried by Boyle into the country; as Maman oversees the search in an effort to find something suitlike, "they cast aside like chaff" the first editions of Pound, Eliot, and Williams, and an Alfred Stieglitz catalogue.[35] Tradition and female authority are brought to bear not on art but on appearance. In a later section of the autobiography, Boyle describes in more detail her initiation into the "impenetrably sealed universe of the family's daily life."[36] Taking up her gendered role in the provinces, Boyle learns how to darn, make mayonnaise, and milk the goat. Boyle's apparent, albeit temporary, acceptance of the gender role allotted her by French provincial society is eased only by a secret rebellion; each morning, carrying her chamberpot "like a chalice," she imagines "Duchamp's nude descend[ing] the staircase with me."[37] Clinging to her private belief in the modern and the aesthetic, Boyle attempts to live within the constraining conventions.

Ultimately, Boyle's discontent with the French provinces and the "closed, finite world" ruled by her mother-in-law drives her to define herself as writer and as American. She records her American years growing up "in Philadelphia, in Atlantic City, in the Pocono Mountains, and in Cincinnati, as if a recounting of these experiences must finally reveal to me who I was."[38] Boyle's foreign experience thrusts her into a search for identity as woman, writer, and American.

While both Wharton and Boyle in their nonfiction attempt to explain the experience of living abroad and to explore the nature of French culture, they are finally able to do so only in relationship to their American roots. Wharton's *French Ways and Their Meanings* and Boyle's *Being Geniuses Together* represent efforts to bridge the cultural divide that were written after some years of living abroad. Nevertheless, both writers did explore the clash of Franco-American cultures relatively early in their careers as well. A study of the earlier efforts to cross the cultural divide reveals even more radical challenges to female and national identity within the expatriate experience.

Wharton's *Madame de Treymes* and Boyle's *Plagued by the Nightingale* represent the clash of cultures in specifically gendered terms; the marriage of an American woman to a French husband drives the narrative line in both texts. The international marriages bring the American wives onto French soil and into French family life. The new role as wife forces each young woman to confront directly the cultural conflict represented by radically differing gender role expectations. The power of the French family focalized in the matriarch represents a threat to the young wife's individual and national identity. Since it is matriarchal power that enforces the rigid social codes and constraining gender roles dictated by tradition, the authority of the foreign mother must be brought to bear on the young wife in order to force compliance with family and custom. The central question in each novel, then, becomes whether or not the young woman can assert her individuality, her Americanness, and construct her own role in the family drama in the face of the powerful authority of the mother.

Madame de Treymes presents a horrifying view of an American woman trapped by the very traditions of family and veneration of female authority that Wharton admires in *French Ways and Their Meaning*.[39] Wharton tells the story through the mediating figure of the American John Durham, who is especially sensitive to the allure of French culture. In the opening of the novel Durham is "struck anew by the vast and consummately ordered spectacle of Paris; by its look of having been boldly and deliberately planned as a background for the enjoyment of life, instead of being forced into grudging concessions to the festive instincts, or barricading itself against them in unenlightened ugliness, like in his own lamentable New York."[40] For Durham, the blending of beauty and order in the cityscape mirrors the larger cultural codes governing behavior—especially interaction between the genders. The reader is told that "Durham, indeed, was beginning to find that one of the charms of a sophisticated society is that it lends point and perspective to the slightest contact between the sexes."[41]

Durham has come to Paris to persuade Fanny de Malrive, formally Fanny Frisbee of New York, to divorce her husband and marry him. Fanny's marriage to the Marquis de Malrive has been an unhappy one, and there is without doubt enough legal evidence of injury on the Marquis's part to warrant a divorce decree. But years of living in France have made Fanny acutely aware of the pitfalls in transgressing tradition; she is unwilling to begin divorce proceedings unless she is sure her husband and his family will not oppose her.

Fanny de Malrive has become quite thoroughly one of them; indeed, it is this transformation that makes her so desirable to Durham. He muses to himself that while the original Fanny Frisbee had been remarkable in her possession of "the showiest national attributes," she had been one of a type.

Fanny de Malrive was unique. Durham's sister notes: "I never saw anything so French!" Durham adds:

> Yes, it was the finish, the modeling, which Madame de Malrive's experience had given her that set her apart from the fresh uncomplicated personalities of which she had once been simply the most charming type. The influences that had lowered her voice, regulated her gestures, toned her down to harmony with the warm dim background of a long social past—these influences had lent to her natural fitness of perception a command of expression adapted to complex conditions. . . . [H]er acquired dexterity of movement seemed . . . a crowning grace.[42]

Fanny's transformation has taken place at a price however. Durham is surprised by "the sense of distance to which her American past had been removed."[43] No longer an American by nature, she has become a kind of spectator of her own country's men and women, who takes delight in spending time with Durham, his mother and sisters, "dear, good, sweet, simple, real Americans."[44]

Fanny's Europeanization is not the only reason she is reluctant to move forward with divorce proceedings. She has a son and in her own way intends to be "a French mother."[45] Ironically, however, the assumption of motherhood also seems to evoke vestiges of Fanny's national pride. The implications of Fanny's motherhood are profound. Her role as mother binds her to the power of the family in a way that no marriage tie can. Connected by a mother's love to a son who carries a dual national heritage, Fanny recognizes the French family's efforts to make the child one of them. Her efforts to preserve some element of Americanness in the boy place her in direct opposition to her husband's family and culture. Fanny explains to Durham:

> There is nothing in your experience—in any American experience—to correspond with that far-reaching family organization, which is itself a part of the larger system, and encloses a young man of my son's position in a network of accepted prejudices and opinions. Everything is prepared in advance—his political and religious convictions, his judgments of women, his whole view of life. He is taught to see vileness and corruption in everyone not of his own way of thinking, and in every idea that does not directly serve the religious and political purposes of his class.

Fanny's desire to redeem her son from familial and national prejudices lock her into a relentless struggle against the power of the family. She tells Durham she cannot "surrender even the remotest hour of his future . . . because the moment he passes out my influence, he passes under that other— the influence I have been fighting against every hour since he was born!"[46]

Curiously, Fanny's motherhood makes her an integral part of the family system even if her role is that of continuing opposition to that system.

Fanny's fear that the family will never consent to the divorce, although they are not without sympathy for her position, prevents her from moving beyond separation from her husband—a move that seems tacitly accepted by the family.

Wharton's text makes clear that the powerful forces at work are familial and national in nature. The extent of Fanny's predicament cannot be fully comprehended by the American Durham, who remains locked in his reliance on an Emersonian individualism. "He noticed that she spoke as though the interests of the whole clan, rather than her husband's individual claim, were to be considered; and the use of the plural pronoun shocked his free individualism like a glimpse of some dark feudal survival." Fanny points out that "their whole world is behind them."[47]

Only later does Durham come to recognize "the sudden concentrated expression of the ancestral will."[48] Having been invited to tea by Fanny's mother-in-law, Durham observes the other "visitors, who mostly bore the stamp of personal insignificance," but he is struck by "the visible closeness of tradition, dress, attitude and manner, as different as possible from the loose aggregation of a roomful of his own countrymen." Gradually he comes to understand that power lies not within the individual members of "the little company of elderly and dowdy persons" but in the "solidarity of this little group."[49] The only exception to the exercise of shared social power is the central and controlling figure of the mother. When Durham attempts to plead Fanny's case to Madame de Treymes, Fanny's friend and sister-in-law, she points out, "I thought you understood that I am simply their mouthpiece." She asserts that she has "a great deal of influence with my mother" but in the end admits, "[W]hat my mother commands we all do."[50]

A sudden reversal in the plot at the end of the story reveals Durham's failure to mediate the cultural divide and to win Fanny and her son's release from the family. He discovers that the family's apparent agreement to allow the divorce and his remarriage to Fanny was a carefully orchestrated plan to wrest control of the boy from his mother and to restore him "to his race, his religion, his true place in the order of things."[51] Madame de Treymes confesses that the family has sought legal advice and has been assured that under French law remarriage of the mother would shift custody back to the father.

Wharton's narrative highlights the naïveté of the American who believes he can penetrate the mystery of the power and authority of foreign tradition. But the ultimate victor in the cultural struggle over national and family values is not entirely clear. Madame de Treymes tells Durham of the plan, certain that he will participate in the deception. But she errs in her assumption that Durham will give up his adherence to his own American tradition for preserving what she dismisses as an "abstract standard of truth." Durham's response is that he has no choice—"it's an instinct."[52] Knowing that Fanny can never give up her son, Durham abandons his hope for their marriage and prepares to tell Fanny the truth.

The narrative's conclusion certainly raises questions about Wharton's take on the international conflict she explores in the story. On one level, the family retains firm control over Fanny by preventing her remarriage and return to America. And yet the family fails to expel the foreign influence from their midst. Their maneuvers to quietly give up on the recalcitrant son and brother but to preserve the family by transferring "allegiance to the child" are checked."[53] The child remains with his mother, who has, in fact, learned much from her foreign relations. This woman, who has taken on French motherhood, has foreseen the struggle. She admits to Durham that church and family own half the child, but goes on to vow:

> But that other half is still mine, and I mean to make it the strongest and most living half of the two, so that when the inevitable conflict begins, the energy and the truth and the endurance shall be on my side and not on theirs![54]

If Fanny's motherhood prevents her from ever returning to America and places her under the matriarchal authority of the family, embracing her own motherhood allows her to work against the constraints of foreign customs and traditions and to reclaim an American identity. Early in the story, Fanny not only agrees with Durham that she has been a "good American" but asserts that she is "a better and better one every day!"[55] Wharton's examination of the Franco-American conflict ends in a stalemate. Perhaps her later tribute to French tradition and matriarchal power in *French Ways and Their Meanings* is her more final word on the subject.[56] But it is curious that the nonfictional treatment erases the conflict over difference represented so vividly in the earlier story. At the very least, the novel complicates our understanding of Wharton's portrait of an American woman abroad.

Boyle's *Plagued by the Nightingale* takes up many of the same themes of national identity, tradition, matriarchal authority and motherhood.[57] As was the case with Wharton's texts, Boyle's earlier fictional representation reflects certain ambiguities toward cultural differences not seen as overtly in the autobiographical version in *Being Geniuses Together*. Although Boyle's scathing critique of French provincial culture is untempered in the autobiography, the female protagonist in *Plagued by the Nightingale* is both attracted to and repelled by the dynamics of the family and the exercise of matriarchal power.

Boyle's narrative establishes the primacy of a feminine realm and female power from the very beginning of the novel. The protagonist Bridget, who is meeting her husband's family for the first time, awakens that summer afternoon to a "feminine world" that "echoed in the stairway," a "strange feminine world" inhabited by Nicolas's three younger sisters as they climb the stairs to awaken the couple.[58] The central figure and seat of authority within that realm is Nicolas's mother, Maman. As the couple descend to meet the waiting family, Maman emerges as "the hard center of movement." It is her "protruding eyes that examined them as she talked."[59]

Her authority is great enough to undermine even the patriarchal authority of the father. Later in the novel, Papa's disgust with one daughter's behavior brings on her "terrifying sobs" until Maman's funny story about the father's courtship makes them all laugh "in the warm summer afternoon" and realize "that Papa himself was perhaps fallible after all."[60] In times of crisis inside and outside the family, Maman takes charge. When a row of thatched houses catches fire in the village, she organizes "the agitated people, moving her hands and directing with her sharp old finger," moving from pump to pump to keep the fire in check until the firemen arrive. When one of her daughters becomes seriously ill, she becomes "like an old general" giving the family "their orders, her wise protective orders, as though she were saving and intrenching [sic] them for coming battle."[61]

While Maman's power is unassailable, it serves to enforce a culture's strict rules governing the behavior of women. Prepared for only their "own known world," the daughters wear "bathing dresses" with "sleeves to the wrists and sagging skirts" that make them look "like ugly ducklings" even on the family's private beach. Bridget, Nicolas' American wife, unwittingly breaks this code when she exposes her "long angular body" at the water's edge.[62] Throughout the novel, she must be schooled in the appropriate behavior by Maman and the girls in order to escape family judgment.

Most importantly, Maman's authority works to ensure the continuance of the family through marriage and reproduction. Bridget soon discovers that her summer with the family is rendered unique not only by Nicolas's marriage to her, an American but also by the possibility of a marriage proposal from a family friend to one of the sisters. The three younger unmarried girls have been led to believe that Luc, a young man they have known for years, now established in a career and serving as a medical associate with their brother Pierre, cannot help but finally choose one of them for his wife.

In fact, Luc is also subject to Maman's authority. Upon his arrival at the family home with Pierre, he is immediately found "talking respectfully to Maman about her strawberry bed" and playing with "the speckled setter dog" he "had presented to her a year ago."[63] In response to the old woman's repeated "Vacances, vacances," Luc agrees to take his summer vacation the following month and in effect accepts the old woman's deadline for his decision. Later in the story, Maman's reading aloud of the telegram that announces his arrival in two days heralds the impending climactic familial moment. The family now waits for Luc to act, this "Luc who was to these three virgin women a French career that they had studied for in cathedral naves, had languished for in convents, in their communion veils had learned to bow before, burn candles to, this man who each of the three knew must mean a lifetime crowned or doomed forever."[64] Boyle's narrative highlights Luc's role as Maman's chosen one.

Maman's drive to preserve the family above all else includes plans for Bridget and Nicolas as well. In the first meeting with her new daughter-in-law, Maman speaks of her five grandchildren: "Her voice rounded and smiled about the babies. . . . Her hands shaped their limbs, their perfect heads, the hair cut across their brows. Her lips receded in fatuous lines of pride." Then turning to Bridget, "she pressed Bridget's knee with her hand, speaking so personally, so meaningly to her, and the girls nodded and smiled in a soft murmur of assent. 'Et vous. . . .' "[65] And so, Bridget is offered her own access into this female world.

By taking on motherhood, she will meet the needs of the family and acquire her own measure of authority. Although Nicolas initially soundly rejects his mother's proposal, Maman's designs continue to shape the couple's choices. Later in the novel, as Nicolas anguishes over their poverty and dependence on the family, he tells Bridget: "I haven't any money at all, I don't know what I'm going to do, and this morning Papa said he would give me fifty thousand francs if I would have a child."[66] Motherhood is simultaneously a trap and a means of escape for the young Frenchman and his American wife. Nicolas and Bridget initially resist family pressure to become parents. They ignore the father's orders, the mother's inexorable faith in the power of family and the forces of nature, and the lure of escape from all such familial tensions by the promise of money for parenthood. But as the novel proceeds, alternative courses of action are progressively eliminated.

Boyle heightens the conflict between the needs of the individual and the values of the larger group by a strategy that works both literally and metaphorically within the narrative. The cultural imperative to preserve the French family is opposed by Nicolas's awareness that his family carries within it the seeds of disease and death. Literally, the males in the family sooner or later develop a progressive wasting away of the legs and eventual paralysis. The disease was a kind of "family's possession that had nothing to do with themselves" much like an element of the estate such as "the pelouse or the gate or the wall."[67] Although the literal fact of the disease explains Nicolas's refusal to bear children, the metaphorical implications further enrich the narrative. The gendered nature of the disease suggests an inherent weakness in the men who are supposed to father the family. The limited power of the matriarchy can enforce the old code to reproduce but cannot repair what has gone wrong.

The family's drive to preserve and perhaps restore itself ultimately takes on an almost vampire-like quality. Nicolas tells Luc, "This desperate family needs you. . . . We are in desperate need of quarts of new blood in every vein of us."[68] Sirens and vampires, the three daughters must seduce the man who will restore the family. Maman thinks to herself, "This handsome man, this gleaming god-like man . . . must somehow, through the flesh of one of her three daughters, be grafted to them all, be one rich fruitful bough upon the decaying family tree."[69]

Bridget's marriage enmeshes her in the efforts to preserve the family. However, Boyle's text reveals that Bridget's struggle, although represented in terms of gender role and motherhood, moves beyond the realm of family to embody a kind of shadow conflict that is played out in terms of national traits identity. Nicolas's introduction of an American wife into the family's closed society raises questions about constructed customs and values once seen as utterly natural.

As a new element, Bridget's American blood represents the possibility of regeneration. The international marriage is clearly "the most astonishing thing that had happened to the family."[70] She brings with her a foreign landscape and system of beliefs that are both original and attractive. When Nicolas sits "talking about America" his sister can only cry, " 'Yes, tell me Nicol. The colors in the rocks there! The red earth! Tell me, Nicol.' "[71] Bridget carries with her a connection to a multitude of people on a scale nearly unimaginable to the family. Maman cries:

> "How peaceful it is!" . . . "What a gentle and peaceful life we have here when we consider the size of the world around us. Consider New York, for instance," continued Maman. "Those postcards of Nicolas' give us some idea at least of how many men that one city alone contains! Bridget, now what would be your idea, approximately, of how many men there are walking at this moment on one side of Broadway?"[72]

On the other hand, Bridget's culture is also a threat to the system of values embedded in French family life. Unable to speak their language, she barely understands his sisters when they tiptoe into the room that first afternoon. She dresses improperly for the beach, chooses the wrong color for a new dress, and wastes money on the whimsical gift of a nightingale. Indeed, her alien presence in some ways represents Nicolas's chosen weapon against the family's drive to reproduce itself.

The clash of cultures and the gender conflict intersect in Bridget's struggles to reconcile family demands, Nicolas's needs, and her own conflicting desires. Bridget is both drawn to and repelled by the solidarity of the family and the foreign traditions of the French culture she encounters. Early in the novel she muses on the isolation that accompanies the individualism native to her culture:

> Bridget had begun to think of her own family and how they had scattered their children out like dice and not held them close together in the hollow of the hand. Everyone was an individual to them, with his own individual way to go and they never interfered.[73]

She recognizes her desire for the kind of intimate connection blood can bring even though she herself sees the longing as a kind of alien thing inside herself. She concludes:

[I]t is the perversity of weakness that asks my own family to be a loving Jewish tribe, to be all the more fierce for each other because there is the same flesh on our bones. . . . There is no necessity to be one person alone, unrelated. I am afraid to have no family at all, she thought; no one, nothing, I am afraid. Gently she put her hand thorough her mother-in-law's arm as she sat talking to her. The responding pressure gave her a curious assurance. She was accepted so because she was Nicolas' wife.[74]

The presence of Nicolas's family awakens in Bridget a desire for a kind of intimacy that extends beyond the love she shares with Nicolas. But she also is repelled by the intrusiveness of this intimacy. She sees its effect on Nicolas, feeling as if "he was turning remote, and he was rankling within her like a dim wound in her spirit. He was growing cold in protest against the family."[75] Her individual love for Nicolas prevents her from an unquestioning acceptance of this female realm of family and motherhood. Bridget reflects on her conflicting desires:

So safe they were, so safe. What a world of women who lived without avarice or despise, what a woman's world built strongly about the men's fortunes and the men's fortitude, what a staunch sweet world that could never fail. . . . And this strange, hard, bitter thing in Bridget that could have cried aloud. This perverted thing in Bridget that closed like a fist in their faces and that said: 'Where is Nicolas?'[76]

Thus, Bridget's personal struggle to negotiate her own relationship with the family comes to represent cross-cultural conflict in the tension between American individualism and romantic love and French tradition regarding primacy of the family.

Eventually Bridget comes to reject the paramount value of the family in part because "it has no pride to it, and it has not made them lift their chins a hair's breadth higher." She laments the lack of her own heritage of heroism with which she "could have shamed them." She goes on:

There was my grandfather . . . and . . . perhaps with a legion like him behind me I could now lift my head among these people. But through lack of education and that tradition of old warriors I should have relished, I resent the purpose of the good family, for I myself have no purpose at all.[77]

Bridget's rejection of the family and assertion of her own individual need to act, however, like that of Fanny Malrive in Wharton's tale, rests on ambiguity and paradox.

Bridget's final rebellion centers on her ultimate refusal to help make Luc part of the family.[78] Luc tells Bridget he will marry whomever she chooses for him, but having fallen in love with her, he proposes that they go away together. Bridget decides that he must escape completely—from all of them. She thinks to herself, "Oh, Luc, . . . what are you doing in this barren country with people who wrench children from you? Oh, flee from them while you are still able to combat them!"[79] In the end, sacrificing her "own small liberty to the deep wide exemption" she can grant him, she both refuses to choose his wife or to run way with him."[80] In freeing Luc from the family, Bridget embraces American values of personal freedom and individual action that run counter to the French tradition in which she now lives. In so doing, she seems to implicitly claim her own Americanness.

Yet, as was the case in Wharton's novel, the female protagonist's successful rebellion against foreign tradition carries with it the abandonment of personal freedom. For Bridget can ensure Luc's complete freedom only by having Nicolas's child. Her decision to take on motherhood severs the possibility of any further ties with Luc and effectively removes him from Maman's sphere of influence.[81] But, by bearing a grandchild, Bridget lives out Maman's wishes, fixes her uncomfortable place in the family hierarchy, and keeps the family's hope for continuance alive. In one action, Bridget both denies the family what it most wants and satisfies its deepest desires. Motherhood for Bridget, thus, is a kind of subversive action which frees Luc from Maman's grand design but at the same time traps her within the family system.

Wharton's and Boyle's fictional accounts of a young American woman's encounter with French traditions highlight in similar ways a kind of cultural crisis that occurs at a deeply personal level. The protagonists in both novels find that their efforts to negotiate an independent course of action force them to reassess and define for themselves their own identities as Americans. The memoirs of Wharton and Boyle reflect similar struggles in the lives of the novelists. Wharton's and Boyle's texts demonstrate their awareness that French culture provides certain freedoms for French and American women living within it; but, at the same time, they seem to recognize that that very tradition exacts a price that runs counter to specifically identified American values of independence and individuality.

Establishing a relationship between the memoirs (which after all, are also constructions of a reality rather than objective "truths") and the more clearly fictional accounts of the expatriate experience can be dangerous. The correlation between lived experience and a fictional exploration of what one knows can never be fully made. Nevertheless, it is tempting to note briefly the ways the lives of Edith Wharton and Kay Boyle parallel and counterpoint their texts. Wharton's muting of the conflict between freedom and constraint in *French Ways and Their Meanings* suggests that she chaffed less under the restrictions than Boyle. Of course, Wharton from the outset occupied a privileged position as a foreign woman. She admits in *A Backward Glance*, " enjoyed a freedom not possible in those days to the native-born, who were still enclosed in the old social pigeon-holes, which they had begun to laugh at, but to which they still flew back."[82] By the time she began to live year-round in France, around 1913, she had begun divorce proceedings. She lived the remainder of her life, unmarried and childless, producing work after work, supporting herself, and wielding much the same kind of power over her own life that she locates in the French wife and mother in *French Ways and Their Meaning*.

Unlike her protagonist, Boyle refused to submit to the provincial traditions of the Brault family. Eventually she left her husband for Ernest Walsh and in 1926 gave birth to Walsh's child. Ultimately, Boyle would marry three times and raise eight children. But she would continue to write and to participate wholeheartedly in a literary life. As in the case of Wharton, Boyle's work was not only important for her sense of herself as an artist, but also enabled her to support herself and those dependent on her.

On the whole, both writers were able to find in Europe a personal freedom that the protagonists of their early works do not possess. Nevertheless, their examination of the cultural clash experienced by an American living abroad in terms of motherhood, family values, and women's roles suggests that they were profoundly aware of the ways in which their lives as expatriates could run counter to the masculine norm. And because of their willingness to explore that difference in memoir and fiction, contemporary readers are invited to recognize the rich diversity of experience within a revised and more complete version of the expatriation narrative.

Notes

1. Robert McAlmon, *Being Geniuses Together 1920–1930,* revised with supplementary chapters and an afterword by Kay Boyle (San Francisco: North Point Press, 1984), 11.

2. In *Women of the Left Bank: Paris, 1900–1940* (Austin: University of Texas Press, 1986), Shari Benstock notes that the prevailing perspective on the expatriates and modernism "was constructed largely by men" (29). Benstock's treatment of women writers who lived and wrote in Paris in the first half of the century specifically addresses the absence of women from the conventional expatriation narrative. See also Mary Loeffelholz, *Experimental Lives: Women and Literature, 1900–1945* (New York: Twayne, 1992); William Wiser, *The Great Good Place: American Expatriate Women in Paris* (New York: Norton, 1991); and Kenneth W. Wheeler and Virginia Lee Lussier, eds., *Women, the Arts, and the 1920s in Paris and New York* (New Brunswick: Transaction Books, 1982).

3. Benstock argues in *Women of the Left Bank* that while it is necessary to recognize the "important variations" within the lives of these individual women, they also share certain commonalities (9). One such parallel was the motivation for expatriation. Benstock notes that "they wanted to escape from America and to find in Europe the necessary cultural, sexual, and personal freedom to explore their creative intuitions" (10).

4. Wharton's long-standing association with France is narrated in her biographies. See R. W. B. Lewis, *Edith Wharton: A Biography* (New York: Harper and Row, 1975) and Shari Benstock, *No Gifts from Chance: A Biography of Edith Wharton* (New York: Scribner's, 1994).

5. For accounts of Kay Boyle's life in France, see Sandra Whipple Spanier, *Kay Boyle: Artist and Activist* (Carbondale: Southern Illinois University Press, 1986) and Joan Mellen, *Kay Boyle: Author of Herself* (New York: Farrar, Straus and Giroux, 1994).

6. Edith Wharton, *French Ways and Their Meaning* (New York: Appleton, 1919) and *Madame de Treymes and Three Novellas* (New York: Macmillan, 1987). *Madame de Treymes* was first published in 1907.

7. McAlmon's memoirs were originally published in 1938. In 1968 Boyle revised the first edition and inserted chapters detailing her own life. According to the dust jacket, Kay wanted to present "[a] binocular view of Paris" (quoted in Spanier, *Kay Boyle,* 210). The most recently completed revision, also edited by Kay Boyle and published in 1984, is the source for all subsequent references.

8. Literary history generally positions Wharton in direct opposition to experimentalists living in Paris in the 1920s. Certainly Wharton's style and subject matter mark her as a more traditional writer. Yet two essays in *Wretched Exotic: Essays on Edith Wharton in Europe,* ed. Katherine Joslin and Alan Price (New York: Peter Lang, 1993), indicate that the boundaries between Wharton and the experimental modernists are less fixed than previously assumed. Kristin Olsen Lauer in "Can France Survive this Defender? Contemporary American Reaction to Edith Wharton's Expatriation" 77–95, cautions against accepting at face value her complete exclusion from the avant-garde. In "The Salons of Wharton's Fiction" 97–110, Robert Martin and Linda Wagner-Martin point out that both Fitzgerald and Hemingway admired Wharton.

9. R. W. B. Lewis and Nancy Lewis, eds., *The Letters of Edith Wharton* (New York: Scribner's, 1988), 481.

10. Lewis and Lewis, *Letters,* 461.

11. Studs Terkel, interview by Kelley Baker, *Twentieth Century Literature* 34 (fall 1988): 304–9.

12. McAlmon, *Being Geniuses Together,* 104.

13. McAlmon, *Being Geniuses Together,* 214.

14. McAlmon, *Being Geniuses Together,* 336. It is interesting to note, given Wharton's disregard for Eliot, that the quotation from *Being Geniuses Together* continues: "Down with the sterility of 'The Wasteland'!" (336). Apparently Boyle disliked Eliot as well, although on entirely different grounds.

15. Wharton, *French Ways,* 136.

16. McAlmon, *Being Geniuses Together,* 39.

17. McAlmon, *Being Geniuses Together,* 14.

18. Wharton, *French Ways,* 9, vii.

19. Wharton, *French Ways,* 17.

20. Critics have noted the oppositional stance between cultures in Wharton's life and work. Millicent Bell in "Edith Wharton in France," printed in *Wretched Exotic,* argues that her "self-reliance" in moving to another country "indicated something about her of the frontiersman" (64–65). Susan Goodman in *Edith Wharton's Inner Circle* (Austin: University of Texas Press, 1994) claims that Wharton "believed that any change in one's surroundings made the self more accessible by throwing it into relief against a foreign backdrop" (13). In "Why Wharton Is Not Very Popular in France" (*Edith Wharton Review* 9 (spring 1992): 19–22), Jean Meral asserts that Wharton's comments on French culture "have meaning only in relation to cultural references and values that are essentially American" (21).

21. Goodman notes in *Edith Wharton's Inner Circle* that Wharton and her expatriate friends defined themselves as people without a country: "As self-styled citizens of the world they belonged nowhere and elsewhere" (x). The complexities of Wharton's "desire" for a place where she could feel at home are explored in Shari Benstock, "Landscape of Desire: Edith Wharton and Europe," in *Wretched Exotic.* Benstock believes that Wharton "desired an America that was more European and a Europe that was more American" (21).

22. Lewis and Lewis, *Letters,* 84.

23. McAlmon, *Being Geniuses Together,* 14.

24. In the forties, Boyle would give her accounting of French culture to Americans. She published two novels intended to explain the French Resistance to Americans: *Avalanche* (1944) and *A Frenchman Must Die* (1946).

25. Critical response to *French Ways and Their Meaning* varies widely. Margaret McDowell in the revised edition of *Edith Wharton* (Boston: Twayne, 1991) calls it "disorganized" and states that it contains "ill-considered judgments about American women" (15). Cynthia Griffin Wolff in *A Feast of Words: The Triumph of Edith Wharton* (New York: Oxford University Press, 1977) dismisses it as "a superficial study" (296). R. W. B. Lewis states "it is a hurried rambling book, though not lacking in the usual perceptive and delicate observations of the French reverence for life" (*Edith Wharton*, 422). In her biography, Benstock notes that "[w]hatever truths about French, German, and American societies emerge in these essays (and there are many), their insights reflect most clearly Edith Wharton's personal values" (348). Millicent Bell says it is "a fine little social study" (62).

26. Wharton, *French Ways*, v, 18. Critics warn that Wharton's views on France cannot be taken as "fact"; instead her representation of French culture is a construction very much shaped by her own needs. Jean Meral suggests that the reader "may reproach her . . . for warping the image of France in order to suite [sic] her own purposes" (21). Susan Goodman says that, for most of the expatriates, France was an "abstraction" since "place becomes . . . the self's objective correlative" (121). Maureen E. St. Laurent, "Pathways to a Personal Aesthetic: Edith Wharton's Travels in Italy and France," in *Wretched Exotic*, claims that Wharton "is the author of the 'France' and 'Italy' that she presents in her travel writing" (175). Shirley Foster, "Making It Her Own: Edith Wharton's Europe," in *Wretched Exotic*, notes that Wharton was "at once the eager recipient of foreign influences and the active colonizer of her land of promise" (144). Viola Hopkins Winner, "The Paris Circle of Edith Wharton and Henry Adams," *Edith Wharton Review* 9 (spring 1992): 2–4, states that Wharton's "Paris was an intellectual and social ideal, not a historical reality" (3).

27. Wharton, *French Ways*, xi, x.

28. Sandra Gilbert and Susan Gubar point out in *Sexchanges*, No Man's Land, vol. 2, (New Haven: Yale University Press, 1989) that for Wharton, "Europe, especially France, . . . was the only imaginable heaven" (125). Benstock notes in *Women of the Left Bank* that "Edith Wharton wanted a *French* life" and "sought to define herself by the standards of French culture" (39, 65). Penelope Vita-Finzi in *Edith Wharton and the Art of Fiction* (New York: St. Martin's, 1990) argues that French culture provided Wharton with a sense of "order" in contrast to the "anarchy" she found in America and guaranteed the "stability" of tradition (19, 9).

29. Wharton's most direct examination of French culture occurs in *French Ways and Their Meaning*. But she revisits the subject in her autobiography, *A Backward Glance* (New York: Scribner's, 1934). A brief survey of the autobiography suggests that, even 25 years later, Wharton's complex and contradictory attitudes about France remain unchanged. She admires the "social quality" of French culture and the "power of absorbed and intelligent attention" possessed by Frenchwomen that enables them to provide the "perfect background for the talk of men" (261, 274).

30. Wharton, *French Ways*, 100, 102, 116, 120. Wharton's opposition to her own country's treatment of women has been well documented. See Elizabeth Ammons, *Edith Wharton's Argument with America* (Athens: University of Georgia Press, 1980).

31. Wharton, *French Ways*, 117–118, 105, 106. Julie Olin-Ammentorp, "Wharton's View of Woman in French Ways and Their Meaning," *Edith Wharton Review* 9 (fall 1992): 15–18, examines some of the apparent contradictions regarding women in *French Ways and Their Meaning*. Olin-Ammentorp believes that the work "suggests Wharton's unstated belief in the fundamental inferiority of women" and that it "asserts a very conservative, even Victorian, model for women" (15, 17). She finds Wharton's position "perplexing in light of both her life and her art" (17).

32. Wharton, *French Ways*, 24, 112, 11.

33. McAlmon, *Being Geniuses Together*, 41–42.

34. McAlmon, *Being Geniuses Together*, 44.

35. McAlmon, *Being Geniuses Together*, 43.

36. McAlmon, *Being Geniuses Together*, 64.

37. McAlmon, *Being Geniuses Together*, 67.

38. McAlmon, *Being Geniuses Together*, 67, 68.

39. Critics have noted the ambiguity in Wharton's perception of France as a place liberating to a woman and a barely recognized awareness that this place is also subject to the patriarchy. Gilbert and Gubar, *Sexchanges*, admit that "Wharton's depictions of Europe, which we have called her only imaginable heaven, were consistently constrained by what she saw as the limits of the probable, and in patriarchal culture . . . all that was probable for women seemed to her to be the chance of developing their minds" through conversation with men (130). Judith Saunders claims that both Gertrude Stein and Wharton "[r]epeatedly, and in a variety of contexts, . . . characterize France as a place where basic contradictions co-exist. They express the bottommost layer of the paradox as a clash between freedom and confinement" (8). See Judith Saunders, "Edith Wharton, Gertrude Stein, and France: The Meanings of Expatriation," *Edith Wharton Review* 9 (spring 1992): 5–8.

40. Wharton, *Madame de Treymes*, 205.

41. Wharton, *Madame de Treymes*, 207.

42. Wharton, *Madame de Treymes*, 221, 222.

43. Wharton, *Madame de Treymes*, 222.

44. Wharton, *Madame de Treymes*, 208–9.

45. Wharton, *Madame de Treymes*, 211.

46. Wharton, *Madame de Treymes*, 213.

47. Wharton, *Madame de Treymes*, 217.

48. Wharton, *Madame de Treymes*, 237.

49. Wharton, *Madame de Treymes*, 233.

50. Wharton, *Madame de Treymes*, 243, 244

51. Wharton, *Madame de Treymes*, 269.

52. Wharton, *Madame de Treymes*, 273.

53. Wharton, *Madame de Treymes*, 269.

54. Wharton, *Madame de Treymes*, 214.

55. Wharton, *Madame de Treymes*, 210.

56. Cynthia Griffin Wolff says the novel "reflects the author's own astonishments at the tortured patterns of the ancient civilization that she was coming to know better and better during her protracted visits to France" (*Feast of Words*, 138). R. W. B. Lewis finds in the story Wharton's "sense of herself in 1906." He believes Wharton is "suggesting that the psychic imprisonment of women could occur anywhere and even under the most gracious of conditions" (*Edith Wharton*, 165). In their introduction to *Wretched Exotic*, Joslin and Price note the discrepancy between Wharton's attitudes in the fiction and the nonfictional piece. They suggest the contradiction reflects Wharton's "unsettling knowledge that she was a hybrid" and "[t]hat her allegiances {were} often blurred" (12).

57. Some critics have suggested Boyle's interest in issues perceived as female explains the lag in critical attention to Boyle's work. Suzanne Clark in *Sentimental Modernism: Woman Writers and the Revolution of the Word* (Bloomington: Indiana University Press, 1991) argues that many women writers have been systematically excluded from the modernist movement for "representing attachments to everyday life that were not literary." Both men and women "repressed the specific innovations of women writers because they denied these feminine connections" (127). In *Women of the Left Bank*, Benstock includes Boyle in the list of "women who continued writing, editing, and translating activities while raising children and assisting in furthering their husbands' literary careers" (451). Spanier in *Kay Boyle* claims that Boyle's contri-

butions remain unacknowledged because of her "subject matter—often the trials of a woman groping for an identity and a context in which to live" (215). She hypothesizes that such content "simply did not interest critics concerned with more 'substantial' issues." Boyle's early novels "expressed in terms of a woman's experience—apparently were considered so much female fluff" (215). In *Metamorphosizing the Novel: Kay Boyle's Narrative Innovations* (New York: Peter Lang, 1993), Marilyn Elkins points out, "Because much of her longer fiction incorporated themes that focused upon female experience, reviewers and critics often found Boyle's innovative content discomforting" (7).

58. Kay Boyle, *Plagued by the Nightingale*, (1931; reprint, London: Penguin, Virago Modern Classics, 1990): 7.

59. Boyle, *Plagued by the Nightingale*, 8.

60. Boyle, *Plagued by the Nightingale*, 58, 59.

61. Boyle, *Plagued by the Nightingale*, 38, 153.

62. Boyle, *Plagued by the Nightingale*, 7, 14, 11.

63. Boyle, *Plagued by the Nightingale*, 23.

64. Boyle, *Plagued by the Nightingale*, 45.

65. Boyle, *Plagued by the Nightingale*, 10.

66. Boyle, *Plagued by the Nightingale*, 51.

67. Boyle, *Plagued by the Nightingale*, 46.

68. Boyle, *Plagued by the Nightingale*, 96.

69. Boyle, *Plagued by the Nightingale*, 94.

70. Boyle, *Plagued by the Nightingale*, 139.

71. Boyle, *Plagued by the Nightingale*, 125.

72. Boyle, *Plagued by the Nightingale*, 66.

73. Boyle, *Plagued by the Nightingale*, 59.

74. Boyle, *Plagued by the Nightingale*, 60.

75. Boyle, *Plagued by the Nightingale*, 34.

76. Boyle, *Plagued by the Nightingale*, 44.

77. Boyle, *Plagued by the Nightingale*, 159.

78. Critics read the ending of the novel in radically different ways. See Spanier's summary in *Kay Boyle*, 61–62.

79. Boyle, *Plagued by the Nightingale*, 117.

80. Boyle, *Plagued by the Nightingale*, 190.

81. Elkins' reading of the novel emphasizes the protagonist's "autonomy" in making choices that "negotiate within that context" of "family structures" (*Metamorphosizing the Novel*, 22). Thus even though, "[h]er resolution to have Nicolas' child appears to be an act of desperation, . . . Boyle shows that it is, nonetheless, an act she *chooses*, however reluctantly" (27).

82. Wharton, *A Backward Glance*, 258.

Advancing Literary Women:
Edith Wharton, Kay Boyle, and *My Next Bride*

ABBY H. P. WERLOCK

Before the recent upsurge in research on and reappraisals of both Edith Wharton and Kay Boyle, to argue similarity between Wharton, born in 1861, and Boyle, born in 1902, would have seemed laughable. The erroneous but traditional image of Wharton was of an aristocratic, monied, humorless, corseted, and conservative writer who by the 1920s must have seemed, as she wrote to F. Scott Fitzgerald, the representative of "tufted furniture and gas chandeliers."[1] Conversely, the erroneous but popular image of Boyle—if one remembered her name at all—was of a bohemian, dazzling, witty, unorthodox, and politically involved writer who, as Sandra Whipple Spanier notes, signed the 1929 literary manifesto "Revolution of the Word" and joined Raymond Duncan's toga-wearing artists' colony.[2] Until recently, neither woman's works were studied widely in either high school or university level classes; indeed, until very recently, Wharton was never mentioned in considerations of modernism, while Boyle was likely to be buried in a footnote. Some fifty years later, however, Boyle clearly recalls the mandates of those formulative days of modernism: "Our slogans were 'down with Henry James, down with Edith Wharton, down with the sterility of *The Waste Land.*' "[3] Ironically, a contemporary review of Boyle's first novel praised her precisely because the *New York Times* book reviewer found *Plagued by the Nightingale* "as powerful as Edith Wharton's *Ethan Frome.*"[4]

Although their personal backgrounds provide a fascinating study in contrasts,[5] the similarities between Wharton and Boyle occur in their professional commitments to a lifelong literary career and to similar interests in their writing. Both received numerous literary honors.[6] Wharton set standards for women's magazine fiction; Boyle invented the story now commonly known as the "New Yorker story," and both demonstrated considerable skill in dealing with agents, editors, and publishers.[7] Both spoke fluent French and lived primarily in France at the time of their greatest achievements as

This essay was written specifically for this volume and is published here for the first time by permission of the author.

writers—Wharton in the 1920s, Boyle in the 1930s. Both took their expatriate status seriously,[8] and both inevitably suffered from the mistaken notion of
some critics that they had stayed too long in Europe, thereby ceasing to be
"American" writers.[9] And although neither called herself a feminist, Wharton
pointedly distanced herself from the women writers who evoked romantic
"rose-and-lavender" impressions and who lacked her realism,[10] while Boyle
disdained the term "lady novelist."[11]

In fact, Wharton and Boyle share a good deal more than their common
expatriate American status, their talent, and their literary productivity. Both
writers broke with tradition and depicted, with varying degrees of openness,
issues of sexuality and gender that sometimes baffled and often outraged
their readers. Further, both invented new ways of writing the *Bildungsroman,*
peopling their fictions with women characters who face the inequities of their
patriarchally dominated societies. Wharton, unlike Boyle, remained popular
throughout her lifetime, but both readers and critics overlooked what Margaret MacDowell calls her "persistent questioning of the role of women in
both historical and contemporary American society—and sometimes Europe
and Africa."[12] In a similar vein, Gerald Sykes wrote for the *Nation* that
Boyle's strength was in her depiction of female sexuality, in her understanding of "feelings which could have been generated in no other place than a
woman's body." Boyle "put to shame nearly every other emancipated woman
writer who has attempted to deal with this subject."[13]

Ultimately, both Wharton and Boyle consistently and courageously
introduced into their fiction serious issues which affected both men and
women, but especially their women characters, and, predictably, were criticized when their depictions of their women heroes swerved from the expected
norm. Neither wrote many happy endings. R. W. B. Lewis observes that
Wharton's writing provides "testimony to the modes of entrapment, betrayal
and exclusion devised for women" during the first decades of the twentieth
century; Spanier observes that Boyle's theme for six decades has been "that
love is a fundamental human need and that tragedy results when this vital
force is thwarted, stifled, or destroyed."[14] Both writers addressed such issues
as drug- and alcohol-induced behavior,[15] psychological and/or physical abuse,
and incest;[16] and both depicted the internal as well as the external struggles
of their female protagonists faced with such abuse.

To an extent we are just beginning to appreciate, Wharton and Boyle
wrote novels remarkable for the range of women's situations they presented.
Wharton wrote entire novels depicting various stages and options in women's
lives—novels such as *The House of Mirth* (1905), *The Custom of the Country*
(1913), *Summer* (1917)—whereas Boyle managed in one novel, *My Next Bride*
(1934), to incorporate many of the women's problems Wharton had
addressed in individual works. Wharton's extensive presentations of women
such as Lily Bart, Undine Spragg, and Charity Royall helped prepare the way

for a writer like Boyle who, in *My Next Bride*, incorporated most of these stages in her depiction of her heroine Victoria John.

Notably, Wharton's last two (and interconnected) novels, *Hudson River Bracketed* and *The Gods Arrive*, appeared in 1929 and 1932, respectively, just before the appearance of *My Next Bride* in 1934. In these three works, all published within five years of each other, Wharton's strongest woman-as-artist character, Halo Spear, shares striking parallels with Boyle's woman-as-artist character, Victoria John.

Although, like Boyle, Wharton's first full-length commercial publication was a short story collection,[17] her first novel, *The House of Mirth*, catapulted her to instant success. Her protagonist, Lily Bart, as beautiful and innocent as her name, has been educated only in the arts of courtship and marriage; the novel charts Lily's gradual initiation into the darker aspects of sex and her realization of her own powerlessness. Lily's only "power" is in her beauty and her appeal to numerous men, but she ultimately refuses to trade on her beauty, succumb to sexual propositions, or engage in blackmail, instead choosing poverty and death over dishonor. Edith Wharton emphasizes Lily's status as ornament (an early title of the novel was "A Moment's Ornament")[18] implicitly and explicitly throughout the novel and brilliantly evokes her confusion and terror as she narrowly escapes rape by Gus Trenor, the man she believes has been her friend. Lily's tragedy is that no one else in the wealthy circle from which she is eventually expelled is capable of appreciating her quietly rebellious strength of character. Finally, after learning that she is not equipped to earn her own living, Lily chooses an overdose of chloral, a sleeping drug.

Lily tries to articulate her identity, both verbally and in writing, but fails, and she literally chooses silence rather than become a wife, a mistress, a blackmailer. For a time she listens to Selden, another man she believes to be her friend; she thinks for a time that she, too, can join his "republic of the spirit,"[19] where all are free to behave without artifice. Finally, though, she realizes that her instincts have been correct all along: this freedom exists only for men. Prepared neither for the hypocrisy her "set" endorses for women's "advancement" nor for honest work to earn her living, Lily would literally rather die than capitulate to the existence sanctioned by the circles in which she moves.

Wharton illuminates Lily's missed opportunities through her friend Gerty Farish, who works for a living and returns home each night to her own flat. But Lily is woefully unprepared, both emotionally and physically, for earning her keep, and her lack of preparation literally kills her. "I have tried hard," Lily tells Selden just before her death, "but life is difficult, and I am a very useless person" (498). At the end, only in death—and only through the unreliable Selden—does Wharton suggest that a "word" would clarify her predicament (533). Since we are never privy to that word and since Selden, rather than Lily, is its articulator, I believe that her corpse most clearly "articulates" her identity.

Wharton would never again present a woman with no recourse but suicide. Nor would she ever present a central female figure who behaves promiscuously, as would Boyle in *My Next Bride*. However, Wharton's clearest statement on marriage as a socially sanctioned form of prostitution, of selling oneself, occurs in *The Custom of the Country,* for it is the American "custom" to sell its women to the highest bidders, and Undine Spragg is the "monstrously perfect result of the system."[20] In *The Custom of the Country,* Undine, trained like Lily to enter the marriage marketplace, keeps "improving" her situation by marrying and remarrying, moving ever higher in terms of wealth and social position. Despite her "business sense," Undine, like Lily, is naive and, after going to bed with Peter Van Deegan, finds that he does not plan to marry her. Significantly, however, in Undine's case the experience only teaches her to reckon more carefully next time. Even in the aptly named St. Desert, the French chateau of her third husband, Undine remains a virtual prisoner. Her chains are less obvious than the braceleted manacles that defeat Lily, but they confine her nonetheless.

Like Lily, Undine lacks formal education—indeed, in her few attempts to "improve her mind," she finds she has neither the training nor the attention span to help her profit from the lectures she attends—and, at the end of the novel, Wharton portrays Undine indefatigably plotting her next marriage. Wharton's irony is double-edged: Undine, unlike Lily, enters the market, studies its logistics, takes calculated risks, and survives: the difference is that whereas Lily spirals ever downward from a Fifth Avenue house to hotel room to boarding house, Undine climbs ever upward, from modest midwest home to New York mansion to French chateau. But finally Undine, like Lily, fails to articulate her identity, mistakenly seeking it over and over in the wrong places with the wrong men.

In *Summer,* Wharton unleashes a powerful number of dangers threatening to engulf the young Charity Royall, including illegitimacy, incest, sex without marriage, pregnancy, and abortion. At the opening of the novel Charity pauses at the doorstep, sees a man, retreats, then reemerges and steps over it. For the rest of the novel her stepfather, Lawyer Royall, and the attractive young architect, Lucius Harney, move across her threshold almost as through a revolving door while they play their roles in initiating her into the outside world. Like Lily and Undine, Charity has utterly no preparation for life; she refuses a chance at an education (although the dreary library in which she works suggests that the education would teach her nothing she needs to know) and, like Undine, chooses the route that seems to place her in a position of dominance, of power: falsely secure in her obvious attractiveness to men, Charity believes that she can hold Lawyer Royall at bay and maintain the affections of Lucius Harney. She is mistaken, of course, for after her lover abandons her, pregnant with his child, she returns to her stepfather, who marries her.

Her stepfather is addicted to drinking binges that last for days and, when Charity encounters him with a prostitute, he calls her a "damned whore!"[21] Like Lily and Undine, Charity has vague longings of realizing herself, of escaping the narrow confines of North Dormer. But her sense of power is illusory; she is stopped by her encounters with the male representatives of education, law, and the Church—as well as by Harney, who demarcates even the houses to which men consign their wives.[22] Like Lily, Charity feels terror when her stepfather tries to enter her space—he awakens her at night pleading, "Charity, let me in . . . I'm a lonesome man" (28); and like Lily with Gus Trenor, she escapes that one time. As with Lily and Undine before her, however, Charity finds herself ultimately trapped. Even her attempt to escape her pregnancy is doomed; the abortion clinic where she and other unfortunate single pregnant girls seek help is so distasteful and belittling that Charity chooses not to abort her child. Although she "had given [Harney] her all, it was not enough" (198), and she falls back into the ironically conventional if slightly incestuous arms of her stepfather.[23]

In her two novels *Hudson River Bracketed* and *The Gods Arrive*, Wharton portrays the "modern" Halo Spear and Vance Weston who decide, as the Emerson source for the second title suggests, to "give all for love." Herein Wharton addresses in detail the options and ramifications of divorce, extramarital love and sex, and "illegitimate" pregnancy. Only in these two connected novels, her last complete published work, does Wharton finally present a women hero who speaks up and asserts herself. After experiencing the unhappy confinement of a socially approved marriage to a man who belittles her talent, Halo decides to live with her lover Vance Weston in Spain and France. Although the evidence suggests that Halo possesses more talent as a writer than does Weston, she subsumes her talent to that of her lover—who repays her by abandoning her for another woman.

Despite the suffering Weston causes Halo by his desertion, Wharton clearly has invented a gifted woman who will not succumb to her temporary depression. Part of Halo's strength lies in the fact that, unlike her predecessors, Halo has an admirable, viable female model who provides her with the means to independence and self-respect. This aunt, who bears a marked resemblance to Wharton herself, bequeaths to Halo a legacy that includes not only the house on the Hudson but a woman's library (in pointed contrast to the male library of *Summer* or "my father's library" which Wharton used as a young girl).[24] Halo not only leaves Weston and returns to the house on the Hudson, but, unmarried and pregnant, she nevertheless determines to have the child. In her newly assertive voice, she announces her wish to return to her maiden name: "I want to be Halo Spear again. That's all."[25] Halo's pregnancy is heavily metaphorical, signifying her acknowledgment of her own creative abilities, so long used only to bolster those of Weston. Indications are that Halo, a talented writer in her own right, now has the means to articulate herself.[26]

" 'It's a history of women,' Kay wrote to [her agent] Ann Watkins, 'and of that nameless and nonsexual thing that can bind women to each other closer than can any relationship with men.' "[27] And indeed, in *My Next Bride,* Boyle seems both to reenvision the hopeless fates of some of Wharton's earlier women characters, and to reaffirm the possibilities suggested by Wharton's most recent artist-hero, Halo Spear. *My Next Bride* opens through the wary eyes of two middle-aged Russian sisters who watch Victoria John come up the walk and cross the threshold. These ladies, so obviously products of the older era, in their long black silk dresses, are "as alike as prisoners,"[28] and certainly, like Wharton's helplessly unschooled "ladies" before them, they are not equipped to support themselves. Yet despite their literal and metaphorical status as ladies imprisoned in a bedroom, timid as "birds" and suffering spasms of "queer, helpless fright" (16), Boyle imbues them with a shy pride and latent courage as they warn Victoria not to stay in this house and urge her to leave immediately. In her depiction of these women from an earlier era, Boyle at once delineates them as foils to Victoria, the "modern" woman, and reimagines their future: unlike Wharton's similar "useless" women, the Misses Fira and Grusha have the chance to change their circumstances—and will do so with the help of the younger woman.

Victoria, whom they can tell is "fresh from somewhere else" (9), nevertheless moves into this house owned by yet another woman who signifies the dead past: nameless and wraithlike, incapable of focusing her eyes or of moving, her "blinded voice" (12–13) barely capable of speech, this other "lady" and her grotesque crippled servant who attends her, complete the picture of women incarcerated in a dead house from a dead era. Yet even the fact that this house and the one to which Victoria eventually moves are or were owned by women signals her difference from Lily, Undine, and Charity—all either tenants in various men's houses, or propertyless women—and evokes the strong image of Wharton's houseowning Halo Spear.

Victoria not only intends to find work to support herself (her short dress emphasizes simultaneously her modernity and her childlike naïveté), but also "to paint" (33). Her initial conversation with Miss Fira (who is a pianist) and Miss Grusha further emphasizes their seeming differences: Victoria wants to support herself with work, but Miss Fira's understanding of the word "work" derives from the era when ladies painted flowers on china in the summer: "sometime . . . we'll show you the miniatures our mother did" (34). Like Wharton's Lily Bart, these ladies are "useless"; their concept of "work"— addressing Mr. Sorrel's programs, for example—is as frivolous and meaningless as Lily's employment as social secretary-cum-advisor to wealthy arrivistes. Because they do not work and thus lack means, Miss Fira and Miss Grusha exist in a state far worse than genteel poverty, a state that helped drive the unprepared Lily to suicide, the woefully misguided Undine into socially sanctioned prostitution, the hapless Charity to marriage with her guardian.

Yet these two Russian exiles are prepared to break the rules of the house and to help Victoria in any way they can. Thus they join ranks with the three women whose photographs Victoria has brought with her, images of women who serve as inspirators and mentors. The first is a former art teacher from Victoria's midwestern home, an unnamed woman whose very silence, Victoria says, "sent me out looking for whatever there is" (20). The second is Victoria's mother, who hoped to inspire her daughter with the examples of Brancusi, Duchamps, and Gertrude Stein. The third is an Australian vaudeville singer, Mary de Lacey, who advised Victoria not to "go looking for jobs in every city. Go looking for something else. Maybe you'll find it" (25).[29] Thus Boyle's Victoria, like Wharton's Halo, possesses images of women whose encouragement enables her to endure and survive her trials and emerge (in ways similar to the Wharton female hero whose strength is in her name) the "victor."

Potentially undercutting their roles as mentors, however, or at least suggesting the dangers Victoria must face on her road to "whatever there is," lurk the dark undertones of Victoria's memories of these women. The art teacher hardly ever spoke, and remained a "stranger" to Victoria (20). Victoria's mother's eyes betray her unhappiness in a marriage marred by infidelity and "a sensitivity . . . stabbed to death a thousand times a life by fear" (21). And Mary de Lacey, whose eyes reveal a defiance "mitigated by panic" (21), committed suicide in a rented room. Lacey's death follows that of her mother, who accompanied Lacey and her three-year-old son in a wild escape from Lacey's husband, who was "after" them (22). Lacey traveled with cyanide and was prepared to kill herself should her husband catch up with her. As events unfold, her mother is the one who dies first, and her corpse—reminiscent of Charity's mother Mary's corpse, which lies "like a dead dog in a ditch" (*Summer,* 250)—becomes food for the sharks; Lacey learns that "they pitch your innards right over the edge there when they're through cutting you up" (25). The callous contempt for female life depicted in *Summer* not only reappears here in *My Next Bride,* but adumbrates Boyle's later description of the "cutting" that takes place in the abortion house.

At the invitation of her new friends, Victoria accompanies them to yet another house, one no more auspicious than the one in which she lives: "standing in cold and vacant confusion," it is "a dismantled, disreputable caricature of what it had once been" (38). At first it seems a modern and spiritual distance from the other house; it was a gift to the visionary artist-writer-dancer Sorrel, a "divine" or "preacher" who inhabits a "temple" (41). The women do not yet know that the "gift" is from Sorrel's wife, a dancer. Miss Fira, Miss Grusha, and Victoria are literally taken in by the breathless ambiance of the dancers and by the visionary presence of Sorrel. In just such a way is Lily taken in by Selden, Undine by Van Deegen, Charity by Harney, and Halo by Weston. The seductive way in which Sorrel combines religious and sexual energy recalls particularly the similar combination in Vance Weston, who dreams of founding a "new religion" (*HRB*, 3) but who is in fact interested only in pleasing himself. Victoria is too innocent at this point to understand the meaning of Sorrel's interest in her, an interest that will later manifest itself in a sexual invitation. In this depiction of a father figure lusting after the young girl, Boyle's Sorrel follows Wharton's Lawyer Royall. Moreover, the quasi-incestuous motif is clearly intentional in both novels.

Once ensconced in the toga-clad commune where the words "father" and "mother" are forbidden, Victoria sees yet another woman's photograph: she stares at the picture "of Sorrel's dead wife" (67); she is referred to by no other name. Sorrel's wife was "a woman of poetic vision" (123), an assertive and talented woman whose dancing brought her audience to tears, and whose heart was made "of gold" (62). She evicted the commune members when she discovered Sorrel's adultery with Mathilde, who bore his child. But Sorrel's wife achieved only a Pyrrhic victory, for, according to Miss Fira and Miss Grusha, "she went away and died" (62). And, as Wharton demonstrated in nearly all her novels, the sympathy is rarely with the woman, no matter how justified her behavior (in this case Sorrel's wife)—or how reprehensible (in this case his mistress, Mathilde). Miss Fira and Miss Grusha, representatives of the old order, habitually defend Sorrel: "Out of their own virgin infatuation for his sainthood there came a delirium of blame on the woman who was close to him as they could never be" (63). As Wharton shows, for example, in Bertha Dorset and other women in *The House of Mirth*, the phenomenon of female defenders of the patriarchal orders remains remarkably strong because their very survival depends upon their adherence to the male codes. Thus Boyle's message here, like Wharton's, is that if women assert themselves, no matter how justifiably, the results are devastatingly predictable: married or single, the woman who declares her independence from men seems doomed to suffer or to die.

Like Lily, Charity, Undine, and Halo, Victoria stares at her reflection in the mirror, "the question lying like a ring of breath on the tall glass, asking what am I here for, what am I doing here?" (61). At this stage of her education, however, she thinks the answer lies in men, and when one of the children asks why she always paints "strong old men with beards," she replies, in essence, that she distrusts both her gender and her size, saying that if she draws enough men she might succeed in changing her "own face. It's too small" (77). Although Victoria remains still oblivious to the subtle messages embodied in Boyle's text, they provide alternative information that Victoria must eventually acknowledge. Contrary to Victoria's admiration for the "saintly" male principals, these messages depict maleness not only in terms of men who do not listen to women and who think only of themselves, but also in the unpleasantly erotic imagery embodied in Peri, a "swarthy, covetous man" who stands "short and thick" and squats, eyes "bright as an animal's," emitting the smell of "evil" as he leers at Victoria (234). The personification of raw maleness, Peri resembles Wharton's men who lust after Lily, Undine, and Charity.

As she paints at the back of the shop, Victoria naively anticipates the object of her sexual awakening that will walk through the door, that is, enter her life. Like the uninitiated Charity, she does not know what it will be, but surely it "would come quick, lean through the door, it would roll rich as an Italian face, warming like the sun, it would open its throat wide and roar with laughing. . . . Here's sun as rich as butter, olive-skinned, mouth wild as wine" (79). The warm, sensual abandon of Victoria's longing is notably similar to Charity's sun-drowsed anticipation of her awakening sexual interest, which culminates in the affair with Harney.

However, just as Charity mistakenly anticipates Harney and finds instead her stepfather at several points, Victoria realizes that at the door is not a lover but Mathilde, the sexually experienced mistress to Sorrel, who walks in and sits "plump, soiled, nunlike" next to Victoria, (80) "like a Mother Superior initiating a novice" as, metaphorically, indeed she is (81). Moments later, Victoria again anticipates the doorbell and waits for "blood rich and strange and new enough that could not be denied"—and again she is disappointed, as the visitor is one of the American "painted up" ladies who visit Mr. Sorrel (83). The blood here not only suggests the surging blood of her own sexual and creative urges, but also foreshadows the blood of the abortionist, which will haunt her memory with its "dripping."

Finally, just as Harney enters the library because he had seen Charity from the outside, Antony Lister enters the shop because, he explains to Victoria, "I saw you from the street" (99). Yet although Boyle depicts Lister more sensitively than she portrays the other men, she also imagistically reveals the traits that link him with their shared maleness. Lister is reflected in the mirror, filling "the shop with several lightish, quick-eyed men" (99) and recalls Wharton's Weston, who sees himself as having "innumerable" selves (GA, 284). Unlike Wharton's Harney, however, who leads several lives, seduces Charity, and hides from her his engagement to a rich young woman of his own class, Lister immediately mentions his wife Fontana, who, like himself (although he says he's given up painting), is an artist: she "makes things out of clay" (100). It is Lister's repeated mentioning of Fontana that provides a clue to Victoria's future: her odyssey to self-discovery will succeed ultimately because of women, not because of the narcissistic if sympathetic Lister, or the self-serving Sorrel.

On a superficial level, then, Lister proves more sympathetic than some of Wharton's male characters. In fact, because he cannot break free of the patriarchal tradition, he seems more like Ralph Marvell, Undine's second husband; indeed, like Marvell, who also comes from a patrician family, Lister commits suicide. Yet Lister's earlier preoccupation with his own considerable problems precludes his being of substantive help to Victoria. When he asks how many lovers she's had, she replies: "I—I am a puritan. I live by myself. I'm of no importance at all" (107). At this point, Victoria's low opinion of herself echoes Lily's perception of her irrelevance and Halo's understanding of her mediocre talents. Victoria still has a long journey to self-esteem.

As Victoria falls in love with Lister, she believes with all the urgency of the young that love has come to her too late. She thinks to herself, "I'm going to wilder, deeper places, Lister. Next week or the week after I'll be twenty. You might be afraid to come along" (136). This stubborn—and at this point unrealizable—sense of independence recalls nearly all Wharton's women characters—but especially Undine—with their naive beliefs in their own power.

Like Weston and Harney, Lister tells Victoria what he would like, never asking what she wants (159). His self-centeredness and his inability to hear Victoria's words link him with Sorrel. A comparison of the two men's "wilderness" stories—Lister has camped in the Catskills, Sorrel has ridden the Western plains—suggests that in their own ways both Lister and Sorrel have "lighted out for the territory," a land where they leave the women behind, "safe" in their protected spaces. Like Vance Weston, who moves east from his midwest home but then continues to travel, leaving Halo behind, Boyle's men travel at will.

As is always the case with Wharton's men, Sorrel is the one who holds the real power throughout most of Victoria's life in the commune. Like Wharton's Selden, who teaches Lily about the "republic of the spirit" where people are free and equal, or Harney, who introduces Charity to "free" love, or Weston, who advocates modern love and art, the hypocritical Sorrel in fact believes only in his own freedom to do as he wishes. Like Weston, especially, Sorrel believes in himself as an artist and is astonishingly conceited and self-centered.

In a scene reminiscent of the "Old Home Week" scene in *Summer,* the hypocritical Sorrel gives a speech remarkably similar to the one delivered by Lawyer Royall; Sorrel's speech, too, reveals the ultimate self-centeredness of men and its tacit undermining of women: "I can only say to you that I believe in man—not in what man has erected all around him . . . but in the reality of man . . . which casts out all but the simplest needs of man . . . and so the revolution of love will be performed" (252). In *My Next Bride,* with its emphasis on the female protagonist and her "education," Boyle—like Wharton in *Summer*—appears to reiterate the word "man" intentionally for ironic purposes;[30] Sorrel's speech merely announces publicly the congregate male principle that runs through the text of *My Next Bride.*

Sorrel's taste in women literally compares to his love of sweet food, "spread under glass, endless in shape and size and their names spoken, that filled him weekly with tireless, unquenchable delight. . . . He wanted them all, his mouth full with them. . . ." (146). His seeming shyness and gentle "fatherliness" with Victoria (147) proves, as with Wharton's Harney, an easy mask to pierce, and finally Boyle reveals him in his arrogance and male lust-fulness. Like Lawyer Royall who stands "erect" and powerful in his maleness (*Summer*, 150), Sorrel stands "strong and white," with "muscles waiting hard as stone" (260). " 'Kiss me,' " he says to Victoria, "and his mouth was an old man's mouth moving over her face" (261). The revulsion implicit in this description recalls that felt by Lily for her "friends" Gus Trenor and Sim Rosedale, Undine for her third husband Raymond de Chelles, and—espe-cially—Charity for Lawyer Royall. Differing from Charity, however, who escapes from the father figure Royall only to be trapped into marriage with him through Harney's betrayal and her refusal to terminate her pregnancy, Victoria finds her way out of the frustrating and demanding world of the men.

Thus Victoria's pregnancy does not permanently entrap her. Certainly she suffers in the aftermath of her sexual initiation and subsequent disillu-sioned promiscuity. Victoria cannot ascertain the identity of her first lover or of her baby's father, although Michel, a "short, thick" man with perfume in his hair, seems a likely candidate for either role, if only as one more embodi-ment of the undiscriminating, demanding male principle. But like Halo Spear, Victoria emerges from her blank misery and, with the aid of her many women friends, begins to ascertain her identity. Indeed, in the midst of her personal crisis, Victoria goes to the aid of her Russian friends, who are being evicted. "She could not say, put your heads down here on my knees, little women, let me take the pins out of your hair, let me draw the bones from your lace like taking splinters from your flesh. . . . You must believe in me for I am not afraid of anything the world can do" (154–55). Like Lily for a time, seeing women who are even worse off than herself gives Victoria strength and courage. She actually enables Miss Fira and Miss Grusha to realize their dream of settling in Monte Carlo. But whereas Lily cannot even succeed at making hats with other working women, Victoria envisions a future in which, neither as "stenographer" nor "salesgirl" (161), she becomes the artist-entrepreneur who runs a printing shop for poets and writers and perhaps even displays and sells her own paintings.

Victoria is named after her mother, suggesting a woman's tradition that extends forward to Victoria's female mentors and friends. Moreover, all the women who help her enjoy an empowerment utterly lacking among the friends who try to aid Lily, Undine, and Charity. Unlike Gerty Farish of *The House of Mirth*, Indiana Frusk of *The Custom of the Country*, or Ally Hawes of *Summer*, Victoria's friends range across the social spectrum, from the vaude-ville singer Lacey to the actress Estelle to the aristocratic Russian sisters to the wealthy artist Fontana.

The other incident that initiates Victoria's recovery from her bouts with the twin ailments of despair and promiscuity occurs in the form of a letter from Fontana. Although she throws the letter away, the writing and words of this woman seem connected to Victoria's illumination and rejuvenation. She finally hears the false words she has been using about Sorrel and the printing press: "I no longer believe in it, she thought. I no longer believe in Sorrel's intention. I must say it louder. Perhaps if I say it loud enough it will come true again" (263). Even before the two women actually meet, Fontana's words apparently encourage Victoria to use her real voice rather than continue as the mouthpiece for Sorrel. She finally admits and refuses to enable Sorrel's hypocrisy.

Fontana and Victoria find a *sage-femme* who performs abortions "three flights up in the dark," a woman with "soiled hands folded over, her eyes sombre and small and sly" (301). Although Wharton's abortion house in *Summer* has an air of faux respectability, it proves fundamentally no different from Boyle's, for the abortionists—described as hypocrites in both stories—demonstrate concern only with money and with making questionable boasts about their prominent clientele. In one of her most memorable passages, Boyle describes the very nearly unutterable horror of the place as, like Charity, Fontana and Victoria refuse to do business with the abortionist: they leave to the sound of "the dripping, the endless dripping of the life-blood as it left the bodies of those others; the unceasing drip of the stream as it left the wide, bare table and fell, drop by drop, to the planks beneath it, dripping and dripping on forever like a finger tapping quickly on the floor" (303).

The next sound Victoria hears, however, is metaphorical "music," for Fontana has discovered a real doctor who will put Victoria to sleep and perform the abortion. Thus Victoria, like Wharton's Halo, instead of facing the end, now believes that "this was only the beginning" (312). As Fontana explains that she has developed the strategy of laughing to hide her pain, the two women fall asleep, arms about each other's necks, "as if some kind of peace had been suddenly and at the same instant given to their hearts" (320). Although she has yet to forge an entire identity, Victoria, with her new knowledge, new outlook, and new woman friend, now possesses a solid basis on which to continue to explore herself and to pursue her career as an artist.

In a single novel, then, Kay Boyle explores the same dilemmas faced by women appearing in a wide range of novels by her pioneering predecessor Edith Wharton. Victoria John's odyssey toward selfhood embodies much of the self-doubt, pain, and frustration that plagued Lily Bart, Undine Spragg, Charity Royall, and Halo Spear. Finally, however, empowered by actual or metaphorical legacies from women in their respective novels, Wharton's 1932 heroine Halo Spear and Boyle's 1934 heroine Victoria John affirm their dignity and talent as artists. Nullifying the lingering images of either "gas chandeliers" or "toga-clad communes," Wharton and Boyle have advanced the literary depiction of women's ever-expanding possibilities. In so doing, they leave us a powerful legacy of their own.

Notes

1.   Letter dated 8 June 1925, quoted in *The Letters of Edith Wharton,* ed. R. W. B. Lewis and Nancy Lewis (New York: Charles Scribner's Sons, 1988), 581.

2.   Sandra Whipple Spanier, *Kay Boyle: Artist and Activist* (Carbondale: Southern Illinois University Press, 1986), 25–27.

3.   Quoted in Leo Litwak, "Paris Wasn't Like That," *New York Times,* 15 July 1984.

4.   Charles Hansen Towne, "Kay Boyle's Novel," *New York Times Book Review,* 5 April 1931, 94, quoted in Joan Mellen, *Kay Boyle: Author of Herself* (New York: Farrar, Straus and Giroux, 1994), 154.

5.   Although their differences in family background, education, philosophical leanings, and political commitments fall outside the scope of this essay, of particular interest is the difference between these writers' relationships with their mothers. Wharton claimed to be afraid of her mother, who forbade her to read most contemporary authors and who disapproved of her writing, whereas Boyle was close to her mother, who, believing her daughter a prodigy, read Gertrude Stein's "Tender Buttons" to her at a young age.

6.   Among Wharton's numerous honors are a Pulitzer Prize, an honorary doctorate from Yale, and gold medals from the American Academy of Arts and Letters and the National Institute of Arts and Letters; Boyle's include two O. Henry Awards and membership in the American Academy of Arts and Letters.

7.   See R. W. B. Lewis, *Edith Wharton: A Biography* (New York: From International Publishing Corporation, 1985), 458, 507; and Mellen, *Kay Boyle,* 155, 157.

8.   Both had misgivings about New York, which Edith Wharton found to be an "ugly, patchy, scrappy" depressing place (Lewis and Lewis, *Letters,* 313). Boyle quipped, "If allowed to enter New York, I must recite the names of the presidents and prove that I can write my name" (quoted in Mellen, *Kay Boyle* 161).

9.   Margaret B. MacDowell, *Edith Wharton* (New York: Twayne Publishers, 1992), 17; Mellen, *Kay Boyle,* 164.

10.   Edith Wharton, *A Backward Glance* (New York: Appleton Century, 1934), 293–94.

11.   Spanier, *Kay Boyle,* 215. See also Mellen, *Kay Boyle,* 147, 152–53.

12.   MacDowell, *Edith Wharton,* 131.

13.   Gerald Sykes, "Too Good to Be Smart," review of *Wedding Day and Other Stories, Nation,* 24 December 1930, 711–12, quoted in Mellen, *Kay Boyle,* 153.

14.   Lewis, *Edith Wharton,* xiii; Spanier, *Kay Boyle,* 56.

15.   Although Boyle's references to these phenomena are well known, Edith Wharton's are less so. For example, between writing *The Custom of the Country* and *Summer,* Wharton wrote *Bunner Sisters,* a novella in which one sister leaves the small enclosed space where she and the other sister operate a dressmaking business. She marries a man who takes her west to St. Louis, where he proves himself a "dope fiend," punches her in the breast, and abandons her. She loses her baby and returns home to die. The surviving sister has lost all faith in the way the world operates and, at the end of the book, is walking the streets of New York, seeking employment as a sales girl.

16.   Again, refuting outdated views of Wharton's so-called prudishness, are her more explicit descriptions of sexual desire and the sexual act, which remained unpublished in her lifetime. In the incomplete story "Cold Greenhouse," written about 1928, Wharton depicts the incestuous love of mother for son. In the "unpublishable" Beatrice Palmato fragment, written about 1919, Wharton explicitly describes sexual intercourse between a stepfather and daughter. Knowing that she could write this way, it is not surprising that a passionate sexuality underlies much of her rather more chaste published descriptions. Perhaps her most memorable published treatment of sexual climax occurs in *Summer,* where her genius and wit cloak the description in the metaphor of a Fourth of July fireworks display wherein "A long 'Oh-h-h'

burst from the spectators: the stand creaked and shook with their blissful trepidations" (*Summer*, 148). See also Lewis, *Edith Wharton*, 544–548; and Cynthia Griffin Wolff, *A Feast of Words: The Triumph of Edith Wharton* (New York: Oxford University Press, 1978), 407–15.

17. Kay Boyle, *Wedding Day and Other Stories* (New York: Jonathan Cape and Harrison Smith, 1930); Edith Wharton, *The Greater Inclination* (New York: Scribner's, 1899).

18. Wolff, *Feast of Words*, 109.

19. Edith Wharton, *The House of Mirth* (New York: Charles Scribner's Sons, 1905), 108. Subsequent references to this edition are parenthetically cited in the text.

20. Edith Wharton, *The Custom of the Country* (New York: Scribner's, 1913), 208. Subsequent references to this edition are parenthetically cited in the text.

21. Edith Wharton, *Summer* (New York: Harper and Row, 1979), 152. Subsequent references to this edition are parenthetically cited in the text.

22. See Abby H. P. Werlock, "Whitman, Wharton, and the Sexuality of *Summer*," in *Speaking the Other Self: American Women Writers*, ed. Jeanne C. Reesman (Athens: University of Georgia Press, forthcoming).

23. That Wharton was conscious of the incest hidden behind closed New England doors is evident in several documents. For example, in a conversation with Henry James at the Mount in 1904, Wharton commented on "the dark unsuspected life—the sexual violence, even the incest—that went on behind the bleak walls of the farmhouses" in little New England villages" (Lewis, *Edith Wharton*, 40). In her "Subjects and Notes, 1918–1923"—the same "donne book" that contains the Beatrice Palmato fragment—she outlines "The Family," an idea for a story about incest involving a brother, a sister, and the sister's daughter, at the end of which she notes, "The above is absolutely true, but if I were to use it as a subject all the critics would say it was not like real life, that such 'unpleasant' things may exist singly, but don't occur in 1 household, whereas that is just where and how they do occur, one source of corruption" ("The Family," in "Subjects and Notes, 1918–1923," box 22, folder 701, item 51 Edith Wharton Archives, Beinecke Library, Yale University).

24. Wharton, *A Backward Glance*, 52.

25. Edith Wharton, *The Gods Arrive* (New York: D. Appleton and Company, 1932), 362. See also Edith Wharton, *Hudson River Bracketed*, (New York: D. Appleton and Company, 1929). Subsequent references to these editions, hereafter referred to as *GA* and *HRB*, respectively, are parenthetically cited in the text.

26. See Abby H. P. Werlock, "Edith Wharton's Subtle Revenge? Morton Fullerton and the Female Artist in *Hudson River Bracketed and The Gods Arrive*," in *Edith Wharton: New Critical Essays*, ed. Alfred Bendixen and Annette Zilversmit (New York: Garland Publishing, 1992), 181–200.

27. Quoted in Mellen, *Kay Boyle*, 188. For speculations on the lesbianism implications of the descriptions of Victoria and Lacey, and Victoria and Fontana, see Spanier, *Kay Boyle*, 89; and Mellen, *Kay Boyle*, 178, 221.

28. Kay Boyle, *My Next Bride* (London: Virago Press, 1986), 16. Subsequent references to this edition are parenthetically cited in the text.

29. For extensive discussion of these female images, see Spanier, *Kay Boyle*, 87; Marilyn Elkins, *Metamorphosizing the Novel: Kay Boyle's Narrative Innovations* (New York: Peter Lang, 1993), 46–48; Deborah Denenholz Morse, "My Next Bride: Kay Boyle's Text of the Female Artist," *Twentieth Century Literature* 34, (1988): 334–46; and Donna Hollenberg, "Abortion, Identity Formation, and the Expatriate Woman Writer," *Twentieth Century Literature* 40, (1994): 499–517.

30. In *Summer*, 192–95, the "Old Home Week" speech delivered by Lawyer Royall is replete with Royall's references to "illustrious men," "young men," "gentlemen," and "select men"; at its conclusion, other men congratulate Royall among themselves with the pronouncement, "That was a *man* talking—" [Wharton's italics].

Absence and the Figure of Desire
in Kay Boyle's *Monday Night*

BURTON HATLEN

Kay Boyle's sixth novel, *Monday Night,* may seem to represent a sharp change of direction from her previous work.[1] There is here no strong female protagonist such as we find in most of Boyle's earlier novels. Instead the central characters in *Monday Night*—a middle-aged American writer named Wilt and a young American doctor named Bernie—are male; and Boyle's decision to focus on such characters may suggest that she has shifted her attention away from the issues of gender and sexuality that are central to her earlier novels. At the same time, *Monday Night* is more stylistically self-conscious, even mannered, than any of Boyle's previous novels. Point of view and authorial perspective often shift violently; the narrative is regularly interrupted by extended lyric "arias"; and the plot is both telescoped (the action takes place in a period of twelve hours), mysterious (the quest of Wilt and Bernie for the enigmatic Monsieur Sylvestre seems, at best, quixotic), and unresolved (although they spend the whole book searching for Sylvestre, Wilt and Bernie never find him). And along with its bravura stylistic flourishes, *Monday Night* is an insistently literary novel, alluding to or otherwise engaging a range of writers and literary traditions. Despite all its ostentatiously belletristic qualities, however, *Monday Night* does not represent a turning away from issues of gender politics to issues of aesthetic form, but rather a critical examination of the gender politics of literary form itself. For the novel brings into play a range of literary traditions that effectively deconstruct one another, and this deconstructive process points us toward new literary *and* new moral and political possibilities.

Monday Night locates itself in an intertextual space between two broad literary currents of the 1920s and 1930s. On the one hand, the novel has some identifiable affinities with the works of certain experimental French writers whom Boyle came to know in the late 1920s, when she was living in Paris and spending much of her time with the writers grouped around the

This essay was written specifically for this volume and is published here for the first time by permission of the author.

276

magazine *transition*. Eugene Jolas's magazine celebrated and disseminated the work of the French Surrealists, and *Monday Night* has affinities to what I shall call the "Surrealist quest romance"—a form developed by writers, especially Breton, Desnos, Soupault, and Crevel, whom Boyle admired and in one case (Crevel's novel *Babylon*) translated. At the same time, *Monday Night* also shows a debt to certain distinctively American literary modes, ranging from the detective story; through the broader genre of the "tough guy" novel as developed in the late 1920s and early 1930s by such writers as Hemingway, Faulkner, Cain, and Hammett; to the still broader genre of the "innocents abroad" novel as practiced by Hawthorne, James, Wharton, Hemingway, Fitzgerald, and others.

The distinctive tone of Boyle's novel results from its merging of these variously "French" and "American" modes. Most of the genres that Boyle invokes have traditionally been identified with male writers; but Boyle always makes her own whatever she borrows, reshaping formal possibilities in accordance with her own politically radical and specifically feminist perspective. Thus in *Monday Night*, the intertextual merging of the "French" and "American" modes points toward a critique of both these literary traditions. In brief, Boyle melts down the tough guy detective—or at least his first cousin, the investigatory reporter—into a dreamer who is driven by his own inner compulsions to an endless and finally fruitless quest of the Figure of Desire. But by casting such a quintessentially macho (and quintessentially American) figure in the role of the quester, Boyle also uncovers the implicit male orientation within the Surrealist quest narrative, which for her becomes an exploration of how *men* specifically (not "people") invent Figures of Desire, and of how these fantasy quests determine both the ways men live their own lives and the ways they reshape the lives of the women onto whom they project their desires. Rather than abandoning her political concerns, then, Boyle has in *Monday Night* carried these concerns to a new level, to explore the sexual politics implicit in two important fictional genres of our century.

I

Kay Boyle began reading the French Surrealists in 1922, when, as a nineteen-year-old Midwesterner trying to find a place in the New York literary world, she became the editorial assistant to Lola Ridge, the American editor of *Broom*. Interspersed among the works of American writers like Gertrude Stein, Sherwood Anderson, Wallace Stevens, and William Carlos Williams, *Broom* published English translations of poems by the Comte de Lautréamont, one of the godfathers of the Surrealists, as well as works by several members of the Surrealist movement itself, including Paul Eluard, Benjamin Peret, and

Louis Aragon.[2] A few years later, temporarily living with her young child in England, Boyle read the first issues of *transition,* and there she encountered, for the first time, the writings of "Philippe Soupault, and also Robert Desnos, whose two poems, 'The Dove of the Ark' and 'I've Dreamed So Much About You,' immediately became part of my singing repertoire for the baby falling asleep in her rocking, rolling pram."[3] A few months later, now living in Paris, Boyle met and became a close friend of Eugene Jolas, and through him she also became friends with many of the French writers whom *transition* praised and published: Breton, Desnos, Crevel, Soupault. And in 1929, when *transition* published its famous "Revolution of the Word" manifesto, Jolas's attempt to lay out the principles of an English-language surrealism ("The imagination in search of a fabulous world is autonomous and unconfined," "narrative is not mere anecdote, but the projection of a metamorphosis of reality," etc.), Boyle's name appears first among the signers.[4] The fiction that Boyle wrote during the *transition* years—roughly, 1927–1930—and collected in her first book, *Wedding Day and Other Stories,* is distinctly more experimental than her later work, as it explores the evocative power of verbal dislocations, hallucinatory imagery, and fragmented narrative lines.[5] I would not suggest that Boyle ever "became a Surrealist," in the narrow sense of that term; for even the *Wedding Day* stories remain rooted in the conventions of realistic character-, plot-, and scene-centered fiction, in a way that the Surrealists eschewed. Nevertheless, it is clear that Boyle felt a strong personal affinity for at least some of the Surrealist writers and read their work with interest.

It also seems probable that Boyle felt a considerable sympathy for the Surrealist project of human liberation through erotic liberation. To André Breton and his followers, the carnage of World War I had definitively demonstrated that the social order is dedicated to death. Thus Surrealism set itself the task of undoing the social order by opening it up to the Freudian id itself. Through automatic writing, an exploration of dream experiences, a deliberate flirtation with schizophrenia, and sometimes the use of hallucinatory drugs, the Surrealists attempted to recover the voice of desire.[6] Furthermore, Surrealism in all its various incarnations always insisted that this liberatory project was not only psychological but also political: witness, for example, the efforts of Breton to affiliate the movement *en masse* with the Communist Party, his flirtation with Trotsky after the Surrealists were expelled from the party, and the long term communist affiliations of two notable Surrealists, Paul Eluard and Louis Aragon. Both Freud and the Marxists looked on these putative disciples with suspicion, but it is precisely their determination to have it both ways, to bridge the gap between Marx and Freud, that makes the Surrealists interesting today. In a broad sense, Boyle certainly shared both the liberatory goals of the Surrealists and their leftist political perspective. Both her scathing contempt for people who base their self-esteem on their conformity to social proprieties and her sympathy for characters who violate these proprieties as they explore new sexual possibilities are apparent in all her early fiction. And she also saw the struggle for erotic liberation as part of a larger political struggle for human liberation. Boyle was always too rebellious to fit comfortably inside any political party, whatever the McCarthy blacklisters may have thought. And in her early writings the political concerns are more latent than overt, although that would change when, in the late 1930s, she enlisted in the struggle against Fascism, and then in the postwar years found herself resisting the American-style Fascism of Senator McCarthy, and then in turn committed herself during the 1960s to the struggle against racism and the Vietnam war, and so on. But Boyle felt a need to put her commitments on the line as early as the Sacco-Vanzetti trial;[7] and while her "lost generation" writings may not explicitly treat political issues, nevertheless they perceive the world in terms of power relationships, especially the power of men over women, and implicitly call for a revolution in such relationships. Thus while Boyle may not have felt as strongly as did the Surrealists either about the necessity of disrupting traditional linguistic and literary structures or about the need to enlist under the banner of the Communist Party, she was clearly sympathetic to the liberatory moral and political goals that they were pursuing.

Monday Night shows the particular influence of one specific sub-genre within Surrealist writing, the "Surrealist quest romance." The Surrealists are generally better known for their poetry than for their fiction. But in the 1920s and early 1930s, several well-known Surrealists published extended prose works, more or less narrative in form, more or less fictional in mode; and almost all of these works display at least some of the characteristics of the quest romance—as do, indeed, some later Surrealist narratives that I will not discuss here, such as Michel Leiris's *Aurora*. The quest romance form descends, of course, from the Middle Ages: a dream of love sends the knight on his way, in quest of the *summum bonum*—the Holy Grail, or whatever. As elaborated by generations of poets, both the inspiration and the goal of the quest generally take the form of a woman: the Rose of *Le Roman de la Rose,* Dante's Beatrice, or the Faerie Queene in Spenser's poem. The quest pattern has so disseminated itself throughout our literature that it has seemed to some an archetype of the collective unconscious; in an inverted form, for example, the pattern establishes the basic structure of the Gothic novel, as the visionary dream figure becomes a ghost or perhaps a vampire. To see the questers of *Monday Night* as deriving specifically from Surrealist prototypes may thus seem gratuitous. But it is clear that the Surrealists rediscovered the quest pattern with a vengeance and that they redefined this genre as specifically a quest for the Figure of Desire; and this specifically Surrealist version of the quest romance seems to have influenced Boyle. For the Surrealists, the immediate prototype was primarily Nerval's *Aurelia.*[8] Nerval was schizophrenic, and his narrative graphically describes his psychotic hallucinations. But he was also a student of *Le Roman de la Rose,* and his visions assume the form of a dream quest for the evanescent beloved who embodies the always unreachable mystery of being itself. Moreover, Nerval wove into the form various forms of occult lore, including the Cabalistic concept of the Shechinah, the female power that makes and unmakes the material world. This modernized version of the visionary quest narrative proved uniquely suited to the preoccupations of the Surrealists, as the inspiration and object of the quest become for them both the Muse and the object of desire itself—desire now conceived in a distinctly modern, post-Freudian sense, as the id insatiably hungering for a sensory plenitude forever lost.

The archetypal Surrealist quest narrative is Breton's *Nadja,* the apparently true story of the poet's relationship with a young woman who is drifting rapidly toward a psychotic breakdown.[9] In the first fifty pages of this book, Breton roams restlessly through Paris accompanied by his Surrealist friends, encountering various women who seem to give him a glimpse of something *beyond:* an actress named Blanche Derval, whom he returns obsessively to watch in the role of an enigmatic murderess, a "magnificent predatory beast";[10] a nameless woman who leaves him one of her gloves as a token;[11] and so on. Then, more than one-third into the book, Nadja accosts the narrator on the street. "She told me her name, the one she had chosen for herself: 'Nadja, because in Russian it's the beginning of the word hope, and because it's only the beginning.' "[12] (But also, inescapably, the name suggests Nada, nothing, the eternal Negative.) At this first meeting, Breton asks Nadja, "Who are you?" She replies, "without a moment's hesitation, 'I am the soul in limbo.' "[13] These enigmatic messages draw Breton toward Nadja, as she comes to represent for him the hope of a pure spontaneity: she can and will say or do *anything.* But Nadja's spontaneity is, we and Breton quickly realize, a symptom of increasing madness—a madness that, however, liberates her creativity, for Nadja begins to make surreal drawings that carry a powerful if obscure meaning for Breton. In the end Nadja's behavior becomes so bizarre that she is committed to an asylum, leaving the poet to lament the destructive effects of such institutions—but why, then, doesn't he attempt to get her out?—as he hurls "at myself or at anyone who comes to meet me, the forever pathetic cry of 'Who goes there? Is it you, Nadja? Is it true that the beyond, that everything beyond is here in this life? I can't hear you. Who goes there? Is it only me? Is it myself?' "[14]

Nadja is not, however, a novel. For examples of the Surrealist novel, we must turn to Breton's friends and disciples, in particular Robert Desnos, Rene Crevel, and Philippe Soupault. First published in 1927, Desnos's *La liberté ou l'amour* gave Boyle, she declared forty years later, "my first tentative understanding of surrealism."[15] In the opening section of this novel, translated in *transition* and quoted at length by Boyle in *Being Geniuses Together,* the narrator declares that his "door was always open to mystery then, but mystery came in, closing it behind her. . . ."[16] Mystery takes the form of a woman named Louise Lame. Her first appearance in the novel is signaled when the leaves falling from the trees in the Tuileries turn into a torrent of women's gloves:

gloves of every description, kid gloves, suede gloves, long Lisle gloves. A woman is taking off her gloves in front of a jeweler's to try on a ring and have her hand kissed by Corsair Sanglot. . . . The crowd trampled these memories of kisses and embraces. . . . I alone avoided treading on them. Sometimes I even picked up one of them. . . . I felt it tremble in my trouser pocket. Its mistress must have trembled just like that in a fleeting moment of love.[17]

As the narrator follows Louise Lame through the streets of Paris, she leaves for him a trail of various other items of clothing: her panties ("I unfolded them and plunged my head into them with delight. They were impregnated with Louise Lame's most intimate odours"),[18] then her dress, and so forth. The last garment is a leopard skin coat: the leopard itself, Desnos fantasizes, was a vast and magnificent animal who flayed himself and crawled to Paris, to lay "the supreme homage of his fur . . . at the feet of the fatal, adorable girl."[19]

A few more steps and then she unfastens this last item of clothing. It falls to the ground. I run faster. Louise Lame is now naked, completely naked in the Bois de Boulogne. The cars flee, trumpeting like elephants. . . . A storm of anguished sounds spreads through the surrounding districts. . . . Paris bars its doors and windows, extinguishes its lamps. . . . The naked woman knocks on every door, lifts each closed eyelid.[20]

Clearly, Louise Lame is a mythical figure, in a way that Nadja is not. But like Breton's heroine, Louise Lame came as Mystery into the world and draws the soul of the quester toward the Beyond.[21]

For a second example of the Surrealist novel, we may turn to Crevel's *Babylone,* also first published in 1927 and translated into English by Boyle herself.[22] Less experimental than Desnos's novel, Crevel's is on one level a reasonably traditional study of the repressive structure of the bourgeois French family—the same kind of family that Boyle's herself dissects in her first published novel, *Plagued by the Nightingale.*[23] In this respect Crevel's novel may seem more interested in the social structures that encode themselves in the superego than in the Surrealist quest for a "convulsive" (the term is Breton's, at the end of *Nadja*) beauty. However, the central character of *Babylone* is a nameless child—later, a young woman—who restlessly projects her imagination and desire onto the people around her. Thus Crevel, uniquely among the Surrealists, creates a female quester and asks the reader to explore the subtleties of female desire. Crevel himself was homosexual, and the anonymity of his heroine suggests that she may be in some measure himself. In any case, the novel's focus on a female protagonist may explain Boyle's particular interest in this book. There are also homoerotic overtones to the child's desires, for her inchoate longings focus above all on Cynthia, the beautiful red-haired cousin of the child's mother. Cynthia has run off with the child's father, and by this act she has entered a mysterious realm of transcendent sexuality:

Cynthia remained a flaming idol in her memory, in turn brightening the gray heavens or warming the finical azure of the minutes to the color of a painting between two showers. But after the flaming passage of the young woman with a helmet of fire across that azure, the little girl, her eyes still dazzled by the miracle, could not repudiate that beautiful comet.[24]

One after another, most of the characters in the novel—the only exceptions are the child's mother, the missionary that the mother marries, and the child's grandfather, a psychiatrist locked within his own mental categories—plunge into the sensual fires represented both by Cynthia and, more broadly, by a mythical Africa that the missionary couple attempts, unsuccessfully, to tame. At the end of the novel, the child herself stands, shakily, on the brink of womanhood, intoxicated and terrified by her own desires. Will she too leap into the cauldron?

There is abundant evidence that Boyle knew well the novels of Desnos and Crevel. On the other hand, to my knowledge Boyle never mentioned Philippe Soupault's *Les derniers nuits de Paris*.[25] Yet it seems likely that she knew this novel too; for Boyle and Soupault were friends, and she was also a close friend of William Carlos Williams, who translated Soupault's novel into English. In any case, Soupault's novel is more similar to *Monday Night* than any of the other three Surrealist narratives that I have here described. Like all of the other books, *Les derniers nuits* centers on a mysterious and powerful woman, Georgette:

Georgette . . . went on, dispelling sorrow, solitude or tribulation. Then more than ever did she display her strange power: that of transfiguring the night. Thanks to her, who was no more than one of the hundred thousands, the Parisian night became a mysterious domain, a great and marvelous country, full of flowers, of birds, of glances and of stars, a hope launched into space.[26]

Several other men, members of a criminal gang grouped around a shadowy journalist-politician named Volpe, share the narrator's obsession with Georgette. She is, it seems, the infinite and absolute object of desire, embodying the night and the city through which these men move. The members of this gang may or may not also be involved in a series of mysterious deaths; and as he traces Georgette's path through the city, the narrator of Soupault's novel is also in quest of an explanation for these crimes. "All the night-prowlers of Paris," the narrator says early in the book, are finally "in search of a corpse,"[27] and these parallel quests suggest that Georgette, as the embodiment of night, may represent death as well as love. At the climax of the novel, Georgette mysteriously disappears, and all her devotees, the narrator as well as the members of the gang, initiate a massive search for her, fearful that "if she should disappear forever, . . . there would be no more night."[28] Then in the last page of the novel, no less mysteriously, she reappears. But is it she? Indeed, "who" "is" "she"?

II

Monday Night does not offer us the kind of monstrous or hallucinatory events we might expect in a Surrealist novel. Nevertheless, Boyle's novel, like the Surrealist narratives summarized above, is primarily concerned with exploring the modalities of desire through a quest narrative. The plot of *Monday Night* revolves around two Americans, Bernie and Wilt. Bernie, a recent medical school graduate, has just arrived in Paris from Chicago. Throughout his years in school, he has been saving his money for a post-graduation trip to pay homage to his hero, the French toxicologist Monsieur Sylvestre, whose expert testimony on the effects of various substances on the human body has sent a series of apparent murderers to prison, or to the guillotine. "This man," Bernie says in one of his few articulate moments, "to me there's nothing like him, he's as great as anyone in history. . . . This man, . . . he's got the knowledge all right, and then he's got something else which gives him just about the whole sacred show." And when Bernie's own words can no longer express his longing, Boyle supplies her own:

> Beyond this there were other things to say, to speak of that immemorial and profoundly ennobling power which may be a man's faith in his own vision or which may more truly be the faith a man has in the passion of his own divinely intelligible blood. . . . Because of his own hesitancy, his own trembling upon the brink of being, [Bernie] thought wondrously of this man who had not feared; because of his own chaste reverence for truth, he saw him as . . . Quixotic in the flesh, an enigma . . . , not comprehended and therefore betrayed.[29]

Bernie's quest for M. Sylvestre provides the trigger of Boyle's plot. Who is M. Sylvestre? Is he worthy of Bernie's adulation? These are the questions that draw Wilt—and us—into Bernie's quest.

On his first day in Paris, Bernie has met Wilt, an American newspaperman and long-time resident of Paris, and the novel begins a few hours later. In these few hours, Wilt, entranced by Bernie's youth and enthusiasm, has appointed himself Virgil to Bernie's Dante: he will lead the quester through the inferno and purgatorio of Paris, to the promised goal. And if Bernie is only marginally and intermittently articulate, Wilt is a compulsive and eloquent talker, so that his voice very quickly takes over the novel. Boyle herself says that her portrait of Wilt is based on a man well-known to Americans living in Paris during the 1920s, Harold Stearns: "I wrote a book about this man, and it is to me the most satisfying book I ever wrote."[30] Stearns was "the Peter Pickem of the Paris edition of the Chicago *Tribune*, . . . who picked the winners at the racecourse at Maisons-Laffitte (or else failed to pick them)."[31] Clearly, it was Stearns's voice that inspired Boyle to write *Monday Night:*

once he began to talk you forgot the stubble-covered jowls packed hard from drink, and the stains of food on his jacket lapels, and the black rimmed fingers holding his glass. . . . I knew if the things he described had not happened in this lifetime they had happened sometime, somewhere else, or else they should have happened; and if they had not happened to him, he believed by this point that they had, and one had no right by any word, or look, or gesture to take this desperately accumulated fortune of belief away.[32]

In the novel, Stearn's ability to make other people's experiences his own takes the form of Wilt's passionate identification with Bernie's quest. Wilt hungers to "be a writer," not just a newspaperman. To him, this means immersing himself in other people's lives, making their hopes and fears his own. He sees all human beings as questers, inspired by some kind of vision of what might be. It is such a vision that he sees in Bernie, and when we meet him he has already impulsively and generously given himself over to helping Bernie in his quest.

Bernie, however, proves at best a fickle quester. While Wilt wants to press on with the search for M. Sylvestre (he isn't at the drugstore that he owns, so is he perhaps at his country home?), Bernie is almost immediately distracted by thoughts of dinner. And like most young American men of the time, it quickly turns out that he has come to Paris, not to pay homage to the Truth, but to get laid. He falls soulfully in love with a woman well past forty, the proprietress of a bar where he and Wilt take refuge; and then, somewhere around 2 A.M. on this adventurous night, he loses his money—and, presumably, his virginity—to a prostitute who picks him up on the street. As Bernie's interest in M. Sylvestre fades, the young American doctor becomes little more than a reluctant piece of baggage, and Wilt's own quest—not so much for M. Sylvestre himself as for the "good story," and for the human truth about everyone involved—takes over. When they finally arrive at the toxicologist's country house, Bernie and Wilt learn that he is not home, but they spend an hour or more—fifty pages of text—talking to the butler, the housekeeper, and the cook. And the more Wilt learns about M. Sylvestre, the more skeptical he becomes of Bernie's vision of him: as Sandra Spanier says, Wilt "begins to spin another history of the great doctor, arriving at quite a different 'truth' about the man."[33] The people that Sylvestre has sent to prison or to the guillotine were, Wilt and we begin to realize, all driven by passion. In all cases the presumed "victims" appeared to have died of natural causes, until Sylvestre's testimony persuaded the court that they had in fact been poisoned; and in all cases the presumed murderers had protested their innocence to the end. As he learns more and more about Sylvestre's loveless marriage and his betrayal of the one woman he had truly loved, Wilt begins to speculate that perhaps Sylvestre has been falsifying evidence, out of a demonic malice toward anyone still capable of experiencing genuine desire. Wilt arrives at this hypothesis somewhere around midnight, at the end of

Part I of the book, the "Monday Night" section; and he will spend the rest of the book—the "Tuesday Morning" section, which runs from around midnight to about 7 A.M.—in search of evidence that might support this hypothesis.

Nothing explicitly monstrous or fantastic happens in the course of the twelve or so hours that Bernie and Wilt spend together. Nevertheless, the narrative has a distinctly surreal feel to it, principally because of M. Sylvestre, who remains an enigma. Bernie and Wilt never find him, and so we never meet him either. We get story upon story *about* him, but how are we to verify the truth of these stories? Even at the turning point of the novel, as Wilt begins to elaborate his hypothesis about Sylvestre-as-jealous-murderer in an extended monologue, Sylvestre's butler voices, in counterpoint to Wilt, an alternative vision of the toxicologist as a kind of Christ-figure, suffering in his own flesh the human agonies of the people he is condemning to punishment, all in the name of Truth. (But it is not entirely clear that the butler actually sees his employer in this way. The butler's "monologue" is entirely in indirect discourse, as Wilt "reads" the Sylvestre-as-Christ narrative from the butler's facial expressions, but it seems quite possible that this narrative too is merely invented by Wilt.) Which narrative is "right," Wilt's or the butler's? How can we decide? In the last chapter of the novel, on his way to Lyons to confront Sylvestre himself, Wilt picks up a newspaper and reads a headline, "Eminent Toxicologist May Be Proven Criminally Insane." Wilt has, it seems, lost his big scoop once again. Relatives of some of the men that Sylvestre sent to prison or to death have been, we learn, pushing for a reopening of these cases, and they have just persuaded the courts to do so. So Wilt's hypothesis, it appears, is "right." But note the conditional verb in the headline. The press, it seems, has turned against Sylvestre, but by this point in the novel we have had abundant reasons to feel a certain distrust of the press. And as the novel breaks off in this indeterminate way, the point becomes, not the long sought Truth about M. Sylvestre, but rather the way the other characters weave their own fantasies around him: the ways they invent and reinvent him as the Figure of Desire, just as the questers in the Surrealist narratives discussed above all invent their own such figures, named Nadja, or Louise Lame, or Cynthia, or Georgette.

Boyle interweaves into the story of Bernie and Wilt accounts of several other questers, all also driven to pursue an imagined Figure of Desire. Early on, in chapter 5, she gives us, in what amounts to an interpolated short story, an account of one of the cases that Sylvestre has presumably "solved," the story of André Roux, of the woman he loved, and of the mother he supposedly murdered so he could marry the woman he loved. André is a rich, spoiled young man. After a dissolute youth, he has fallen desperately in love with a woman who rides horses bareback in the circus:

> Night after night there was the same physical stab at the heart, the exquisitely trapped moment of delirious fear at the sight of her waiting to spring from the

sawdust to the horse's back, the same tremor for the split fraction of a second right or wrong; or at the skip of her criss-crossing legs in pink or blue cutting fast over the ring in a desperate and pathetic imitation of confidence and grace. . . .[34]

This love intoxicates and transforms André, fills him with "a core of impersonal and endless wonder,"[35] but the circus rider refuses to marry him, because he has no money of his own, and she is fearful of being poor. Does André murder his own mother to get the money that will allow him to live comfortably with the bareback rider? The court thinks so and sends him to the guillotine. We, in the end, have our doubts. But in either case, the point for Boyle lies, not in André's innocence or guilt, but in the poignancy and tenderness of his love itself.

At other points in the novel too, we are invited to pause over the absences, longings, hungers that motivate Boyle's secondary characters. For two chapters (180–206), we move inside the consciousness of a child, the son of a man whom Sylvestre has sent to prison, M. Coutet. The son, we learn, craves his mother's presence, the taste and smell of her, in a way that nothing can appease. As a result, he is fiercely jealous of all male interlopers. A classic Oedipus complex, in short—but the Freudian term here becomes, in fact, simply another name for desire itself. As for Madame Coutet, we learn something of her hungers too, which have led her to invite into her home first a lesbian lover who dresses up in M. Coutet's old army uniform and then a succession of men whom she picks up in the streets: all, suggests Wilt, are substitutes for M. Coutet, "because having lost him at the outset you've had to go on making pictures of somebody, anybody who might be like him only you couldn't do it, . . . because the model's stand happens to be empty, the sitter, whether you like it or not, just doesn't happen to be sitting for his portrait any more."[36] Thus Madame Coutet too, at least in Wilt's imagination, is engaged in an endless process of inventing and reinventing the Figure of Desire.

I offer one final example of the way the characters in this novel are molded by desire and remold the world accordingly. Bernie and Wilt spend two chapters in a bistro near Sylvestre's country house. There, Bernie becomes infatuated with the proprietress—but she herself, we learn, has thoughts only of her son, a bicycle racer participating at that moment in the Tour de France, as a member of the Monacan team. As the woman speaks of her son, her own ardor transforms him into a mythical figure:

So that in the end the Tour de France was no longer composed of a knot of men in striped sweat-shirts pedaling, or a string of men along a road-side pumping with bare sinewy legs, the mud-stained shorts they wore clasping hairy and sweat-drenched and rain-drenched thighs. . . . [A]s she talked of them they became a legion of the young and the exalted, as vulnerable as poets, recruits

to an intrepid company that strove with only honor, or at the most achievement the reward as well as the goal. . . . [F]or she talked of them not as one
would talk of bicycle-racers or even as athletes but as if they were part-explorers
seeking another strata of atmosphere or sea, part-knights defending an even
purer conception of the Grail.[37]

The mother's desire transforms the bicycle racers into semi-mythical beings.
But, Boyle implies, the desire for victory also transforms the racers themselves: "I know guys who'd rather have the Maillot Jaune"—the prize
awarded the winner of the Tour de France—"than the Nobel Prize," says Wilt
just before the lyric passage quoted above.[38] Significantly, the bicycle racers
return at the very end of the novel. Waiting at the station for a train to Lyons
where he hopes to talk to Sylvestre, Wilt meets instead the Monacan bicycle
team, which has resigned in protest from the Tour de France. As the bicyclists
speak to the waiting reporters, the ugliness and violence and treachery of the
media-manipulated sporting world becomes clear. Yet the men are still in
some fashion heroic, and thus this final chapter sustains the peculiar double
vision created by the mother's aria to her son. The vision of desire, Boyle tells
us, cannot obliterate the inescapable physical and social circumstances of our
existence in this world; in this respect she remains a realist. But neither can
these physical realities destroy the power of desire to transform the world,
and in this affirmation of the powers of desire Boyle reveals her continuing
affinities with the project pursued by the Surrealist friends of her Paris years.

III

Monday Night has, however, affinities not only with French Surrealist narrative but also with several distinctively American fictional modes, starting
with the detective story. As Sandra Spanier notes, "The plot of Boyle's novel,
stripped bare, is a detective story."[39] Notoriously, Poe invented the modern
detective story, and he also haunts the pages of *Monday Night*. In the first part
of the novel, Bernie and Wilt are in search of a supersleuth, a modern version
of Poe's Dupin: if Dupin solves complex crimes through the sheer power of
ratiocination, Sylvestre does so scientifically, dissecting body tissues in his laboratory. But then, midway through the novel, the scientist begins to meta-
morphose into a madman (also a distinctly Poe-esque transformation—and
indeed the whole atmosphere of the book, especially the visit to Sylvestre's
country house, is pervasively Gothic), and the supersleuth becomes (or *may*
become) a monstrous criminal. With this transformation of Sylvestre, Wilt
assumes the role of the detective. From the beginning, Wilt's general seediness gives him a distinct resemblance to the private eyes of 1930s tough guy
fiction:

> He might have been fashioned of almost any other substance except flesh, a great scoop of what might have been wax or even lard slapped into human shape and crammed, while still malleable, into a suit of clothes somebody else had already worn and stained. If he had been conceived in logic, veined with blood, he must have remembered sometime to wash, to send a shirt to the laundry or else buy a new one, to acknowledge the lineaments of cataclysm once come face to face with in a glass.[40]

So Boyle describes her hero in the opening chapter. Wilt also has a mutilated ear, which he hides beneath a hat worn indoors and out, in the manner of a '30s detective. And the question of when the next drink will come and where it will come from determines much of Wilt's behavior. In all these respects, Wilt could have, physically, stepped out of any one of a number of "tough guy" novels of the 1930s, by Hemingway or Faulkner or Cain or Hammett.

As the novel proceeds, furthermore, Wilt also *sounds* more and more like a detective: " 'I want to begin at the beginning, if it is not too painful for you, Madame Coutet,' he said, his eyes on her face, his voice exactly imitating the sound of that professional and purely impersonal urgency (the exigencies of duty, the taste even of regret), which would deceive her into telling him everything in the end."[41] In fact, of course, Wilt is not a detective. But he is a reporter, and in the mythology of the '30s the investigative reporter is at least a first cousin of the private eye: think of the tough guy reporters of *Front Page*. And as Wilt himself notes, the archetypal tough guy writer, Hemingway, came out of the newspaper world.[42] As we approach the end of the novel, Wilt increasingly begins to act as a reporter. Thus when he accidentally meets the Monacan bicycle team in the last chapter, he immediately slips into a professional newspaperman role and begins trying to worm out of these men the "real" story of why they pulled out of the Tour de France. So too, earlier, he has attempted to speak to Madame Coutet's emotions, hoping to persuade her to help in his investigation. As we watch Wilt at work, we see some reasons why the private eye and/or the investigative reporter became so central to the culture of the 1930s. To get the "real story," Wilt, like any reporter or detective, must find the human reality in the situation, get close enough to the participants so that they will tell him all. He must truly empathize with the people involved by projecting himself into their lives. Yet he does so finally for ulterior motives: to solve the crime or to get the big scoop. Thus to protect himself, he must cultivate a tough, cynical demeanor. Nevertheless, the tough guy pose itself becomes proof of his sensitivity and vulnerability: only this pose, we are asked to believe, protects him from being overwhelmed by the human reality of the lives he is struggling to understand. If Wilt is a Christ-figure, as both Spanier and Elkins propose, so too are the other tough guy detectives and reporters of the 1930s writers; for these modern heroes offer themselves as willing to bear the burden of the mystery—and misery—of human weakness and guilt, and thereby they suffer for us all.[43]

The literary filiations of the tough guy strains in *Monday Night* are harder to trace than the Surrealist affinities described above. I know of no evidence that Boyle was reading Cain or Hammett in the 1930s—although she read widely and constantly, so some direct knowledge of their work seems quite possible. However, Boyle was a close friend of Robert McAlmon, whose literary reputation she sought to foster throughout her life; and both in his life and in his writing, McAlmon cultivated tough guy poses. McAlmon was also homosexual, so Boyle's friendship with him may have given her an insight into the homoeroticism implicit in the tough guy tradition within American culture. In Paris Boyle also moved in the same circles as Hemingway, and she certainly knew his writing well, although she disliked him as a person and expressed strong reservations about the macho posturing of his writing.[44] On the other hand, Boyle repeatedly voiced her enthusiasm for the writing of William Faulkner—indeed, McAlmon chastised her for allowing herself to become an imitator of Faulkner.[45] *Monday Night* in particular has a strong Faulknerian flavor, as Boyle herself acknowledged: in a 1953 letter, she wrote, "I believe Faulkner has influenced my style in several things I've written, particularly in 'Monday Night.' "[46] Furthermore, as Spanier reports, "In the same year that she published *Monday Night*, [Boyle] reviewed Faulkner's *The Unvanquished*, calling him 'the most absorbing writer of our time' and herself 'one who loves Faulkner's work and has followed it closely and impatiently.' "[47] These comments suggest that Boyle very probably read *Absalom, Absalom!,* published a year before *The Unvanquished* and *Monday Night*, and possessing strong affinities with the latter. For like Boyle's novel, Faulkner's narrates an imaginative quest by two men to discover the truth about a mysterious and inaccessible (in this case because he is dead) figure, the half-mythical plantation owner Henry Sutpen; and as the story develops we learn that Sutpen's life, like Monsieur Sylvestre's, may revolve around a secret crime.[48] Significantly, Faulkner was in the 1930s often associated with the tough guy school in American writing, primarily on the strength of *Sanctuary,* a book that does indeed have some striking similarities to James M. Cain's early novels. We also know that Boyle read *Sanctuary;* and although she expressed a fierce revulsion against the book,[49] it clearly had a strong impact on her.

Its "tough guy" overtones locate *Monday Night* firmly within a specifically American literary tradition, and certain other characteristics of the book also serve to place it within such a tradition. Like *The Sun Also Rises* and *Tender Is the Night,* most of Boyle's novels play variations on the Jamesian theme of the American in Europe, and *Monday Night* conforms to this pattern. Bernie is the innocent abroad, a lineal descendent of Daisy Miller and Isabel Archer. He brings to Europe a purity of heart, but not much else. Wilt is a more complex figure, but he too is in his way an innocent, and he embodies a distinctively American generosity and enthusiasm for new possibilities. As Boyle herself suggests, Bernie and Wilt also seem to belong *together,* in a pairing that also seems uniquely American: "[Wilt] led Bernie down the sidestreet, the hopelessness of the one drawn meanderingly in the wake of the other's purpose and resolve. Mutt and Jeff, Laurel and Hardy, names given to those qualities as familiar as the dollar and cent mark."[50] Or, we might add, Leatherstocking and Chingachgook, Huck and Jim, the Lone Ranger and Tonto, Dean Martin and Jerry Lewis. The straight man and the clown. Two *men*, drawn together in the face of an implacably wild continent, or in the face of a civilization that threatens to tame the boyish will—or, perhaps, in the face of a generic Woman who, because she seems both civilized and wild, threatens to engulf the lonely male ego. At one level, then, *Monday Night* is about male bonding: and this theme, so exhaustively explored by Leslie Fiedler,[51] in itself serves to define Boyle's novel as quintessentially American. As Fiedler might also note, and as Boyle makes clear, Bernie and Wilt are drawn together precisely because both are terrified of women and are, therefore, hopelessly incompetent in dealing with them. Bernie has left behind a "nice" American fiancée. In Paris he is entranced by a woman old enough to be his mother—and he is drawn to her precisely *because* he wants a mother. Then he ignores the advances of a woman who *is* interested in him, the maid at Sylvestre's. And then he buys the services of the first prostitute he meets— a scene over which Boyle discreetly draws a veil of silence. In short, every move Bernie makes, vis-à-vis women, is wrong.

As for Wilt, when we first meet him his alcoholic and other obsessions seem to have carried him beyond sexuality: "The girl sat watching him," Boyle tells us on the sixth page of the novel, "coldly, immunely, the way a man is looked at who is now exempt forever from any feminine interest."[52] While Wilt sees himself as having passed beyond sexuality, however, he retains a capacity to invent Figures of Desire, although unfortunately he is interested only in fantasy women, impossibly idealized literary archetypes. "The women he spoke or dreamed of now" are all

> the dream-figures of his own or other men's lives: the Thérèse, the Eugénie, the Elise of Heine's passion, or the Friderike, the Charlotte, the Maximiliane, the Lili as sublime, as warm and living as when they lay in Goethe's arms. . . . In his blood, in his senses, he could feel them ahead, perhaps wandering with their arms locked in each other's under the boughs of the invisible trees, the phantasmagoric shadowy shapes of drifting women whose passion and whose scent mounted like drink to the far, unignited asylum of his mind.[53]

Locked into a fantasy of desire, Wilt has, it seems, lost the ability to experience real desire. Is Boyle suggesting that there is something typically American about this preference for the myth over the substance? Perhaps, for many of the Europeans in the novel—André and his circus-rider, the Coutets— seem capable of genuine passion.

As Monday night gives way to Tuesday morning, however, Wilt does at last begin to recognize the flesh and blood reality of a living woman, Madame Coutet. Fearful lest she escape from him before he can convince her of his theory concerning Sylvestre, Wilt asks for her glove as security, and she replies, "Very well, take it then, take it off":

> He ran his fingers in under the glove's cuff and with a shock came to her naked wrist and now that he touched this flesh and felt the heart's shy quivering pulsing in this skin, he saw exposed in all its desperate poverty the endlessly enacted farce of dream substituted for nothing more tangible than dream, whore succeeded by nothing but whore performing in the allegory of desire. . . .[54]

Here, for one dazzling moment, Wilt touches the true Body of Desire, not merely the invented Figure of Desire. And Boyle strongly implies that the sexual currents flowing from Wilt toward Madame Coutet at this moment are reciprocated: to her, this man, however bumbling and verbose he may be, is by no means beyond sexuality.

But Wilt has already dedicated himself wholly to the service, not of his own desire for Madame Coutet, but of the myth he has created about her presumed desire for her imprisoned husband. As Marilyn Elkins points out, "When Madame Coutet removes her glove, he is shocked by his sudden vision of her hand; he is still unable to accept her as flesh and blood instead of as a character of his imagination."[55] Two pages after the brief erotic exchange over (and inside) the glove, Wilt is saying to Madame Coutet, "If I thought you wanted him back, if I thought for two minutes that you wanted him, if I thought you wanted that man home in bed with you at night instead of eating his guts out in jail—"[56] Wilt's inability to resolve this sentence grammatically suggests a deeper inability in him to live in the moment. And as Madame Coutet recognizes his preference for the splendors of his imagination over the too real skin beneath his fingers, she laughs:

> He heard her begin to laugh, the clear, soft, not hysterical but utterly senseless sound of laughing a woman makes shamelessly and artlessly before the solemn and vulgar devices of a circus clown, or at the obvious and unvarying point of a travelling-salesman's story; laughing and laughing in silvery or golden or crystal notes, beautiful as a bird's or a coloratura's aria, and as discordant and disastrous as breaking glass.[57]

This laughter both ends the scene and dissolves any lingering possibility that Wilt might shed the clown persona and become instead a lover. Thus he remains trapped—sadly, it would seem, forever—in the endless circulation of the fantasy of desire, the endless flow of the language of desire, to which he has sacrificed the possibility of erotic contact with another human being.

IV

The conflation of continental avant-garde literary modes with American popular culture that I have here described is not unique to *Monday Night*. The
Surrealists themselves were interested in the new mass-media cultural forms
issuing out of the United States: in 1930, for example, Philippe Soupault
published an essay titled *The American Influence in France,* focusing primarily
on the impact of American movies on the literary culture of Europe.[58]
Soupault himself was particularly interested in the American detective story,
and in the late 1920s he published a short story titled *Le mort de Nick Carter,* a
brilliant little parody that, for two chapters, recreates the mood of a Nick
Carter mystery story, and then abruptly kills off the famous American detective and his two faithful sidekicks Chick and Patsy, thus instantly decon-
structing the whole genre—for the one possibility that the genre rigidly
excludes is the murder of the detective himself.[59] The Surrealists were drawn
to American popular culture in part because the latter already seemed in
some ways "surreal": witness the newspaper comic strip and then its ani-
mated form in the Walt Disney cartoon. Surrealism in turn may have had
some influence on American writers like Faulkner, although the affinities
between some of his novels and the works of the Surrealists probably attests
more to a common devotion to the Gothic mode than to a direct influence on
the part of the French writers. (But it also is possible that Faulkner too was
reading *transition* in the late 1920s.) At least a few of Boyle's own contemporaries in Paris also saw some potential overlap between the Surrealist vision
and American popular culture. In the mid-1920s, Robert McAlmon's Contact Press published a novel by Robert M. Coates titled *The Eater of Darkness,*
a deliberate (if distinctly contrived) interweaving of Surrealist imaginative
flights with the American detective story.[60] I know of no evidence that Boyle
and Coates were friends, but they certainly had many mutual friends, and
both he and his novel were very much "on the scene" during her Paris years.

But while the conflation of these modes may not have been original with
Boyle, the effect of this conflation in *Monday Night* is certainly unique. What
happens within the intertextual space that Boyle opens up between the
French Surrealist quest narrative and the American tough guy novel? First,
the tough guy is eroticized. The tough guys of Hemingway, Faulkner, and
Hammett occupy a bleak landscape that lies, if not beyond sexuality, at least
beyond eros. (Thus my insistence on including Popeye in this group is by no
means gratuitous.) The tough guy has seen too much: no longer can he give
himself wholly to desire. Or, perhaps more precisely, the pleasure of feeling
someone's skin split open beneath one's knuckles has become more compelling than any less violent pleasures a woman might offer. And when the
tough guy does give way to a sexual impulse, as in some of Cain's and Hammett's novels, it is with the virtual certainty that the object of desire will
prove unworthy—every woman, in this literary milieu, is suspect. But Boyle

uncovers the longing hidden behind the tough guy's tight-lipped smile. She also deftly and expertly dissects the ways in which the tough guy pose masks a fear of women. The tough guy hopes to find in male friendship a substitute for an erotic relationship with a woman, but at this point the tough guy pose itself becomes the problem. For how can a tough guy admit his need to another man? Thus by overlaying onto the tough guy story the Surrealist narrative of desire, Boyle unmasks the American tough guy himself.

At the same time, Boyle also unmasks the unacknowledged phallocentrism of the Surrealist quest narrative itself. In the examples of such narratives described earlier in this essay, the object of the quest, the Figure of Desire, is always female; and in all but one case, the quester is male. By substituting an enigmatic male figure as the object of the quest, Boyle brings to the surface the latent gender implications of the Surrealist quest narrative. For this dislocation reminds us that, while the woman may take on great power as the embodiment of the Figure of Desire, she nevertheless remains *object,* the invention of the male imagination. The "real" woman is always already absent—and can represent the Figure of Desire only *because* she is absent. What of the woman who refuses to be absent? Boyle doesn't ask this question explicitly—except perhaps in Madame Coutet's laughter, which calls everything into doubt. But the male absence at the heart of this novel ironically underscores for us the female absence at the heart of the Surrealist quest romance—and of all other genres in which male desire projects itself onto an imagined Other.

In thus reinventing both the Surrealist quest narrative and the private-eye mystery, Boyle also deconstructs the very concept of Truth itself: whether the scientific truth that Monsieur Sylvestre purportedly serves; or the "facts" that Wilt, the private eye/reporter/novelist, wants to uncover; or the sentimental "truths" that preoccupy Bernie. At the center of this novel stands an Absence: Monsieur Sylvestre, who may or may not be one of the great intellects, one of the great lovers, or one of the great criminals of history—or who may not even exist, since he never becomes present within the text, except as a fantasized projection of the fears and hopes of the other characters. In its fascination with this Absence at the Center, *Monday Night* echoes both Kafka's *The Castle,* the archetypal modernist narrative of failed quest, and, as we have already seen, Faulkner's *Absalom, Absalom!* The figure of Wilt may also remind some readers of Djuna Barnes' Doctor Matthew O'Conner, who frantically tries to fill the void with the sound of his own voice. And indeed, a preoccupation with the Void is characteristic of much Modernist writing of the period between the wars. In its concern with the absence at the center, *Monday Night* also anticipates some of the preoccupations of postmodernist theory, especially in its suggestion that the attempts of the male characters to fill this absence with the projections of their own desires have destructive consequences both for these men and for the women on whom they project their longings. What would happen if these men simply accepted that Absence, and gave up the attempt to fill it with Presence? This is a question that some of Boyle's women characters—especially Madame Coutet, whose laughter announces the final absurdity of Wilt's quest—seem to want to ask. And by the time we get to the end of this novel, it begins to seem that Boyle herself wants to ask this same question.

The sign that points toward Absence, as Derrida has taught us, becomes the Trace, and *Monday Night* also displays a pervasive concern with the Trace. In the penultimate chapter, as Wilt and Bernie are riding in a cab toward the train station, Wilt tells a long story about "a friend once who had to have his leg cut off, . . . and it seems you can have your choice when you have an amputation: either you can take it away with you when you leave the hospital or else you can donate it."[61] The friend chooses to take the leg with him, "preserved in alcohol,"[62] as a tangible signifier of what he has lost. Then Wilt segues into a story within a story. Many years before he lost the leg—in, we eventually learn, a street-car accident in Cincinnati[63]—the friend had worked as a cook on an expedition into the Congo, and "it seems they had an American horse on board with them."[64] An African chief sees the horse and wants it, and the expedition leader gives it to him. Several years later, Wilt's friend is again traveling by boat up the Congo River, and one day

> he saw an animal stick its head out of the foliage or underbrush and bare a set of teeth like tombstones at him. . . . There was this thing barring his way, with long wild black hair all over its neck, coarse as a lion's mane and ears like an ass's, and its snout held up with the teeth bared in it. Then he saw it was staring at him with soulful long-lashed eyes, like his mother's eyes looking broodingly from paradise at him.[65]

A few moments later, the friend sees the same African chief coming along the path and asks him what this strange animal could have been. The chief explains that the

> American horse . . . used to love grazing along the side of the river at night, and one night last Fourth of July one of the alligators slumbering in the mud awoke and yawned and when he closed his jaws again they closed on the grasses and on that horse's nose, and the American horse aroused the jungle with his screaming, and when we got him free he had lost a portion of his face.[66]

We pass from the man's missing leg to the horse's missing nose by pure metonymic association: the missing leg has no relevance to the story of the horse in the Congo, except that missing body parts play a role in both. Both incidents, however, point us toward the gap, the wound: a part of the living tissue, torn out. Here is the Void, inscribed upon the body itself.

All human beings, Wilt's fable implies, have suffered a wound. We have all lost a part of ourselves. And all quests—*male* quests at least—are attempts to recover that plenitude lost. Wilt himself acknowledges as much at the end of his fable, when, turning to Bernie, he attempts to sum up the meaning of their night together: "we have sought all night together the flesh of our libido, you the suckler seeking the breast, I the phantasy maker seeking through fabrication the substance of his unaltered childhood dream."[67] But the breast, the fantasy, the leg, the horse's nose—these are in fact gone forever, leaving us only the trace. Wilt's fable self-consciously echoes Conrad's *Heart of Darkness:* indeed, at one point Wilt suggests that his friend had at one point "walked ashore at Boma . . . with Conrad," and that "he'd gone upriver time and again . . . into the heart of the elephant country."[68] And just as Kurtz finally learns that he cannot fill the Darkness with the projections of his own willful fantasies, so Wilt and Bernie must finally stand, in the dismal morning light of the train station, before the void opened up by the failure of their dreams. Yet the night does leave Wilt a trace, to remind him of how desire shapes the lives of men: and, interestingly, the last sentences of Boyle's novel invoke the same symbol of longing that Desnos creates at the beginning of *La liberté ou l'amour,* a woman's glove, stripped from her hand, left to tantalize those who will never possess the figure of desire:

> [Wilt] dropped one hand into his pocket, feeling for a cigarette, but there were none; only the black kid glove was there. Before he went back to the buvette he took it out and sat looking at it for a minute, the crumpled fingers inside-out still, the wrinkles still marked at the wrist where the bracelets had been.[69]

Desnos's novel, as we have seen, begins with a rain of gloves falling from the sky. Boyle's novel, in contrast, ends with one glove, redolent with the odors of a woman's skin. But in both cases the glove becomes the tangible trace of a lost plenitude, paradise discovered—and when else can we discover it?—at the very moment of its loss.

The quest for the Figure of Desire, I have here suggested, links Boyle to the Surrealists and, in a very different way, to the traditions of American culture. The (male) French writers that she read in the 1920s and 1930s celebrated desire, but desire for them is always gendered male: the only exception is the homosexual Crevel, who was, therefore, clearly Boyle's favorite among the Surrealists. The (male) American writers of the time denied or deflected desire: the virgin or the whore—these were, still, the only kinds of women that the American male writers of the time could imagine, however they might try to move beyond this dichotomy. America, the Parisian expatriates liked to say, was a Puritan country, and Boyle clearly agreed: thus her decision to live in Europe, where an American woman could begin to explore her own sexuality. Yet Boyle also knew from personal experience—see, in particular, *Plagued by the Nightingale*—that French society too, in its own way, can deny and distort Eros. In developing the male characters at the center of *Monday Night,* Boyle is primarily interested in the way the cultural circumstances of

America and Europe have structured the modes of male desire—a subject of obvious interest to a heterosexual woman like Boyle. On both sides of the Atlantic, Boyle suggests, male desire is distorted, directed either toward lost mothers (that is, usually, the American way, although the story of Madame Coutet's son suggests that Europeans are also subject to this impulse) or toward unattainable, mythical dream-women (that is the usual European way, although Wilt shows that American men can dream such dreams too). An intertextual reading of *Monday Night* allows us to recognize both Boyle's acerbic view of male desire and her awareness that the issue is not simply personal but cultural: in both France and America certain assumptions have encoded themselves in literary forms and in popular myths, and in both countries these assumptions are fundamentally patriarchal. Thus while *Monday Night*—unlike most of the often autobiographical novels that Boyle had written in the previous ten years—does not offer us a strong female protagonist, gender politics is nevertheless at the center of this book. Yet at the same time as the book critiques the distorted gender relations of patriarchy, it also reaches out generously to men, welcoming and celebrating male desire even as it asks men to look again at how the myths that men generate affect the women around them. Wilt is, obviously, a crippled man: his wounded ear suggests a transposition upward of a wound in his sexuality itself. But Boyle's portrait of him, while clear-eyed and ironic, is also tender and loving: whatever he may think of himself, she does not see him as having passed beyond sexuality. This mix of feminism and sexual warmth toward men makes Boyle's a distinctive voice among the writers of her generation; and if I may speak, finally, as a specifically male reader, this voice seems to me both attractive and salutary.

Notes

1. Kay Boyle, *Monday Night* (Mamaroneck, N.Y.: Paul P. Appel, 1977). All quotations from and citations to the novel are to this edition. *Monday Night* was originally published in 1938.

2. Harold Loeb, ed., *The Broom Anthology* (Boston: Milford House, n.d.).

3. Robert McAlmon, *Being Geniuses Together 1920–1930*, revised with supplementary chapters and an afterword by Kay Boyle (San Francisco: North Point, 1984), 213.

4. *In Transition: A Paris Anthology* (London: Secker & Warburg, 1990), 19.

5. Kay Boyle, *Wedding Day and Other Stories* (New York: Jonathan Cape and Harrison Smith, 1930).

6. For a full description of the Surrealist project, see Jacqueline Chénieux-Gendron, *Surrealism*, trans. Vivian Folkenflik (New York: Columbia University Press, 1990).

7. Boyle and McAlmon, *Being Geniuses Together*, 217–19.

8. Gerard de Nerval, *Selected Writings*, trans. Geoffrey Wagner (Ann Arbor, Mich.: Ann Arbor Paperbacks, 1970), 111–78.

9. André Breton, *Nadja*, trans. Richard Howard (New York: Grove, 1960).

10. Breton, *Nadja*, 50.

11. Breton, *Nadja*, 55–56.

12. Breton, *Nadja*, 66.

13. Breton, *Nadja*, 71.

14. Breton, *Nadja*, 144.

15. Boyle and McAlmon, *Being Geniuses Together*, 267.

16. Robert Desnos, *Liberty or Love!* trans. Terry Hale (London: Atlas, 1993), 39.

17. Desnos, *Liberty*, 40.

18. Desnos, *Liberty*, 41.

19. Desnos, *Liberty*, 43.

20. Desnos, *Liberty*, 43.

21. The principal quester in Desnos's novel is the Corsair Sanglot, who at times seems to forget entirely about Louise Lame; in this respect the novel is by no means a pure example of the quest narrative. But Louise Lame dies and is reborn more than once in the course of the novel, and each time she reappears Desnos suggests that the Corsair and Louise are engaged in an eternal quest for one another; at these moments the novel veers back toward the quest romance pattern.

22. Rene Crevel, *Babylon: A Novel*, trans. Kay Boyle (San Francisco: North Point Press, 1985). Boyle apparently completed this translation in the early 1930s.

23. Kay Boyle, *Plagued by the Nightingale* (Carbondale: Southern Illinois University Press, 1966). Originally published in 1931.

24. Crevel, *Babylon*, 16–17.

25. Philippe Soupault, *Last Nights of Paris*, trans. William Carlos Williams (New York: Full Court Press, 1982).

26. Soupault, *Last Nights*, 73.

27. Soupault, *Last Nights*, 41.

28. Soupault, *Last Nights*, 166.

29. Boyle, *Monday Night*, 52–53.

30. McAlmon, *Being Geniuses Together*, 291.

31. McAlmon, *Being Geniuses Together*, 290.

32. McAlmon, *Being Geniuses Together*, 291.

33. Sandra Whipple Spanier, *Kay Boyle: Artist and Activist* (Carbondale: Southern Illinois University Press, 1986), 128.

34. Boyle, *Monday Night*, 60.

35. Boyle, *Monday Night*, 63.

36. Boyle, *Monday Night*, 227–28.

37. Boyle, *Monday Night*, 85–86.

38. Boyle, *Monday Night*, 85.

39. Spanier, *Kay Boyle*, 126.

40. Boyle, *Monday Night*, 16.

41. Boyle, *Monday Night*, 214.

42. Boyle, *Monday Night*, 34.

43. Spanier, *Kay Boyle*, 129–30; Marilyn Elkins, *Metamorphosizing the Novel: Kay Boyle's Narrative Innovations* (New York: Peter Lang, 1993), 149–50. I should add, however, that I do not share the belief of Elkins (148–50, 155–56) and Spanier (see esp. 129–31) that Boyle wants us to see Wilt as a heroic figure, a prototype of the questing artist, and/or as a saint whose devotion to the truth and to human possibility redeems a corrupt world. He wants to be a great writer, but there is no evidence that he can or will achieve this goal, and Boyle's portrait of him seems to me deeply ironic.

44. Spanier, *Kay Boyle*, 24–25.

45. McAlmon, *Being Geniuses Together*, 253.

46. Letter to Richard Carpenter, quoted in Spanier, *Kay Boyle*, 132.

47. Spanier, *Kay Boyle*, 132.

48. William Faulkner, *Absalom, Absalom!* (New York: Modern Library, 1951). See also Elkins, *Metamorphosizing the Novel*, 150: "Perhaps Boyle was trying to adopt what she saw as Faulkner's method in her presentation of Bernie's truth as constructed from conversations and the imagination; the similarities to *Absalom, Absalom!* seem apparent."

49. Spanier, *Kay Boyle*, 132.

50. Boyle, *Monday Night*, 44–45.

51. Leslie A. Fiedler, *Love and Death in the American Novel* (Cleveland: Meridian Books, 1962).

52. Boyle, *Monday Night*, 8.

53. Boyle, *Monday Night*, 93–94.

54. Boyle, *Monday Night*, 235.

55. Elkins, *Metamorphosizing the Novel*, 154–55.

56. Boyle, *Monday Night*, 239.

57. Boyle, *Monday Night*, 246.

58. Philippe Soupault, *The American Influence in France*, trans. Babette and Glenn Hughes (Seattle: University of Washington Chapbooks, 1930).

59. Philippe Soupault, *Mort de Nick Carter* (Paris: Lachenal et Ritter, 1983). Originally published in 1926.

60. Robert M. Coates, *The Eater of Darkness* (New York: Capricorn, 1959).

61. Boyle, *Monday Night*, 247.

62. Boyle, *Monday Night*, 249.

63. Boyle, *Monday Night*, 254.

64. Boyle, *Monday Night*, 249.

65. Boyle, *Monday Night*, 255.

66. Boyle, *Monday Night*, 257.

67. Boyle, *Monday Night*, 257.

68. Boyle, *Monday Night*, 248.

69. Boyle, *Monday Night*, 274.

Life-Giving: Kay Boyle's Innovations in Autobiography in *Being Geniuses Together*

CHRISTINE H. HAIT

The autobiographical nature of much of Kay Boyle's fiction, especially her early fiction, is well known. Boyle, however, came to repudiate the autobiographical approach to fiction and to take pride in her work that demonstrated her willingness to explore a point of view other than her own. She claimed as a favorite her novel *Monday Night,* which is based on her observations of the life of her friend Harold Stearns in Paris, because she took in it a male point of view. She told one interviewer, "I always feel very happy when I can get away from that American girl, that American woman. . . . I have tried to get away from that autobiographical figure."[1] It is no surprise, then, that Boyle approached writing an autobiography warily. It would be another friend of her Paris days, writer and publisher Robert McAlmon, who provided her with a means by which to escape to some extent, even in the autobiographical act, the American girl or woman. In a 1980 preface to *Plagued by the Nightingale* she said of the autobiographical heroines of her early novels, "It is all too evident that I present these quiet-spoken, romantic, and self-sacrificing young women as victims of circumstances or of less sensitive individuals than they, and I deplore the overweening justification of self this signifies."[2] Such self-justification is the very stuff of traditional autobiography. To avoid it, she needed to find a fresh approach to the form. She made a daring choice: turning to an existing autobiographical text, McAlmon's *Being Geniuses Together* (1938), a memoir of Paris in the twenties. She revised it and added her own chapters that recall her life in the twenties and, in particular, her relationship with McAlmon. Her writing took as its purpose not self-justification but the defense of another. Autobiographical writing became an occasion to revive a friend and to recover an important, yet undervalued, literary figure of the twenties.

Boyle's approach to autobiography is distinctive, and it results in a distinctive form, the dual autobiography. Yet it may appear that this form

This essay was written specifically for this volume and is published here for the first time by permission of the author.

thwarted her purpose. For in 1968, when the revised edition of *Being Geniuses Together* was published, few reviewers of the memoir judged in favor of Boyle's defense of McAlmon. Instead, they pitted the defendant and the defender against each other, in a contest of duelling autobiographers, with Boyle usually winning out as the more accomplished writer. Or they were reminded by Boyle's defense of the jokes made about McAlmon during the twenties and thirties and revived them in their reviews. Or they accused Boyle of opportunism, of using McAlmon's earlier memoir to further her own version of history.[3]

Boyle reports in *Being Geniuses Together* that McAlmon often chided her for her romantic views, which are revealed in her effort to reform autobiography. "A reluctant autobiographer,"[4] she overcame her reluctance to assume the "awkward" pronoun "I,"[5] believing that the first person might be used to advance the cause of a third-person "he," that the autobiographical act need not be self-serving. Yet the form resists her higher purposes. Although her aim is not to "save face," Boyle, writing autobiography, cannot help but present a portrait of herself that draws attention to itself. And readers, as the reviews show, are unaccustomed and resistant to reading autobiography in a way that would allow Boyle to achieve her aims. Many of them come to autobiography interested not in social justice primarily but in the compelling life story of a singular person. And when confronted with two authors, bedded together in this unusual way, they understandably find it difficult not to compare and contrast them, to place them in competition with each other, and to choose a loser and a winner. The tendencies of the form and its readers are not as easily elevated as the author's aims.

But the dual autobiography does achieve desirable results. A rich tension is created between its alternating voices. The voices compete for our attention and approval, yet they also complement each other. Boyle never suggests that her chapters are designed to enhance McAlmon's, but they achieve that purpose nonetheless. His chapters gain interest because Boyle's portray him as a mysterious and complex character. More interesting, Boyle's chapters are enhanced by the presence of McAlmon as a competing focal point within them. Although, again, not her stated aim, Boyle uses McAlmon to distance herself from her own excesses and from the excesses of her chosen form. He keeps her honest, and he keeps the form honest. His character allows Boyle to address her own susceptibility to illusions and to expose the illusions of self-redemption and self-recollection lurking behind the autobiographical act.

Although the dual autobiography is a distinctive approach to the form, Boyle's desire to avoid the trappings of traditional autobiography places her in the company of the twentieth century's most inventive autobiographers. In addition, the strategy that she selected to circumvent the self-justification of traditional autobiography is the same strategy employed by many other modern autobiographers, especially women: "the strategy of the Other." Lillian Hellman used this strategy in her autobiographical writings, Marcus Billotson and Sidonie Smith note, because it helped her "to avoid self-indulgence while committing to paper experiences that are uniquely hers and to sustain a fragile balance between the imperatives of self and the integrity of the 'other.' "[6] According to Julia Watson, who notes the frequency of the "shadowed presence" in modern women writers' autobiographies, "the tactic of writing in the shadow of an Other can be an act of liberation from the constraints of conventional accounts of female lives."[7] Perhaps most relevant to Boyle's particular employment of the strategy of the Other is Bella Brodzki and Celeste Schenck's comment on Gertrude Stein's challenge to the ideology of individualism in *The Autobiography of Alice B. Toklas:* "Being *between two covers* with somebody else ultimately replaces singularity with alterity in a way that is dramatically female, provides a mode of resisting reification and essentialism, and most important, allows for more radical experimentation in autobiographical form than recent critics . . . have been willing to attribute to women writers."[8] Writing the self through reflection on an Other, then, has been recognized as a particularly modern and feminist act, which not only challenges traditional notions of selfhood and conventional narratives of female experience but which also opens up the genre of autobiography to reinvention.

On the other hand, Boyle's reluctance to celebrate her autonomy and her personal and public successes can be viewed as further evidence of the debilitating effects of women's oppression under patriarchy. A woman autobiographer's use of the strategy of the Other may suggest her acceptance of society's notions of ideal feminine behavior. Writing the self through the Other allows her to appear self-effacing and sacrificing, traditionally feminine characteristics, thus neutralizing the potentially explosive power of a woman claiming significance for herself. Patricia Meyer Spacks refers to the "selves in hiding" in the autobiographical works written by women that she studied: "[T]o a striking degree they fail directly to emphasize their *own* importance, though writing in a genre which implies self-assertion and self-display. Although several find indirect means of declaring personal power and effectiveness, they do so, as it were, in disguise."[9] Carolyn Heilbrun deplores the lack, until recently, of honest autobiographies by accomplished women and blames it on their fear of losing their femininity. "Because [confronting power and control] has been deemed unwomanly, and because many women would prefer (or think they would prefer) a world without evident power and control, women have been deprived of the narratives, or the texts, plots, or examples, by which they might assume power over—take control of—their own lives."[10] Women autobiographers will challenge traditional notions of female selfhood, these points of view suggest, only when they refuse to hide behind masks or to disavow their own desires for power and autonomy.

How, then, do we interpret Boyle's decision to devote her remembrances of the twenties to the revival of a male friend and to center her recollections of the period, in which she also played a major role, around the significance of another? Does her desire to avoid self-justification reflect a modernist and feminist challenge to the ideology of individualism or a traditionally feminine tendency toward self-effacement? The key lies in the autobiography itself, in which she takes a position that precludes either/or answers and that privileges a both/and position, and in which the term *self-effacement* is complicated and tested. Although Boyle's approach to autobiography is seemingly self-effacing, the story she tells of her development in the twenties is the story of a woman gradually gaining control and power over her life. It is the story of a woman who learns the value of suffering and self-sacrifice, but who also acquires the authority and the critical skills that enable her to articulate what and who she stands for and against. It is not the story of a woman who stands in the background out of focus, or in the shadows. In fact, her features are more clearly defined because of the sharp relief McAlmon provides. And her love and appreciation for McAlmon are only part of her story; another significant part is her ability to love and appreciate much that McAlmon scorns, her ability to feel his influence yet not be effaced by him. She maintains in her autobiography what Suzanne Clark finds in the fiction: a "multiple sympathy."[11] She replaces the "paranoid logic of the subject" with the "logic of sympathy" and "works to rewrite the extreme imagination of reason which erases woman from the place of the subject or installs her as the singular Other of male discourse. Hers is instead a lyric refiguring of the story which produces more multiple possibilities."[12]

Thus, Boyle's relationship with McAlmon is placed within a constellation of relationships, composing a multidimensional figure. These relationships are so interwoven that in order for her to discuss one of them—her relationship with McAlmon—she must touch on them all. Her relationship with her mother, for example, who seems to have no connection to McAlmon on the surface, is central to the narrative Boyle tells.[13] In fact, Boyle's autobiography might easily be read as a daughter's story, so integral is the mother-daughter relationship to her narrative.[14] But again demonstrating the "multiple possibilities" toward which Boyle's narratives move, the autobiography is both the story of a daughter's attachment to her mother and the story of a daughter's necessary separation from her.

Her attachment to her mother was profound, for her mother, Boyle writes, gave her "definitions" and "offered the milestones to measure the distance of [her] understanding, and these milestones . . . never altered."[15] The "autograph" of her mother in this autobiography is the scar in her palm, "the ineffaceable signature of her bravery" (22), which she acquired as a child when she tried to save the hot glass chimney of a lamp from toppling to the floor. The scarred mother makes a lasting impression on her daughter: "She alone, with her modest but untroubled intuitions about books and painting, music and people, had been my education" (19).

Yet Boyle's discussion of her mother comes at the start of her story, which begins in 1920. In the decade that she recounts, she learned primarily from others. Although she built upon the education she received from her, her mother was not effaced, Boyle makes clear, by the daughter's accumulation of other knowledge, through reading and personal experience, much of which seems to counter the mother's "modest . . . intuitions."

Without stating explicitly that the education she received from her mother was inadequate, Boyle presents herself in the early twenties as full of illusions. At this time, she writes, she was terribly illiterate, disdaining the knowledge that books could provide. Having just arrived in New York, just married, and just gained employment at the literary journal *Broom,* which provided her the opportunity to meet the artists she idealized, she was deliriously happy. She refused to believe that her happiness was illusive, unreal because it had not yet been earned. During the decade that Boyle remembers in her memoirs, she learned the value of suffering. To earn her happiness, she, too, would be scarred. Like her mother, she would have to earn, on her own, the badge of her bravery.

References in the autobiography to two other "daughters" whom Boyle encountered during her time in Paris in the twenties subtly indicate Boyle's understanding of a woman's potential loss of identity when the daughterly role is played out to the exclusion of other roles. She remembers encountering Lucia Joyce, the daughter of James Joyce, and feeling as if she were looking in a mirror, so acutely did she identify with the daughter's struggle to find an identity for herself: "She was (as perhaps I too was then, and as perhaps all daughters are until they cease being merely daughters) precariously only half a person, and the other half she sought for in panic first in one direction and then in another, not knowing in whose mind or flesh or in what alien country it might lie" (353). Boyle suggests that the lack of an integrated self and the desire that such a lack provokes are the daughter's lot, until she is able to integrate her daughterhood into a larger sense of self. Part of what the reader of her autobiographical chapters discovers about Boyle in the twenties is that, despite her eloquently stated devotion to her mother, her development during this time period involved becoming something other than "merely" a daughter.

The failure to develop beyond the daughterly role and the loss of self that results are represented in the autobiography by the Princess of Sarawak, who contracted Boyle to ghostwrite her own memoirs. Boyle struggled to draw from the "strangely inarticulate" Princess "the bare facts of her life." But her "mind appeared to function in a state of shock," and "her valiant attempts to relive the memories of all she had been, or had not been, served no purpose except to stun her into silence" (289). Her memories were "dimmed and blurred, and the meaning of life itself somehow effaced, by the charm and grace and beauty of her mother," and as a result, her life "had actually never been hers" but her mother's (290). She recalled the events of her mother's life, "[b]ut the events (not to mention the emotions) of the Princess's own life had been reduced to names and dates, their significance lost, obliterated, in some year and by some occurrence that she could not at the moment recall" (290). Unable to give substance to her existence, she willingly allowed Boyle and Archie Craig, her cousin, to invent the details of her life, accepting the story that they gave her of herself. "Frantically, tragically, . . . she was asking anyone who came and went in the room, or came and went in her life, to give her a description, however inadequate, of her own reality" (290–91). The Princess was unable to write her autobiography herself because she was truly and, apparently, irrevocably effaced. Overshadowed by an Other, her mother, she was passive, aphonic, and completely unable to "collect" herself or to see meaning in her own experiences.

A poem by McAlmon that Boyle quotes at the beginning of her chapters of the autobiography speaks to the condition of the Princess of Sarawak. It introduces the themes of integration and recollection and demonstrates that, even before Boyle met him, McAlmon was associated with her desire to move beyond the daughterly role and to integrate and to collect the multiple elements of herself, to literally come into being. Before she met McAlmon, she read his poetry and committed to memory the following lines:

> Oh, let me gather myself together.
> Where are the pieces
> quivering and staring and muttering
> that are all to be a part of me? (12)

The poem expresses the desire, associated with both youth and autobiography, to collect and integrate the "quivering and staring and muttering" elements of the self into an active, insightful, articulate, and unified identity. The poem speaks of desire, but not of agency. These lines spoke her indecision, as well as McAlmon's, Boyle writes. The ability to make choices became very important to Boyle, and she has highlighted it elsewhere. In a preface to the 1981 Virago edition of *Plagued by the Nightingale,* an autobiographical novel that covers many of the same experiences recounted in *Being Geniuses Together,* she claims that "the meaning of the book [*Plagued by the Nightingale*] may perhaps be that there is always in life the necessity to choose" and that the book "is one of the many records of a young woman's troubled search for the old landmarks by which we choose the way that we must go."[16] The indecision and uncertainty of youth, Boyle asserts, must yield to the urgency of choices and commitments.

The question McAlmon asks in the poem initiated the search for identity that Boyle's chapters present. Boyle describes herself at the beginning of this search in terms that relate her to the Princess of Sarawak, who asked others to give her her reality. Boyle, when we first encounter her in the early twenties, feels "excluded from knowledge" that is possessed by others. "I believed that everyone—and writers in particular—had been given information of a nature quite unknown to me, which endowed them with their marvelous authority"

(12). Without such knowledge, she often felt absurd, and a skeptical look could make her question her very existence. The "dark and baleful" eyes of a secretary at the *New Masses* in New York, to whom she announced her desire to contribute to the magazine because she believed in its goals, seemed to say to her that she was absurd and that she could not believe in anything. Cowed, she walked out "less certain than ever who or what {she} was" (13).

Borrowing the words of writers, endowed with their "marvelous authority," Boyle began a search for her own authority. McAlmon's poem about collecting the pieces of himself expressed her indecision, and later, in Paris, lines from George Moore's novel *The Lake*, "There is a lake in every man's life and he must ungird his loins for the crossing," expressed her growing awareness that the search for direction and identity must conclude with action. Questing and questioning ("Where are the parts of me . . . ?") must not exclude taking a stand and choosing answers. The lines from George Moore's novel provided inspiration for her future efforts to take decisive steps toward a goal (108–109).

But when she first arrived in Paris and met McAlmon, she was still unable to say who or what she was, to give an autobiographical account of herself, so to speak. In her description of their first encounter, and in subsequent descriptions of other encounters, she emphasizes his eyes, which seemed to operate like lasars, penetrating the masks and presumptions of the people he encountered. "His eyes had scarcely left my face, and their icy blueness had not altered as he asked (as he must have asked everyone he met), using quite other words, exactly what and who I was, and I did not know what answers to give" (96). She walked away, unable to look into his eyes.

During the twenties, Boyle struggled to shape an answer to McAlmon's question. As Boyle tells it, during this time, she literally wrote and read herself into existence. Self-definition became increasingly important to her at the same time that she came to acknowledge its difficulty. It was inextricably tied for her to the written word, her own and others. The statements in *transition* about "the revolution of the word" were important because they "at least approached a definition of the nature of my own undefined revolt" (264). For her, letters to others were both the process by which self-definition was achieved and its product. "In the endless letters I wrote . . . I was doing no more than submitting a full and doubtless inaccurate account of who I thought I was, or was seeking to be" (239). And a moment of crisis is characterized by her failure to write letters: "That kind of definition had failed me" (355). She tried to draw conclusions from the facts of her life and to understand the meaning of her own experiences, even when the conclusions were arguable and the meaning shifting.

The horror of living life without recognition of its meaning and without access to one's own memories is represented in the autobiography in the character of the Princess of Sarawak. The Princess is the antithesis of all that McAlmon stands for in Boyle's autobiographical chapters. McAlmon asked the Other to represent itself; the Princess of Sarawak asked the Other to give her representation. In all he stood for, "[McAlmon] was saying that if a man and his situation are difficult to explain by tactile argument, then the definition by other means must be as solid as a statue, maybe bigger than life size, but anyway something you can acknowledge with your hand" (96). Give me a picture of your reality, McAlmon demanded of all he met. Give me a picture of my own reality, the Princess of Sarawak begged all who entered her life. Through her portrayals of McAlmon and the Princess, Boyle gives shape to the autobiographical urge and to the autobiographical failure, to her inspiration and to the model she works against.

In Boyle's chapters, and in his own, McAlmon emerges as a champion of unblinkered self-knowledge and tough realism, intent on exposing all grandiosity, mysticism, and sentimentality. "Maybe it's time you stopped putting things between yourself and reality," he told Boyle one night in a bar (320). Later, he said of her friends Harry and Caresse Crosby and of the people gathered at their home on New Year's Eve in 1928, "They're wraiths, all of them. They aren't people. God knows what they've done with their realities" (368). He mocked Boyle's projected collection of the greatest poetry of the day as a "crazy, senseless [undertaking]," and looking her "straight in the eye with his glacial blue stare," tore up the announcement for it (355). Her friend Eugene Jolas earned McAlmon's most bitter scorn because his journal *transition* privileged not tangible reality, but hallucinations and dreams. McAlmon, in contrast, privileged the present moment, announcing to Boyle at their first meeting, "As for me, I'll take my future now" (96).

From McAlmon, Boyle learned to value presence and solidity, those things "acknowledge[d] with [the] hand" (97). His role in her life, and his role in the autobiography, is that of the iconoclast and the skeptic. In the early twenties Kay Boyle attended literary gatherings in New York, "listening, listening, [her] critical faculties wholly numbed, believing that not one indispensable word could be spoken" there, and believing that the gatherings confirmed the lesson her mother taught her, that the "one meaning of value in life" was "the search for and affirmation of that which the hand could not touch" (19). For this often starry-eyed, youthful Kay Boyle, McAlmon was a revelation. He was the other side of her uncritical, venerating, youthful self that must be brought into focus in order for her to find her own authority and voice.

Yet in the end she remained loyal to Jolas, to the Crosbys, to those dreamers, drawn to the shadowy past or to the still insubstantial future, whom McAlmon scorned. The critical skills that she gained allow her to point out McAlmon's weaknesses: his "violent dissatisfaction" with himself, his "impatience" that he tried to calm through drink (192), "his almost pathological distrust of the subconscious," and his too easy and too quick ridicule of that which he distrusted (266–67). In her chapters, she shows that she values his perspective at the same time that she demarcates the differences between his and her own. Her ability to appreciate both the realist and the dreamer defines her finally. In reference to her simultaneous admiration of McAlmon and Jolas, she writes: "I was grateful then, and I am still grateful now, that I lacked the intellectual effrontery, and subsequent embitterment, that might have diminished my acknowledgment of all these two men stood for and all that they had done" (338). Her lack of intellectual presumptions makes possible her "multiple sympathy." Part of her autobiography's testimony to McAlmon's influence, ironically, is her ability to take a critical position distinctively her own.

In the twenties, McAlmon demanded that the young Kay Boyle present a clear and honest picture of herself to him. In the sixties, McAlmon makes the same demands of Boyle the autobiographer. Boyle begins and ends her reminiscences with references to her tendency to romanticize. McAlmon, she notes in both the introduction and conclusion, pointed out this tendency in her writing. At the beginning, she promises the reader that she will attempt to write the memoir that follows "without romanticizing and without going 'Irish-twilighty,' the two things that McAlmon kept shouting out to me about my writing" (11). She ends her portion of the memoir by quoting a letter McAlmon wrote Bill Bird in 1929, in which he deplored the failure of readers to discover and appreciate both Boyle and Katherine Anne Porter. He then compared and contrasted the two writers, and according to Boyle, judged Porter the better writer because "she wrote with greater authenticity, while Kay, come hell or high water, had to romanticize every situation" (373). Her response to his remark, "This may very well be true" (373), concludes the autobiography.

McAlmon's criticism of her is placed in emphatic positions within the autobiography. Boyle presents her chapters as "part of a dialogue I have never ceased having with Robert McAlmon" (11), who, shouting out to her about her tendency to romanticize in her writing and complaining to a friend about it, tends to get the first and last word in the writers' conversation. Boyle conveys the impression that McAlmon, who died in 1956, continues to speak to her, admonishing her, challenging her to rid her writing of its romanticism. Her closing statement, with its use of both the conditional auxiliary and the present tense, "This *may* very well *be* true," invites the reader's speculation that, despite her initial promise, the situations narrated in her memoir have been romanticized and that her struggle against such tendencies continues.

McAlmon's criticism of her, then, gives Boyle a way to address the difficulties of writing honestly about her own experiences and motivation. Because of his criticism, she suggests, she is, if not a less romanticizing writer, a more self-conscious one. As a result, she places both her younger and her present self under continual critique. Seemingly writing with McAlmon's voice in her ear, she points out her pretenses, scrutinizes her behavior, and questions her motivations as a young girl in the twenties. In addition, she questions her authority as an autobiographer to evaluate her younger self. (At one point, she stops the narrative to ask "But how do I know that I am telling the truth now about what I believed and wanted then?" [114].) Not only does she write with McAlmon's voice in her ear, but she also engages in self-reflection by repeatedly recalling his eyes, by recreating his scrutiny of her. He serves as an autobiographical muse, who not only asks the question "Who or what are you?" but who also demands an honest, self-critical answer. His "ruthless honesty which drew people to McAlmon demanded that those he faced with his icy stare look closely at themselves and their pretenses. It was a demand that made the presumptuous turn the other way" (26). Determined not to be one of the presumptuous, she fixes her attention throughout her chapters upon his icy stare.

Boyle's continued attachment to McAlmon is evident throughout her chapters. She depended upon him in her youth and depends upon him in her autobiography for inspiration. Their friendship continues to have meaning for her, and in homage to it, she literally stands by him in the pages of the autobiography. Yet she also acknowledges their separate natures and the loneliness at the heart of human experience that not even an act of sympathy can efface. A poem by McAlmon placed at the beginning of the dual autobiography emphasizes the individual's isolation:

> But the days go on, and the tides
> endlessly recoil; and one is still alone
> after the passing of people,
> and the turning of events, scarring
> with their experience;
> alone, and the winds are still blowing.
> Desolation abides, and primitive fear
> and watching with primitive eyes, and why—
> why does one heed the fall of a leaf,
> or note
> the size of a raindrop in a shower,
> while the covert thought runs on. . . . (xiii)

The poem stands in stark contrast to the sly and witty title of McAlmon's autobiography, *Being Geniuses Together*. It also gives an intentionally ironic twist to Boyle's interventions: she may place herself side by side with McAlmon in the pages of the text, but this act cannot be romanticized. Her actions cannot entirely compensate for the ultimate desolation and suffering that McAlmon confronts in the poem. People and events do not abide; they do not soothe and heal. They pass on, leaving scars. Yet the hope in the poem resides in the fact that although people and events leave one scarred, they do not necessarily render one numb, senseless, shocked. Somehow, for some reason, at least for some people, the senses remain alive; the creative and intellectual apprehension of experience continues. Thus, in the pages of Boyle's autobiography, scarring becomes a positive image, representing the opposite of obliteration and effacement. Those who have been scarred yet not effaced, Boyle suggests, are those who scar her, that is, leave an indelible mark on her life, never to be erased.

McAlmon's poem about gathering himself together, which Boyle quotes at the beginning of her chapters, also allows Boyle to emphasize their separate natures and to suggest that he would ridicule her efforts to save him from obscurity. She recalls the night in 1928 that she told McAlmon that she had been reciting to herself this poem since 1923 and remembers his response: "For Christ's sake, six years saying the same poem? When are you going to grow up, kid?" (369). He rankled at the romantic hero worship that her recitation suggested and at the notion that he served as some kind of master or mentor. He tried to repulse her by making a mockery of the poem and of himself, calling the "quivering pieces" of himself "[s]tinking" and "[f]ouled up" and declaring that he was "fed up" with what he carried around inside himself (369). Striking his chest, he commanded Boyle, "For Christ's sake, don't care about me! Stop it, will you? Let the God-damned pieces fall apart!" (369).

McAlmon would have none of Boyle's admiration or her solicitations. His violent speech followed Boyle's comment that she hoped that the Crosbys' Black Sun Press would publish a collection of his poetry. Poetry collections and recollection of the self seem connected in McAlmon's command to Boyle to "[l]et the God-damned pieces fall apart!" He would not be saved by her—by her hopes for his career or by what he viewed as her desire to patch up the pieces of him into a coherent whole. Placed at the end of this autobiography, which begins with Boyle's expressed hope that this "present revision will do more than provide a deeply sympathetic portrait of a writer and publisher who deserves to be remembered for his unique qualities, but that it will as well help to accord to Robert McAlmon his rightful and outstanding place in the history of the literary revolution of the early nineteen-twenties" (xiii), the scene is ironic. Boyle's autobiography has as its goal the redemption of McAlmon from disregard. Yet in this scene, he refuses her redemption. Stop caring, McAlmon pleads, stop trying to put the pieces together. Forty years later in 1968, refusing not to care, and perhaps relishing the irony of the act, Boyle recollected him.

Modernists like Virginia Woolf recognized that "redemption and the action of recollection (in the sense of 'gathering again') by which it claims to be achieved are . . . the deadly temptations of the autobiographical."[17] Boyle proves to be a self-conscious modern autobiographer aware of these temptations. She resists self-justification and problematizes the actions of memory and recollection in autobiographical writings, recognizing the dangers involved in constructing a coherent narrative of the self. In 1984, when *Being Geniuses Together* was reissued, she made her position on self-justification in autobiography and the complicated actions of memory explicit. In an afterword to the 1984 edition, she argues that autobiography should be more than an "exercise in self-absolution." Autobiography, she states, can only achieve "a worthy purpose" when it provides a defense, not of the self, but of "those who have been unjustly dealt with in one's own time, and whose lives and work ask for vindication." Extending the legal language, she argues that autobiography should be a "brief presented in exoneration of the inequitably judged."[18] She also quotes Rene Crevel on the subject of memory: "Memory is the tattooing by which the weak, the betrayed, the exiled, believe they have armed themselves. . . . Memory is the ink which corrodes all flesh, all splendor!"[19] The operations of memory may be defensive or even destructive. Yet it is possible that they may be used to achieve "a worthy purpose": in this case, to commemorate a man of "fierce integrity" who "does not deserve oblivion."[20]

Thus, Boyle unapologetically uses autobiography to redeem and recollect another, to try to save him from oblivion, from effacement. She resists a different kind of "deadly temptation": an acceptance of discontinuity and displacement in our relationships with the people who have left their mark on us. Like the story of her relationship with her mother, the story of her relationship with McAlmon is a story of both separation and attachment. Yet his significance in her life, like her mother's, she declares ineffaceable. Of her mother, Boyle states, "She prevailed, while the men of the family were effaced, line by line, a little more every year" (22), and of McAlmon, "all McAlmon had been to me, and had not been, all that he had said, or had not said, was never to be effaced" (372). Boyle bears the marks of her relationships; *her* signature act in the autobiographical chapters is to expose the signatures of others upon her. It proves not so much a self-effacing act as a representative act of "multiple sympathy," giving significance to the expression of comfort and hope that Boyle, in the autobiography, assigns to Nancy Cunard: "nobody is ever betrayed, darling, nobody ever dies" (340).

Notes

1.   Quoted in Elizabeth S. Bell, *Kay Boyle: A Study of the Short Fiction* (New York: Twayne, 1992), 93.

2.   Kay Boyle, preface to *Plagued by the Nightingale* (London: Virago, 1981), vi–xii, vii.

3.   Jean Stafford, "Spirits," review of *Being Geniuses Together 1920–1930,* by Kay Boyle and Robert McAlmon, *New York Review of Books,* 24 April 1969; Malcolm Cowley, "Those Paris Years," review of *Being Geniuses Together 1920–1930,* by Kay Boyle and Robert McAlmon, *New York Times,* 9 June 1968, sec. 7; Anthony Powell, "Knocking Around the Latin Quarter," review of *Being Geniuses Together 1920–1930,* by Kay Boyle and Robert McAlmon, *London Daily Telegraph,* 9 April 1970.

4.   Leo Litwak, "Kay Boyle—Paris Wasn't Like That," *New York Times,* 15 July 1984, sec. 7, p. 1.

5.   Kay Boyle, afterword to *Being Geniuses Together 1920–1930,* by Robert McAlmon revised with supplementary chapters by Kay Boyle (San Francisco: North Point Press, 1984), 333.

6.   Marcus K. Billotson and Sidonie A. Smith, "Lillian Hellman and the Strategy of the 'Other,' " in *Women's Autobiography: Essays in Criticism,* ed. Estelle C. Jelinek (Bloomington: Indiana University Press, 1980), 164.

7.   Julia Watson, "Shadowed Presence: Modern Women Writers' Autobiographies and the Other," in *Studies in Autobiography,* ed. James Olney (New York: Oxford University Press, 1988), 182.

8.   Bella Brodzki and Celeste Schenck, introduction to *Life/Lines: Theorizing Women's Autobiography* (Ithaca, N.Y.: Cornell University Press, 1988), 11.

9.   Patricia Meyer Spacks, "Selves in Hiding," in *Women's Autobiography: Essays in Criticism,* ed. Estelle C. Jelinek (Bloomington: Indiana University Press, 1980), 113–14.

10.   Carolyn G. Heilbrun, *Writing a Woman's Life* (New York: Ballantine Books, 1988), 17.

11.   Suzanne Clark, *Sentimental Modernism: Women Writers and the Revolution of the Word* (Bloomington: Indiana University Press, 1991), 130.

12.   Clark, *Sentimental Modernism,* 137.

13.   For a discussion of the role of mothers in women's autobiographies, see Stephanie A. Demetrakopoulos, "The Metaphysics of Matrilinearism in Women's Autobiography: Studies of Mead's *Blackberry Winter,* Hellman's *Pentimento,* Angelou's *I Know Why the Caged Bird Sings,* and Kingston's *The Woman Warrior,*" in *Women's Autobiography: Essays in Criticism,* ed. Estelle C. Jelinek (Bloomington: Indiana University Press, 1980), 180–205.

14.   Robert McAlmon, *Being Geniuses Together,* 19–20; hereafter cited by page number in the text. Unless otherwise noted, references are to supplementary chapters written by Boyle.

15.   Boyle, preface to *Plagued by the Nightingale.* Compare to Georges Gusdorf's often-cited definition of autobiography as the genre in which the writer "calls himself for witness to himself": Georges Gusdorf, "Conditions and Limits of Autobiography," in *Autobiography: Essays Theoretical and Critical,* ed. James Olney (Princeton: Princeton University Press, 1980), 29.

16.   Shari Benstock, "Authorizing the Autobiographical," in *The Private Self: Theory and Practice of Women's Autobiographical Writings,* ed. Shari Benstock (Chapel Hill: University of North Carolina, 1988), 28.

17.   Boyle, afterword to *Being Geniuses Together,* 333.

18.   Boyle, afterword to *Being Geniuses Together,* 334.

19.   Boyle, afterword to *Being Geniuses Together,* 343.

20.   Boyle, afterword to *Being Geniuses Together,* 343.

Index

♦

The Volume Editor

Dr. Marilyn Elkins, Associate Professor of English and Co-coordinator of Liberal Studies and Women's Studies at California State University Los Angeles, is the author of *Metamorphosizing the Novel* (Peter Lang, 1993). She edited and wrote the introductions for *The Heart of a Man* (Norton, 1973; Naval Institute Press, 1991; Dell, 1992) and *August Wilson: A Casebook* (Garland, 1994). Her articles on women writers and African American literature have appeared in scholarly journals and books of collected essays, and her writing on the Vietnam War has been published in military history journals and is frequently anthologized. The recipient of a 1994 Fulbright Award for lecturing in France, Dr. Elkins is currently working on a book-length study of women's use of fashion as literary trope.

The General Editor

Dr. James Nagel, J. O. Eidson Distinguished Professor of American Literature at the University of Georgia, founded the scholarly journal *Studies in American Fiction* and edited it for 20 years. He is the General Editor of the Critical Essays on American Literature series published by Macmillan, a program that now contains over 130 volumes. He was one of the founders of the American Literature Association and serves as its Executive Coordinator. He is also a past president of the Ernest Hemingway Society. Among his 17 books are *Stephen Crane and Literary Impressionism, Critical Essays on* The Sun Also Rises, *Ernest Hemingway: The Writer in Context, Ernest Hemingway: The Oak Park Legacy,* and *Hemingway in Love and War,* which was selected by the *New York Times* as one of the outstanding books of 1989 and which has been made into a major motion picture. Dr. Nagel has published over 50 articles in scholarly journals and has lectured on American literature in 15 countries. His current project is a book on the contemporary short-story cycle.